Change in Contemporary English

Based on the systematic analysis of large amounts of computer-readable text, this book shows how the English language has been changing in the recent past, often in unexpected and previously undocumented ways. The study is based on a group of matching corpora, known as the 'Brown family' of corpora, supplemented by a range of other corpus materials, both written and spoken, drawn mainly from the later twentieth century. Among the matters receiving particular attention are the influence of American English on British English, the role of the press, the 'colloquialization' of written English, and a wide range of grammatical topics, including the modal auxiliaries, progressive, subjunctive, passive, genitive and relative clauses. These subjects build an overall picture of how English grammar is changing, and the linguistic and social factors that are contributing to this process.

GEOFFREY LEECH is Emeritus Professor of English Linguistics in the Department of Linguistics and English Language at Lancaster University.

MARIANNE HUNDT is Professor of Linguistics in the Department of English at the University of Zürich.

CHRISTIAN MAIR is Professor of English Linguistics in the Department of English at the University of Freiburg.

NICHOLAS SMITH is Lecturer in English Language and Linguistics in the School of English, Sociology, Politics and Contemporary History at the University of Salford.

STUDIES IN ENGLISH LANGUAGE

General editor
Merja Kytö (Uppsala University)

Editorial Board
Bas Aarts (University College London), John Algeo (University of Georgia),
Susan Fitzmaurice (Northern Arizona University), Charles F. Meyer
(University of Massachusetts)

The aim of this series is to provide a framework for original studies of English, both
present-day and past. All books are based securely on empirical research, and represent
theoretical and descriptive contributions to our knowledge of national and international
varieties of English, both written and spoken. The series covers a broad range of topics
and approaches, including syntax, phonology, grammar, vocabulary, discourse,
pragmatics and sociolinguistics, and is aimed at an international readership.

Already published in this series:

Change in Contemporary English

A Grammatical Study

GEOFFREY LEECH
Lancaster University

MARIANNE HUNDT
Universität Zürich

CHRISTIAN MAIR
Albert-Ludwigs-Universität Freiburg, Germany

NICHOLAS SMITH
University of Salford

CAMBRIDGE
UNIVERSITY PRESS

CAMBRIDGE UNIVERSITY PRESS
Cambridge, New York, Melbourne, Madrid, Cape Town,
Singapore, São Paulo, Delhi, Mexico City

Cambridge University Press
The Edinburgh Building, Cambridge CB2 8RU, UK

Published in the United States of America by Cambridge University Press, New York

www.cambridge.org
Information on this title: www.cambridge.org/9781107410466

© Geoffrey Leech, Marianne Hundt, Christian Mair, Nicholas Smith, 2009

First published 2009
Reprinted with corrections 2010
3rd printing 2011
First paperback edition 2012

A catalogue record for this publication is available from the British Library

Library of Congress Cataloguing in Publication Data
Leech, Geoffrey N.
Change in contemporary English : a grammatical study / Geoffrey Leech . . . [et al.].
    p.   cm. – (Studies in English language)
Includes bibliographical references and index.
ISBN 978-0-521-86722-1
1. Corpora (Linguistics)   2. English language – Grammar.   3. Computational
linguistics.   I. Title.   II. Series.
P128.C68L43   2009
425 – dc22   2009019728

ISBN 978-0-521-86722-1 Hardback
ISBN 978-1-107-41046-6 Paperback

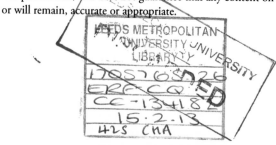

Contents

Figures

List of Figures in Appendix III

Tables

Preface

This book aims to give an account of how the English language has been changing recently, focusing especially on (a) the late twentieth century, (b) the written standard language, (c) American and British English, (d) grammatical rather than lexical change, and using the empirical evidence of computer corpora.

Corpus linguistics is now a mainstream paradigm in the study of languages, and the study of English in particular has advanced immeasurably through the availability of increasingly rich and varied corpus resources. This applies to both synchronic and diachronic research. However, this book presents, we argue, a new kind of corpus-based historical research, with a narrower, more intense focus than most, revealing through its rather rigorous methodology how the language (more especially the written language) has been developing over a precisely defined period of time in the recent past.

The period on which the book concentrates is the thirty years between the early 1960s and the early 1990s, and the four corpora that it studies in most detail are those which go increasingly by the name of the 'Brown family': the Brown corpus (American English, 1961); the Lancaster–Oslo/Bergen corpus (British English, 1961); the Freiburg–Brown corpus (American English, 1992); and the Freiburg–Lancaster–Oslo/Bergen corpus (British English, 1991).[1]

These corpora, described in more detail in Chapter 2 (section 2.2) and in Appendix II, are reasonably well known, and have been studied as a group, not only by ourselves, but by others, since the completion of this corpus quartet in the mid-1990s. All four corpora are available to researchers around the world, and can be obtained under licence from either ICAME at the Aksis centre, University of Bergen, or the Oxford Text Archive, University of Oxford.[2] However, we venture to claim that as authors of this book we have been more intimately engaged with these corpora than any other research group: in their compilation, their annotation and their analysis. Indeed, this

---

[1] An informative manual of information for the Brown family of corpora, including their POS tagging, is provided by Hinrichs *et al.* (forthcoming).
[2] The web addresses of these two corpus resource agencies are as follows: http://icame.uib.no/ and http://ota.ahds.ac.uk/.

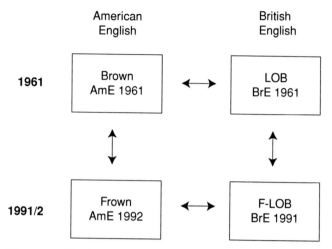

Figure o.1 The four matching corpora on which this book focuses

intimacy entitles us to feel a certain familial affection for these textual time-capsules, and almost invariably (like many others) we refer to them by their acronymic nicknames: Brown, LOB, Frown and F-LOB.[3]

The strength of these four corpora lies in their comparability: the fact that they are constructed according to the same design, having virtually the same size and the same selection of texts and genres represented by 500 matching text samples of c. 2,000 words. This means that we can use the Brown family as a precision tool for tracking the differences between written English in 1961 and in 1991/2. How has the English language changed, in these two leading regional varieties, over this thirty-year generation gap? The findings brought to light by this comparison between matching corpora are fascinating: they reveal, for the first time, or at least with a new sense of accuracy, how significant are the changes in a language that take place over even such a short timespan of thirty years. Even though these changes, as we report them, are almost entirely matters of changing frequency of use, they often show a high degree of statistical significance.[4]

The affection we feel for this corpus family does not blind us to their considerable limitations (see section 2.1), notably their restriction to the standard written language. We have therefore taken care to supplement the evidence they provide with analyses of other corpora relating to the later twentieth century, so as to enlarge and corroborate our findings on how the language has recently been changing. In extending our range in this way, most

---

[3] The explanations of these names for corpora, as well as other abbreviations, are found in the list of 'Abbreviations and symbolic conventions', pp. xxvii–xxx.

[4] Significance levels are shown, where appropriate, by asterisks: *, **, *** in the quantitative tables – see the table of Abbreviations and symbolic conventions.

important have been the corpora that record indications of what has been happening to the spoken language. The Diachronic Corpus of Present-Day Spoken English (DCPSE),[5] released in 2006, has made it possible to study, over the sample period of time, changes in the spoken language, though not under the same rigorous conditions of comparability that apply to the Brown family. In addition, the British National Corpus (BNC), though it has no reliable diachronic dimension, gives us a large (ten-million-word) well-sampled subcorpus of spoken English from the early 1990s. Both of these corpora are limited to British English: but we have been able to consult the CIC (Cambridge International Corpus) and LCSAE (Longman Corpus of Spoken American English, comparable in date and method of collection to the spoken demographic subcorpus of the BNC) to see how that presumably most trail-blazing variety of the language – spoken American English – compares with others. Again, there is only an indirect diachronic dimension here, through the study of 'apparent time' by comparison of different age groups of speakers. But at least we are able to speculate on tangible evidence about how the spoken American variety has been moving in the period under review.[6]

Apart from these (necessarily imperfect and incomplete) comparisons between corpora of speech and writing, we have also been able to extend our range, when need arises, along the diachronic dimension. In the months preceding the publication of this book, we were able to make limited use of the newest member of the Brown family – though oldest in date – the Lancaster 1931 Corpus[7] (inevitably nicknamed 'B-LOB' for 'before-LOB'), sampled from a seven-year period centring on 1931, and so effectively providing us with three equidistant reference points, 1931 ($\pm$ 3 years), 1961 and 1991/2, for further diachronic comparison. For even greater historical depth, we have occasionally used the ARCHER corpus and the *OED* citation bank. These valuable resources again lack the strict comparability criterion of the Brown

---

5 The DCPSE, consisting of 885,436 words, and compiled by Bas Aarts and associates at the Survey of English Usage, University College London, consists of transcribed British spoken texts originally collected as parts of two different corpora: (a) the Survey of English Usage corpus (of which the spoken part was later largely incorporated into the London–Lund Corpus) collected in 1958–1978; and (b) the ICE-GB corpus collected in 1990–1992. Geoffrey Leech is grateful to Bas Aarts for letting him have an advance copy of DCPSE at a point when it was timely for drafting certain chapters of this book.
6 It should be mentioned that there are several corpora of present-day spoken English of which we have not made detailed use, since, although admirable for other types of research, they are either two small for our present purposes (e.g. the Santa Barbara Corpus of Spoken American English) or too genre-restricted (e.g. MICASE, Corpus of Spoken Professional American English, the Switchboard corpus).
7 This corpus, now in a provisional pre-release form, has been compiled by Nicholas Smith, Paul Rayson and Geoffrey Leech with the financial support of the Leverhulme Foundation. With further support from the Leverhulme Foundation, we will shortly have yet another member of the Brown family, with a corpus of BrE at the beginning of the twentieth century (1901 $\pm$ 3 years to be precise). However, this corpus, provisionally called Lanc-1901, was not completed in time for its results to be used in this book.

family, but allow corpus-based investigations of trends going back to EModE (in the case of ARCHER) and to OE (in the case of the *OED* citation bank). Turning towards the future: we have not been able to draw on more recent progeny of the Brown family, since none are yet available; but the 'corpus of last resort' these days, the World Wide Web (see a number of contributions to Hundt *et al.* 2007), has sometimes given us persuasive evidence about what has been happening since the early 1990s.[8]

What has become obvious is that the corpus resources available for recent diachronic research do not comprise a static platform for research, but a moving staircase: every year new text resources become available, in increasing numbers and increasing size, enhancing our evidential basis for researching the recent development of the language. In such a situation of continuing advance, it is a reasonable compromise to adopt the position we have taken – to focus on the four tried-and-tested Brown family corpora, while using other corpora where it is particularly rewarding or important (as well as feasible) to do so.

The unavoidable assumption of incompleteness is familiar in many fields of scientific endeavour: if researchers before publication waited until complete results and complete answers were available, there would be no publication. Certainly, it would have been easy for us to engage in further research on the range of topics we have investigated here, collecting or consulting further corpora, carrying out deeper analyses, and so on, without reaching a natural endpoint. We hope that in spite of its existing limitations, this book will be felt to have achieved a valuable conspectus of new or recent findings across a wide variety of grammatical topics. Although we have taken care to achieve a consistent perspective and framework of research throughout the book, readers may notice some lack of consistency in the kinds of coverage of corpus analyses offered in individual chapters. In the 'moving staircase' scenario described above, this is almost inevitable, and there is after all no harm in a book which reflects to some extent the different emphases, interests and strengths of individual chapter authors.

One of the most positive achievements of our collaboration is the uniform part-of-speech annotation (or POS tagging) of all four corpora – all five, if one includes the 1931 corpus. We have used the same software annotation practices (the Lancaster tagger CLAWS, the supplementary tagger Template Tagger and the enriched C8 tagset of grammatical categories – see Appendix II and also the detailed tagging guide in Hinrichs *et al.* forthcoming). This has enabled the corpora to be compared, grammatically, on an equal footing, using equivalent search and retrieval patterns to extract instances of abstract constructions, such as progressives, and in some important instances (e.g.

---

[8]   Paul Baker of Lancaster University has provisionally compiled a twenty-first century web-derived corpus on the Brown model, and this will eventually take its place in the Brown family of corpora.

zero relativization) even grammatical categories not explicitly realized in surface structure. Here again, however, we have not managed to achieve complete consistency of treatment: the three corpora LOB, F-LOB and Frown have all been manually post-edited after automatic tagging, while the Brown corpus, the earliest of all to be compiled and tagged, has not undergone the manual post-edit with the new set of tags. This has meant a lower degree of confidence (with an initial error margin of c. 2 per cent) in the correctness of some results in the American English (AmE) comparison of Brown and Frown, alongside the more accurate British English (BrE) comparison of LOB and F-LOB. However, this margin of error has been minimized by employing a corrective coefficient based on the tagger's error rates observed in the comparison of pre-corrected and post-corrected versions of the Frown Corpus – see further p. 24, footnote 27.[9] The dictum that 'Most corpus findings are approximations' (see section 2.3) is particularly to be taken to heart in interpreting our findings for grammatical constructions and categories in AmE, and this has sometimes led us to give more attention to the results for BrE than those for AmE.

Given that the book focuses on changes in grammar, the POS tagging combined with powerful CQP search software (see section 2.4 C) has enabled us, without aiming at comprehensiveness, to achieve a broad grammatical coverage of the language.[10] After two introductory chapters, the next seven chapters concentrate on topics relating to the verb phrase. They cover the subjunctive (Chapter 3), the modal auxiliaries (Chapter 4), the so-called semi-modals (Chapter 5), the progressive aspect (Chapter 6), the passive (Chapter 7), expanded predicates such as *have/take a look* (Chapter 8) and non-finite constructions (Chapter 9). In Chapter 10 we move on to the noun phrase, enquiring particularly into noun–noun sequences, genitives and relative clauses. In the last chapter, Chapter 11, we seek a synthesis, dealing with social and linguistic determinants of the short-term changes demonstrated in earlier chapters, and extending the book's coverage by illustrating these determinants with a number of additional linguistic trends.

The book abounds with statistical tables and charts, comparing frequencies (often normalized to occurrences per million words) according to period of

---

[9] Tables and figures relying on approximations based on adjusted automatic tagging counts in this way occur mostly in Chapters 10 and 11, or in the part of Appendix III relating to these chapters. Such tables and figures are indicated by a warning note '(automatic)' or '(AmE automatic)' beneath the relevant table or figure.

[10] A simple and obvious point has to be made here: we have naturally given primary attention to areas of English grammar known or suspected to be undergoing change. (In some cases the 'knowledge' or 'suspicion' comes from our own exploratory study of the corpora.) There are, however, interesting areas of contemporary English grammar that we have not dealt with: for example, we will have nothing to say about corpus findings relating to the choice of singular or plural verb after a collective-noun subject (*The team is/are . . .* – a construction that has, however, been more than adequately studied elsewhere – see Levin 2001, 2006; Depraetere 2003; Hundt 2006). Our failure to treat a particular topic is not a reliable signal of its lack of interest from the present-day diachronic viewpoint.

time (mostly 1961 vs 1991), region, genre, etc. We have aimed to provide sound corpus description, using inferential statistics to generalize beyond corpus observations, looking at single dependent variables at a time, and interpreting the findings in the framework of a reasonable and robust usage-based model of language change. To avoid cluttering up the descriptive chapters (Chapters 3–11) with statistical details that might obscure the main findings and lines of argument, we have consigned many of the statistical tables and diagrams, particularly the more complex ones, to Appendix III.

The four authors are jointly responsible for the whole work in its final form; nevertheless, it may be of interest to know which authors took particular responsibility for which chapters. They are here identified by their initials: GL: 2, 4, 5, 10, 11; MH: 3, 7, 8, also the References; CM: 1, 9; NS: 6, Appendices. It should be added, however, that the relative input of individual authors can by no means be measured in this way.

This is the appropriate point to acknowledge gratefully our debt to those who helped us in various ways; to Merja Kytö as series General Editor, and to Helen Barton, editor at Cambridge University Press, we owe a great deal for their encouragement, support and forbearance. We also owe much to the research assistants who helped us in the processing of textual data: Lars Hinrichs, Barbara Klein, Luminiţa-Irinel Traşcă and Birgit Waibel in Freiburg; and Martin Schendzielorz in Heidelberg. We are grateful, too, to Paul Rayson and Sebastian Hoffmann, colleagues at Lancaster; to Gunnel Tottie, for expert guidance on American and British English; and to Chris Williams for comments on Chapter 6; also to the funding agencies without whose support our research reported here would not have been possible. Thanks are due, on this score, to the Deutsche Forschungsgemeinschaft (DFG) for grant MA 1652/3 to Christian Mair and the University of Freiburg, to the Arts and Humanities Research Board (AHRB; subsequently changed to AHRC), the British Academy, and the Leverhulme Trust for research grants awarded to Geoffrey Leech at Lancaster University. We also record our gratitude to Cambridge University Press for making available to us relevant sections of the Cambridge International Corpus (CIC), and to Pearson/Longman for allowing us to consult the Longman Corpus of Spoken American English (LCSAE).

Abbreviations and symbolic conventions

A. Abbreviations for corpora, corpus collections and subcorpora
(listed approximately in order of importance for this book)

1	Brown	the Brown (University) Corpus (see 2.1, Appendix I)
2	LOB	the Lancaster–Oslo/Bergen Corpus
3	Frown	the Freiburg–Brown Corpus
4	F-LOB	the Freiburg–Lancaster–Oslo/Bergen Corpus
5	The Brown family	the four corpora above, regarded as a group
6	Lanc-31	the Lancaster 1931 Corpus, matching the four corpora above
7	B-LOB	a nickname for Lanc-31, meaning 'before LOB'
8	Press,	Four subcorpora into which the corpora of
9	General Prose,	the Brown family are divided. For the
10	Learned,	composition of the Brown corpus (and hence
11	Fiction	of the other corpora of the Brown family), see Appendix I.
12	BNC	the British National Corpus[1]
13	the BNC demographic subcorpus (BNCdemog)	a part of the BNC, consisting of largely spontaneous spoken English discourse by 153 individuals and their interlocutors, sampled from the population of the UK on demographic principles
14	BNC Sampler	A subcorpus of the BNC, consisting of c. one million words of writing and c. one million words of speech. The POS tags are more refined than for the whole BNC, and have been post-edited for correctness.
15	ICE	the International Corpus of English

---

[1] We have used the World Edition of the British National Corpus.

16	ICE-GB	the International Corpus of English (Great Britain) – one of the constituent corpora of ICE
17	DCPSE	the Diachronic Corpus of Present-Day Spoken English
18	DSEU	a mini-corpus consisting of an early part of the DCPSE
19	DICE	a mini-corpus consisting of a later matching part of the DCPSE
20	ANC	the American National Corpus
21	ARCHER	A Representative Corpus of Historical English Registers
22	LCSAE	the Longman Corpus of Spoken American English
23	CIC	the Cambridge International Corpus
24	ACE	the Australian Corpus of English
25	CONCE	Corpus of Nineteenth-Century English
26	MICASE	the Michigan Corpus of Academic Spoken English

Alphabetical index to the above list:

B. Abbreviations for Geographical and Historical Subdivisions of English

AmE	American English	LModE	Late Modern English
BrE	British English	ME	Middle English
ModE	Modern English	OE	Old English
EModE	Early Modern English	PDE	Present-Day English

C. Other Abbreviations

C8 — The C8 tagset: a set of part-of-speech tags used for annotating the Brown family of corpora (the C8 tags are listed in Appendix II)

CLAWS — Constituent-Likelihood Automatic Word Tagging System (a POS tagger)

CLAWS4 — The newest version of CLAWS

CQP	Corpus Query Processor (software: a tool for interpreting corpus queries)
LL	Log likelihood (a measure of statistical significance)
NP	Noun phrase
N+N	Sequence consisting of noun + noun
N+CN	Sequence consisting of noun + common noun
OED	*Oxford English Dictionary*
pmw	Per million words (in statistical tables, frequencies are often normalized to this standard frequency measure)
PN+PN	A sequence of proper noun + proper noun
POS	Part of speech (used especially in the collocation 'POS tagger/tagging')
XML	Extensible Markup Language (an artificial metalanguage used for the encoding and processing of textual material, including corpora)

D. Conventions

[Brown L12], [LOB A09], and the like	These are address labels used to identify the whereabouts, in the Brown family of corpora, of a particular example, sentence, etc. After the corpus name, the letter indicates the text category and the two digits the number of the text sample in that category. Similar address labels are used for examples from the BNC and other corpora.
*	An asterisk before an (invented) example indicates its status as an unacceptable or ungrammatical usage.
?	A question mark before an example (invented or otherwise) indicates its questionable acceptability.
[. . .]	In a corpus example, an ellipsis in square brackets indicates where the example has been simplified by the omission of part of the original corpus sentence.
*, **, ***	Placed next to a numerical quantity in a statistical table or bar chart, these are indicators of increasingly higher statistical significance.
*	* means 'significant at the level $p < 0.05$ (LL > 3.84)'.
**	** means 'significant at the level $p < 0.01$ (LL > 6.63)'.

***	*** means 'significant at the level $p < 0.001$ (LL > 10.83)'.
N* etc.	In referring to POS tags, an asterisk is occasionally used as a 'wildcard symbol', standing for any number (including zero) of characters, excepting a space or other delimiting character. For example, N* will identify any tag beginning with N, which means, in fact, any noun in the C8 tagset.
HAVE got to, SHE, HAVE, NEED to, and the like	In certain chapters, the small capitals indicate that the word cited is understood as a lemma, not as an individual word form. For example, *HAVE to* signifies any form of the verb *HAVE* followed by *to* (i.e. *have to, has to, had to, having to*). The chapters in which this convention chiefly applies are 4 and 5. It is important to avoid confusion in some contexts by using this convention. In other contexts the convention is unnecessary, as the interpretation of a graphical form like *be going to* is clear from the context. Hence we use this convention only in some chapters.

1   Introduction: 'grammar blindness' in the recent history of English?

Surprising though this may be in view of a vast and growing body of literature on recent and ongoing changes in the language, there is very little we know about grammatical change in written standard English in the twentieth century. No one would seriously doubt that grammar constitutes a central level of linguistic structuring, and most people would agree that standard English, while being one variety among many from a purely descriptive-linguistic point of view, has nevertheless been the most studied and best documented one because of its social and cultural prominence. What, then, are the causes of this apparent 'grammar blindness'?

1.1   Grammar is more than an arbitrary list of shibboleths

Among lay commentators on linguistic change what we have is not really complete blindness but an extreme restriction of the field of vision. Rather than see grammar as the vast and complex system of rules which helps us organize words into constituents, clauses and sentences, the term is restricted to refer to a collection of variable and disputed usages which have been selected arbitrarily in the course of almost 300 years of prescriptive thinking about good grammar and proper English.

Let us illustrate this restriction of the field of vision with a first example. English has a complex and highly differentiated inventory of noun-phrase post-modification by means of relative clauses. This inventory comprises several types of finite and non-finite clauses which differ greatly in grammatical structure, in logical status (as 'restrictive' or 'non-restrictive' specification of the head) and also in stylistic connotation. All the highlighted structures listed in (1) below would be considered part of this system. The first is an authentic instance from a standard digital reference corpus of present-day written English; the others are variations on the theme:

(1)   a.   Interestingly, Mr John Major is acquiring a high profile as a foreign statesman *to whom more and more heads of state are willing to turn, and*

1

 whose voice is regularly listened to in international councils. [F-LOB
 B06]¹

b. Mr John Major is acquiring a high profile as a foreign statesman
 who(m) more and more heads of state are willing to turn to [. . .]

c. Mr John Major is acquiring a high profile as a foreign statesman *that
 more and more heads of state are willing to turn to* [. . .]

d. Mr John Major is acquiring a high profile as a foreign statesman *for
 heads of state to turn to* [. . .]

e. Mr John Major is acquiring a high profile as a foreign statesman *to
 turn to* [. . .]

f. Mr John Major is acquiring a high profile as a foreign statesman *to
 be turned to* [. . .]

In the history of English, not all these forms are of equal age and spread, and
there is no reason to assume that historical developments in this fragment of
the grammar of English should have come to a halt in the twentieth century.
Many interesting questions arise which might well be worth exploring. For
example, we might ask whether non-finite relative clauses are spreading,
possibly at the expense of finite alternatives, as this would be an expected
development in view of a general tendency for non-finite clauses to become
more important in the recent history of English (see, e.g., Chapter 9 of the
present book and Mair 2006b: 119–140). Or we might look at the statistical
or semantic relationships between active and passive infinitives in examples
such as (1e) and (1f) above.

However, most discussions on recent changes in the use of relative clauses
in English will instantly home in on one issue, namely the choice between
who and *whom* as a relative pronoun in object function. Similar variability
between the two forms is, of course, found in independent and dependent
interrogative clauses (cf., e.g., *Who(m) did you ask?*; *I didn't know who(m) to
ask*), so that – unless indicated otherwise – the following comments on *who*
and *whom* can be taken to refer to both types of constructions. Usually, the
issue is framed around the question of whether English is losing a traditionally
'correct' form, *whom*, and whether the resulting loss of distinction between
the subject and object uses of this relative pronoun should be seen as a
desirable simplification – the minority view – or as a sign of possible decay
in the language.

At this stage, we do not want to anticipate the results of a detailed investigation of the use of relative clauses in present-day English, which will
be offered in Chapter 10 (section 10.5) of the present book. However, we

---

¹ When quoting examples from standard corpora or digital databases, the usual conventions
are followed. In this particular example, which is from the F-LOB (Freiburg–Lancaster–
Oslo/Bergen) Corpus of written British English, 'B' refers to the textual category, in this
case 'Press/ Editorial' and '06' is the number of the 2,000 word text sample the quote is
taken from. Readers unfamiliar with corpus-linguistic conventions and/or the corpora used
for the present study are referred to section 1.2 below and Chapter 2 for more information.

would like to use the example to point out the most important ways in which prescriptivism tends to narrow our field of vision in the study of linguistic change in progress and in some instances even promotes positions which are at odds with the facts of language history.

As for the use of *whom* in questions, the prescriptive tradition has identified the historical developments correctly in very general terms. *Who* and *whom* go back to the Old English interrogative pronouns *hwā* and *hwǣm*, which functioned as the nominative and dative case forms, respectively.[2] The use of uninflected *who* in object function is a historically younger development, which the *OED* (2nd edn., 1989: s.v. *who* 5) labels as ungrammatical but as 'common in colloquial use'. The same *OED* entry, however, also shows very clearly that English is not losing the form *whom* now (as is commonly alleged), but lost it in informal spoken English long ago. The first of many instances of the colloquial use given in the entry is from a letter written in 1450 (*Paston Lett.* I. 112: *I rehersyd no name, but me thowt be hem that thei wost ho I ment* 'I mentioned no name, but felt that they knew who I meant'), and the usage is attested continuously to the present day.

The facts are a little more complicated in the case of relative clauses, as both *who* and *whom* were added to the inventory of English relative pronouns relatively late, in the thirteenth and fourteenth centuries. While it is plausible to assume that the distribution of the two forms was governed by inflection and *whom* was the primary choice for objects, the historical record shows hardly a time lag between the first attestation of relative *who* in restrictive clauses (1297, *OED*, s.v. *who* 9) and the first possible case of the modern 'ungrammatical' use in a fourteenth-century work (*OED*, s.v. *who* 13).[3] Not unexpectedly, the use is attested in Shakespeare. For example, Macbeth can bewail the fall of him 'who I myself struck down' (*Macbeth*, iii.1). In view of this, it is difficult for prescriptivists to construct an argument for the historical priority of *whom* over *who* as a relative pronoun.

For both the interrogative and the relative uses it seems that the past few centuries have seen little genuine grammatical change, as the facts have been clear and stable. In all the examples below the (a) options have been the normal ones in spoken and informal English, and the (b) variants have been available as additional options in written and formal spoken English.

(2) a. *Who* did she come to see? [F-LOB P06]
    b. *Whom* did she come to see?

(3) a. 'There is Doris Jones, for instance, *who* I go away with, and Mary Plumb, and the Fosters –' [F-LOB L02]

---

[2] The generalized use of *whom* for all kinds of objects is a later development.
[3] 'Qua þat godd helpis wid-all, Traistli may be wend ouer-all' (= 'whom God helps . . .'). Note that *be* may be a misreading here for *he*, and that the use of the nominative might be prompted by the continuation of the sentence, in which 'the one who is helped by God' functions as subject.

    b. 'There is Doris Jones, for instance, *with whom* I go away, and Mary
       Plumb, and the Fosters –'

This being so, any statistical shifts in usage which we might observe in twentieth-century language data would not be due to direct grammatical change. The grammar, seen as the system of rules and options underlying usage, has been very stable for the past few centuries. What might have changed, though, are stylistic conventions or expectations of formality. For example, a writer of a sports feature in a newspaper had both options available in the year 1900 as well as in 2000. If a corpus analysis were able to show late twentieth-century sportswriters to favour the informal (a) options more often than their predecessors, it would be an interesting finding – not about the evolution of the grammar of English, but about the evolution of newspaper writing style in a changing market. Of course, there is an obvious relation between style change and grammar change in the long term. If, for example, a linguistic form becomes marginal generally or across a very broad variety of genres, it will eventually disappear as an option from the structural system and either die out or live on as a fossilized expression in the lexicon.

    If we are looking for clear-cut grammatical change in the use of *whom*, we have to concentrate on a very specific syntactic environment, namely the one illustrated in example (3b). Currently, the position immediately following a preposition (cf. (3b) – *with whom*) is the only one in which grammatical descriptions of present-day English regard the use of the inflected form as obligatory, and this – in addition to an occasional desire on the part of speakers and writers to sound formal and elegant – is probably what has protected it from extinction. Real grammatical change would be demonstrated if we were able to show that relative clauses of the type:

(4) 'There is Doris Jones, for instance, *with who* I go away, and Mary
      Plumb, and the Fosters –'

were not possible a hundred years ago, are being used now and are possibly becoming more frequent. We will return to this question in section 1.2 below.

    The most heated phases in the arguments over the proper use of *who* and *whom* are, it is safe to say, behind us, and even conservative commentators on the state of the English language may have begun to acquiesce in the 'ungrammatical' use of *who* as an oblique form – much as they have got used to *it is me* instead of *it is I* or the use of *will* instead of *shall* to refer to the future with the first persons singular and plural.

    However, the satisfactory conclusion that this particular debate has found does not mean that we are generally living in an enlightened age which has moved beyond such linguistic prejudice and merely needs to wonder about the curiosities of a misguided past. Even today, prescriptive rules are being enforced which are as unfounded in fact as any eighteenth-century traditional recommendation but advocated with no less vigour than their predecessors.

As it happens, a case in point is provided by another instance of variable usage in the field of relative pronouns, namely the choice between *which* and *that*. Especially in the United States, the prevailing opinion among educators and editors is that *that* is the only legitimate way of introducing a restrictive relative clause with a non-human antecedent and that *which* should not be used for this purpose. However, an unprejudiced look at historical data shows beyond doubt that *which* has not been confined to introducing non-restrictive relative clauses at any period in the history of English. In fact, it has served as a frequent alternative to *that* in restrictive relative clauses in educated usage – throughout the entire history of the English language in North America and for almost a thousand years in British English.[4] Of course, a neat one-to-one mapping of form and function – *which* for non-restrictive and *that* for restrictive post-modification, as in (5a) and (5b) below – appears tidy and makes theoretical sense (at least on the not unproblematical assumption that the logic of natural languages follows formal logic rather closely):

(5)   a.   Already he was asking Hemingway about his next book of stories, a book *that* Pound strongly advised against. [Frown G38]
      b.   Already he was asking Hemingway about "Men without Women," *which* Pound strongly advised against.

However, this distribution has never been obligatory in any variety of English past or present.[5] Instead, there is an untidy asymmetry. *That* cannot normally be used for non-restrictive post-modification, but *which* is normal in restrictive relative clauses.

(5)   c.   Already he was asking Hemingway about his next book of stories, a book *which* Pound strongly advised against.
      d.   *Already he was asking Hemingway about "Men without Women," *that* Pound strongly advised against.

Interestingly enough, American usage manuals and US editorial practice for almost a century now have been based on the fiction that a clear functional separation between *that* and *which* should exist – which is either an interesting case of a collective illusion taking hold among educated members of a speech community or a modern-day revival of the eighteenth-century impulse to bring natural language into line with logic and thus remove its perceived defects. Whatever its motivation, prescriptive teaching in this case has not been without effect: a comparison between matching British and American databases undertaken in Chapter 10 shows restrictive *which* to be seriously under-represented in American English in comparison to British English.

---

4   The earliest *OED* attestations date from the twelfth century. Use of *that* as a relative pronoun is attested from Old English times.
5   Indeed, the American Frown corpus itself contains numerous examples of restrictive *which*, for instance the following one from a – presumably professionally edited – newspaper source: 'That's the verdict which repeatedly emerges from the polls.' [Frown A10]

Here we shall conclude by referring our readers to an instructive jeremiad on this issue in which eminent linguist Arnold Zwicky, after referring to an episode in which the 'sacred That rule' generated considerable extra income for the legal profession,[6] summarizes the many but usually futile battles he has fought in order to get instances of restrictive *which* past avid but misguided American editors.

Every so often, I've had to deal with editors from presses who are genuinely puzzled by the passion I have invested in protesting the That Rule. It's just a matter of house style, they say; it has nothing to do with syntax. You say how capitalization works, you tell people what fonts to use and how paragraphing is indicated and all that. And you tell people which subordinators to use in restrictive relative clauses. Why are YOU getting your knickers in a twist? I mean (they say), this is basically all arbitrary stipulation, the only function of which is to create and maintain consistency in the press's publications. (Some writers, like Louis Menand, even revel in arbitrary 'rules' for their own sake.)

Twice, my aggressive truculence about the That Rule (and a collection of other zombie rules) has prompted editors to cave in to my craziness and let me do whatever I want. Me. Not anyone else, just me, for this one book. They were then baffled that I didn't view this response as really satisfactory. I pointed out that the scholarly books their firms published on English grammar uniformly failed to subscribe to the That Rule, so that their presses looked like packs of hypocrites and fools. They simply didn't get it. For them, one thing is scholarship, the other thing is practice. They're just different. ('Language Log', posting by Arnold Zwicky at 22 May 2005; http://itre.cis.upenn.edu/~myl/languagelog/archives/002291.html#more)

In this connection it is interesting to note that a major recent reference grammar of English explicitly condemns this ill-founded rule in one of its 'prescriptive grammar notes' (Huddleston and Pullum 2005: 191), which are otherwise devoted to more traditional shibboleths such as the use of 'singular' *they*, the split infinitive or the choice between *I* and *me*.

---

[6] Zwicky points to a disturbing legal case in which the perfectly obvious meaning of a sentence was turned into its opposite in court: 'The Texas statute furthers no legitimate state interest which can justify its intrusions into the personal and private life of the individual'. [US Supreme Court, Lawrence v. Texas] In debating technicalities of a complex judgement, legal experts seriously, and in print, appealed to the 'That rule' to support their reading of the *which*-clause as non-restrictive – never even minding the fact that, as Zwicky points out, a non-restrictive reading is not even possible in this example because 'no legitimate interest' is not a referential noun phrase. The possibility of a completely absurd misinterpretation of the statement, with *which* introducing a sentential relative (with a paraphrase such as, roughly, 'The Texas statute furthers no legitimate state interest, and this can justify its intrusions into the personal and private lives of the individual') was fortunately never pursued.

1.2 Grammatical changes: proceeding slowly and invisible at close range?

Grammar is probably the level on which the English language has changed most radically in the course of its recorded history, and this is noted in treatments of Old and Middle English. By contrast, studies of change in the more recent past generally place much more emphasis on phonological and lexical phenomena than on grammatical ones (cf., e.g., the small number of pages devoted to grammar in standard treatments of changes in present-day English such as Barber 1964, Foster 1968 or Potter 1975). Barbara Strang, herself the author of a classic history of the English language, has noted this imbalance, arguing that it is most likely not rooted in the facts of language history but in our ability to perceive and analyse them:

> One possible explanation can hardly be proved false, but should be entertained only as a last resort: namely, that although there has been considerable grammatical change in the past, English grammar in our own lifetime is somehow uniquely stable and free from change.
>
> The most promising direction of search for an explanation would seem to lie in the assumption that there is grammatical change in progress at the moment, as in the past, but that we are considerably less perceptive of it than of other kinds of linguistic change. (1970: 59–60)

What is it that makes grammatical change difficult to perceive? For a lay observer, especially in a language such as English with its largely analytical grammar, part of the difficulty may lie in the fact that so little of the grammar is audible/visible directly – for example in the form of inflectional endings on words – and so much of it is abstract, involving, for example, the position of elements in a clause relative to each other or, as in the case of re-analysis, the development of a new underlying form for an established surface sequence. Thus – to take an instance of a simple 'visible' change – it does not take a degree in linguistics to note that the plural of *postman* remains irregular (*postmen*) in present-day English, while the plural of *Walkman* tends to be *Walkmans*.

The following example, by contrast, raises a few more complicated issues about the status of *following*:

(6)   *Following* the signing of the peace treaty and British recognition of American independence, Washington stunned the world when he surrendered his sword to Congress on Dec. 23 1783 and retired to his farm at Mount Vernon. [Frown G13]

Following looks like a present participle, and indeed similar constructions would make decent enough non-finite adverbial clauses in many syntactic contexts, for example in *Following the suspicious stranger, they ended up in a rather unpleasant part of town*. Such an analysis, however, is not available here, and at least in this example and similar ones *following* is therefore most appropriately analysed as a deverbal preposition roughly equivalent to *after*. The gradual expansion of some participles into the prepositional domain is by no means a unique phenomenon, but illustrates a well-trodden path of grammaticalization. Earlier instances from the history of English include *regarding*, *concerning*, *barring* or even *during* and *notwithstanding*, and similar phenomena are common in other languages. However, the long time taken by such shifts, their gradual nature, the involvement of abstract grammatical categories rather than concrete words and morphemes, and not least the structural ambiguity of many relevant examples all make it very difficult for lay observers to spot such changes and to make explicit the linguistic processes involved.[7]

For lay and expert observers alike, an additional difficulty in perceiving grammatical change, in particular grammatical change at close range, is that it generally proceeds more slowly than lexical and phonetic change. While a lifetime devoted to observing lexical or phonetic developments in English will generally be enough to arrive at a fair number of definitive conclusions, the same timespan is insufficient to allow testable statements about the direction and speed of grammatical trends. For grammatical changes, therefore, even linguistically trained observers will need more solid orientation than their own necessarily subjective and partial observations provide. As David Denison has made clear in his magisterial study of grammatical change in nineteenth- and twentieth-century English, practically all grammatical change involves a gradual and statistical element during the long process in which an innovation establishes itself in the community of speakers (or, conversely, a formerly common but now obsolescent form is phased out):

Since relatively few categorial losses or innovations have occurred in the last two centuries, syntactic change has more often been statistical in nature, with a given construction occurring throughout the period and either becoming more or less common generally or in particular registers. The overall, rather elusive effect can seem more a matter of stylistic than of syntactic change, so it is useful to be able to track frequencies of occurrence from EModE through to the present day. (Denison 1998: 93)

---

[7] Minimally, the person would have to have the metalinguistic competence necessary to conduct standard linguistic re-formulation tests and interpret their results. For example, an analysis of *following* as a verbal participle is unlikely because the construction cannot be expanded into a finite adverbial clause which shares its subject with the main clause (in this case 'Washington'):

*When he *followed* the signing of the peace treaty and British recognition of American independence, Washington stunned the world when he surrendered his sword to Congress on Dec. 23, 1783 and retired to his farm at Mount Vernon.

For a more detailed analysis of this particular instance of grammaticalization, see Olofsson (1990).

In view of this, there is no way around the systematic compilation of statistics and frequencies which are based on large machine-readable bodies of textual data.

The present work is thus based on the following three premises, namely that (1) the systematic study of such corpora will refine our understanding of recent and ongoing grammatical change in standard English, that (2) such research will help us to correct current misperceptions and that (3) the method will occasionally point us towards interesting developments in the language which have not even been noticed before.

The corpora used for the present study are first and foremost the four matching one-million-word corpora of British and American English known as the 'Brown family' (after the pioneering Brown corpus which set the pattern for many similar ones subsequently compiled). The Brown corpus, named after Brown University in Providence, Rhode Island, where it was compiled by W. Nelson Francis and Henry Kučera in the 1960s, is – as its official title describes it – a 'Standard Corpus of Present-Day Edited American English, for Use with Digital Computers'. It contains about a million words of text, sampled in 500 extracts of c. 2,000 words each spanning a range of 15 different textual genres, and representing the state of written American English in the year 1961.[8] The LOB (Lancaster–Oslo/Bergen) corpus was compiled under the direction of Geoffrey Leech and Stig Johansson in the 1970s to provide a matching database for British English. In the 1990s, F-LOB (the Freiburg update of the LOB corpus) and Frown (Freiburg update of the Brown corpus) were compiled under the direction of Christian Mair at the University of Freiburg, in order to bring the comparison of British and American English closer to the present and, even more importantly, to make possible the systematic corpus-based study of how regional variation interacts with short-term diachronic change. The 'Brown family' of corpora has spawned a considerable amount of research on grammatical change in progress in present-day English, both by the authors of the present book and by others. Most of this research has been based on the plain-text versions of the corpora, with the obvious limitations on linguistically sophisticated access to the material that such a restriction entails.

However, the present book is not merely a continuation and summary of previous research, but represents a new departure in at least two respects. First, it is now possible to complement research on the plain-text corpora with investigations of versions of the corpora which have been grammatically annotated for parts of speech. As will be shown, this opens up interesting possibilities of accessing the material in novel ways, and studying aspects of ongoing grammatical change which have never been covered before. To give an illustration: a study of inflectional and analytical comparison of

---

[8] See the Preface, Chapter 2 and Appendix I for further information on this corpus and other corpora used for the present study.

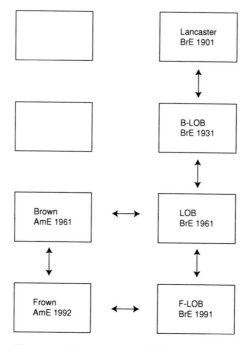

Figure 1.1 Matching one-million-word corpora of written English

adjectives (see section 11.6.3) based on untagged corpora is confined to searching for individual pairs such as *politer* vs *more polite*, or *commoner* vs *more common*. It would not be possible to search for the category 'inflectionally graded adjective' as a whole, nor would we be able to determine the share of comparative and superlative forms as a proportion of the total number of adjectives (i.e. the forms which are potential carriers of the marking investigated). In other words, we would be almost certain to miss many important generalizations about ongoing change in this fragment of the grammar. Second, work on the Brown family of corpora was often hampered by the fact that in a timespan of a mere thirty years it is difficult to differentiate directed diachronic developments from random fluctuation. To remedy this, the two UK-based authors of the present book have started work on compiling matching corpora documenting the development of British English in 1931 ('B-LOB,' for 'before LOB') and in 1901 ('Lancaster 1901').

The relationship between these corpora is visually represented in Figure 1.1.

As the blanks in the 'American' half of the diagram show, the symmetry is not perfect yet, and much of Lancaster 1901 remains to be completed. Nevertheless, the corpus-linguistic working environment illustrated generally makes it possible to sketch the development of high- and medium-frequency lexico-grammatical phenomena in written British and American English in the twentieth century and to get an idea of the relation between the two major international reference standards at two points of time in the latter half of the century.

Again and again, in the course of the analyses offered in the present book, we shall see that British and American English are not the monolithic entities they sometimes appear to be in popular perception. Particularly at the level of grammatical organization which is the focus here, the relations between the two varieties are complex, and so is the interplay between synchronic regional contrast and short-term diachronic change. Nevertheless, we would like to offer a few general remarks at this point, if only to help the reader's orientation. Among the several existing and emerging standards which have arisen in the wake of a process of linguistic–cultural de-colonization going back at least to the US Declaration of Independence in 1776, British and American English still occupy a unique position in that they still are the only two standard varieties with a truly global reach, and hence more likely to influence the future shape of the language than standards with a regional or national scope.

In phonology, it may well be possible (and useful) to describe British and American English (or Indian English, New Zealand English or any other variety, for that matter) as separate systems characterized by their own categorically distinct features. On the lexico-grammatical level, however, such categorical 'either–or' contrasts are the exception rather than the rule. It is our view that standard varieties of English all over the world share the same basic system of grammatical options, and that regional contrasts among varieties in most cases manifest themselves in different statistical preferences in the choice of variants, or in the extension of shared constructional patterns to new lexical items. This has obvious implications for the assessment of mutual influences between British and American English, an important concern of the present study. Whereas in popular perception, particularly in Britain, there is often fear of a blanket 'Americanization' of British English, our analyses will show that documenting the true extent of the grammatical influence of American English on British English is a complex business. There are fragments of the grammar in which American influence is absent and even some divergence between the two varieties can be observed, as in the spread of *from*-less gerunds after verbs of prevention (cf., e.g. *that'll stop him calling again*), which is a British development as yet not paralleled in American usage. There are a few limited instances of presumably direct American influence on British usage, as in the area of the 'mandative' subjunctive (e.g. *we request that this be made public*). But the most common constellation by far is that American English reveals itself to be slightly more advanced in shared historical developments, many of which were presumably set in motion in the Early Modern English period, before the streams of British and American English parted.

A further caveat concerns the way in which the grammatical features investigated present themselves in our corpus data. Inevitably, we encounter grammatical forms and constructions embedded in particular text types and discourse contexts. Thus, it may well be the case that the averaged contrasts in, say, modal-verb usage which we observe between British and American English are far outweighed by the contrasts between two text types within one British or American corpus (see Table 4.1). Taking account of the role of genre and text-type is, of course, vitally important in all those cases in which one of two variants investigated is informal or colloquial. For the corpus linguist, this should not be seen as a cause for despair but as a challenge – a challenge to produce a differentiated description of how short-term changes in stylistic fashions and discourse conventions are related to and ultimately help bring about the structural changes that remain the focus of the book.

Given that many grammatical innovations start out in spoken English and then gradually spread into writing, the Brown family's restriction to edited written English is problematic. Where necessary, we have therefore consulted spoken data from two late-twentieth-century corpora of British and American English, chiefly the British National Corpus and the Longman Corpus of Spoken American English. At least for the British National Corpus, extensive speaker information is given which makes possible research into ongoing change on the 'apparent-time' model, that is by differentiating between the usage of older and younger speakers.[9] A small but richly annotated 'real-time' diachronic corpus of spoken English has been compiled by Bas Aarts and colleagues at University College London (DCPSE – 'Diachronic Corpus of Present-Day Spoken English'); it has been used for this study where appropriate, as have other standard electronic resources for the study of the history of English, such as, for example, the quotations database of the *OED*.

To illustrate how these resources can be combined in the study of ongoing diachronic trends, let us return to one of the two instances of variable usage discussed above, namely the alleged disappearance of the form *whom* from standard English. On the evidence obtained from the Brown family, worries about the imminent demise of *whom* in late twentieth-century English turn out to be unfounded.

The figures in Table 1.1 show random fluctuation, possibly even convergence between the two major regional standards, but definitely not a parallel and directed diachronic trend in the two varieties. Figures from the one-hundred-million-word British National Corpus (BNC) are also instructive. At a total frequency of 12,596, or c. 129 words per million, *whom* cannot exactly be called a rare word in contemporary English. Its function as a style marker, however, becomes obvious as soon as one looks at the frequencies

---

[9] The apparent-time assumption was first introduced into the sociolinguistic study of variation and change in Labov (1963). See Labov (1994: 43–72) for a detailed discussion of the conditions in which it holds.

Table 1.1. Whom *(interrogative and relative function) in four matching corpora*

	1961	1991/92
American English (Brown/Frown)	144	166
British English (LOB/F-LOB)	217	177

in different textual genres: more than 200 words per million in some of the more formal written genres, and figures as low as 5 per million words in the spontaneous dialogues.[10] Yet the study of ongoing change is not just a matter of compiling statistics but must involve theoretically guided qualitative analysis, as well.

Such an analysis reveals interesting cases of hypercorrect usage such as the following, in which *whom* is used in place of an expected *who*:

(7)   I went in to look at kitchen units and saw Mrs Major in deep conversation with a man in a grey suit *whom* I thought was a salesman. [F-LOB A09]

Even towards the beginning of the twentieth century Otto Jespersen (1909–49: III, 197–200) noted the currency of such usages, pointing out that their predictable occurrence in certain environments might have more to do with the grammatical structure of the English language than the sloppiness of individual speakers and writers. On the basis of attestations from the Early Modern English period onwards, he was additionally able to dispel the notion – widely held at the time – that they were recent. Obviously, speakers and writers have long been confused about the historically appropriate rules for the use of the inflected form *whom* and increasingly employ it for its stylistic prestige only.

More interesting than the occasional use of *whom* in cases in which an inflection is not required, however, is the question whether *whom* is under threat in the one niche in which it remains more or less obligatory in contemporary standard English, i.e. after prepositions. Are we, for example, beginning to find sentences of the type illustrated in (8b) below?

(8)   a. Harry Hopkins, *by whom* Christian Asman was employed, said [...] [Frown L09]
      b. *Harry Hopkins, *by who* Christian Asman was employed, said [...]

Even the expected collocation, *by whom*, is a rare combination of words. In the four corpora of the Brown family it is attested a mere nine times, of

[10] This goes against previous research based on other corpora, in which results did point towards a decline in the discourse frequency of *whom* in spoken and written English in the late twentieth century (Aarts and Aarts 2002: 128). For some more fine-grained analyses of *whom* in the Brown family and the BNC, see de Haan 2002.

which seven instances are relative constructions of the type illustrated in (8a). Not surprisingly, given that we are dealing with relatively small amounts of written text, *by who* is not found at all.[11] In order to determine the status of *by who* in contemporary English, we need more material, and in particular more material from informal writing and speech.

And indeed, *by who* is attested in the British National Corpus, as the following examples show, even though the frequencies are still fairly low.[12] Here are some typical examples, covering various spoken and written genres:

(9)   A: Don't they worry about you not doing games? Cos I've been asked a question before <unclear>

    B: I've been asked loads of questions.

    A: Have you?

    B: Yeah.

    A: *By who?*

    B: Erm some lady who works for the council or something. [BNC KNY; spontaneous conversation]

(10)   A: It is indeed a self-serving statement statement [sic!], so, so what does that give us? <'clears throat'> <pause> If you were to characterize this, this interview, what would you call it?
<pause> It's a text. *By who?*

    B: <unclear> <'too quiet to hear'>

    A: Part of the confession is a self-serving part, it's a er, possibly mixed statement. Er, in which he blames somebody else, okay? What is the effect of that? [BNC HYH; law school tutorial]

(11)   He turned to Hitch. 'You heard the geezer the other night, John; he didn't sound like he was joking, did he?'
Hitch shook his head.
'I agree with Joe,' he added. 'It *could* be a set-up.'
'But *by who?*' Plummer wanted to know, a note of exasperation in his voice.
[BNC G01; fiction: Shaun Hutson, *Captives* (1992)]

---

[11] Of course, a search in a tagged corpus need not limit itself to individual strings of words such as *by whom* or *by who*. A search in the tagged F-LOB corpus for 'any preposition' followed by relative *whom* revealed a raw total of 122 instances (which had to be reduced slightly after manual post-editing of the concordance), whereas the corresponding search for prepositions followed by either relative or interrogative *who* produced not a single relevant case and only a handful of spurious examples of the type 'a matter of who is in control'. There were two instances of interrogative *whom* preceded by prepositions. See Section 10.5.4 on the recent history of preposition stranding in relative clauses for further details.

[12] The raw total is 41. This, however, includes a majority of spurious hits: some in which WHO ('World Health Organization') was misidentified as the pronoun; a number of structures of the type, 'You judge people not by who they are but by what they do and how they behave' (BNC ADP 2299), which are not relative clauses. After subtracting additional scanning errors and the residue of uninterpretable passages inevitable in the transcription of spontaneous speech, a mere eleven pertinent instances remain.

(12)   Strangely, lesbians have come to be categorised as a 'low risk group' for HIV infection. At least our sexual behaviour (as defined *by who*, we need to ask) has been classified as low risk – though this appears to have been interpreted by every corner of society as *no risk*.
BNC ARW [journalism: *Spare Rib*]

Like the few other attested cases, most of these examples are from informal conversation or written genres such as narrative fiction, which often imitate spoken conventions. Note also that none of these examples has *who* used as a relative pronoun.[13] The typical use is in elliptical questions. True relative clauses, such as the following one, which is modelled on an authentic BNC example (BNC CEW 199) in which *whom* was used, seem to be unattested:

(13)   For the next 15 years she was to lead an undistinguished life of secluded domesticity until her marriage to a middle-aged magistrate, *by who* she bore three children.

Of course, what will not be attested in a corpus of one hundred million words can always be obtained in fair quantities from the World Wide Web, as a search for the phrase *by who he had* will easily prove.[14] While we realize that web-based corpus linguistics is developing into a booming subfield at the moment (see Hundt *et al.* 2007), for the present book we have nevertheless decided to heed Brian Joseph's recent warning 'caveat Googlator' (Joseph 2004). This means that the exhaustive and fine-grained analysis of small corpora will be the starting point and foundation for most of the analyses presented in the present book, and ancillary material from larger databases, including the World Wide Web, will be used occasionally only, and if it serves to illustrate an important point which could not be made otherwise.

When it comes to the study of ongoing change in grammar, small corpora are still superior to large but less structured textual archives, especially if – as in our case – they have a rich annotation and are closely controlled for regional, diachronic and stylistic variation. Also, in Edward Sapir's memorable words,

---

[13] In a BNC-based study covering a large number of prepositions in addition to *by*, de Haan (2002: 215–16) reports eight relative clauses featuring prepositions followed by *who*, involving *about, for, in, of, with, upon*. One typical example (from a periodical publication) is:

A passionate lover of the Savoy Operas, she was a founder member of the Bradford Gilbert and Sullivan Society, with who she had a long association. (BNC C8G: 418)

[14] A Google search undertaken on 10 October 2005 yielded c. 421 returns for the whole web, c. 15 for the .uk top-level national domain, and c. 5 for the predominantly American top-level domain .edu. A typical example is, 'He married Elizabeth, daughter of John de Mohun, 9th Lord de Mohun of Dunster, by who he had a son and two daughters', from the Wikipedia entry for William Montacute, 2nd Earl of Salisbury: http://en.wikipedia.org/wiki/William_Montacute,_2nd_Earl_of_Salisbury [accessed 1 October 2006].

'all grammars leak', and it would be surprising indeed if we did not come across instances of contextually licensed flouting of grammatical rules or plain performance errors in the vast quantity of language data accessible in web searches. This is true today, and it may have been equally true for the following example from the early seventeenth century, in which the performance error seems to have survived cast in stone:[15]

(14)   Here lieth the Bodies of Henrie Sacheverell Esqier who married 3 Wives, Marie, Daughter of Robert Gittins in ye County of Kent Esqr. *by who* he had issue one sonn and 2 daughs. She died ye 27th of October 1600. His second wife was Elizath [sic!] daughter to Willia Copleay, of Spratborowe in ye County of Yorke Esqr who died ye 13th of Maie 1616. His third wife was Lucie daughtr to Willia Boughton of Lawton in the Cou'ty of Warwick Esqr which Henrie died ye 7th of Januarie Ano Dni 1625. [Holy Trinity Church, Radcliffe-on-Soar,   http://nottshistory.org.uk/articles/summerexcursion1924/radcliffe5.htm]

Before we start rewriting the history of English syntax on the basis of this single early instance of an unusual form, we had better ask ourselves whether we might be dealing with dialect usage in a period of emergent standardization or, even more practically and simply, whether the person who transcribed the original lapidary inscription did not miss a small superscript *m* (*who^m*) of the kind which was regularly used in writing at the time. Even if we – provisionally and for the sake of argument – accept the example as authentic, we have no evidence that such experimental forms have increased markedly in frequency in the course of the past few centuries.

1.3   A frame of orientation: previous research on recent and ongoing grammatical changes in English

In the study of grammatical change in present-day English, the 'tip of the iceberg', that is the collection of disputed usages that has aroused the concern of prescriptivists, has been covered regularly, though not necessarily in the dispassionate and empirically sound way that is characteristic of the best research on older stages in the history of English.

Among the works which have guided us in our choice of phenomena to study and in formulating our hypotheses, we would like to mention three treatments of ongoing change in English published in the 1960s and 1970s, namely Barber's (1964) *Linguistic Change in Present-Day English*, Foster's

---

[15] Much like today, sequences of 'preposition + *who*' seem to have been somewhat more common in interrogative clauses, especially of the echo and elliptical types, than in relative clauses in Early Modern English (see Jespersen 1909–49: V, 484–485).

(1968) *The Changing English Language* and Potter's (1975) *Changing English*. These works offer many insightful comments but, unsurprisingly in view of their dates of publication, the amount and quality of the documentary evidence offered leaves a lot to be desired by the standards of contemporary corpus-linguistic practice. A first tentatively corpus-linguistic approach to change in progress is presented by Bauer (1994) in his *Watching English Change*. It is not to deny the merit of Bauer's pioneering effort to point out that it is comprehensive neither in its coverage of the phenomena nor in its use of the available corpora and textual resources,[16] thus leaving many important topics for the present study and others to explore.

The two publications providing the most important and most immediate frame of reference for the present book are David Denison's (1998) survey of 'Syntax' in volume IV of *The Cambridge History of the English Language* and Mair's (2006b) *Twentieth-Century English* – both works which are recent and based on systematic evaluation of corpora. Again, it is not to detract from their merits to point out that neither of these two publications has been able to cover its subject comprehensively. Denison, for example, deals with the evolution of English grammar from 1776 to 1997 and generally highlights nineteenth-century developments rather than the very recent past. Mair (2006b), on the other hand, is a general history of standard English in the twentieth century which also covers developments in pronunciation and the lexicon and is therefore somewhat restricted in the coverage of the grammar in comparison to the present book. In addition, the author was unable to make full use of the tagged versions of the Brown family of corpora, which prevented him from covering some important topics that will be dealt with in the present work. We also owe an intellectual debt to the abundant work on change in progress in the sociolinguistic literature (cf., e.g., Labov 1994, 2001; Romaine and Lange 1991; Rickford *et al.* 1995), although – in view of a widespread disregard in sociolinguistic circles for the study of the standard dialect – the influence has often been indirect.

Of course, innovative impulses for the study of language history have not come from sociolinguistics alone. Today is an exciting time for diachronic studies in other ways, as well, as is witnessed by a recent convergence of

---

[16] Among the data Bauer uses for his study is a corpus of editorials from *The Times* newspaper, compiled by himself, which contains the relevant texts from the first ten days of March of every fifth year. It seems that the method of analysis was traditional-philological and did not rely on computer-aided retrieval techniques. For the study of lexical innovation, he seems to have relied mainly on the printed version of the *OED*, in particular the supplements, rather than the second edition published on CD-ROM (which in turn would not have afforded the full range of digital search options provided by the *OED Online* today). It is, in fact, impressive testimony to the speed of progress in corpus development to consider how many of the corpora and digital text archives in general use in the linguistic community today were not available to Bauer a mere fifteen years ago. The completed versions of F-LOB and Frown would be an obvious case in point.

interests between corpus linguistics and grammaticalization studies (e.g. Hoffmann 2005, Krug 2000, or the contributions to Lindquist and Mair, 2004b). Typically, students of grammaticalization focus on the long historical range, and studies of grammaticalization processes in English tend to focus on earlier stages in the development of the language. There is no reason to doubt that the same forces are at work today, and in fact the present book will discuss some instances of incipient or ongoing grammaticalization.

What the present book undertakes is thus a fresh look at grammatical change in twentieth-century English. Typically, a starting point for our investigations will be provided by the many current hypotheses and assumptions about changes going on in English grammar. These are rarely completely unfounded, but documentation is usually very patchy, impressionistic and coloured by prescriptive prejudice. This being so, state-of-the-art corpus-linguistic methodology is, we feel, precisely the strategy to use in order to flesh out, to refine and, where necessary, to correct the picture.

A consensus list of grammatical topics worth exploring in this spirit might take the following form (based on Barber 1964: 130–144, with additions):

- decline of the inflected form *whom*
- use of *less* instead of *fewer* with countable nouns (e.g. *less people*)
- regularization of irregular morphology (e.g. *dreamt* → *dreamed*)
- a tendency towards analytical comparison of disyllabic adjectives (*politer, politest* → *more polite, most polite*)
- spread of the *s*-genitive to non-human nouns (*the book's cover*)
- revival of the 'mandative' subjunctive, probably inspired by formal US usage (*we demand that she take part in the meeting*)
- elimination of *shall* as a future marker in the first person
- development of new, auxiliary-like uses of certain lexical verbs (e.g. *want to* → *wanna* – cf., e.g., *the way you look, you wanna see a doctor soon*)
- further auxiliation of semi-auxiliaries and modal idioms such as *be going to* (→ *gonna*) or *have got to* (→ *gotta*)
- extension of the progressive to new constructions (especially modal, present perfect and past perfect passive progressives of the type *the road would not be being built / has not been being built / had not been being built*)
- use of *like, same as*, and *immediately* as conjunctions
- omission of the definite article in combinations of premodifying descriptive noun phrase and proper name (e.g. *renowned Nobel laureate Derek Walcott*)
- increase in the number and types of multi-word verbs (phrasal verbs, *have/take/give a* + verb)
- placement of frequency adverbs before auxiliary verbs (even if no emphasis is intended – *I never have said so*)

— *do*-support for *have* (*Have you any money?* and *No, I haven't any money* →
  Do you have/have you got any money? and *No, I don't have any money/I
  haven't got any money*)
— spread of 'singular' *they* (*Everybody came in their car*) to formal and
  standard usage.

The list could be extended easily. Chapter 7, for example, will show that
there have been fairly drastic shifts in the frequency and use of various types
of passive, although the passive is rarely mentioned among the grammatical categories possibly undergoing change at the moment. This should not
come as a surprise, as systematic corpus-based study will regularly reveal
current assumptions about the nature of ongoing changes as incomplete and
partially mistaken. In particular, the systematic analysis of corpus data cor-
rects a bias in the previous literature toward rare, unusual and bizarre usage
(which is naturally what most attracts the attention of the impressionistic
observer). In corpora we can document both the unusual/innovative *and* the
usually more powerful continuity of usage. Corpora make clear that language
change, in particular grammatical change, is rarely dramatic but proceeds
gradually, slowly and – most importantly – at differential speeds in different
varieties/text types. Corpora, as records of actual usage, also help correct
the bias introduced into the study of ongoing changes by prescriptive concerns. Where, to use a convenient distinction introduced by William Labov
(1972), the prescriptive tradition is concerned with social 'markers', that
is those variable usages which are salient in the community and the subject of conscious debate, corpora make it possible to additionally investigate
social 'indicators', the often more interesting and ultimately more important
changes which proceed below the threshold of conscious awareness. The
corpus linguist's moment of deepest satisfaction is probably reached when
the unprejudiced analysis of diachronic trends in the corpora reveals changes
which have not been previously suspected.

The present study is constructed around a collection of matching corpora
which are stratified with regard to text type or genre, and which document
the two major regional standards of English at successive points of time
in the twentieth century. This arrangement is ideal for anyone wishing to
study grammatical change against the background of changing traditions
of speaking and writing, changing genre conventions or evolving norms
of sociolinguistic and stylistic propriety. As we shall see, these 'discourse'
norms are subject to much faster changes than the 'structure' norms of the
grammar and play an important role in the spread of grammatical innovations,
by speeding up or slowing down certain developments in certain contexts.
The discourse level also provides the link between the language-internal
forces that determine the evolution of the grammatical system, and the
socio-historical factors that shape the communicative context in which the
language is used. One trend which has massively impacted on the shape of

written English in the course of the past century is what we will refer to as 'colloquialization', i.e. a tendency for written norms to become more informal and move closer to speech.[17] The present study will provide ample statistical documentation of this trend based on corpora, for example by showing that there have been increases of informal contracted negatives of the type *isn't*, *doesn't* or *hasn't* at the expense of the formal two-word alternatives *is not*, *does not* or *has not* (see section 11.3.1). On the discourse level, paragraphs in popular written genres have become shorter, and newspaper reports now come with more passages of direct quotation – whether real or fictitious – than they used to.

To gauge the extent of the colloquialization of written norms in the twentieth century at this stage, it is enough to present one typical early twentieth-century advertisement and think about why similar marketing strategies would be unthinkable today (Figure 1.2).

Clearly, some things have not changed much. Then as now, cosmetics are among the most heavily advertised consumer goods, and women are an important target audience in this case. On the other hand, the type of gender-stereotyping in evidence in this advertisement is not very popular today. But of course it is the very grammar of the text which would prevent it being used in similar contexts today. The very first sentence – 'Should you want it, even on washing days, you can have all the time desired for gossip or any other form of entertainment.' – contains a very formal grammatical structure, inversion of auxiliary and subject in the dependent clause. The next sentence has three instances of the passive voice, which is a grammatical marker of formality, now seriously in decline even in extremely formal and stylistically conservative genres such as academic prose. The copywriter has managed to include the construction *by the fact that* + clause twice in a text that comprises a total of only a little more than a hundred words.[18]

As the *OED* entry for *Americanism* shows,[19] British writers have been aware of, and not always comfortable with, a trickle of lexical borrowings

---

[17] While generally speaking the written language is formal and the spoken language informal, the correspondence is not perfect. For example, in recent journalistic writing there has been an increase in noun phrases of the type *San Francisco Redevelopment Agency Executive Director Edward Helfeld* [Frown A02], which are certainly more informal than the alternative, *Edward Helfeld, the Executive Director of the San Francisco Redevelopment Agency*, but which would nevertheless be rare in spoken language.

[18] In the BNC the form *the fact that* occurs at an overall frequency of c. 134 per million, which rises to extremes of c. 439, 335 and 334 respectively in formal text types such as the Parliamentary *Hansard*, academic tutorials or school essays, and sinks to around 31 per million for spoken conversational texts. It occurs just once in 558,133 words of advertising literature in the BNC. Of course, our interpretation assumes that what is a marker of formal syntax today functioned as such at the beginning of the twentieth century. This assumption is plausible for the features discussed here.

[19] Sense 3 of the word, the one relevant here, is illustrated with the following quotations, among others: 'Society has been progressing (if I may borrow that expressive Americanism) at a very rapid rate' from an 1826 source and 'There are many Americanisms which in the course of time will work their way into the language of England' from 1833.

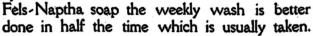

Gossip.

Should you want it, even on washing days, you can have all the time desired for gossip or any other form of entertainment.

This is easily proved by the fact that with Fels-Naptha soap the weekly wash is better done in half the time which is usually taken.

This is accounted for, in its turn, by the fact that Fels-Naptha soap is much more than soap—Naphtha with soap—which loosens the dirt in half an hour's soaking instead of the ordinary hard rubbing. Consequently, the washing needs only the half instead of the whole day.

The best argument is made by Fels-Naptha soap itself.

Sales Co., Ltd., 30, Wilson Street, London, E.C.

Figure 1.2 Advertisement for Fels-Naptha Soap, *The Times*, 31 December 1915, page 15

from American English since the early nineteenth century. From about the middle part of the twentieth century, however, there has been increasing concern among speakers of British English that their variety might be being 'Americanized' on a large scale. Although it is clearly not on the grammatical plane that we find the most salient contrasts between British and American English, this is a hypothesis worth investigating, and we shall return to it in Chapter 11, where we show that there is not much cause for alarm.

British English often follows American English in those long-term grammatical drifts which were set in motion centuries ago and in which different varieties of English have basically followed the same course at slightly different speeds. Well-described cases would include the tendency to use main-verb syntax for *have* (*Don't you have any sense of responsibility at all?* rather than *Have you no sense of responsibility at all?* – see Table 11.3) or the use of *will* rather than *shall* for the future in the first persons singular and plural. On the other hand, our corpora show that even in the twentieth century British English is still capable of independent grammatical innovation which will lead to divergence from current US norms (or – admittedly the more unlikely case – will eventually motivate Americans to change their norms on the British pattern). A case in point is provided by structures such as *Can we stop/prevent this happening?*, which unlike the alternatives with *from* (*Can we stop/prevent this from happening?*) have virtually disappeared from American English in the course of the twentieth century but have remained firmly established as standard usage in Britain.

Like Americanization, colloquialization does not proceed unchecked, either. Written communication today has to cope with unprecedented amounts of information, and our corpora strongly suggest that this has left a mark on the structure of the noun phrase. In particular, premodification of nouns by other nouns has increased markedly (see sections 10.2–3), so that noun phrases of the type illustrated below are now far more common in written texts than they were a hundred years ago:

(15)   Black Country car sales group West Midland Motors [F-LOB A38]

West Midland Motors, the car sales group based in the Black Country (or a similar re-formulation) would have been the traditionally preferred structure in such cases. It would have delivered the same information using some more words – a 'luxury' contemporary writers seem increasingly unwilling to afford.

1.4   Conclusion

The example just mentioned makes an important general point. More often than not there are links between grammatical changes, on the one hand, and social and cultural changes, on the other. Such links may not be as obvious as the links between social change and lexical change, and they are certainly more indirect. Again and again, however, the authors have discovered that, especially when it comes to explaining the spread of innovations through different styles and genres, apparently disparate grammatical 'symptoms' can be traced back to common 'causes' at the discourse level. Exploring the connections between the observed shifts in grammatical usage (the nuts and bolts of the system, as it were) and the broader changes in the communicative climate of the age, which are reflected in the performance data that the corpora are made up of, is a fascinating challenge not only for the linguist.

The latter part of the twentieth century, the era in focus here, seems to have been a period shaped by a growing appreciation of the informal and colloquial in writing, by a pervasive and growing influence of American usage on all varieties of English (which, of course, does not preclude occasional counter-movements), and, certainly in the written language, by the effects of an 'information explosion', which forces writers to compress ever-increasing amounts of information in texts of limited length. Needless to add, these trends may sometimes work hand in hand – American forms are often more informal than those preferred in traditional British usage – but in other instances they do not. For example, there is a conflict between the 'competing demands of popularization vs. economy' (Biber 2003a). It is a great advantage of the use of corpora that they allow us new insights both into changing grammatical constructions and the changing discourse and social contexts in which they are used.

2 Comparative corpus linguistics: the methodological basis of this book

This chapter concentrates on the foundations of corpus linguistics and the methodology used for the investigation of the four corpora (Brown, LOB, Frown and F-LOB) belonging to the Brown family. As explained in Chapter 1, our study of recent grammatical change focuses primarily on these corpora. But there are also other corpora, which extend the study into spoken English or take it further back into the past. For these, the same methodology applies in outline, although there may be some differences. We argue that the present study represents, in some ways, a new kind of corpus linguistics. We can label this **comparative corpus linguistics**, or more specifically **short-term diachronic comparable corpus linguistics**. We will seek to explain this somewhat long-winded phrase by starting with the last words 'corpus linguistics' and gradually working leftwards to take in the other defining words one by one.

2.1 (Computer) corpus linguistics: the Brown Corpus and after

Although the term **corpus linguistics** was apparently not in use until the 1980s,[1] it is generally agreed that this sub-discipline of linguistics has been in existence longer – at least since the earlier 1960s. The term can be simply defined as 'the study or analysis of language through the use of (computer) corpora'. The landmark event for the development of corpus linguistics in the modern sense (involving the use of electronic or machine-readable corpora) was the creation of the Brown Corpus by Nelson Francis and Henry Kučera in 1961–64. It is necessary to say a little about this corpus, because, however dated it may seem by present-day standards, it is actually the prototype of the Brown family of corpora, our primary source of data. Many readers of this book will know about the Brown Corpus; some will know it in the more familiar sense of having consulted it, searched it or analysed its contents. The Brown Corpus has been a stand-by for English language research and teaching since the beginning of modern corpus linguistics.

---

[1] The term 'corpus linguistics' first appeared in the title of a book by Aarts and Meijs (1984).

In its early days, however, the Brown Corpus was not seen as a landmark achievement. When its compilers made it available to the world, it was not greeted with fanfares of applause, as a great breakthrough in the subject. Leaders of opinion in linguistics, as memorably retold by its chief compiler Francis (1979: 110), regarded the making of a computer corpus as a waste of time,[2] and decades passed before the Brown Corpus came to be cited as a source of evidence for serious mainstream research. A description of the contents of the corpus is found in Appendix I (pp. 273–5).

Nowadays, although Brown is probably the most used corpus in the history of corpus linguistics, it is considered far from ideal. Advances in corpus linguistics have been so dramatic, following in the wake of technological progress, that Brown can no longer be recommended as the blueprint for corpus construction of the present day.

There are three reasons for this. First, by current standards Brown is small, consisting of 500 text extracts of approximately 2,000 words each, and therefore of one million words in its entirety (actually slightly more – see Table 2.1).[3] Second, it is limited in its range of coverage of the language. It exemplifies only the written language, and is restricted to texts that have been edited for publication. Further, the types of texts sampled excluded certain varieties which were considered somewhat marginal to general standard written usage: for example, advertisements, poems and play texts. In terms of time and place, Brown was also restricted to texts written by native speakers of American English, and published in 1961. This time-frame, which was bang up to date for its compilers in the early sixties, now seems, for many users, sadly dated.

A third drawback of the Brown Corpus lies in its composition, in terms of (a) the text categories and (b) the number of text extracts sampled for each category. Francis and Kučera did the best they could, in that era, to ensure that the corpus would be well designed. They assembled a group of eminent 'corpus-wise scholars'[4] who decided on the text categories (or genres), and on what proportion of the million-word corpus would be assigned to each.

---

[2] Francis (1979: 110) reports that when he mentioned his corpus-building project, Robert Lees, leading disciple of Chomsky, responded: 'That is a complete waste of your time and the government's money. You are a native speaker of English; in ten minutes you can produce more illustrations of any point in English grammar than you will find in many millions of words of random text.'

[3] The reason why the Brown Corpus consists of more than a million words is that each text sample continued until the first sentence break after the 2,000th word. The same practice was employed in compiling the other corpora in the Brown family.

[4] Francis: 'we convened a conference of such corpus-wise scholars as Randolph Quirk, Philip Gove, and John B. Carroll. This group decided the size of the corpus (1000000 words), the number of texts (500, of 2000 words each), the universe (material in English, by American writers, first printed in the United States in the calendar year 1961), the subdivisions (15 genres, 9 of 'informative prose' and 6 of 'imaginative prose') and by a fascinating process of individual vote and average consensus, how many samples from each genre (ranging from 6 in science fiction to 80 in learned and scientific).' (Quoted from Francis 1979: 117.)

Table 2.1. *Brown and LOB Corpora compared in terms of genres, number of texts and number of words*

Genre category	Brown Corpus		LOB Corpus	
	No. of texts	No. of words	No. of texts	No. of words
A press reports	44	88,629	44	88,727
B press editorial	27	54,529	27	54,295
C press reviews	17	35,350	17	34,214
Press subcorpus: SUBTOTAL	88	178,508	88	177,236
D religion	17	34,575	17	34,226
E skills, trades, hobbies	36	72,578	38	76,569
F popular lore	48	97,239	44	88,679
G biography and essays	75	152,137	77	155,121
H miscellaneous	30	62,442	30	60,593
General Prose subcorpus: SUBTOTAL	206	418,971	206	415,188
J learned	80	162,070	80	161,235
Learned subcorpus: SUBTOTAL	80	162,070	80	161,235
K general fiction	29	58,338	29	58,477
L adventure fiction	24	48,231	24	48,210
M science fiction	6	12,043	6	12,025
N mystery fiction	29	58,433	29	58,274
P romance/love story	29	58,675	29	58,149
R humour	9	18,277	9	18,069
Fiction subcorpus: SUBTOTAL	126	253,997	126	253,204
Overall total for each corpus	500	1,013,546	500	1,006,863

The method of sampling was also determined in a scientific way: there was to be a randomized stratified sampling of extensive libraries of new publications in the United States in 1961, at least those most accessible to the corpus compilers,[5] so that the corpus would be, as far as could be managed, representative of the edited written American English of its time. It was a pity that in those days the study of genre or register variation was virtually *terra incognita*, so that some of the categories that the 'corpus-wise scholars' came up with (such as 'Popular Lore') have not been judged particularly well founded. Over 40 per cent of the corpus, as Table 2.1 shows, consists of a broad cross-section of specialist and non-specialist prose non-fiction labelled 'General Prose' – categories such as Religion, Skills Trades and Hobbies, and Miscellaneous – where differences of genre, as opposed to differences of subject matter, are difficult to detect.

Why, despite these shortcomings, does the Brown Corpus merit its key place in this study? The answer is clear: because it was there from the beginning. It is the earliest electronic corpus that can claim to represent

[5] These were the Brown University library, the New York Public Library and the Providence Athenaeum.

a major cross-section of the English language. To choose a later starting point than 1961 for our diachronic comparisons would not have allowed a reasonable period of time to elapse before the dates of the later corpora. As it is, we can happily exploit a thirty-year gap – the span of a generation – separating the earlier and the later corpora in the Brown family. Despite its limitations, the Brown Corpus design covers a wide range of texts from journalism and academic writing to various types of fiction: a varied and balanced sample of the language. This makes it, admittedly in a limited sense, **representative** of the English language in a way that, for example, a much larger body of material from the *Wall Street Journal* or the *Guardian* could not be. It is significant that this term 'representative', which has already occurred twice in this chapter, featured in Francis's definition of the word 'corpus' as he applied it to his own creation:

a collection of texts assumed to be representative of a given language, dialect, or other subset of a language, to be used for linguistic analysis. (Francis 1979: 110)

Since that time the Holy Grail of 'representativeness' has been a recurrent topic in corpus linguistics. If a corpus cannot be considered representative of (some variety of) a language, then how can it be used as evidence for something beyond itself?[6] What we say we find in a corpus, without representativeness, is simply valid for that corpus. But few corpus linguists would accept the full force of this argument. They believe that corpora, with varying degrees of success, have been designed to be more or less representative of a language or some variety of it. The designers of the Brown Corpus were the first to grapple with that idea seriously, and the result was praised by Biber (1993: 243–244), in his seminal article on representativeness, as a well-constructed corpus with a 'good sampling frame'.[7]

2.2 Comparable corpora and comparative corpus linguistics

However, what makes the Brown Corpus more worthy as our starting point is that it has already become an exact model for other corpora, which differ from it only in terms of time or region of provenance.

Just as the Brown Corpus was the first electronic corpus with pretensions to representativeness, so the Lancaster–Oslo/Bergen (LOB) Corpus (begun

---

[6] On the topic of representativeness, see Biber (1993), Váradi (2001), Mukherjee (2004), Leech (2007) and Lüdeling and Kytö (2008).

[7] Whereas the corpus as a whole can claim a degree of representativeness, the same cannot always be claimed for each text category or genre it contains. Moreover, there is an 'elitist bias' in any corpus of published textual material: the author population in general consists of writers who are much more highly educated and skilled in writing than the average. This bias was no doubt greater in the 1960s than in the 1990s, and is one of the uncontrollable determinants of differences between Brown and Frown, or LOB and F-LOB.

in 1970 and completed in 1978)[8] was the first to aim at comparability. The term **comparable**, applied to two or more corpora, means that whereas their composition and sampling design are the same, the corpora differ in respect of one variable, the comparative variable. (Alternative terms sometimes applied to comparable corpora are 'matching', 'equivalent' and 'parallel'.) In the case of Brown and LOB, the year of publication was 1961 for both corpora, so that the only comparative variable was regional provenance (American versus British). Although the LOB Corpus did not quite reach the ideal of complete comparability with Brown,[9] it was close enough to be used confidently as a basis for contrasting the main grammatical features[10] of the two regional varieties, American and British English, in their written form.

Other comparable corpora followed in the next twenty years: there were Indian, Australian and New Zealand instantiations of the Brown model;[11] but their comparison with Brown was complicated by the fact that they differed from it in two variables, time and place, rather than just one. Hence no observed differences between the corpora could be easily attributed to one particular variable, say the geographical one. However, more strictly comparable were the Frown and F-LOB corpora, compiled at the University of Freiburg, which differ in terms of time, but not provenance, from LOB and Brown, respectively.

Hence the four corpora we have already explained and entitled collectively 'the Brown family' have, so far, a unique status. They can be used for six two-way comparisons as shown in Table 2.2.

In this book, we are naturally particularly interested in the second pair of comparisons, (iii) and (iv), because they show the notion of comparability of corpora being applied to the historical dimension. (In (v) and (vi), where we compare two pairs of corpora, (vi) provides another useful diachronic comparison, one in which the American and British corpora together are treated as a single corpus.) Because of the attention given by the corpus compilers to close comparability, the set of corpora provided unprecedented opportunities to track diachronic changes with precision. This was the beginning of **diachronic comparable corpus linguistics**.[12]

---

[8] Early studies comparing AmE and BrE using Brown and LOB as comparable corpora include Coates and Leech (1980), Hofland and Johansson (1982) and Leech and Fallon (1992). See also the ICAME Bibliography (Altenberg 1991) and its later versions on the ICAME website http://gandalf.aksis.uib.no/icame/icame-bib3.htm. This corpus linguistics bibliography is now maintained and updated collaboratively.

[9] Some minor differences in the composition of the corpora are explained in Johansson et al. (1978: 16).

[10] For most lexical comparisons, obviously larger corpora would be needed.

[11] The Kolhapur Corpus (Indian English, 1978); the Australian Corpus of English (Australian English, 1986); the Wellington Corpus (New Zealand English, 1986–90).

[12] However, in the pre-electronic age, there was an interesting precedent in the use of English biblical translations of different periods for diachronic comparisons, notably by Jespersen (1909–49: IV, 177).

Table 2.2. *Comparisons between corpora in the Brown family*

(i)	Brown vs LOB:	American vs British written English 1961
(ii)	Frown vs F-LOB:	American vs British written English 1991/2[i]
(iii)	Brown vs Frown:	American written English, 1961 vs 1992
(iv)	LOB vs F-LOB:	British written English, 1961 vs 1991
(v)	Brown & Frown vs LOB & F-LOB: American vs British		
(vi)	Brown & LOB vs Frown & F-LOB: 1961 vs 1991/2		

[i] For practical reasons, the Frown corpus was collected from material published in 1992, rather than 1991 (as in the case of F-LOB). There is therefore a slight temporal mismatch between the two later corpora, but for grammatical purposes they can be regarded as contemporaneous.

Corpora have, of course, been extensively used for investigating the history of the language before.[13] However, unless some strict basis for comparability of corpora at different stages in a language's history is maintained, it cannot be said with confidence that the incidence of one feature[14] (say the progressive) has increased over a particular period at a certain rate, or that the incidence of another feature (say the modal auxiliaries) has decreased at a certain rate.[15] Diachronic comparability opens up a new precision in historical studies that trace the spreading and diminishing use of linguistic features.

We add, at this point, the initial word **short-term** to our study of 'diachronic comparable corpus linguistics'. This is an appropriate description of our own study of the Brown family, since the separation of Brown and LOB from Frown and F-LOB spans a much shorter period of time than is usual for historical linguistics. It is a strength of the methodology that

[13] Diachronic corpus linguistics of English has a longer history, beginning in 1984 with work on the Helsinki Corpus of English Texts. Since then, diachronic corpora have proliferated, through dedicated hard work by the Helsinki school and other centres around the world. Some examples are: the Penn–Helsinki Parsed Corpus of Middle English (PPCME2), the Penn–Helsinki Parsed Corpus of Early Modern English (PPCEME), the ARCHER corpus (A Representative Corpus of Historical English Registers), the Corpus of Early English Correspondence (CEEC), the Corpus of Late Eighteenth Century Prose, the Corpus of English Dialogues (1560–1760) and the Corpus of Nineteenth-Century English (CONCE). Despite the immense value of such corpora, it is fair to say that in none of them (with the arguable exception of CONCE – see Kytö *et al.* 2000) has the goal of comparability, in the strict sense applicable to the Brown family of corpora, been achieved. Also few of them contain such a wide range of text types as the Brown family. For a survey of historical corpora, see Kohnen (2007) or Claridge (2008).

[14] We use the general term 'feature' in a broad sense referring to grammatical forms, categories, constructions, etc. Compare the similar use of 'feature' by Biber (1988 and elsewhere).

[15] The ARCHER corpus, covering a period from 1650 to the present, is near to the Brown family in providing a roughly equivalent sampling of different periods. In this case the sampling is from fifty-year periods, and each text category is represented by at least ten texts in each period (see Biber *et al.* 1998: 206–208, 252–253). This permits a broad comparison of grammatical frequencies over equivalent periods, although exact correspondence of one textual category or text to another is not maintained in terms of size, genre and textual provenance.

it can trace developments over a period as short as thirty years, which (as we will show) is long enough to demonstrate significant change in progress. But it is difficult to argue that the comparable corpus methodology can be easily extended indefinitely to longer periods of time – say, of a century or more. This is because comparability depends on stability of the 'genre map' of a language over time. Even the stretch of time between 1961 and 1991 saw the emergence of new written genres or sub-genres (for example, free newspapers, electronic mail and computer bulletin boards) and the decline of old ones (such as essays and belles lettres). It could be argued that, being based on the range of varieties represented in Brown and LOB, even the Frown and F-LOB corpora have failed to represent some of the new changes in language usage. But these were not far-reaching enough to impair the general claim of stability of text categories underlying the comparability of these corpora.

More recently, we have been building a 1931 (±3 years) matching corpus as an addition to the Brown family,[16] and this has given rise to some further issues of genre evolution. In category J, for example, the slots for text extracts on psychology and sociology were difficult to fill in a way comparable to those of LOB, since, at least in Britain, these social sciences had not developed into fully fledged academic disciplines at the time (see Leech and Smith 2005: 89–90). They lacked the specialized organs of publication, specialist discourse and specialist readership that existed in the later twentieth century. Similarly, the text category M was difficult to fill, because the genre of Science Fiction was less developed at that time.[17]

Although examples like these teach us to be wary of extending the diachronic comparable corpus paradigm too freely across time, we are already working on one further addition to the Brown family of corpora, in the compilation of a 1901 (±3 years) comparable corpus.[18] When this corpus is completed and available, it will be possible to track the history of written British English (within the limitations of corpus size and design already discussed) comparably from the first decade to the last decade of the twentieth century. We suspect, however, that the difficulty of maintaining the Brown Corpus design model would become rapidly more apparent if it were extended back

---

[16] The bracketed '±3 years' signifies that the corpus, for practical reasons, draws on texts published in the period 1928–34, that is, including three years preceding and three years following the 'target' date 1931. Leech and Smith, with Paul Rayson, have worked on this corpus with the support of a Leverhulme Emeritus Fellowship granted by the Leverhulme Trust.

[17] Ashley (2000: 125) observes that despite the initial popularity of science fiction in Britain, and the pioneering efforts of writers such as H. G. Wells, the late 1920s and early 1930s constituted a period in which very few magazines published science-fiction stories. In America, meanwhile, the first magazines specializing in science fiction (e.g. *Astounding Stories*) were beginning to appear at this time.

[18] Rayson, Smith and Leech's work on the 1901 (±3 years) corpus is supported, again, by the Leverhulme Trust, whose generosity we gratefully acknowledge. The bracketed '±3' again signifies a window of seven years, 1898–1904.

to the later nineteenth century or beyond.[19] 'Short-termism' is ultimately an unavoidable restriction on the methodology.

2.3 The methodological basis of comparative corpus linguistics

It is often commented that corpus linguistics is empirically oriented rather than theory-oriented; that its findings are derived from the observed corpus data in a bottom-up manner, rather than in the top-down, deductive manner associated with more theory-oriented approaches. This is true, to the extent that the conclusions drawn from a corpus linguistic study are, by their nature, conclusions coming ultimately from the empirical evidence of the data. But there are varying degrees of dependence on the corpus evidence; and the use of a corpus may very well serve to support or challenge a theoretical position,[20] or a theory-dependent hypothesis.

In this section we describe a methodology which has been followed, in the main, in the investigations underpinning later chapters. The method follows a partially ordered step-by-step approach, beginning with the most obviously undeniable information derived from a corpus, and ending with abstract explanations, still open to debate and disagreement (though answerable to corpus evidence). However, it has to be borne in mind that corpus-based[21] methodology is apt to be cyclic – involving both a movement away from the data towards more abstract formulations (generalizations, hypotheses and theories), and a movement back to the data to seek further evidence for or against such formulations. The 'movement back to data' can take the form of investigating another corpus covering a similar or overlapping linguistic domain, or taking a look at a fresh aspect of the corpus already examined. Because of the difficulties of achieving exact representativeness and comparability, it might be best to formulate corpus-based claims about a language in the form 'according to corpus A, statement B holds'; or 'according to comparable corpora X and Y, the comparative statement Z holds'. There is no absolute undeniable truth in corpus-based claims

---

[19] In their discussion of diachronic corpus design, Biber *et al.* (1998: 251–53) recall that one concern of the compilers of the ARCHER and the Helsinki corpora was to 'choose registers that have a continuous history across periods'. Despite this, they acknowledge that the evolution of a genre can be considerable. Medical articles in the early eighteenth century were typically 'case studies written as personal letters to the editor of a journal', whereas in the twentieth century, medical articles adopted a dense experimental style (Biber *et al.* 1998: 252).

[20] For theoretical perspectives on corpus linguistics, it is useful to consult Aarts (1991), Gries (2002: esp. 1–11) and Mukherjee (2005).

[21] A distinction is often made between 'corpus-driven' and 'corpus-based' methods (Tognini-Bonelli, 2001), the former being more inductivist or data-driven than the latter. The term 'corpus-based' seems to fit the methodology we advocate, which is a combination of bottom-up and top-down approaches. The corpus-based method does not preclude serendipity (the 'corpus linguist's lucky dip' as it has been called), whereby striking observations from a corpus spark off an investigation to explain previously unsuspected phenomena. This is, indeed, one of the most rewarding aspects of corpus linguistics.

about a language. Fallibility and approximation to the truth are essential to the empirical corpus methodology, just as it is, for different reasons, to the hypothetico-deductive method of science influentially described by Karl Popper (1979: 119, 341–61). Perhaps the term 'hypothetico-inductive/abductive'[22] may be reasonably applied to it.

Another way to characterize the methodology is to make use of the distinction, commonplace in social science, between **quantitative** and **qualitative** analyses. Whereas in other disciplines these terms are often regarded as incompatible opposites, in corpus linguistics quantitative and qualitative methods are extensively used in combination. It is also characteristic of corpus linguistics to begin with quantitative findings, and work towards qualitative ones. But here again the procedure may have cyclic elements. Generally it is desirable to subject quantitative results to qualitative scrutiny – attempting to explain why a particular frequency pattern occurs, for example. But on the other hand, qualitative analysis (making use of the investigator's ability to interpret samples of language in context) may be the means for classifying examples in a particular corpus by their meanings; and this qualitative analysis may then be the input to a further quantitative analysis, one based on meaning (see section 4.5.2 for an example of this: a semantic analysis of some modal auxiliaries).

Yet another distinction useful in describing the stages of investigating corpus phenomena is that between **formal** identification and **functional** interpretation. On a formal level (thinking of grammatical analysis) we are interested in identifying *within* corpora particular distributional patterns of the occurrence (or co-occurrence) of structures and categories. On the functional level, we are interested in understanding and interpreting these patterns in terms of factors *external* to corpus data – cognitive, social or historical factors, for example.[23] However, even in the processes of formal identification we import something from outside the corpus, from the widely accepted categories of linguistic analysis – namely the system of classification that is applied, and the means of recognizing examples of particular categories.[24]

The strength of the comparable corpus methodology is that it is based firmly on observable differences between two corpora. Such differences provoke a search for explanation – something that leads directly or indirectly from quantitative to qualitative analysis, from form to function, or to hypotheses to explain how and why such changes take place.

---

[22] On abduction, see Bundt and Black (2000: 9–12).

[23] For the interaction, in corpus work, between formal (including quantitative) description and functional interpretation, see Biber (1988) and Biber *et al.* (1999: 41–44).

[24] In this corpus-based approach, the annotation of the corpus – for example, through part-of-speech tagging (see section 2.4 B) is an important means to uncovering and characterizing the more abstract grammatical features of the corpus. The use of **consensual** (i.e. relatively uncontroversial) categories in annotation is part of what the corpus linguist brings to the task: see Appendix II (pp. 276–80) for the list of part-of-speech tags used in our analysis.

In section 2.4, we present a list of steps in the methodology for diachronic comparative corpus analysis, focusing mainly on grammar. The particularities of our own research project are added in *italics*. The stages of the analysis will be further clarified in section 2.5.

2.4   Stages of investigation

The stages are presented in a generalized way that might be applied to any language and any period, while the more specific parameters of our own investigation are shown in italics. We assume that we already have two comparable corpora, such as the Brown and Frown corpora.

(A)   *Rationalize the mark-up of the corpora*. The mark-up of the comparable corpora should be standardized or harmonized, so that the orthographic features of the original texts should be identically or equivalently retrievable. *Originally the mark-up coding systems of both Brown and LOB belonged to an early period of computer technology, when the character set for representing texts in machine-readable form was extremely limited (32 characters for Brown, and 64 characters for LOB). Later, new versions of the two corpora (using different mark-up conventions) became available. Before undertaking our comparable corpus analysis, we harmonized the different mark-up systems, to make sure the comparison between the corpora was as consistent and precise as possible.*[25]

(B)   *Undertake annotation of the corpora*, using the same annotation scheme and annotation tool, so that both the corpora and the annotations are comparable. (If the tool performs its annotations automatically, as is generally the case with a POS tagger, a manual **post-editing** stage of error elimination follows, to correct the output.) *Thus, we undertook a POS tagging of all four corpora: Brown, Frown, LOB and F-LOB. The annotation tool used was the CLAWS4 tagger,*[26] *and the set of tags (category labels) used, termed the C8 tagset, was an enriched version of the more detailed tagset (C7) used for the BNC Sampler Corpus. The automatic tagging took place at Lancaster, and the post-editing of F-LOB and Frown took place at Freiburg. Although the Brown and LOB corpora had already been tagged in previous versions, to ensure tagging consistency*

---

[25]   The items that we standardized included, for example, delimiters for sentences, paragraphs, headings, quotations, captions, the representation of foreign text, omitted items (e.g. diagrams and tables), highlighted text (whether bold, italic or underlined) and special symbols (e.g. accented characters, fractions, end-of-line hyphens).

[26]   The CLAWS4 tagger, which achieves a success rate of between 96% and 97%, was supplemented by a further program, Template Tagger, which runs over the output of CLAWS and increases tagging accuracy to approximately 98%. CLAWS4 and Template Tagger are described respectively in Garside and Smith (1997) and Fligelstone *et al.* (1997).

between the corpora, we found it necessary to re-tag them, using the updated tagset and improved tagging software.[27]

(C)   *Use search and retrieval software to identify and extract recurrent formal features in the corpus.*[28] Unless the search target can be specified with total precision, the use of search software may induce errors of overcollection, and another stage of manual error elimination has to follow. At this point, some **derived datasets** may be displayed, both in the form of concordances in which each example found is shown within its context, and in the form of frequency tables, showing the quantitative differences between the corpora in gross terms, with respect to the feature being examined, as exemplified by Table 1.1. *For some purposes it was sufficient to use a search tool designed mainly for lexical retrieval and analysis, such as WordSmith. In searching for more abstract grammatical categories and structures, a more powerful annotation-aware tool, capable of flexibly matching combinations of words and tags, was used: CQP (using its graphical interface, XKwic).*[29] At this stage, also, it is important to define what we call 'features' clearly and consistently, so that instances of categories or structures can be recognized in texts. Categories such as the *of*-genitive and the *s*-genitive (see section 10.4) have unclear boundaries, and some rather arbitrary-seeming decisions may have to be made in drawing the line between genitives and non-genitives. However, as long as the same categorizing decisions are made in the different corpora being compared, results can be regarded as trustworthy.

(D)   *Refine the comparative analysis.* The next three steps (unordered) are ways of refining the gross frequency analysis, to find out more precisely how the corpora differ. (They are placed in a 'box' as a reminder that they are not sequential.)

---

[27] It is important to mention that whereas LOB, F-LOB and Frown have been manually post-edited after POS tagging, the same is not true of Brown, in which there is a tagging error rate of c. 2 per cent. From previous collections of errors in automatic tagging of LOB and F-LOB (see Mair *et al.* 2002: 262–64), and more recently of Frown, we have arrived at estimated frequencies by multiplying the automatic count by a corrective coefficient k, using the formula $k = 1 - ((a - p) / p)$, where a is the automatic count and p is the count after post-editing. The element of approximation in the automatic recognition of grammatical categories has in this way been minimized, the prediction being that the tagger's error rates on new material will approximate closely to error rates observed on comparable material in the past. However, it has to be borne in mind throughout this book that figures based on the tags in Brown (as compared with Frown) are to this extent less reliable than those comparing LOB and F-LOB.

[28] Probably the best and most up-to-date source of information on corpus linguistics tools, including search and retrieval tools such as WordSmith and CQP, is David Lee's website *Bookmarks for Corpus-based Linguists* http://devoted.to/corpora.

[29] For details of WordSmith and CQP, see Scott (1999) and Christ (1994), respectively. Well-known search software such as WordSmith (Concord) and Monoconc (MP 2.2) can be used for searching on tags, using tagged corpora, but we have preferred to use the sophisticated search syntax of CQP.

(D1) *Derive difference-of-frequency tables* not just for the corpora as a whole, but for corresponding parts of the corpora – genres and subcorpora.

The findings are in the form of frequency comparisons between genres and between subcorpora. *As an example, a table showing the decrease in the frequency of the passive[30] between LOB and F-LOB is shown in Table 2.3 (to be discussed further in section 2.5).*

In this and the following chapters, we use tables such as Table 2.3 to present quantitative findings; or, as an alternative and more accessible presentational device, we present findings in the form of a bar chart, as in Figure 2.1. Supplementary tables and bar charts are presented chapter-by-chapter in Appendix III (pp. 281–313). They are identified by the prefix A, as well as by their chapter number: e.g. 'Table A3.1' is the first supplementary table for Chapter 3.

Apart from its omission of the raw frequencies and the total change between LOB and F-LOB, Figure 2.1 presents the same data as Table 2.3.

The term **subcorpus** refers to groupings of genre categories: *for example, in the Brown family of corpora we often found it convenient to divide each corpus into four subcorpora: Press (categories A–C), General Prose (categories D–H), Learned/Academic*

Table 2.3. *Comparison of use of the passive in the LOB and F-LOB corpora*[i]

| Subcorpora | LOB Corpus (1961) | | F-LOB Corpus (1991) | | |
	Raw freq.	pmw	Raw freq.	pmw	Rate of change
Press	2,303	(12,992)	2,025	(11,368)	** −12.5%
Gen. Prose	6,192	(14,983)	5,424	(13,126)	** −12.4%
Learned	3,271	(20,601)	2,743	(17,183)	** −16.6%
Fiction	1,565	(6,113)	1,516	(5,895)	−3.6%
TOTAL	13,331	(13,260)	11,708	(11,614)	** −12.4%

Table A7.1 presents a similar picture of the declining passive, excluding however non-finite and progressive passives. Hence the frequency figures presented there are somewhat lower than in the present table.

[i] These are approximate figures, based on a tag search for a sequence (with allowable discontinuities) of a form of *be* followed by a past participle. Adjectival forms such as *prepared* in *be prepared* were excluded from the count.

[30] From now on, the term 'passive' in this chapter refers more specifically to the *be*-passive (rather than the *get*-passive). See sections 7.1–3.

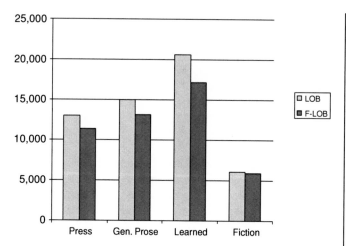

Figure 2.1 Comparison of the use of the passive in LOB and F-LOB Corpora (frequencies normalized to number of passives per million words)

(category J) and Fiction (categories K–R).[31] *These broader sub-divisions of the corpora were particularly helpful in analysing relatively rare features, where any systematic patterns of difference between individual genres were irretrievable, owing to the sparseness of data.*

(D2) *Derive difference-of-frequency tables from inter-corpus comparisons* – i.e. comparisons between Corpus A and Corpus B and other relevant corpora, such as **contemporaneous** corpora, i.e. corpora of the same period of time (*e.g. Brown and LOB are contemporaneous; so virtually are Frown and F-LOB*). *We also made comparisons between the Brown family and spoken corpora, as indicated in Chapter 1. These will be described in section 2.5.*

(D3) *Undertake further categorization of instances of features found in the corpora* – e.g. classify examples in terms of lexical, syntactic and semantic levels of analysis. This can be effectively undertaken using a database or spreadsheet program. Findings can take the form of frequency comparisons refined across lexical, syntactic or semantic categories. *For our own investigation, we made use of Excel spreadsheets, which enabled concordance examples to be displayed and classified in a varying number of fields (or columns), including*

---

[31] These four groupings were backed up by studies showing patterns of homogeneity and heterogeneity of the most frequent vocabulary in the LOB Corpus – see Hofland and Johansson (1982: 27).

> *fields for text category and text number, syntactic and semantic features, notes on individual contextual peculiarities of examples, etc.* It is self-evident that the classifications should be as far as possible identically applied for each corpus, if the results of this multi-field analysis are to yield true comparability.

(E) *Further qualitative analysis, examining individual instances, or clusters of instances, in both corpora,* focusing especially on the categories identified at stage D3. From this, we can arrive at more refined and targeted interpretations of the differences between the corpora.

(F) *Functional interpretation of findings* on all levels of C, D and E above, trying to account for identified patterns of change, looking at not just one feature, but whole groups of features. For example, the increasing frequency of noun–noun sequences and *s*-genitives is attributed (in sections 11.2–3), along with a declining frequency of prepositions, to the 'densification' process affecting written English, whereby content is condensed into a smaller number of words.

2.5 Further details and explanations of the stages of investigation

A little more needs to be said about all six stages above (except for A, mark-up, which will from now on be taken for granted) to illustrate how they work and what results they can yield.

2.5.1: (B)   Annotation

The C8 tagset employed for our research was an augmented version of the C7 tagset used for the BNC Sampler Corpus.[32] The C8 tags are listed in Appendix II. The tag labels, ultimately modelled on the original Brown tagset (Francis 1980: 198–200), consist of a sequence of two to five alphanumeric characters: e.g. NN1, VVG, RG, PPHS1. Generally, these tags are complex symbols (i.e. sets of distinctive features, along the lines of Chomsky 1965: 81–90), each character having a particular symbolic function. For example:

Any tag beginning with N . . . represents a noun
Any tag beginning NN . . . represents a common noun
Any tag with . . Q . . in third position is a *wh*-word
Any tag beginning with V . . . is a verb
Any tag beginning with V and ending with G is an *-ing* form of a verb

---

[32] See http://www.comp.lancs.ac.uk/ucrel/bnc2sampler/sampler.htm.

The analysability of tag labels in this way means that searches can be more grammar-sensitive. For example, if * is used as a wildcard for any intervening characters, the search argument N*1 finds any singular noun, from the set ND1, NN1, NNL1, NNT1, NNU1, NP1, NPD1, NPM1,[33] representing different classes of singular nouns. On the other hand, NP* will find any proper noun (NP1, NP2, NP), whether singular, plural or neutral for number. In this way, the tagset can be flexibly used for searches varying in granularity.[34]

The additional tags in the augmented C8 tagset are: (1) those used for recognizing *wh*-words (*which, who, whom, whose*) that are relative rather than interrogative (or exclamative) pronouns; and (2) those used for recognizing forms of the primary verbs *be*, *have* and *do* which are auxiliaries rather than main verbs in function. The introduction of these additional tags such as VAHG (= *having* as an auxiliary) made it advisable to change the labels for corresponding main verb tags by adding an extra discriminating character: e.g. VHG (= *having* as a main verb) became VVHG. The relevance of such refinements of annotation will become clear in C below.[35]

2.5.2: (C) Search expressions in CQP

The retrieval of grammatical phenomena from the Brown family could have been made much more powerful if the corpora had been parsed (i.e. if they were in treebank form, as the DCPSE is). Although this was not practicable in our case,[36] we were able to make more use of the considerable power of CQP, a retrieval program capable of searching on: (a) sequences with wild cards; (b) differentiation between tags and their accompanying words; and (c) the range of operators (negation, conjunction, disjunction) associated with

---

[33] The interpretation of these tag labels is as follows: NN1 'singular common noun'; ND1 'singular noun of direction' (*north*, etc.); NNL1 'singular locative noun', such as *Mount* in *Mount Everest*; NNT1 'singular temporal noun' (*day*, etc.); NNU1 'singular unit-of-measurement noun'; NP1 'singular proper noun'; NPD1 'singular proper noun for a day of the week' (*Tuesday*, etc.); NPM1 'singular proper noun for a month' (*July*, etc.).

[34] In CQP the wildcard symbol representing 'any sequence of characters' is in fact .* (rather than *).

[35] The accuracy of automatic tagging is improved by manual post-editing. One of the corpora (Brown) has not yet been post-edited in its new comparable format. The other three corpora have been post-edited, and so error is virtually eliminated, although the possibility of some minimal error and inconsistency in tagging even after post-editing cannot be ignored. However, as explained in the Preface, we have relied on automatic tagging in some figures and tables comparing Brown and Frown, where it would not be feasible to undertake manual post-editing. These figures and tables, mainly in Chapters 10 and 11, are indicated by the warning signal '(automatic)' or '(AmE automatic)'.

[36] The immensely complex task of automatic parsing has not yet reached a stage of success where syntactic annotation of the Brown family could be achieved without a prohibitive amount of time spent in the correction of erroneous analyses. Successful large-scale syntactic annotation projects – notably those of the Penn Treebank and the ICE-GB (International Corpus of English: Great Britain) – have invested resources in this task over many years. Regrettably, we could not hope to match this in our own research.

regular expressions. To give a simple example: the search for progressive verb constructions can be specified as VAB* V*G: i.e. an auxiliary form of the verb BE followed by an -*ing* participle form: as in *is coming, could be having, should have been working*, and so on. This does not find all progressives, though, as the auxiliary may be separated from the following verb by various intervening words and constructions: for example, by *not*, by an adverb or adverbial phrase, or by a noun phrase in the case of subject–auxiliary inversion:

Where *am* I *sleeping?*" he said. [F-LOB K09]

President Bush *is* quite properly *pressing* ahead . . . [Frown B12]

. . . and *were*n't they always *emphasizing* that . . . [Brown P21]

Hence the search formula for progressives, if intended to be exhaustive, has to be much more complex than the simple example given above, VAB* V*G, even though that finds more than 80 per cent of all progressives in a corpus.[37]

The problem with even an exhaustive search formula such as this is that it may well fail to find a few instances, where some unforeseen type of sequence occurs between the auxiliary and the following verb. The limit on the number of intervening words cannot be increased indefinitely, as the number of 'mishits' – examples mistakenly retrieved as progressives – also increases rapidly. The optimal number of unspecified words to allow between the two verbs of the progressive is determined by a balance between *over*collection and *under*collection (or put more positively and technically, between precision and recall);[38] that is, between the number of non-progressives erroneously retrieved from the corpus, and the number of *bona fide* progressives which are erroneously omitted from the retrieval set.

The problem of overcollection is solved by manual post-editing, which weeds out the erroneously collected cases from the output file. The problem of undercollection can only be handled by opening up the search argument to accept more non-progressive cases including many more erroneously retrieved cases, a tactic which eventually becomes impractical. We have to acknowledge, then, that while all reasonable efforts are made to reduce undercollection to an absolute minimum, this kind of tag-based search can lead

---

[37] The general query used in CQP to retrieve progressives was: [pos="VAB[oMZRI]|| VABD[ZR]|VAH[oZDI]"] [pos="R.*|MD| XX "] {0,4} [pos="AT.*|APPGE"] {0,1} [pos="JJ.*"] {0,1} [pos="PPH1|PP.*S.*|PPY|N.*|D.*"] {0,2} [pos="R.*|MD| XX "] {0,4} [pos="VABN"] {0,1} [pos="R.*|MD|XX "] {0,4} [pos="V.*G"]. The first item in this sequence is any form of the verb *be*, used as an auxiliary, and the last item is a present participle. The other character strings represent optional items that may appear between *be* and the participle. For example, [pos="R.*|MD| XX "] {0,4} means 'between 0 and 4 instances of any of the tags for adverbs (R–), ordinal number used as an adverb (e.g. *first, last* MD) or negative particle (tag XX)'. The pipe symbol (|) represents 'OR'; i.e. it separates alternative tags in each word position. The other tags are listed in Appendix II.

[38] On the distinction between precision and recall, see Salton (1989).

Table 2.4. *A partial repetition of Table 2.3: passives*

Subcorpora	LOB corpus (1961)		F-LOB corpus (1991)		Rate of change
	raw freq.	pmw	raw freq.	pmw	
TOTAL	13,331	(13,260)	11,708	(11,614)	** −12.4%

to the omission of a very few highly unusual cases of the progressive from the count. The good news is that this problem is the same for each of the comparable corpora: that is, if a small number of examples is omitted from the count of Corpus A, a similarly small number is likely to be omitted from Corpus B. The proportional frequency of the progressives in one corpus relative to the other will be virtually unaffected. It should also be emphasized that this problem arises principally with searches based on grammatical tags, where these are used to retrieve syntactic constructions. Searches based on individual words, or a combination of words and tags, are not vulnerable to this kind of hazard.

2.5.3: (D1)   Frequency across genres and subcorpora

The gross frequency comparison of two corpora is not likely to yield anything definitive, except for the indication (if there is a significant contrast between the two corpora) that there is something here worth investigating. For example, if we simply look at the totals on the bottom row of the passive table, Table 2.3, we know at least that there is a highly significant contrast between the frequency of passives in LOB and in F-LOB.

In Tables 2.3 and 2.4 are included not only the raw frequency, but the frequency per million words (a normalized figure which permits the exact comparison of like with like in the two corpora).[39] The far-right-hand column gives a measure of how significant the difference between the two corpora is, *, ** and *** showing progressively higher levels of significance, as explained in the list of 'Abbreviations and symbolic conventions'. This column (here −12.4%) shows the rate of change – a decline of 12.4 per cent (of the frequency in the earlier corpus) between LOB and F-LOB. (A plus figure would show an increase in frequency: for example, +28.9 per cent is the rate of change between LOB and F-LOB for the (active) present progressive – a remarkable increase.)

If we are interested in the loss of passives, the most obvious thing to investigate as a next step is the comparative frequency of the passive in the fifteen different genre categories A–R, or the four subcorpora shown in

---

[39] For this purpose we use the raw frequencies (*n*) and the corpus word count, as normalized figures do not indicate the size of the data being compared.

Table 2.5. *Another partial repetition of Table 2.3: passives*

Subcorpora	LOB corpus (1961)		F-LOB corpus (1991)		Rate of change
	raw freq.	pmw	raw freq.	pmw	
Press	2,303	(12,992)	2,025	(11,368)	**−12.5%
Gen. Prose	6,192	(14,983)	5,424	(13,126)	**−12.4%
Learned	3,271	(20,601)	2,743	(17,183)	**−16.6%
Fiction	1,565	(6,113)	1,516	(5,895)	−3.6%

Table 2.3. Broadly, in this kind of comparison two different tendencies are likely to be observed: either the parts of the corpus will show a uniform trend in a particular direction, or there will be notable discrepancies between the rates or directions of change. The passive table, Table 2.3, is particularly interesting: (a) it shows a uniform direction of change (in that all subcorpora show a decline of passive frequency); but (b) it shows that the rate of change differs markedly. Although the first three subcorpora (Press, General Prose, and Learned) show a highly significant decrease, the Fiction subcorpus shows only a slight decrease of 3.6 per cent. This data is repeated in Table 2.5.

This result is worth pondering. The general finding is that the passive declines across the whole range of texts in the corpora. The Fiction section of the corpora shows an exceptionally low rate of change, and one obvious hypothesis to help explain this is that Fiction is less affected by the trend, because in any case passives are comparatively rare in Fiction writing (less than half as frequent as they are in any of the other subcorpora). Stylistically, Fiction is already towards the non-passive end of the scale in 1961, and further reduction is not surprisingly limited. This will be discussed further in Chapter 7: our purpose here is simply to show that this type of refinement of quantitative data can lead to some exceptional statistic in need of explanation, prompting hypotheses which require further analysis in greater detail.

In later chapters, in Tables such as 2.3–2.5, we often omit either the raw frequency figure, or the normalized figure pmw. In cases like Table 2.4, where whole corpora are being compared, omitting one of these figures loses very little information, since the corpora themselves approximate to a million words. But in cases like Table 2.5, where subcorpora or genres are being compared, the normalized figure is valuable in indicating the frequency of a particular linguistic feature (here the passive) relative to the size of the different subsections of a corpus.

More questions arise where the directions of change are different. An intriguing example is provided by the table for the frequency of first-person pronouns in Brown and Frown, Table 2.6.

Table 2.6. *First-person singular pronouns* (I, me) *in the Brown and Frown Corpora*

Subcorpora	Brown corpus (1961)		Frown corpus (1992)		
	raw freq.	pmw	raw freq.	pmw	Rate of change
Press	546	3,059	882	4,985	*** +63.0%
Gen. Prose	1,866	4,454	2,468	5,957	*** +33.7%
Learned	226	1,394	156	973	*** −30.2%
Fiction	4,326	17,032	5,572	22,004	*** +29.2%
TOTAL	6,964	6,871	9,078	9,034	*** +31.5%

Here the odd one out is the Learned subcorpus, which shows a sharp decrease in the use of *I* and *me*, whereas the other three subcorpora show a sharp increase. All the changes are highly significant, but one goes in the opposite direction. In 1961, Learned was already the maverick category, with first-person pronouns five times less frequent than the average. By 1992, apparently, it had not only stoutly resisted the general change towards a more personal, subjective style, but had followed a strikingly contrastive trend. Again, hypotheses suggest themselves. The lowering of frequency in J may reflect the fact that some genres (especially the Learned genre) are more conformist and resistant to change than others (see Hundt and Mair 1999). It is plausible that academic writing, indeed, has moved in the opposite direction, aiming at a greater degree of objectivity, which manifests itself in greater suppression of reference to the speaker or writer.[40] However, there are further complicating factors, such as the increasing extent to which quoted material is included in the written corpora between 1961 and 1991/2 (see pp. 248–9). Further qualitative research will be needed to explore the reason for these diverging trends – see, however, the discussion of first-person pronoun usage in section 11.3.6.

To conclude, the more refined quantitative analyses serve to consolidate results already noted, but also, where anomalies are brought to light, to raise issues provoking further investigation. When the four subcorpora (or even more, the fifteen genres) show the same direction of change, this consolidates the across-the-board result for the corpora as a whole. It indicates that the overall trend is indeed pervasive. On the other hand, when the subcorpora or genres show a mixture of contrary trends, or exceptional cases bucking an overall trend, this is a signal that these findings need to be probed in greater detail – particularly by using the methods outlined in section 2.5.4 (D2) and 2.5.5 (D3) below.

[40] The tendency for medical writing (as a specific variety of Learned discourse) to become progressively more 'informational' and less 'involved' over the period 1650–1990 is demonstrated by Biber *et al.* (1998: 211–15), using the ARCHER corpus. In Biber's methodology, 'informational' writing is strongly associated with the agentless passive, whereas involved writing is strongly associated with the use of first-person pronouns (p. 148).

2.5.4: (D2) External comparisons

By external comparisons we mean comparisons outside the two corpora (say, the Brown and Frown corpora) that are under investigation at present. One type of comparison, of course, is within the Brown family of corpora: that is, the comparison between the two pairs of contemporaneous corpora, changes from Brown to Frown being compared with changes from LOB to F-LOB. Comparisons of the American and British corpora can be particularly illuminating with reference to trends that we have called Americanization in Chapter 1 (see section 11.5). However, leaving aside cases where there is no significant change in either corpus, a number of distinct patterns can in principle be observed from the diachronic point of view (cf. Mair's 'typology of contrasts', 2002: 109–112):

(a) *Regionally specific change:* There is a significant change in one corpus-pair, but not in the other. (The opposite of this is *regionally general change.*)

(b) *Convergent change:* The comparative frequencies show greater similarity after the change than before. (The opposite is *divergent change.*)

(c) *Parallel change:* There is a significant change in the same direction in both the AmE and the BrE pair. (The opposite is *contrary change*: changes in the opposite direction.)

(d) *Different rates of change:* Even if the significant changes are in the same direction, the rate of change can be considerably higher in one corpus-pair than in the other. (The opposite is *similar rates of change.*)

(e) *Different starting/ending points:* Significant differences show up at the starting point (1961) and/or the ending point (1991/2) of the period of time under consideration. (The opposite of this is clearly *similar starting/ending points.*)

(f) The *follow-my-leader* pattern is a subtype of parallel change. In this, probably the most interesting pattern, one corpus-pair shows a move in the same direction as the other, but is already further advanced in that direction in 1961, and is again further advanced in that direction in 1991/2. This pattern is illustrated, for example, by the decline in modal auxiliary usage (see section 4.1), where the trend shows AmE in advance of BrE, along the same track.

With the aid of the third British corpus (B-LOB), it is also possible to trace another kind of diachronic variability. We can tell if there is *consistency of change* between the one period and the other (between 1931–61 and 1961–91), or whether change is observed only in the earlier or the later period, or indeed whether there is *inconsistent* change (change in one direction 1931–61, but in the opposite direction in 1961–91). We can also observe whether there is an *accelerating* or *decelerating* rate of change. Thus it is plausible that some changes that can be attributed to Americanization, such as the declining use of modals just mentioned, have been accelerating because of increasing American influence after the middle of the twentieth century.

Further comparisons can be made with other corpora, and especially (since our main study is focused on written language corpora) with corpora of spoken language. Particularly relevant to our study is the recently released DCPSE (Diachronic Corpus of Present-Day Spoken English),[41] the nearest approximation to a short-term diachronic comparative corpus of spoken language matching the Brown family in period and comparability. The DCPSE is not a perfect match to the Brown family for various reasons:

(i)   It consists of British English speech only, mainly from the south-east of England.

(ii) It is derived from two corpora originally compiled with somewhat different sampling and corpus design features and collected over periods of different length: the LLC (London–Lund Corpus) collected over the period 1958–77 , and the ICE-GB corpus (International Corpus of English – Great Britain) collected over the period 1990–92). For example, the text samples of the LLC were approximately 5,000 words in length, whereas those of the ICE-GB were approximately 2,000 words in length.

(iii) The two subcorpora described in (ii) consist of approximately 400,000 words each, rather than the one million words each of the Brown family corpora.

(iv) The collection of the LLC spoken material – undertaken in the Survey of English Usage (SEU) – apart from extending over twenty years, varied greatly from one year to another and from one decade to another in terms of range of text types. Because of this, we found it necessary, to approximate to the comparability of LOB and F-LOB, to make a selection from the SEU texts of 1960–69,[42] and to make a selection as similar as possible from ICE-GB (1990–92), while maintaining a balance between different kinds of spoken texts in the two corpora. The resulting mini-corpora, which we called DSEU and DICE, respectively, consisted of approximately 130,000 words each. On this basis, although the size of these mini-corpora was regrettably small, we were able to make comparisons within spoken British English roughly parallel to those between LOB and F-LOB. Unfortunately, there was no similar way of sampling spoken American English of the same periods, owing to the lack of corpora of spoken AmE from the 1960s.

---

[41] We are grateful for Bas Aarts, Sean Wallis and their team at University College London, compilers of the DCPSE, for making the beta version of the corpus available to us before its official release, together with the accompanying advanced ICECUP 3.1 software. The corpus is issued in a fully parsed version, and the advanced search facilities of ICECUP allow searches based on abstract syntactic categories and patterns, as well as more routine searches based on lexical forms.

[42] A small part of the DSEU (about 18,000 words) consisted of material collected in 1958–59.

In one respect, however, DCPSE is a close parallel to LOB and F-LOB: its material was collected mainly from the south-east of England among middle-class educated people, approximating to the authorial population sampled in the written corpora. All in all, the DCPSE is an important step forward in the study of recent change in the spoken language, and enables us for the first time to test the truth of the common assumption that the spoken language is the leading force in bringing about change in the standard language, and that the written language follows in its wake. In Chapters 4 and 5, we demonstrate that this was found to be the case for the declining frequency of the modals and the rising frequency of the so-called semi-modals (see sections 4.3, 5.2).

Apart from the use of the Brown family and the DCPSE for comparisons between the 1960s and the 1990s in both writing and speech, we found it valuable to use other corpora for particular purposes. For example, spoken demographically sampled data of the BNC from the 1990s (abbreviated as BNCdemog), and the corresponding AmE spoken material of the LCSAE, provided a very large sample (compared with DCPSE) of four to five million words of spontaneous speech from the same period. For more extensive diachronic comparison, the *OED* citation corpus and the ARCHER corpus provided a historical dimension stretching back hundreds of years. Other corpora were used for more specialized purposes.

2.5.5: (D3)   *Further categorization of instances found in the corpora*

If step D2 above is a means to a *broader* analysis of the data across a wider range of language variety, step D3 take us to a *deeper* analysis. Suppose we start with a display of instances of a grammatical feature, as in a concordance, or in a database, with one or more fields automatically filled in (e.g. an address field indicating in which text and genre the example is located) and a number of fields left blank, to be filled in by the analyst. These 'manual coding' fields are necessary where the categories we wish to investigate are not capable of automatic recognition – and this is likely to be true of semantic and pragmatic categories, in particular.

Consider the case of modal auxiliaries (see Chapter 4 *passim*). We have noticed that some modals especially, such as *may*, *must*, *shall* and *should*, have steeply declined in frequency in the corpora between 1961 and 1991. One obvious question was whether particular senses or usages of these modals were chiefly responsible for this change, in having declined more than others. The semantic classification of modals is somewhat controversial, but we chose to adopt the semantic modal categories of Coates (1983), a well-known framework. In broad terms (to be elucidated later) some of these modals were found to be growing less polysemous. Certain rather rare formal usages appeared to be obsolescent. But other usages were holding their own – for example, the deontic use of *should* and the epistemic use of *may* accounted

	A	B	C	F	I	K	Q	R
1	kwic 1	file	regist	spt	subj: anim	given /new?	pragm: interp etc	notes
22	21 controversy stoked up by the decision to force Mr Withers to take early retirement had taken a fresh turn when the former governor broke his silence over the affair. In a report in the London Evening Standard , Mr Withers said: " I { 'm being blamed } for things which were absolutely outside of my control. It is not in my power to move prisoners. "I made a report to my superiors indicating that these men should not be in Brixton/	A28	prov.q pol	qs	a1	g	itp	
51	50 to achieve. Playing with youngsters ' lives can not be justified. Their achievements now will colour their future paths - and they have every right to demand a good grounding ; in fact, the very best the country can offer. We { are forever being told} about increased competition from overseas once the Single market comes into being next year, and we must be in position to meet that challenge. We can only do that if our education system	B26	p.editl		a1	g	always	IndObj
112	107 enerally leave the viewer dissatisfied. In a recent article for Screen</hi>, Paul Kerr identifies the principal cause of this dissatisfaction as the tendency for televised versions to flatten a text so that, it is less a novel as such that { is being adapted } than its plot, characters, setting [and] dialogue. The reason for this flattening is a direct consequence of the elevation of the written text over the film (and especially over	G40	essay	qs	a0	g	itp?	Sem: LGSWE p743 adapt = effort, facilitation, hindrance. Prec passive: 6 back same verb

Figure 2.2 A fragment of an annotated database of the progressive passive, using Excel

for an increasing proportion of all uses of these modals in the 1991/2 corpora.

The method was to establish an exhaustive set of semantic categories for each modal. It is important to define these as precisely as possible, and at the same time to be aware that there are fuzzy boundaries which may lead concordance lines to be labelled 'uncertain'. Other fields can be reserved for co-occurrence patterns between the semantic categories and other lexical, syntactic and semantic variables – for example, first- or second-person subjects, negation, interrogatives, existential *there*, main verbs classes, aspectual patterns – all potentially relevant co-occurring variables (as elaborated in Coates 1983). It is also sometimes found that a less frequent modal usage is likely to occur only in a handful of more or less formulaic lexical combinations: for instance, the permission use of *may* (now relatively rare in both speech and writing) is only likely to occur in speech or fictional writing in certain formulae such as *If I may say . . . , May I ask . . .* :

(1)   *May* I ask you something, Aunt Carrie? [Frown K05]
(2)   If I *may* say, sir, that would be ill-advised at present . . . [Frown P12]

These conventionalized forms can also be marked in another field coded for 'formulae'. Thus each initially empty field in the analysis can be coded with a determinate set of notations applicable to particular textual examples.

Figure 2.2 shows a screen shot of an Excel spreadsheet containing part of the dataset for the progressive passive, with a concordance field alongside a number of different fields for manual analysis.[43]

---

[43] There is also a semi-automatic method of semantic classification using the USAS semantic tagging software (Rayson *et al.* 2004), which achieves a success rate of over 90 per cent, and can be used as an approximate way of identifying semantic patterns in corpus output in the

One problem is: since the categorization of a concordance can be extremely time-consuming if done manually, we find it impracticable to analyse a concordance of (say) 3,000 instances unless the concordance list is 'thinned', that is, reduced in size by systematic selection in such a way as to avoid skewing or bias in the resulting subset,[44] so that every subdivision of the corpus is proportionately represented in the resulting subsample.

The advantages of a database analysis are that the lists and fields can be sorted, filtered and rearranged according to need, and frequency counts and other quantitative calculations made automatically. Subsets can be extracted and examined in isolation from each other, whether they represent genres, semantic classes, co-occurrence factors or 'unclear' cases. The analysis can be progressively edited and refined, so that errors or inaccuracies or unclear cases can be ultimately reduced to a minimum. At any intermediate stage, an analysis comparable to that of D1, comparing the two corpora quantitatively, can be carried out using the new 'deeper' categories. Such an output ultimately provides the results of this step of analysis.

2.5.6: (E)   Further qualitative analysis

From steps D1, D2 and D3, a much more targeted understanding can be achieved as to the differences between the 1961 and the 1991/2 corpora. Hypotheses are formed, and ways of checking these by examining more instances qualitatively are likely to suggest themselves – not only using the Brown family, but also other corpora. At this further qualitative stage, the explanation of a significant change of frequency in one linguistic form also takes account if possible of other, competing forms.

If we talk of *variants* and *variables* here, it has to be borne in mind that in syntax and semantics, unlike phonology and morphology, there is rarely a clear 'either–or' relation between two or more forms or constructions perceived as in some sense 'equivalent'. Consider the contrast between active and passive (Chapter 7) as an example. The major variable of *voice* subdivides into active and passive variants. However, the passive variant again subdivides into three variants: *be*-passive (section 7.2), *get*-passive (7.3) and mediopassive (7.4), and of these the mediopassive, as its name suggests, shares some

form of concordance-based listings. This can be used, for example (see section 4.5.2), to identify some instances of epistemic use of modals, notably those occurring in what Coates (1983) calls 'harmonious combinations', including cases preceded by existential *there* (e.g. *There must be some mistake*) or followed by a perfect participle (e.g. *She must/should have taken*). But in general, semantic analysis to the degree of detail and accuracy required has to be manual.

[44] Assuming a concordance is listed in 'corpus order' by text and genre, the simplest and most satisfactory way to ensure this is to select every *n*th example in the concordance. In this way, while the number of instances examined is reduced to manageable proportions, the broad aim of analysing a representative sample is maintained.

characteristics of both active and passive, so that a determinate split between active and passive cannot be enforced. They form an active-to-passive cline rather than a set of functionally and semantically fully equivalent constructions. In other cases (e.g. the variation between a mandative subjunctive and a periphrastic construction with *should* discussed in Chapter 3) we are dealing with functional (if not semantic) equivalence of two syntactic expressions.[45] Although the competition between two or more variants under one variable is typically a good basis for investigating syntactic change, different ways of expressing the same or similar content are often in only partial competition with one another, and this is illustrated by the following list showing declining and increasing frequency of quasi-synonymous constructions:

LOSING GROUND	GAINING GROUND[46]
modal auxiliaries	semi-modals such as *have to*, *want to*, *be going to* (see section 5.2)
be-passives	*get*-passives (see 7.2–3)
of-phases	*s*-genitives (see 10.4)
wh- relativization	*that* or zero relativization (see 10.5.1–3)
gender-neutral *he*	singular *they*; coordinated pronouns (*he or she*, etc.) (see section 11.6.1)

Using the written Brown family corpora alone, one forms the impression that the competition between the forms above can by no means explain everything. Frequency of colloquial constructions such as certain semi-modals (section 5.2) and the *get*-passive (7.3), for instance, is so sparse that it could not account for the declining frequency of corresponding constructions on the left of the list. The examination of the incidence of these constructions in spoken corpora is much more revealing. It also rarely seems to be the case that two forms alone are in competition. Consider the semantic area of strong obligation and epistemic necessity (see section 4.5.2; also Smith 2003a). The sharp decline of *must* in BrE appears to have much to do with the rising use of *have to*, which more than matches it in frequency in the 1991 F-LOB corpus. But there are other potentially competing forms expressing deontic or epistemic modality: the modal *should*, the semi-modal *need to*, adjectival constructions such as *it is essential/necessary that*, and adverbials such as *necessarily* and *no doubt*, to mention but a few (see section 5.4). Corpus linguistics provides the means to investigate the ecology of such semantically overlapping forms: but it is often a complex story, and few examples can be dealt with in detail in this book.

---

[45] For a more detailed discussion of syntactic variability, see Jacobson (1980), Sankoff (1988) or Kortmann (2006).
[46] This is a simplified version of a list first published in Mair and Leech (2006).

2.5.7: (F)   Functional interpretation of findings on all levels

At this most abstract stage (i.e. most remote from the data) we are concerned with explaining changes of frequency by relating them to other changes, so that they can be regarded as instances of a particular diachronic pattern of evolution, or instantiations of some general theoretical framework. We have already referred to colloquialization as one general trend that appears to account for a range of cases where a construction gains ground (e.g. contracted forms of verbs – *don't*, *he's*, etc.) or alternatively loses ground (e.g. the *be*-passive). We have independent corpus evidence, should any be needed, that contractions are strongly associated with spoken language and passives with written language (Biber *et al.* 1999: 476, 1129). This is enough to make colloquialization a plausible explanation of these changes.

We associate colloquialization with the label 'functional', because it is presumably attributable to external, social factors, rather than purely internal, linguistic change. Fairclough (1992: 98, 201–207) describes the tendency for public media discourse to take on informal speech habits as part of a more general evolution, the 'democratization of discourse' in modern times.

A different kind of evolution can be invoked to explain in part the increasing use of the progressive construction and also semi-modals, like *be going to* and *have to*. In the history of English, these verbal constructions have been recognized as classic cases of the **grammaticalization** process (sections 1.2, 11.3) 'whereby lexical items and constructions come in certain linguistic contexts to serve grammatical functions, and, once grammaticalized, continue to develop new grammatical functions' (Hopper and Traugott [2]2003: xv). This has been regarded as a language-internal type of change, but Croft (2000) and Krug (2000) are among those who see grammaticalization as taking place within a usage-based, utterance-oriented or discourse-oriented theory of language change. Croft emphasizes the diachronic collaboration between innovation or actuation (the creation of novel forms of language) and propagation or diffusion (the way the use of these forms spreads into more general language use). The converse mechanisms of change – attrition and loss – also need fuller consideration. Our quest is for a theoretical framework to explain the decline of modals, as well as the growth of semi-modals: an account that begs the question of how far the definition of the modal auxiliary category itself has been changing (see Cort and Denison 2005).

Although grammaticalization has in the past provided a neat explanation of how main-verb constructions have progressively evolved towards auxiliary-verb constructions, it has not until recently been seen as a theoretical framework sensitive to frequency evidence (but see Bybee 2007). With regard to the progressive construction, the comparable corpus methodology supplies a new form of precise quantitative evidence, confirming that even hundreds of years after the major effects of grammaticalization have taken place (for example, in the case of the progressive), an aftersurge of frequency continues.[47]

Theorizing about diachronic changes has focused primarily on the processes whereby new forms are initiated and spread, and until recently has paid comparatively little attention to the processes by which the range and frequency of usage contracts, and eventually disappears from the language. Insistence on the unidirectionality of grammaticalization has tended to obscure the need for an account of decline and obsolescence that is an essential complement to an account of innovation and diffusion. An account of how a construction progressively loses its range of grammatical functions may provide some explanation for the declining use of the modal auxiliaries. To take an extreme case, the modal auxiliary *need(n't)* (see section 4.5.1), as contrasted with the full-verb construction *need to*, has lost virtually all its functional flexibility as a verb. It has no tense contrast, no non-finite forms and occurs only in non-assertive contexts (usually with negation). Both in terms of its very low and declining frequency (as a modal) and its functional inflexibility, this particular auxiliary seems to be reaching the end of its useful life.[48]

In Chapter 11, such explanatory factors as grammaticalization and colloquialization are discussed in greater depth (see sections 11.2–3), as well as other likely trends such as those we have labelled 'densification' (11.4), 'Americanization' (11.5) and 'democratization' (11.6.1).

2.6 Conclusion

We will develop the above more theoretical issues further in Chapter 11. The main point to observe now is that the diachronic comparable corpus methodology elaborated in this chapter is not purely data-driven, but engages with theoretical and functional explanations. This may mean not just providing confirmation or disconfirmation of such explanations, but modifying and clarifying them in the light of new kinds of evidence. Such evidence is primarily formulated in terms of frequency of use, and one of the messages we wish to convey is that frequency evidence is far more important in tracing diachronic change than has generally been acknowledged in the past.

---

[47] Smitterberg (2005: 57–58, 115) includes increase of frequency, as well as semantic bleaching, 'obligatorization' and formal expansion of the construction within the paradigm of which it is a part, among the effects of increasing *integration* of a construction such as the progressive within the language system. See also Lindquist and Mair (2004a: ix–xiii) on the *rapprochement* between grammaticalization studies and corpus studies, including a focus on frequency.

[48] However, it is prudent to avoid forecasts of a grammatical form's or category's extinction. Repeatedly, the death bells have been tolled for structures that survive in a particular functional niche. The use of *whom* discussed in section 1.1 is an instance; another is the subjunctive (see 3.1); yet another is the passival construction (see 7.1) which, although 'disappearing' two hundred years ago, still survives in patterns like *coffee is now serving.*

3   The subjunctive mood

3.1   Introduction

The analytic part of this book begins with a series of studies of major verb categories: modality, aspect and voice. As part of this, the present chapter will investigate recent changes in the use of the subjunctive mood, an inflectional category of the verb. Semantically, the subjunctive mood is closely related to the modal auxiliaries, which will be the topic of the following chapter. Just like some modal auxiliaries, the subjunctive in English can be used to express obligation or necessity (*he demands that the evidence be/ must be/ should be demolished*). In *if*-clauses it can express 'irrealis', similar to the use of such modals as *could* and *might*.[1]

These semantically interrelated verbal categories, mood and modal auxiliaries, have been much studied both synchronically and diachronically. The demise of the subjunctive is one of the reiterated putative changes in English – both in terms of long-term developments[2] and ongoing change in PDE. Bevier (1931: 207) calls the subjunctive a 'disappearing feature of the English language'; Foster (1968: 220) remarks that 'the subjunctive mood of the verb is a rather feeble and restricted device in modern English' and Harsh (1968: 98), on the basis of his textual evidence, concludes that the 'inflected subjunctive forms decline to the point of non-existence in present-day English'. Towards the end of the twentieth century, Givón (1993: 274) points out that 'the old grammatical category of subjunctive has almost disappeared', and according to Peters' most recent comment (2004: 520), the 'subjunctive is a pale shadow of what it used to be'. Before we start tolling the death bell for the subjunctive, however, we have to pause and distinguish between the paradigmatic poverty of the subjunctive on the one hand and its use on the other hand. By paradigmatic poverty, we refer to the fact that English,

---

[1]   On the relation of modality and mood, cf. Palmer (1999). For a full discussion of the semantics of the subjunctive, see James (1986).
[2]   Harsh (1968), on the basis of Bible translations from 910 to 1923 and plays written between the middle of the fifteenth to the twentieth century, traces the decline of the subjunctive in both genres. He does not specifically focus on the mandative subjunctive, which might be one of the reasons why the recent revival of this particular context for subjunctives is not mentioned.

which had a fully fledged subjunctive that was formally distinct for most person/number/tense combinations in the Old English period (cf. Mitchell and Robinson, 1992: 43ff. and 51), has been reduced to remnants of the paradigm in the third-person singular present tense forms (example 1a), the verb *be* in its bare form (examples 1b and 2) and the past subjunctive *were* with the first- and third- person singular (examples in 3).

(1) a. When he called again, demanding that she *sing* him his favourite song, ... [F-LOB K23]
     b. Both cases demand that people as individuals ... *be judged* fit ... [Frown B02]
(2) a. If the truth *be* told, ... [Frown D10]
     b. If this argument *be* right, ... [F-LOB J49]
(3) a. The oriental girl wiped her mouth with the back of her hand, but delicately, as if this *were* the proper thing to do, ... [F-LOB N11]
     b. And if I *weren't* such a workaholic, ..., I wonder what eventually might have happened. [Frown P20]

As far as the use of the subjunctive is concerned, it survives in a few fossilized contexts, e.g. such as *if need be, be it that...*, *God save the Queen* or in subordinate clauses introduced by *lest*, to name a few examples. Verbal mood cannot, however, be relegated solely to linguistic palaeontology; previous research has shown that it is on the increase again in subordinate clauses following mandative or 'suasive' expressions such as *important* or *demand* (cf. Övergaard 1995 and Hundt 1998b).[3] This is a development in which (written and spoken) AmE is leading world English in an essentially twentieth-century (post-colonial) revival, as we will see in section 3.2. For other uses of the subjunctive, patterns seem to have stabilized at a low level. The present subjunctive in *if*-clauses seems to be a fossilized feature of English, with only a sprinkling of examples in standard corpora such as Brown (5), LOB (9), Frown (4) and F-LOB (7).[4] Quirk *et al.* (1985: 158) regard the *were*-subjunctive as 'something of a fossil'. In order to be able to answer the question whether the past subjunctive is on the wane, Kennedy (1998: 138) calls for further corpus-based analysis of more recent corpora. Our analysis in section 3.3 is an attempt to fill this gap.

3.2   The revival of the mandative subjunctive

Comments on the diachronic development of constructions following mandative expressions such as *require*, *move* or *demand* have often been contradictory: AmE has been found to be lagging behind BrE in the use of the

---

[3] Anderson (2001: 162) claims that mandative subjunctives are also 'recessive' but does not back up his claim with evidence. Serpollet (2001, 2003) also uses the evidence from the Brown family of corpora for her study.
[4] There are four 'ordinary' instances and three instances of the formulaic *if need be*.

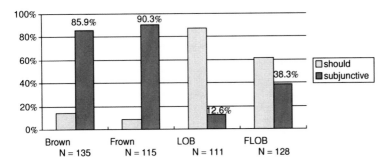

Figure 3.1 *Should*-periphrasis vs mandative subjunctive in written AmE and BrE*

*Figures for LOB and Brown are from Johansson and Norheim (1988:29) For more detail, see Table A3.2.

periphrastic construction with *should*; at the same time it has been suspected of leading World English in a revival of the mandative subjunctive.[5] An earlier study of suasive expressions in Brown and LOB only (Johansson and Norheim 1988) found that the subjunctive was more frequent in the American corpus. The most comprehensive investigation of the diachronic development of the mandative subjunctive in the twentieth century is Övergaard's (1995) study. Even though she includes LOB and Brown among her data, her approach is not based on truly parallel corpora: her additional material, which was estimated to be approximately one million words per corpus, was taken from fewer texts and the samples varied in length.[6] On the other hand, her extra material was not computerized, which means that her method of collecting the data differed significantly from that of previous studies and the approach taken in this book: she read whole texts or parts of texts and did not limit her search to a set of suasive expressions, as Johansson and Norheim had done.

3.2.1   Overall developments of the mandative subjunctive

Since a full set of mandative subjunctives cannot be retrieved automatically even from a POS-tagged corpus, the data in Figure 3.1 are based on a manual analysis of the seventeen most common suasive verbs and related nouns and adjectives.[7] As a syntactic variant, the periphrastic construction with *should*

---

[5] Here we only report on the ongoing change in BrE and AmE. Evidence from other inner-circle varieties of English is discussed in Peters' (1998) study (Australian English) and in Hundt's (1998b) paper (Australian and New Zealand English). Outer-circle varieties (Indian and Philippine English) are covered by Schneider (2005).

[6] Övergaard also added an additional text category in all periods that is not sampled in our family of corpora, namely drama (1995: 12).

[7] These verbs were *advise, ask, beg, demand, desire, direct, insist, move, order, propose, recommend, request, require, stipulate, suggest, urge* and *wish* in all their forms. The related nouns

was chosen.[8] Another variant, namely the indicative (e.g. *I recommend that she uses fewer passives*), is really only an alternative in BrE. We will come back to indicative VPs after suasive expressions below.

In many instances, English verb forms show formal syncretism between indicative and subjunctive. In other words, sentences like *It is important that they leave on time* or *If they were here I would not have to go upstairs again* are formally ambiguous between indicative and subjunctive. We could also argue that they are 'neutral' with respect to the category of mood. These ambiguous or 'neutral' instances were not included in the statistics.[9] With a past tense verb in the matrix clause, however, the unmarked form following a plural pronoun was interpreted as a subjunctive (e.g. *He insisted that they go*). Likewise, all instances displaying preverbal negation with *not* (e.g. *I ask that they not leave*) were counted as subjunctive.

These results show that the *should*-variant has not 'virtually disappeared' from AmE, as Övergaard (1995: 24) claims. The spread of the subjunctive in AmE has been slowing down again after the marked increase in the first half of the last century (cf. p. 53): the difference between Brown and Frown is below the level of statistical significance. This hardly comes as a surprise if we consider that even back in the 1960s with almost 90% subjunctives in mandative contexts, a saturation point had practically been reached in written AmE, and the expectation that the subjunctive would become obligatory is probably an unreasonable one. For the parallel British corpora, the data show a significant increase in subjunctives and a concomitant decrease of the periphrastic construction ($p \leq 0.001$). The expanding use of mandative subjunctives in BrE is not quite as dramatic as that reported in Övergaard (1995: 16): she found only 14 occurrences of the periphrastic variant with *should* in her British data for 1990, but 44 subjunctives. In the F-LOB data, on the other hand, the subjunctives are still less frequent than the periphrastic

---

were *demand, desire, proposal, recommendation, request, requirement, suggestion* and *wish*, but not *directive* or *move/motion* since these had also been excluded in the previous study by Johansson and Norheim (1988). The set of adjectives consisted of *anxious, essential, important, necessary* and *sufficient*. The set of triggering expressions was used throughout this study. According to Crawford (2009: 263), verbs are stronger triggers than nouns, which, in turn, are stronger triggers than adjectives. His study, based on the newspaper section of the Longman corpus (a little over 5.5 million words each of American and British data), provides interesting details on language-internal lexical variation. He found that 'weaker triggers have greater variation'. Moreover, his evidence suggests 'a direction of change where the subjunctive has made its way into BrE in the strongest triggers'. Schlüter (2009), in a longitudinal study of American and British English, has shown that the mandative subjunctive has also been spreading after the conjunction *(up)on (the) condition (that)*.

[8] The mandative semantics is also expressed in constructions with *must* or *have to*, but these are a lot less frequent in both American and British English than *should* (Crawford 2009); they were therefore excluded in our definition of the variable, as were other modals. For a detailed discussion of the definition of the variable, see Hundt (1998b: 159–163).

[9] Johansson and Norheim (1988) show that, when included in the statistics, non-distinct verbs amount to 18.2% and 9% in Brown and LOB, respectively. Excluding the non-distinct forms from the definition of the variable leads to more pronounced preferences in either variety, as Hundt (1998b: 160) shows.

variant, which is not 'losing ground at an accelerating speed', as Övergaard (1995: 31) finds on the basis of her data. This might have to do with the fact that she did not limit her search to a set of triggering expressions and even included subjunctives without an overt trigger. This difference in the search procedure might, at least to some extent, account for the different results. Actual usage of mandative subjunctives in BrE is also lower than the figures that Turner (1980) obtained in his elicitation experiments (41% subjunctives, 34% periphrastic constructions and 25% indicatives) might lead us to expect. This is hardly surprising, however, if you consider that elicitation data do not reflect people's actual usage and are, in addition, 'blind' to register variation, whereas corpus data are not. A stratified corpus of written English registers is thus more likely to be conservative (i.e. show a higher proportion of *should*-periphrasis) compared with elicitation data. Elicited data, in other words, make BrE appear more innovative with respect to the subjunctive option which, being more formal, people may perceive as the more 'correct' option.

As regards regional differences, our parallel corpora provide us with statistical evidence that BrE has not yet caught up with AmE in the use of subjunctives: the differences between Brown and F-LOB as well as between Frown and F-LOB are highly significant ($p \leq 0.001$). An additional difference between BrE and AmE lies in the range of variants that are used in mandative sentences: Johansson and Norheim (1988: 28) report only one indicative in the LOB data. As the following examples indicate, the pattern is slightly more frequent:

(4) In the testing of Rh negative women antenatally, for instance, it is *recommended that* the [. . .] techniques *are used* in parallel. [LOB J13]

(5) May I venture to *suggest that* when the Minister of Works investigates the microphones, he *considers* not only new microphones but the possibility of reverting to the pre-war practice of not having microphones . . . ? [LOB H19]

(6) . . . and it is *essential that* the ripening *is stopped* at the correct degree of acidity, and the temperature subsequently reduced quickly and evenly. [LOB E33]

(7) . . . for plane frameworks it is merely *necessary that* they *are made* of material which obeys Hooke's Law of linear elasticity, to a chosen layout scale. [LOB J76]

In F-LOB, the indicative has remained a low-frequency option, below the 25% level that Turner (1980) observed in his elicitation data. Greenbaum and Whitcut (1988: 684) point out that the subjunctive or periphrastic *should* are preferred over the indicative in formal writing. It is very likely that the indicative is more frequently used in informal spoken than in written English in Britain. Quirk and Rusiecki (1982: 389–93) obtained relatively high ratings for the indicative in their elicitation data (a restricted choice test), indicating that in some contexts the indicative was preferred over the subjunctive (though periphrasis with *should* was preferred to both). Hundt (1998b) reports 167 subjunctives (28.5%), 228 periphrastic constructions with *should* (38.9%) and a substantial 191 instances (32.6%) of indicatives in the 10-million-word spoken subcorpus of the BNC.[10] The following are typical examples from spontaneous conversation:

(8)   it is very *important that* nobody *takes* anything off the shelf automatically... [BNC, KD8 7846]

(9)   I *suggested that* Jack *goes* in [BNC, KB8 9699]

(10)   then today I've had a letter from an architect friend in America *suggesting* he *gets* in touch with an architect in <unclear> for another job... [BNC, KC0 4207]

Note that the proportion of indicatives chosen in the test item 'He wanted to see the play, so I urged/insisted/suggested/recommended that he.... (go/should go/went)' also amounted to 32.6% in Quirk and Rusiecki's (1982) experiment. Their proportions for the subjunctive and the periphrastic option are also similar to the results obtained from the BNC. It might thus well be that spoken BrE has not undergone a substantial change but that the locus of change for the mandative subjunctive is primarily the written language.

For a more detailed comparison of spoken vs written usage of the indicative in BrE, we looked at data from ICE-GB. Figure 3.2 gives the results for a search based on the same set of mandative expressions that were used for the analysis of the Brown family of corpora.

Note that the figures are based on relatively small overall frequencies of the variable in ICE-GB (36 and 30 relevant hits in the spoken and written components, respectively).[11] But the data in Figure 3.2 show that the indicative is a viable alternative in both spoken and written BrE. In spoken English, the indicative is used much more frequently than the subjunctive, whereas in written BrE, it is the least frequent alternative. At a ratio of 56:71 occurrences per million words, the relevant mandative contexts are appreciably a lot less frequent in spoken texts than in written material. We will return to this point in section 3.2.2.

Algeo (1992: 611) claims that the indicative after suasive expressions is a Briticism. Indicatives are not attested in Brown and Frown, and even the

[10] Note that about half of these data are so-called context-governed spoken texts, i.e. actually quite formal. For conversation-only data, see our Table 3.3.

[11] Even in the written component of ICE-GB, subjunctives are relatively infrequent. But this has to be attributed to the fact that the ICE corpora sample a wider range of written texts, including printed and unpublished material. The relative frequency of the indicative in the written component of ICE-GB at 30% even slightly exceeds the 25% mark that Turner observed in his data.

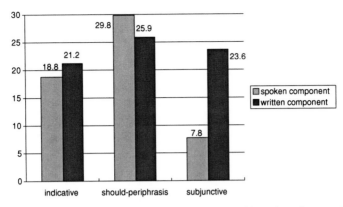

Figure 3.2 Indicative, *should*-periphrasis and subjunctive after mandative expressions in ICE-GB (frequency per million words)*
* For absolute figures, see Table A3.2. Non-mandative uses of the triggers (e.g.
suggest in the sense of 'imply') were not included in the tally for indicative verbs.

approximately five million words of the LCSAE yield only the following
example:

(11)   They require that all their teachers are there at seven fifteen.
       [LCSAE161602]

And since one swallow does not make a summer, we may safely confirm that
the indicative after suasive expressions is indeed a syntactic Briticism.

3.2.2   Is the mandative subjunctive losing its formal connotations?

Various grammarians have commented on the formal character of the
(mandative) subjunctive: Jespersen (1924: 318), for instance, claims that
its revival is 'literary'; Quirk *et al.* (1985: 157) mention that it is 'formal and
rather legalistic in style'. To test this hypothesis, three different aspects will
be considered: (a) the use of the mandative subjunctive across text types in
our written corpora; (b) co-occurrence with another 'formal' construction,
namely the passive; and (c) absolute and relative frequencies in written and
spoken English.

   With respect to register variation, Johansson and Norheim's (1988: 30)
results seem to largely confirm previous statements on the subjunctive's
formal nature, at least in BrE: 'All the examples except one occur in the
categories of informative prose of the LOB corpus.' A look at the distribution
of subjunctives across text categories in F-LOB, however, shows that BrE
is approaching the more even distribution found in the Brown and Frown
corpora (Table 3.1).

Table 3.1. *Distribution of mandative subjunctives across text categories (figures in brackets give the frequency per million words)*

Subcorpora	Brown	Frown	LOB	F-LOB
Press	27 (151)	19 (107)	3 (17)	5 (28)
Gen. Prose (D–G)	50 (140)	29 (82)	5 (14)	15 (43)
Miscellaneous (H)	13 (208)	14 (232)	2 (33)	7 (117)
Learned (J)	14 (86)	15 (94)	3 (19)	14 (87)
Fiction (K–R)	13 (51)	28 (111)	1 (4)	8 (31)
TOTAL	117 (115)§	105 (104)	14 (14)	49 (49)

§ The total number of subjunctives in this table deviates from the total in Table A3.1 (116) because the figures in Table A3.1 are based on those in Johansson and Norheim (1988) whereas the distribution of subjunctives in Brown across text types is based on a search that we did with WordSmith. The deviation is so small (1 instance), however, that the overall results are not affected.

In both BrE and AmE, administrative texts (category H) are the most likely source of mandative subjunctives, as expected. In terms of differential change, however, academic prose (category J) is the text category in which BrE has caught up with AmE. This is all the more interesting because we found this genre to be conservative with respect to other innovations (cf. Hundt and Mair, 1999). At the same time, it is hardly surprising that a genre which is resisting the trend towards a more colloquial written style should be in the vanguard of change that is reviving a (previously) formal syntactic option. Additionally, we can argue that the more even spread across genres in F-LOB indicates that the subjunctive is beginning to lose its former stylistic connotations in BrE.

In BrE, the mandative subjunctive has become more frequent in all text types sampled in the corpus. In AmE, this is not the case, and this has to be attributed to the fact that – despite an increase in the relative frequency of the mandative subjunctive against *should*-constructions – the overall frequency of the subjunctive has decreased from Brown to Frown, a change that did not prove statistically significant, however.[12] This decrease has not affected all genres in the same way: mandative subjunctives have become less frequent in Press and General Prose, but they have increased slightly in administrative writing, academic prose and most substantially in fiction, where they are now as common as in the Press section of the Frown corpus. Of the 28 instances in the fiction section of Frown, 12 mandative subjunctives are used in romance and love stories, not one of the more experimental fiction genres. Other uses of the mandative subjunctive in fictional writing are from contexts which are close to legal and administrative writing in tone and style:

[12] The decline in absolute frequencies of the subjunctive in written AmE is a development that fits the trend to colloquialization, as we will see below.

Table 3.2. *Mandative subjunctives and periphrastic constructions: active vs passive VPs*

	LOB	F-LOB	Brown	Frown
subjunctive	3 : 11	25 : 24	54 : 63	66 : 39
should-periphrasis	69 : 37	30 : 49	15 : 7	6 : 4

(12) a. 'I ask that the court excuse Mrs. Williams's outburst. [...]' [Frown L11]

   b. The defense attorney insisting that she repeat the color over and over again [...]. [Frown L11]

   c. 'Sire,' he said, 'an emissary just arrived from the mighty King of Spain urgently begs that Your Majesty receive him.' [Frown K25]

These examples are an important reminder that the fiction section is probably the least stylistically homogeneous category in our corpora and increases in this part of the corpus are therefore more difficult to account for.

In LOB, the majority of mandative subjunctives co-occur with the passive, whereas the Brown corpus shows a more even distribution of active and passive subjunctives. Johansson and Norheim interpret this as further proof of the subjunctive's formal nature in BrE. The growing use of mandative subjunctives in BrE goes hand in hand with an increase in active subjunctives, resulting in a more even distribution of active and passive subjunctives in F-LOB than in LOB (see Table 3.2). This can be taken as evidence that the subjunctive in BrE is indeed losing its formal connotations. In Frown, active subjunctives now even outnumber passive subjunctives.

Passive subjunctives are also found in text categories which are at the forefront of the ongoing colloquialization, namely the Press section of our corpora:

(13) Both cases *demand that* people as individuals, not as part of arbitrary classifications, *be judged* fit – or not – to contribute to the welfare of children. [Frown B02]

(14) 'Conditions have *dictated that* operations *be scaled* down [...]' [F-LOB A38][13]

(15) The political parties are now disintegrating into ethnic or other groups that rightly *demand* they no longer *be mulcted* by a graft from the centre, [...] [F-LOB B12]

---

[13] Note, incidentally, that this particular example was retrieved differently, namely by searching for subordinating *that* and a following *be*, allowing for one word to occur between the conjunction and the subjunctive. This was the only example from the whole search that was not also included in the previously retrieved set of subjunctives.

Table 3.3. *Mandative subjunctives and periphrastic constructions in written and spoken English (percentages are given for subjunctive only)*

	F-LOB	BNCdemog (conversation)	Frown	LCSAE
subjunctive : *should*	49 : 79	19 : 41	105 : 11	56 : 4
% subjunctive	38.3%	31.7%	90.5%	93.3%

The last example is particularly interesting because it is from a sentence where the subordinating conjunction *that* has been omitted (*that*-omission being another marker of informality). Overall, *that*-omission in mandative sentences occurs more often in spoken than in written texts. Of the mandative sentences in F-LOB, only slightly over 8% show deletion of the subordinating conjunction (see Hundt 1998b: 168); Hoffmann (1997: 71), in his analysis of *be*-subjunctives, found *that*-deletion in 19% of the mandative sentences collected from the spoken BNC.

In addition to the passive uses of mandative *be*, there are also occasional active uses, but the data in Table 3.2 indicate that the verb *be* may not remain the stronghold of the subjunctive that it was in the past, as passive subjunctives are becoming relatively less frequent. Data from spoken corpora provide further evidence that the mandative subjunctive is, indeed, losing its former formal connotations; it is occasionally used in spoken BrE but is especially frequent in spoken AmE (see Table 3.3).

The relative frequency of the subjunctive against the *should*-periphrasis in the written and spoken corpora is remarkably similar – more similar within BrE and AmE than across varieties. The findings are statistically significant (the difference between F-LOB and Frown as well as that between the BNC and the LCSAE is significant at $p \leq 0.001$). The differences within the varieties (F-LOB vs BNC and Frown vs LCSAE) are not statistically significant. In BrE, the ratio of subjunctives to *should* is higher in writing than in speech, whereas in AmE it is higher in the spoken than in the written corpus. The following are typical examples of subjunctives in spoken contexts:[14]

(16)   They, they *asked that* it *be done* on a Friday and a Saturday . . . [BNC, KBK 4702]

(17)   Gilbert *insisted that* we *provide* coffee for all the people [BNC, KBW 14225][15]

[14] The BNC also yields an interesting instance of backshifting of a present to a past subjunctive in reported speech: 'I *insisted that* it *were* open doors for you as jobs were so hard to get, . . . ' (BNC, KC9 5595).

[15] This instance was counted as a subjunctive because the triggering expression is in the past tense. In a present tense context, a verb following the pronoun *we* would have been non-distinctive between subjunctive and indicative usage.

(18)   Er well as far as I can see erm <pause> with, with a few minor
       reservations, the <pause> the elders would prefer not to *recommend*
       to the church *that* a call *be issued*. [BNC, KBo 3872]

An obvious and important caveat here is that the previous comments all relate
to relative frequency. With respect to absolute frequencies, the mandative
subjunctive is vastly more common in writing than in speech. Note also
that in Figure 3.2 above and the data presented in Table 3.3, mandative
contexts as a whole are more common in writing than in speech: the one-
million-word corpora F-LOB and Frown provide 128 and 126 potential
contexts, respectively, whereas the 4.2 million words of spoken BrE and five
million words of spoken AmE each produce only 60 potential contexts for
choice between a subjunctive and a modal periphrasis.[16] This might account
for the widely held notion of the subjunctive being a feature of written
English.

3.3   The *were*-subjunctive

While there is corpus evidence on the fate of the mandative subjunctive from
previous studies, the development of the *were*-subjunctive in the second half
of the twentieth century has oddly been neglected so far. The recent, corpus-
based grammar by Biber *et al.* (1999) only mentions it in passing. The focus in
this section is on the past subjunctive *were* or, more precisely, the variation
between subjunctive and indicative in the (adverbial) subordinate clause
of a hypothetical sentence. The examples in (19) illustrate the subjunctive
pattern:[17]

(19) a. If cancer *were* to start in one liver cell in each animal and proliferate
         at the same rate of speed, which animal would be the first to die?
         [Frown J31]
      b. The best thing we can do is to behave as if nothing *were* further from
         our thoughts. [F-LOB P10]
      c. I looked at him as though he *were* speaking Swahili to someone else
         and went about my business. [Frown R01]

---

[16] This only holds for the definition of the variable that we used here. Alternative patterns that
      avoid the choice between subjunctive, *should*-periphrasis and indicative altogether (such as
      non-finite clauses) would result in much lower relative frequencies of the subjunctive.
[17] There is also a marginal use of the *were*-subjunctive in conditional sentences with an
      inverted protasis (*Were she a little more friendly, I would certainly call her more often*), but
      this is an extremely formal option which Denison (1998: 300) shows to be very infrequent
      in ARCHER, increasingly so towards the twentieth century. A search for *I, he, she, it, this*
      and *that* preceded by directly adjacent *were(n't)* in four corpora of Present-Day English
      (Frown, F-LOB, the Wellington corpus of written New Zealand English and the Australian
      Corpus) only yielded a total of 15 *were*-subjunctives of this type (7 American, 6 British and
      2 Australian).

In the journal *American Speech* from 1961, we find an article on 'pseudo-subjunctive' *were*, lamenting the hypercorrect use of the subjunctive in such contexts as reported speech or instances like *I wonder if it were possible*. The author sees the *were*-subjunctive as the clearest indicator of the subjunctive mood and concludes that 'the apparently increasing popularity of *were* as a hypercorrection is an indication of the security of its future' (Ryan 1961: 49). The first corpus-based approach to *were*-subjunctives in BrE and AmE is again the article by Johansson and Norheim (1988), who found that the subjunctive was preferred to the indicative in hypothetical conditionals. In terms of the overall frequency of forms, the *were*-subjunctive was more frequent in LOB, but relative frequencies of subjunctive *were* and indicative *was* suggest that AmE is the more conservative variety. Peters (1998: 98) ascribes the overall conservatism to the influence of prescription.[18] Both the previous remarks on hypercorrect usages and the following judgemental comment from the *Contemporary Review* indicate that this might, indeed, be the case:

To ignore the subjunctive . . . means that we no longer consider it important in our speech to separate fact from possibility, that which has happened from that which could occur – or prefer to do so in awkward parenthetical phrases, such as 'hypothetically speaking . . .' or 'theoretically'. [. . .] the language which has lost its subjunctive has lost its soul. (Elsom 1984: 36, 37)

Peters (1998) provides evidence from the Australian Corpus of English compiled in the mid-1980s. Her data indicate that there might be a 'substantial shift away from the use of *were* subjunctives, in favour of indicative *was* and a wide range of modal paraphrases' (p. 100) and that 'in Australia the use of the *were* subjunctive is stiffening into a formulaic *if x were* [. . .]' (p. 101). With respect to the diachronic comparability of Brown, LOB and ACE, she concedes that:

the comparison does of course incorporate a time difference of twenty-five years between the Australian English of ACE and the American and British English of Brown and LOB. This difference may nevertheless have historical value in reflecting the influence of the two older varieties of English on the younger one and help to calibrate directions in usage. (p. 97)

On the basis of evidence from the more recent Frown and F-LOB corpora, we are able to add to the existing body of evidence and distinguish between

---

[18] Prescriptive condemnation of indicative *was* instead of subjunctive *were* has a long tradition in English grammar writing, as Auer (2006: 41f.) points out. Interestingly, however, the grammar checking facility of a word-processing programme such as Word does not identify indicative *was* as ungrammatical.

ongoing change and regional variation (although obviously not for Australian English).

Anecdotal evidence points to another possible and related change, namely the spread of *would* to the subordinate clause of conditional sentences. Fillmore (1990: 157) states that 'the conditional perfect is used, in American English, in past counterfactuals (if you *would have fixed* it, it would have worked)', a pattern that is also attested in non-standard Late Modern English (Denison 1998: 300). It might be the non-standardness of this variant that provoked Fillmore's somewhat judgemental comment:

For much of the time during which I've concerned myself with conditional sentences I've been unwilling to believe that this was common enough to deserve my attention, but in the meantime I've come to believe that it might actually be the dominant form in this country. I've recently heard it used by a Senator, a Presidential Press Secretary, several university professors, and a number of my dearest friends. (Fillmore 1990: 153)

Note, however, that in the example that Fillmore quotes, *would* does not replace subjunctive *were* but counterfactual *had*.[19]

Previous research thus indicates that the *were*-subjunctive is likely to have decreased in frequency in twentieth-century English. With respect to regional differences, this change might turn out to be more advanced in BrE than in AmE, which, in turn, might be the leading variety in a growing change to *would* in counterfactual *if*-clauses.

As in the case of the mandative subjunctive, automatic retrieval of *were*-subjunctives is not possible. Using WordSmith, we searched for the relevant subordinating conjunctions *as if*, *as though*, *even if* and *if*[20] followed either by *were(n't)* or *was(n't)*, allowing for a space of up to seven words to the right of the conjunction.[21] The resulting concordances of the searches were post-edited, eliminating all plural subjects and singular *you*.[22] Clauses with collective nouns or otherwise ambiguous subjects were not included in the final dataset, either. Furthermore, instances where *if* was used in the sense of 'whether' (introducing an indirect question) were not included, among them instances of what Ryan (1961) called pseudo-subjunctives (20a–d), where *were* occurs in place of the normal standard *was* of (20e–f):

---

[19] Anderson (2001: 163) considers *would* in the *if*-clause (**If that would be true, I would resign*) to be ungrammatical but points out that it is commonly used by speakers with 'Germanic' first languages.

[20] We did not include *unless* because it would have made comparison with previous studies impossible.

[21] Note that the subjunctive was only used after *though* in combination with *as*; simple *though* was therefore excluded from the search.

[22] Obviously, instances of *you* followed by indicative *was* (as in 'Neither could you if you was as poor as me', F-LOB R03) were also left out of the count.

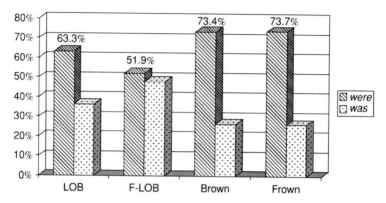

Figure 3.3 Subjunctive *were* vs indicative *was* in hypothetical/unreal conditional constructions

(20) a. ... he simply didn't care if she *were* a snake charmer from India or the whore of the island, which he supposed she was. [Frown P09]
   b. He wondered if she *were* even twenty-one yet. [Frown P26]
   c. Even as she wondered if she *were* imagining things, the woman's friend appeared at her car ... [Frown L23]
   d. ... she asked a colored man staying in the hotel if he *were* free. [Frown G55]
   e. When the judge asked Lilly if he understood his rights and if he *was* satisfied with his lawyer, Lilly said 'yes.' [Frown A30]
   f. It would help if I could find out if the driver *was* ever found. [Frown L02]

To test the hypothesis of a growing use of *would* in *if*-clauses we searched for *if* followed by *would*, again allowing for a maximum of up to seven words between the two search strings. We will begin by looking at overall frequency developments.

3.3.1 *The* were-*subjunctive: diachronic development*

Figure 3.3 gives the overall results of the comparison between the 1960s and 1990s corpora. The data from our parallel corpora show that the *were*-subjunctive in BrE has decreased over the thirty-year period between LOB and F-LOB and is now used with about the same frequency as the indicative. AmE is clearly lagging behind in this development and, in the 1990s, has not even the same proportion of *were*-subjunctives and indicatives found in the 1960s British corpus. The difference between the 1960s corpora is not statistically significant. While the change within BrE is significant at ($p \leq$ 0.05), the shift from Brown to Frown is below the level of statistical

Table 3.4. *Subjunctive* were *vs indicative* was *in hypothetical/unreal conditional constructions**

	LOB *were : was*	F-LOB *were : was*	Brown *were : was*	Frown *were : was*
as if	33 : 15	19 : 19	35 : 8	32 : 8
as though	22 : 9	13 : 9	19 : 1	9 : 3
even if	7 : 10	2 : 6	3 : 4	4 : 4
if	64 : 38	46 : 40	56 : 28	53 : 20
TOTAL	126 : 72	80 : 74	113 : 41	98 : 35

* Figures for Brown and LOB are from Johansson and Norheim (1988). Note that they also included *even though*, which we felt was not hypothetical and therefore did not include in our definition of the variable.

significance. The net result is a highly significant regional difference between the 1990s corpora (at $p \leq 0.001$).

As the overall figures in Table 3.4 show, the raw frequency of subjunctive *were* in *if*-clauses is now higher in AmE than in BrE. As in Peters' study (1998: 95), the strongholds of the construction are not only simple *if* but also the complex conjunctions *as if* and *as though*.

Even though the indicative seems to be replacing the *were*-subjunctive in hypothetical conditional constructions, its remaining uses are not, as one might suppose, limited to fixed phrases like *If I were you....* In fact, there is only one instance of this phrase, in the Frown Corpus (incidentally, from the fiction part of the corpus).

There are a few examples with *would* or another modal in the subordinate clause of the sentence, but only a sprinkling of counterfactual *if*-clauses containing *would* (none of them involving the verb *be* and thus possible variants of subjunctive *were*). A search for *if* followed by *would be/wouldn't be* in the LCSAE produced some evidence that *would* is used in counterfactual *if*-clauses in AmE:[23]

(21) a. And if everybody would be nice we wouldn't need policemen [LCSAE 124301]
      b. Yes if you would be willing to do it for us. You'd be volunteering for something you may not want to do. [LCSAE 161501]
      c. If Oprah Winfrey would be my teacher, I'll listen to her you know. [LCSAE 141401][24]
      d. If that would be a good alternative, I would have to bill at that point. [LCSAE 125202]

[23] We allowed for up to five items to occur between the subordinating conjunction and *would/wouldn't*. The auxiliary and *be*, however, were directly adjacent in all searches. We therefore missed those instances where an adverbial was placed between *would* and *be*.
[24] Note that this example, with stress on *would*, could also be given an emphatic volitional reading ('if x were willing to...') which would make it more acceptable.

    e. ... if you would be willing to give her money from your organization account or whatever then she would appreciate it I'm sure ... [LCSAE 119601]

Out of the 64 instances in the LCSAE, however, only 10 would require subjunctive *were* or indicative *was* according to the usage guides. The great majority are instances of indirect questions where *if* was used instead of *whether*:

(22) a. ... didn't know if Cassie would be able to get up there or not. [LCSAE 153101]
     b. And so I didn't know if it would be that much difference. [LCSAE 125203]
     c. I was wondering if Mr ... would be available for me to come over and have some forms signed? [LCSAE 156101]

These rather frequent constructions might eventually pave the way for a more widespread use of *would* in counterfactual *if*-clauses. So far, however, *would* is not a frequently used alternative for subjunctive *were* in counterfactual *if*-clauses, even in spoken AmE. The search also returned an interesting case of a self-correction in which the speaker replaces *were* by *would*:

(23) And instead of having a [sic] R A explain it like afterwards, if, if there were would be like a program we could develop. [LCSAE 164301]

3.3.2   The were-subjunctive: a recessive formal option?

One might suspect that the *were*-subjunctive – on its retreat – is specializing as a formal option in written standard English. In this case, we would expect it to co-occur with other formal constructions (such as the passive) and in the more formal text categories of the corpora. With respect to the passive, however, the data from F-LOB and Frown do not indicate a preference for co-occurrence: only 15 of the 80 *were*-subjunctives in F-LOB were passives and 9 of the 98 in Frown. In other words, unlike the mandative subjunctive, the *were*-subjunctive does not favour the passive voice. The distribution across text types does not offer any support for the hypothesis that the past subjunctive occurs predominantly in formal text categories (see Table 3.5).

    Were-subjunctives are still relatively frequent in the Fiction subcorpus of both F-LOB and Frown – a genre that, otherwise, is more open to colloquial usages.[25] This is anything but convincing evidence that the *were*-subjunctive is a formal option in Present-Day English. A striking regional difference is the much more widespread use of *were*-subjunctives in AmE newspapers.

---

[25] There is a tendency, though, for the *were*-subjunctives to occur in narrative passages rather than in quotations.

Table 3.5. *Distribution of* were-*subjunctives across text types (figures per million words are given in brackets)**

	Press	General Prose	Official and Learned	Fiction	Total
F-LOB	6 (33)	25 (71)	17 (77)	32 (124)	80
Frown	14 (78)	23 (65)	11 (50)	50 (194)	98

* The word counts for the calculation of the relative frequencies were based on a Unix count.

To sum up, the data from our corpora confirm that the *were*-subjunctive is definitely losing ground in hypothetical adverbial clauses. From a more global perspective, AmE turns out to be the conservative variety in this ongoing change and BrE, for once, is more advanced. There is no evidence of a growing use of *would* as a variant for subjunctive *were* in counterfactual *if*-clauses – a usage that still seems to be more or less non-standard.

3.4 Revival and demise of the subjunctive? An attempt at reconciling apparently contradictory developments

We may ask why the subjunctive is behaving in this slightly contradictory way: on the one hand, corpus data reveal that the mandative subjunctive is spreading again; on the other hand, we observe a marked shift away from the subjunctive in conditional clauses. The post-colonial revival of the mandative subjunctive has been attributed to language contact in the Mid-West of the United States (immigrants transferring the subjunctive from their native languages in the acquisition of English; Övergaard 1995: 44f.). Redundancy has been suggested as the major reason for the decline of the subjunctive in conditional clauses.[26] One of the Australian respondents in Peters' (1998: 99) style survey pointed out that 'after *if* the use of the subjunctive to suggest counterfactuality is redundant'. The formal syncretism of indicative and subjunctive with plural subjects (*If they were . . .*) may have contributed to this view that the past subjunctive in counterfactual conditionals is redundant. A good example supporting this view comes from the Frown corpus – an essay about historical injustice that uses hypothetical cases to make a point. In this instance, indicative *was* is used instead of subjunctive *were*:

(24)   In the actual course of events, what followed E (events F, G, and H) is simply what results from applying natural laws to E as an initial *condition*. For example, *if E was your seizure* of the only water hole in

---

[26] See Visser (1963–1973: Vol. III, Part II, 885), Gonzáles-Álvarez (2003: 306) and Auer (2006: 46) for a similar explanation concerning developments in earlier stages of English.

the desert just as I was about to slake my thirst, then F – the event that follows E – would be what happens normally when one person is deprived of water and another is not: you live and I die. [Frown G22, emphasis added]

The American conservatism in the ongoing loss of the *were*-subjunctive could be explained by several factors. The fact that the mandative subjunctive has seen such a marked revival, especially in AmE, might have lent support to the receding *were*-subjunctive (maybe also due to language contact) in this variety. As in the case of the mandative subjunctive, the relatively strong status that the *were*-subjunctive has in AmE might not simply have to be attributed to straightforward colonial lag but a more complicated pattern of post-colonial revival.[27] Preliminary evidence that before the 1960s the past subjunctive had reached an even lower point comes from the long-term evidence in Auer (2006) and C. C. Fries' (1940: 106) grammar:

(a) In the ARCHER data that Auer (2006) investigated, the relative frequency of the past subjunctive to the indicative had declined to only 20.8% for the period 1750–1799, but increased again towards the end of the nineteenth-century, to 27.4%. This indicates that the subjunctive might have increased even further again at the beginning of the twentieth century towards the levels found in the LOB and Brown corpora, only to decline again in the second half of the century.[28] Auer does not comment on differential change in BrE and AmE, however.

(b) Before the advent of computer corpora, Fries found 30 instances of indicative verb forms in conditional clauses and only 12 subjunctives (both present and past) in his 'standard' material and a ratio of 24 indicatives against 6 subjunctives in his 'vulgar' English materials. He takes this as a clear tendency to avoid the subjunctive in non-factual conditional clauses (Fries 1940: 107).

Compared with evidence from Johansson and Norheim as well as our own data, these findings suggest that AmE might have seen a short revival of the *were*-subjunctive between the 1940s and 1960s and has recently been following the lead of other varieties towards a more frequent use of indicatives, if somewhat reluctantly. To verify this, however, we will need data from early-twentieth-century AmE and BrE.[29]

Another explanation could be that Americans may be more susceptible to prescriptive influence in this area of language use. This explanation receives

[27] For a critical evaluation of the terms 'colonial lag' or 'colonial innovation', see Hundt (2009a: 13–37). A post-colonial survival of the *were*-subjunctive could possibly have been supported by the prescriptive tradition that seems to be somewhat stronger in the US than in Britain.

[28] Additional evidence from the B-Brown and B-LOB corpora will allow us to verify this point at a later stage.

[29] Compilation work on the 1930s LOB corpus (B-LOB) has now been completed; the American 1930s version of Brown, however, has only been started recently.

support from the fact that hypercorrect usage has been commented on in America but not Great Britain (even though such patterns are attested in both varieties).[30] This line of argument would also offer a plausible explanation of the conservative nature of AmE newspaper usage with respect to the *were*-subjunctive.

Urdang (1991: 12) uses a fairly original explanation for the regional demise of the *were*-subjunctive in BrE that we merely add for entertainment value:

We shall have to wait and see if the changes of Margaret Thatcher's political fortunes are reflected in the language as spoken in Britain, for one might be tempted to infer that the assertiveness of her tenure was partly responsible for the demise of the subjunctive in contrary-to-fact constructions – at least in those perceived by her to be contrary to what she perceived as fact.

Obviously, ongoing grammatical change that is happening on a global scale cannot possibly be attributed to a single individual, not even after a long term of office.

3.5 Summary and conclusion

With respect to long-term developments, Traugott (1972: 148) and Blake (1996: 222) argue that modals (especially *should*) take over from the original subjunctive forms; Denison (1998: 160), however, points out that the indicative is an alternative variant to the modal periphrasis. In the next chapter, we will see that the modal verbs are decreasing in general. This chapter has shown that two of them, namely *should* and *would*, are also failing to replace the subjunctive, *pace* Barber's (1964: 133) claim, but for different reasons.

The mandative subjunctive is in the process of replacing periphrastic constructions with *should*, more so in AmE than in BrE. With respect to absolute frequencies, the mandative subjunctive is still vastly more common in writing than in speech. This is mainly a correlative of the fact that triggering contexts occur more often in the written than in the spoken medium.

Barber (1964: 133f.) doubts that the revival of the mandative subjunctive will lead to a 'serious long-term revival of the subjunctive forms; the present development is probably only a passing fashion'. Both Barber (1964) and Potter (1975: 142) speculate that the long-term effect of this ongoing change will be the final loss of the last regular inflectional ending in the present tense (indicative) paradigm of verbs, i.e. the revival of the mandative subjunctive would, in this case, contribute to a continuation of the change towards a more analytic language type. However, third-person singular present tense verbs without an inflectional ending are still strongly associated with non-standard

---

[30] Interestingly, instances of hypercorrect *were* in non-counterfactual *if*-clauses have remained fairly stable in the American corpora (3 in Brown and 4 in Frown), whereas they have completely disappeared in the 1990s BrE corpus (LOB still has 3 instances).

language use and it is therefore unlikely that this change is going to take place in the near future. The indicative is a syntactic Briticism in mandative contexts. It is a low-frequency option in formal written English: however, our data from ICE-GB show that it is a viable alternative to the subjunctive in spoken and informal written BrE.

Unlike the mandative subjunctive, the *were*-subjunctive in counterfactual *if*-clauses is a recessive feature of standard written English.[31] It is not being replaced by a modal but, instead, by indicative *was*. *Would* + *be* instead of subjunctive *were* in counterfactual *if*-clauses is still largely confined to informal, spoken English. It is meeting with strong prescriptive reaction, especially in the US.[32] One side-effect of this, so to speak, is hypercorrect use of *were* in non-counterfactuals. The revival of a conservative feature, prescriptive reaction to the loss of an old feature and hypercorrection can all be seen as epiphenomena of what Crystal (2004: 523) has called 'a period of transition' in which we have been moving away from dogmatic to pragmatic views on language use. His view is that 'we are coming towards the close of a linguistically intolerant era but – as happens in last-ditch situations – conservative reaction can be especially strong' (p. 525).

As regards the alternative expressions for verbal mood, we see a split of compensation strategies: modal periphrasis (with various modal verbs but a pronounced preference for *should*) is a viable but currently recessive alternative to the mandative subjunctive; the indicative, however, is dispreferred in mandative contexts in AmE but a viable alternative in (informal) written and particularly in spoken BrE. The past subjunctive, on the other hand, is increasingly replaced by the indicative with the modal variant as a proscribed option[33] which is still restricted to spoken colloquial usage. Note that the indicative as an alternative for the *were*-subjunctive is a more viable option than the indicative after mandative expressions since past tense *was* still helps to convey the non-factual nature of the situation. Indicatives after mandative expressions, on the other hand, are less clearly exhortative than the subjunctive or modal periphrasis.[34]

---

[31] The study of nineteenth-century English by Grund and Walker (2006: 103) supports the direction of change towards the indicative rather than modal periphrasis.

[32] That prescriptivism might have had an influence on the usage of the past subjunctive in the eighteenth century has been suggested by Auer (2006). The impact was not as strong as one might expect, however: 'its effect was limited, causing merely a blip in the diachronic development of the subjunctive' (p. 47).

[33] This fits in with results on long-term developments since EModE, cf. Auer (2006: 46), on the basis of the Helsinki and ARCHER corpora.

[34] This also applies to an even more frequent alternative in mandative contexts, namely the *to*-infinitive, which has been excluded as a variable here. For the success story of the *to*-infinitive in English, see Chapter 9.

4 The modal auxiliaries

With this chapter we move from mood – the subject of Chapter 3 – to the closely related topic of modality.[1] In Chapter 4 we examine the modal auxiliary verbs, or *core modals*, as they have been called (e.g. by Facchinetti *et al.* 2003: vi), to distinguish them from the *semi-modals* which are the subject of Chapter 5. In broad terms, our findings have been that the core modals have been significantly declining in use, whereas the semi-modals have been significantly increasing.[2]

The results we discuss in this chapter have been obtained from a comparison not only of the Brown and Frown, LOB and F-LOB corpora, but also of approximately matching BrE spoken subcorpora, from the DCPSE (see section 2.5.4). We have also looked at the frequency of modals and subjunctives in the Longman Corpus of Spoken American English (LCSAE) and the British National Corpus (BNC). From these combined sources it is possible to obtain an intriguing record of differential rates of change between American and British usage, and between speech and writing, but the overall picture of the modal auxiliaries in gradual decline is unquestionable.

4.1 The declining use of the modal auxiliaries in written standard English 1961–1991/2

First, we examine the changing frequency of the modals in written English as observed in the four corpora of the Brown family. Given that all four corpora

---

[1] On mood and modality, see Palmer ([2]2001: 1–23; 2003: 2–4). Palmer sees the mood system as a binary cut between 'modal' and 'non-modal' (or 'realis' and 'irrealis'), whereas the modal system subclassifies the 'non-modal' category into various subcategories, such as epistemic and deontic. In Palmer's view, however, the system of mood no longer operates in English, as 'the subjunctive has died out' (Palmer 2003: 3).

[2] Compared with the subjunctive, the core modals are of course vastly more frequent and central to the grammar of the language. Yet in contrast to the debates on the fate of the subjunctive, the declining frequency of the modals seems not to have been noticed until recently, when diachronic corpus studies of Modern English became possible. This and the next chapter draw on Leech's (2003) and Smith's (2003a) studies of modals and semi-modals in the Brown family. A more general decline of the core modals in the twentieth century has been found in a study of the ARCHER corpus by Biber, Conrad and Reppen (1998: 207) and Biber (2004: 199–200).

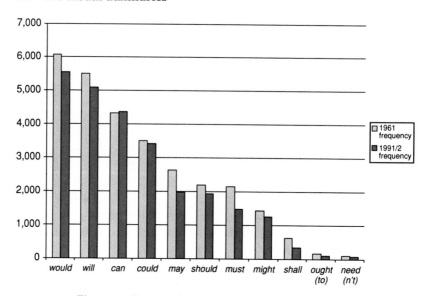

Figure 4.1 Frequencies of modals in the four written corpora: comparing 1961 with 1991/2

are so closely comparable in size and composition, there is no need in this initial survey to provide normalized frequency counts: raw counts are sufficient here. The modals listed in Figure 4.1 are the **core modals** which can be said to express central modal meanings of possibility, necessity, permission, obligation, prediction and volition, as well as to share the syntactic properties associated with the class of auxiliaries in English – including the so-called NICE properties (Huddleston 1984; Palmer [2] 1990: 4; Facchinetti *et al.* 2003: vi, viii). The words which conform to these criteria are *will, would, can, could, may, might, should, shall* and *must*, to which *ought (to)* and *need(n't)* are added as peripheral members. The graphic form *need(n't)* here is a reminder that we are considering not the semi-modal *need to* – see Chapter 5 – but *need* constructed as a core modal, i.e. followed by a bare infinitive, and having the NICE properties, as well as the ability to occur in the contracted negative form *needn't*:

(1)   There *need* be no doubt about that. [LOB E34]

We exclude *used to* and *dare*, which have sometimes been included among the marginal modals (Quirk *et al.* 1985: 137–40) because, although they share in some measure the syntactic properties of core modals, their meanings do not primarily belong to modality. The so-called semi-modals *be going to, have to, (have) got to* and the like, will not be entirely ignored in this chapter, but will receive more detailed attention in Chapter 5.

It is useful to begin by putting the American and British corpora together (see Figure 4.1), in order to show the overall picture of decline in frequency (from 1961 to 1991/2) – a picture which is closely replicated, as we will see, on both sides of the Atlantic. (The size of the combined corpora is approximately two million words for each time period.)

Figure 4.1 and Table A4.1 indicate that the general trend is a significant loss of frequency: the decline is 10.6% for the class as a whole, while the loss for individual modals varies between 2.2% (*could*) and 43.5% (*shall*). (The only departure from this declining trend is in a tiny rise in frequency of 1.3% in the case of *can*.)

The average decline in frequency for the individual modals is as high as 18.9% – a figure that reflects a 'bottom-weighting' of the frequency loss: that is, less common modals have declined more than more frequent ones. The four most common modals *would*, *will*, *can* and *could* account for 67.5% of all modal usage in 1961, and in 1991/2 this figure has risen to 71.9%. These four common modals treated as a group have lost only 4.7% of their usage in the thirty-year period, whereas the bottom seven modals as a group have lost 22.7% (the most notable losers, apart from *shall*, are *may* (with a loss of 24.6%), *must* (31.2%), *need(n't)* (31.6%) and *ought (to)* (37.5%).

Nevertheless, there is constancy in the pattern of change: the order of frequency of the modals is the same in both 1961 and 1991/2, and what is particularly striking (except in the case of *can*) is the consistent pattern of the overall decline.

In our next stage of analysis, we look at the frequency patterns of the AmE and the BrE corpora individually but side by side, shown in Figures 4.2 and 4.3.

From Figures 4.2 and 4.3 we see a remarkably similar pattern in the two pairs of corpora. The order of frequency of the modals is the same in the American and British corpora, except that in F-LOB *would* has fallen below *will*, and *may* below *should*. Similarly, with a relatively small exception, the trend of frequency loss is found consistently on both sides of the Atlantic. (The exception is that in BrE the possibility/permission modals *can* and *could* register a slight increase in F-LOB as compared with LOB.)

There are, however, noteworthy overall differences between the AmE and the BrE figures. The trend is more extreme in AmE in two respects: (a) the decline in frequency is somewhat steeper than in BrE (11.4% compared with 9.8%); and (b) the decline starts and ends at a lower point. It is as if BrE is following in the footsteps of AmE, but tardily.

4.2   The changing use of the modals in different genres and subcorpora

A further step in our analysis is to examine the parts of the corpora, to see if the decline of modal frequency is more noticeable in some text

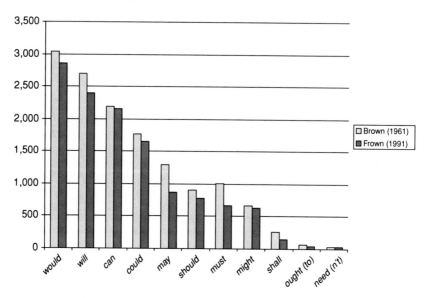

Figure 4.2 Modal auxiliaries in American English, 1961–92

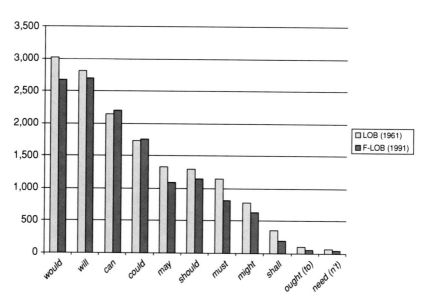

Figure 4.3 Modal auxiliaries in British English, 1961–91

Table 4.1. *Change of frequency of the core modals in subcorpora*

Subcorpus	LOB			F-LOB			change as % of LOB
	raw freq.	pmw	ranking	raw freq.	pmw	ranking	
Press	2,542	14,342	2	2,340	13,207	3	**−7.9%
Gen. Prose	5,685	13,693	3	4,898	11,820	4	***−13.7%
Learned	2,122	13,161	4	2,184	13,571	2	+3.1%
Fiction	4,424	17,472	1	3,961	15,642	1	***−10.5%
TOTAL	14,773	14,672		13,383	13,307		***−9.3%

categories than in others. In this instance we look at the four subcorpora of Press, General Prose, Learned and Fiction, and discover (see Table 4.1) that in one of these – the Learned subcorpus – there has been no decline of modal usage at all; in fact there has been a small (non-significant) rise of 3.1%.

The ranking 1, 2, 3, 4 alongside the normalized frequency counts in Table 4.1 shows the high-to-low order of frequency of the subcorpora in LOB and F-LOB. The ordering for LOB makes good sense, if we recall (see Biber *et al.* 1999: 486) that modals are known to be generally more frequent in conversation than in written genres (see further section 4.4). As fiction writing is, out of these four varieties, the text type most closely related to spoken language, and Learned writing is the most distant from spoken language, it is not surprising that these subcorpora fill respectively the highest and the lowest position in frequency. The two intermediate varieties, Press and General Prose, are again in the order we would expect if closeness to spoken language were the main determinant of modal frequency.

However, by 1991 this ordering has altered, as Learned writing has somewhat increased its frequency of modals (albeit not significantly), instead of following the pattern of decline found in the other varieties. This is seen from the second set of figures 1, 2, 3, 4 in Table 4.1: the Learned category is now in second position, rather than in fourth position. It is difficult to hazard an explanation, without careful qualitative study of the data, of why the Learned subcorpus bucks the trend in this way. Why should a genre that is otherwise very 'written' show an increase of modals, which are favoured by spoken language? In a number of ways, however, as we shall see, Learned writing is more conservative and conformist than other varieties, adhering to fairly strong conventions regarding what are considered 'decent standards' in academic communication. One aspect of this is the habitual avoidance of categorical assertions of truth and falsehood. The qualification of such assertions, through modal concepts such as 'possibility', 'necessity' and 'likelihood', is deeply ingrained in academic habits of thought and expression, and might well be on the increase.

Actually we find that an increased use of two modals – *can* and *could* – accounts for virtually all the frequency difference between the Learned use of modals in LOB and in F-LOB. *Can* has increased from 387 to 531 occurrences (or by 37.5%), while *could* has increased from 144 to 193 occurrences (by 34.3%). The following passage gives a taste of the usage of these 'possibility' modals in the Learned text category:

(2)   But I *can*not see how such private interpretations *could* have any bearing on the objective meaning of the terms, as employed in speech and writing, if, with respect to employment, they are causally idle. [...]

It does not follow from this that the state of affairs which epiphe-nomenalism postulates is one which *could* not obtain – that there *could* not be a world in which the mental had no causal influence on the phys-ical. Nor does it even follow that we *can* know *a priori* that the actual world is not of this kind. For it *can*not be established *a priori* that the mental actually is a topic for overt discussion. [F-LOB J51; italicization of modals added]

Interestingly enough, *may*, another modal of possibility, while decreasing very significantly in general use between LOB and F-LOB, is actually quite buoyant in the Learned category (increasing marginally from 385 to 393 occurrences), being the second most common modal, after *can*, in Learned writing in the BrE corpora. There is no mileage here, therefore, in the idea that the increase of *can* has taken place at the expense of the declining modal *may*. We can guess, on the other hand, that the tendency for Learned writing to buck the trend of modal decline is related to the prominence academic writing gives to the modalities expressed by *can* and *may*.

4.3   The changing use of the modals in spoken vs written corpora

As explained in section 2.5.4, there are no true spoken equivalents of the Brown family of corpora, but for British spoken English, cautious conclu-sions can be drawn from the comparison between two comparable 'mini-corpora' of approximately 140,000 words each, the DSEU corpus (from the 1960s) and the DICE corpus (from the early 1990s). These 'mini-corpora', covering a wide range of spoken data from spontaneous dialogue to broad-cast monologue, have been extracted from the DCPSE corpus of spoken British English (see 2.5 D2) to match as closely as possible the comparability criteria (equality of size and text selection) of the Brown family. The fact that modals have high frequency as grammatical items, especially in spoken English, makes the results meaningful even in the comparison of such small corpora, although necessarily tentative. The results, as it transpires in Figure 4.4, are striking enough to dampen scepticism.

There are some differences in frequency order between the spoken and written corpora. Also, judging from these figures (as well as other sources,

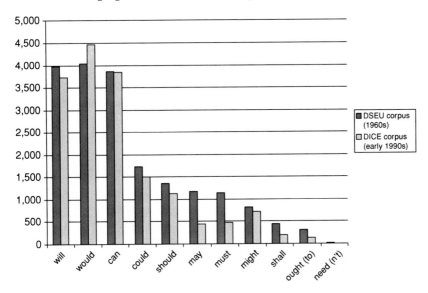

Figure 4.4 Comparison of DSEU and DICE: modals
in spoken BrE in the 1960s and the early 1990s (pmw)

e.g. Biber *et al.* 1999: 486), the general frequency of modals is much higher
(by a margin of 24.8% in 1961 and of 23.7% in 1991) in the spoken data
than in the written data.[3] However, the most notable observation is that
Table A4.3 (giving the numerical data presented in Figure 4.4) shows a
decrease of 11.8% in the use of modals in the spoken mini-corpora – a result
corroborating the findings for the corresponding written corpora, LOB and
F-LOB. The five modals showing a sharp decline in the written corpora
show an even sharper decline in the spoken corpora, in several cases over
50%: *need(n't)* (64.9%), *may* (62.3%), *ought to* (58.4%), *shall* (53.4)%. (It
must be remembered, however, that in the mini-corpora the numbers are
too small to be significant, especially at the lower end of the frequency scale.)

---

[3] The arguably simplistic division between written and spoken data in this section obscures
the extent to which modals vary in different genres both in writing and in speech. However,
the difference of frequency in spoken and written corpora in 1961 is so great that it puts
other genre distinctions in the shade. For example, although in the written texts modals
are significantly more frequent in Fiction than in the other subcorpora (17,472 tokens pmw
in LOB compared with an overall LOB frequency of 14,672 pmw), this is still appreciably
lower than the overall frequency in the contemporaneous DSEU spoken mini-corpus (18,971
pmw). The modals are remarkably variable according to genre, however, and it is worth
noting that (as can be observed in the ICE-GB corpus and the BNC) several genres of
written English, such as business letters, classroom lessons and transcribed parliamentary
debates, have a higher incidence of modals than even informal conversation. Moreover, the
greater decline of modal frequency in speech means that the gap between the spoken and
written corpora declines considerably by the 1990s.

In contrast, the most frequent modals *can* and *would* are changing relatively little, *can* declining by 0.5% and *would* even increasing by 10.4%.

The increasing percentage of usage concentrated in the four most frequent modals *will*, *would*, *can* and *could* – an effect we noticed in the written corpora – is even more striking in the spoken corpora, rising from 71.9% in the 1960s to 81.1% in the 1990s. In general terms, then, the picture of decreasing use of modals in writing, especially among the less frequent modals, is confirmed with even greater emphasis for speech.

4.4   The core modals and competing expressions of modality

A popular supposition might be that declining modal usage is linked – as a possible explanatory factor – with the spreading use of a group of so-called semi-modals, which appear to be in competition with at least some of them. For example, it has been often noted that the grammaticalization process has given rise to verbal idioms such as BE *going to*, which semantically competes with *will* as a future auxiliary (see Heine 1993), and HAVE *to*, which semantically competes with *must* in the areas of obligation and necessity (see Krug 2000, Tagliamonte 2004).[4] This theme, which will be discussed in greater depth in the next chapter, cannot be totally overlooked at this point.

Although the thesis that core modals are being gradually displaced by the semi-modals appears to have some persuasive force, one compelling argument against it, as far as the present study is concerned, is that in the Brown family of corpora, semi-modals are on the whole much less frequent than core modals. The findings to be discussed in Chapter 5 indicate that although the Brown family shows an increase in semi-modals more than proportionate to the loss of core modals (an increase of 14.3% compared with a decrease of 10.6%), the overall frequency of core modals is very much greater than that of the semi-modals in these written corpora.[5] In fact, core modals are nearly seven times more common than semi-modals in the 1961 corpora, and 5.4 times more common in the 1991/2 corpora. The increase in the number of semi-modals (in raw frequency 520) accounts for only 16.4% of the decrease in numbers of core modals (in raw frequency 3,171), so there can be no argument on this basis that the semi-modals wholly account for the decline we have discussed.

However, there are one or two signs that the written corpora are less indicative in dealing with this issue of 'displacement' than adequate compa-rable spoken corpora would be. In the two British mini-corpora of speech (see section 4.3) we find an increase of 27.1% in the use of semi-modals (from 678 to 862 occurrences), three times the increase found in the written British

---

[4] Biber (2004: 199–202) shows from the evidence of the ARCHER corpus that the marked decline of modals in the twentieth century has been largely counterbalanced by a marked increase in the semi-modals.

[5] See Tables A4.1 and A5.1 for the quantitative data from which these and the following statements are derived.

corpora LOB and F-LOB. This yields a ratio of 4.0 modals per semi-modal in the 1960s and 2.7 modals per semi-modal in the 1990s. In other words, the gap between modal frequency and semi-modal frequency has been getting much smaller in British speech than in British writing – but the ratio is still greater than 2 to 1.

Given that American speech is popularly (and with some reason) supposed to be the most influential source of innovation in the language, we must regret at this point the lack of a pair of comparable corpora of American speech analogous to the DSEU and DICE mini-corpora. However, we have been allowed access to an approximately five-million-word corpus of transcribed AmE spontaneous speech of the 1990s, the Longman Corpus of Spoken American English (LCSAE) (see Chapter 1), and from this we have observed that the ratio of core modals to semi-modals is much smaller in American conversational data – collected in the mid-1990s and therefore close in time to the DICE mini-corpus of British speech – than in the varieties we have investigated with our comparable corpora. The detailed figures will be presented in the next chapter, in Figure 5.4, but for present purposes it is enough to state that in LCSAE there are just 1.6 core modals per semi-modal. Thus the 'displacement hypothesis' still appears to have some force, if one focuses on the variety – American spontaneous speech – commonly assumed to have an influence on both British speech and American writing. The most compelling statistic here is that in the LCSAE there are more than eight occurrences of the semi-modal *have to* for one occurrence of the core modal *must*. In this light, we can assume that what is happening in the Brown family of corpora may be merely a pale reflection of more dramatic developments taking place in American speech.

4.5 Shrinking usage of particular modals: a more detailed examination

Going back to Figures 4.1 to 4.3 and the Brown family of corpora, we see that the most extreme cases of decline, in both regional varieties together, are the infrequent modals *shall*, *ought to* and *need(n't)*, and the middle-order modals *may* and *must*. Figures 4.2 and 4.3 show us that these have somewhat different patterns of decline in the AmE and BrE corpora – for example, in AmE *may* and *must* have decreased more drastically, whereas *need(n't)* has decreased much less than in the BrE data. (However, in the last case, the numbers for AmE were already so low even in 1961 that it would be hazardous to build anything on this contrast.)

In comparative corpus studies, it is reasonable to focus, for more careful analysis, on the most striking changes or variations in frequency. This is not an infallible strategy, as it might transpire that a lack of frequency contrast between comparable corpora conceals a more complex picture in which different types of frequency change cancel one another out. However, given that one cannot study everything in depth, we have decided to give some attention here to the five modals just mentioned – *shall, ought to, need(n't), may* and *must*. We will also take a closer look at *should*, because, although its decreasing use is no more than average, it has interesting interrelationships with *shall* and the subjunctive.

4.5.1   The modals at the bottom of the frequency list: shall, ought to *and* need(n't)

The least common modals, which happen to be those that have declined most in percentage terms, show signs of diminishing functionality, and perhaps obsolescence. One of these signs is what may be called 'paradigmatic atrophy'. That is, the number of the various grammatical contrasts which constitute the paradigm of an English verb is reduced, so that only some of the possibilities are available, or at least are likely to occur. This is something common to the modal auxiliary class as a whole. Modals have been called 'anomalous' or 'defective' in that they have no morphological contrast of person and number, and have no non-finite forms. Even the present–past tense distinction, if it is considered to exist for modals, is highly irregular and problematic, and there is no distinct past tense analogue at all of *must*.[6] If we take *shall* as an example of a modal undergoing decline, it has all the paradigmatic limitations mentioned above, and indeed there is virtually no case nowadays (see section 4.5.2) for arguing that *should* is the past tense of *shall*. In addition, as is well known, *shall* suffers from limitations of person: its future use (with or without volitional colouring) is virtually restricted to first-person subjects:

(3)   'I *shall* go into this matter very fully,' said the Bishop . . . [LOB A24]
(4)   I *shan't* be here much longer. [LOB L07]
(5)   Then *shall we* start? [F-LOB P22]

With second-person subjects, *shall* scarcely occurs – and the few occurrences there are (Brown 5, Frown 2, LOB 5, F-LOB 4) show signs of archaism such as the use of *thou* or *ye*, and/or come from quotations from earlier periods of the language (e.g. the Bible or the American Constitution). With third-person subjects, *shall* has a special range of 'stipulative' meaning that tends to be restricted to legal or legalistic English, or to a few other contexts where archaism appears to be at work as a means of stylistic heightening:

(6)   He is determined, come what may, that Algeria *shall* remain French. [LOB B17]
(7)   The agreement *shall* enter into force upon signature. [Brown H22]

---

[6] *Must*, historically the past tense of the obsolete verb form *mote*, is sometimes used in past-tense-like contexts, notably in (free) indirect style:

But she decided she could not face it. She *must* avoid outside distractions at all costs. [LOB K05]

However, it is debatable whether this is a lingering past tense usage or 'a present tense modal in a past tense context' (Denison 1998: 178).

(8)   All our people forced to live in Oldham *shall* come home to a green, working-class Royton again. [F-LOB B23]

The use of *shall* with first-person subjects, especially associated with Fiction texts, is more common in the BrE corpora, but declines appreciably in both the AmE and BrE data (Brown 110 → Frown 81; LOB 202 → F-LOB 147).[7] Its use with third-person subjects, on the other hand, is associated especially with the text category H – 'Miscellaneous' – which in practice consists largely of official or administrative documents. *Shall* with third-person subjects is more common in the AmE corpora, but again shows a large fall in frequency between the 1961 and 1991/2 corpora (Brown 150 → Frown 66; LOB 144 → F-LOB 46).

With *shall* in particular we see a second possible sign of obsolescence, which may be called 'distributional fragmentation'. That is, instead of being dispersed in different varieties of texts in a corpus, the form tends to be increasingly restricted to certain genres and, within those genres, to certain texts.

Possibly an additional factor to be considered under the heading of paradigmatic atrophy is the increasing rarity of the negative contraction in -*n't* with some (though not all) modals. The largely obsolete form *mayn't*, as negative contraction of *may*, does not occur in the Brown family at all: indeed, there are only seven examples of it in the 100 million words of the BNC, three of them in tag questions, e.g.:

(9)   you may be able to get that rectified *mayn't you?* [BNC KC0 3920]

and there are no examples in the five million words of the LCSAE. The evidence of Brown and Frown testifies to the virtual non-existence of *mightn't*, *shan't*, *mustn't* and *oughtn't (to)* in AmE: not only in Frown but also in Brown they are vanishingly rare (putting both corpora together, *mightn't* and *oughtn't (to)* have no occurrences, *mustn't* eleven occurrences, and *shan't* two occurrences), while the British corpora show a marked decline of all three – from 27 tokens in LOB to 8 tokens in F-LOB. The extreme manifestation of this trend is found again in the American conversational LCSAE corpus, where (in approximately five million words) there are virtually no occurrences of *mightn't* or *oughtn't (to)*, and only five of *mustn't* and one of *shan't*. Here again, the evidence, though very limited, suggests that a trend already advanced in AmE is being followed after a time lag in BrE.

As noted in Chapter 2 (section 2.5 F), the Brown family shows a sharp general increase in the use of contracted forms of verbs and negatives between the 1961 and the 1991/2 corpora. This manifestation of colloquialization is

---

7   In both AmE and BrE, *shall* with a first-person plural subject continues to be used quite frequently in polite suggestions, such as *Shall we make a move? What shall we do now?* (see also Tottie 2002: 154). It also tends to survive in formulaic usages like *as we shall see* and *shall we say* in expository texts.

found also among the *-n't* forms of the modal auxiliaries, so that the percentage of all modals that are negative contractions (e.g. tokens of *shouldn't*, as a percentage of all tokens of *should* and *shouldn't*) increases overall in AmE from 4.3% to 6.3%, and in BrE from 3.7% to 5.2%. However, this trend towards greater use of contractions does not apply in BrE to the steeply declining modals we have focused on in this section. If we take *might, must, shall* and *ought (to)* as a group,[8] the proportion of instances that are negative contractions declines from 1.1% to 0.5%. (In AmE the proportion is already as low as 0.3% in Brown, rising to 0.5% in Frown – but this rise is insignificant, representing a minimal increase from six to seven instances.) It seems, then, that these steeply declining modals have become scarcely usable with negative contractions towards the end of the twentieth century. It has been argued (Huddleston and Pullum 2002: 801) that the *-n't* form is in fact an inflectional variant of the plain modal (i.e. that *-n't* is a morphological suffix rather than an enclitic contraction). This point, if granted, supports the claim that in this respect the modals, or at least the more 'fading' of them, have become increasingly restricted in their grammatical paradigm. That is, regarded as a morphological loss, this is arguably an aspect of paradigmatic atrophy and is thus connected with the general loss of frequency of the modals.

Looking at negation from a different angle, we note that the modal auxiliary *need(n't)* is again restricted in terms of polarity – but in this case, the modal is restricted to non-assertive contexts, where negation (or occasionally interrogation) is overtly signalled by forms like *not* in (10), or is implicitly signalled, through forms like *only* in (11) and *all* followed by a restrictive clause in (12):[9]

(10) We searched around for a window-cleaner, but she *need not* have worried. [LOB R08]

(11) One *need only* taste a great Meursault or Chablis to be convinced. [Frown F38]

(12) Her first illusion consisted in the belief that *all* she *need* do was to go to an agent. [LOB R03]

Like *must*, the marginal modals *need(n't)* and *ought (to)* have no past tense analogues (although they can be used in past tense environments, for example, in indirect speech/thought, as in (12)). Their grammatical inflexibility (which

---

[8] This leaves out of account *may*, which has no negative contraction in the Brown family, and *need(n't)*, which, as will be discussed shortly, is a special case of a negatively oriented modal.

[9] There is something paradoxical in the fact that *need(n't)*, despite its low frequency, has to some extent maintained its form with negative contraction in the Frown corpus. In Frown one would expect *needn't* to be less represented than in Brown, but there are in fact six instances of it in Frown, and five in Brown. These are small numbers, but they do hint that the negative orientation of *need(n't)* helps to preserve the negative contraction which has completely or virtually disappeared in the more frequent modals *may, might* and *ought*.

is related, but not identical, to their morphological invariability) suggests that these items are reaching the limits of viability, and their diminishing frequency makes them also the most endangered of the modal auxiliaries.

4.5.2   *The semantics of modal decline:* may, must *and* should

To probe the reasons for the sharp decline in frequency of certain modals, an obvious further step is to examine their usage in terms of semantic categories. For example, in the case of *must*, is it the deontic or the epistemic meaning that has declined? We here focus on the three modals, *may*, *must* and *should*, which are of middle rank in terms of frequency, but have decreased in use more than might be expected. There is considerable indeterminacy in the semantic subcategorization of modals (Leech and Coates 1980), and the close and blurred interconnections between one type of usage of a modal and another have led some to treat each modal as monosemantic: one modal, one meaning. However, more common has been the assumption, in spite of indeterminacy, that the same modal may realize a range of modal meanings, including the major categories of *deontic* and *epistemic* modality.[10] Before each of the following tables, the relevant semantic categories are illustrated by simple examples from the corpora.

(A) MAY
(a) Epistemic possibility: We *may* be able to hide you ... [Frown N11]
(b) Root/event possibility: A blower *may* be installed to increase comfort. [Brown H15]
(c) Permission: *May* I ask you something, Aunt Carrie? [Frown K05]
(d) Quasi-subjunctive/ formulaic: ... however unobtrusive it *may* be... [LOB A39]
(e) Unclear   An area sheltered from strong winds *may* be highly desirable for recreation use. [Brown E21]

---

[10] Here the semantic categories for modals are based on those of Coates and Leech (1980) and Coates (1983), as these have already been used to investigate the LOB and Brown Corpora. For clarity, the term 'root' is coupled with the terms 'event' and 'deontic' as defined in Palmer (²2001: 7–10). Palmer's three main 'kinds' of modality, Deontic, Dynamic, and Epistemic, are familiar in many publications, and it is a reasonable approximation to recognize the first sense in each table as epistemic and the second sense (plus the third sense of *may*) as deontic. Palmer's third kind, Dynamic, does not really apply to the modals discussed here. In principle, it should do, as Palmer defines Dynamic as a 'directive' type of modality in which the control of the happening is internal to the subject. Thus, the two uses of *must* ('obligation') in *I must go* and *You must go* would belong, respectively, to Deontic and Dynamic modality. However, from the viewpoint maintained here, both are variants of deontic modality. The last category in each table represents unclear or indeterminate cases; whereas the preceding senses, in the cases of *may* and *should*, represent increasingly rare usages which are formal, formulaic and old-fashioned.

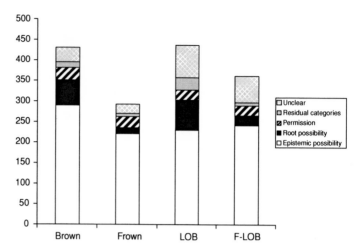

Figure 4.5 *May* – change in frequency of senses (analysis of every third example) in the Brown family of corpora

The epistemic use of *may* can be paraphrased 'It is possible that NP VP$_{fin}$ ...', whereas the root/event possibility use can be paraphrased either (1) by *can*, or (2) by 'It is possible (for NP) to VP$_{inf}$ ...'. The permission use of *may* can also be paraphrased by *can*, as well as by expressions such as 'BE allowed/permitted/permissible to'. Among the 'residual' categories are 'quasi-subjunctive' usages such as the optative *May the Lord bless you abundantly* ..., *I pray to God that he may be spared* ..., and formulaic usages such as ... *as the case may be*. The results in Figure 4.5 are based on every third example of *may* in the corpora.

From Figure 4.5 (see also Table A4.4), it appears that all four of the semantic groupings are in overall decline (although the difference between the 1961 and 1991/2 corpora is not always significant). The major exception to this is the epistemic 'it is possible that' meaning, which is actually more frequent in BrE of 1991 than in BrE of 1961. It is also observed, for both AmE and BrE, that the epistemic meaning is surviving more robustly than other meanings, and in both varieties is now claiming a larger percentage share of *may* than in the 1961 corpora. There is, therefore, a noticeable tendency towards monosemy: *may* is becoming predominantly an epistemic modal.[11]

---

[11] A similar observation is made by Biber (2004: 206): 'the decrease in frequency for *may* seems to be associated with a restriction in meaning', although he says it is because of a 'dramatic decline in ability/permission meanings'. Biber's study is longer-term than ours, and is limited to the genre of personal letters, where permission seeking/granting is more frequent.

The negative side of this observation is that the deontic and residual meanings of *may* have been decreasing apace. These already somewhat marginal meanings have been becoming further marginalized. On the face of it, it is surprising that the 'permission' use of *may*, losing its traditional bolstering by pedants, pedagogues and parents, has not declined more over these thirty years: in fact, it has increased its percentage, though not its raw frequency of occurrence. A possible explanation is that this 'polite' *may* of permission had sunk to a low ebb by 1961, when it was already marginal in comparison with the 'possibility' meanings. More striking in Figure 4.5 is the precipitous decline in the frequency of the 'root possibility' use of *may* since 1961. This usage was getting to feel a little stilted in the later twentieth century, and probably in this case *may* has yielded ground to the competition of the higher-frequency modal *can*.[12] Compare:

(13) The fish, animals, and birds which *may* be found at the site are another interest. [Brown E21]
(14) Nomia melanderi *can* be found in tremendous numbers in certain parts of the United States [. . .] [Brown J10]

One remaining question is: why has the epistemic meaning of *may* decreased in AmE in comparison with BrE? There is a hypothesis still to be tested on the American corpora: that *might* has been gaining at the expense of *may* as a modal of possibility (see Coates 1983: 153, with reference to BrE). At a glance, the percentages of Table A4.2 support this hypothesis. The decline of *might* in Brown and Frown is one of the smallest (a non-significant 3.7%), as compared with a loss of 17.7% in BrE. As the hypothetical past form of *may*, traditionally *might* has been regarded as more tentative as an expression of possibility. However, it has been recently commented that, especially in AmE, it is difficult to discern a difference between *might* from *may* in this sense, and a preference for *might* is apparently setting in – as is certainly the case in conversational English (see Chapter 5, Figures 5.4 and 5.5). In the following examples, it is easy to switch the *may* and *might* without any noticeable difference of meaning:

(15) The Republican Party *may* not even make it to Election Day before a period of mourning sets in. [Frown A11]
(16) Commissioners *might* yet seek a board vote on the issue, but they probably won't. [Frown B07]

---

[12] On this observation, see also Bryant (1962: 48–49) on late-twentieth-century AmE, and corpus-based studies using the ARCHER corpus: Denison (1998: 166) and Biber (2004: 204–206).

(B) SHOULD

(a) Epistemic (weak inference):	There *should* be plenty of time. [F-LOB No5]
(b) Root/deontic (weak obligation):	They *should* be kept out of the reach of children. [LOB B10]
(c) Putative, quasi-subjunctive:	It is right that women *should* control their desires. [LOB K29]
(d) *Should* (1st pers.) = *would*:	I *should* doubt if he has any enemies. [LOB B24]
(e) Unclear:	A decent dealer *should* offer a guarantee. [F-LOB E12]

Of these meanings, (a) and (b) can be paraphrased by *ought to*. The former, labelled 'weak inference' in relation to the 'strong inference' of epistemic *must* (see below), is concerned with probability, whereas the latter (labelled 'weak obligation' in relation to the 'strong obligation' of deontic *must*) is concerned with what is advisable or approvable. Meaning (c) corresponds to the mandative subjunctive in some uses: for example, in *I insisted that he should take part in the concert*, he should take part can be replaced by *he take part* (see section 3.2). In other cases this quasi-subjunctive *should* occurs in *if*-clauses (*If he should call in . . .*) or in a *that*-clause after a predicate conveying surprise, its opposite or some other emotion:

(17)   All the more amazing, then, that a century later our prisons *should* be crowded with debtors. [LOB B13]

What these variants of sense (c) have in common is a semantic weakening such that *should* manifests mood rather than modality: it has no epistemic or deontic flavour, but instead expresses the non-factual nature of the predication pure and simple. Category (d) is another marginal case: it is restricted to first-person subjects, and is the past tense or hypothetical reflex of *shall*. Thus *and I certainly should not think of waking him* could equally be expressed: *and I certainly would not think of waking him*.

Figure 4.6 mirrors for *should* the trend towards monosemy found in the analysis of *may*, except that here deontic rather than epistemic meaning is in the ascendant. Deontic *should*, although slightly less frequent in Frown, becomes even more dominant, with 72% in Brown increasing to 79% in Frown. (In 1961 root *should* was already more strongly dominant in Brown than in LOB and F-LOB, so this finding fits the picture of AmE leading a trend being followed by BrE.)[13] Like LOB and F-LOB, Brown and Frown show a particularly strong trend for the minor and possibly obsolescent uses of *should* (quasi-subjunctive and backshifted-*shall* uses) to lose out. Epistemic

---

[13] However, on the evidence of the raw figures (rather than relative percentages of each sense) in F-LOB and Frown, BrE is now leading AmE in the deontic use.

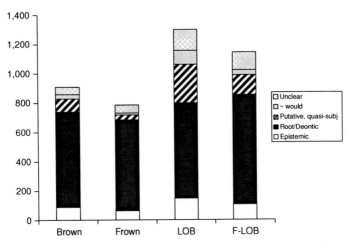

Figure 4.6 *Should* – change in frequency of senses in the Brown family of corpora

should, always playing second fiddle to root *should*, shows a decline from Brown to Frown, as also from LOB to F-LOB.

(C) MUST
(a) Epistemic necessity: I thought I saw the cook, then decided I *must* be mistaken. [LOB G23]
(b) Deontic obligation/   That woman *must* go! [F-LOB P20]
    necessity: I *must* somehow save myself. [LOB N23]
(c) Unclear: But he is a West Point graduate and therefore *must* be born to command. [Brown F18]

The epistemic sense of *must* is sometimes termed 'inferential': it indicates strong inferences made about the truth of the proposition expressed, and means 'the only possible conclusion is that . . . '. The deontic meaning relates to the socio-physical world of obligation and action, and the speaker is often construed as implicitly imposing authority, even if this is authority over oneself, as in the second example of (b) above.

Figure 4.7 shows how *must*, unlike *may* and *should*, has suffered a decline in both epistemic and deontic aspects of usage (see also Table A4.6). However, the deontic use remains dominant in both AmE and BrE, despite decreasing more than 30% in both national varieties.

Why has *must* not been moving appreciably towards monosemy – like the other two modals – with the dominant deontic meaning achieving even greater dominance? One hypothesis is that this 'authoritative' sense of *must*

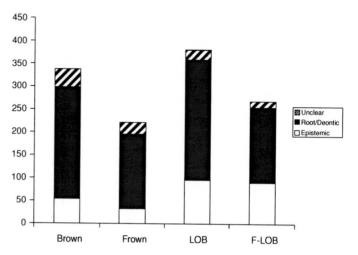

Figure 4.7 *Must* – change in frequency of senses (analysis of every third example) in the Brown family of corpora

has been losing favour for socio-cultural reasons. Investigating nineteenth-century AmE, Myhill (1995) used corpus evidence to arrive at the conclusion that:

Around the time of the [American] Civil War, the modals *must, should, may* and *shall* dropped drastically in frequency, and at the same time other modals, *got to, have to, ought, better, can* and *gonna*, sharply increased in frequency. The "old" and "new" modals overlap in some functions [. . .]. However, within these general functions, [. . .] the "old" modals had usages associated with hierarchical social relationships, with people controlling the actions of other people, and with absolute judgements based on social decorum [. . .]. The "new" modals, on the other hand, are more personal, being used to, for example, give advice to an equal, make an emotional request, offer help, or criticize one's interlocutor. (Myhill 1995: 157)

It could be that a similar 'democratization' trend in society has been taking place in the later twentieth century – or even that the same trend observed by Myhill in the mid-nineteenth century is still continuing, in some form, today, in both AmE and BrE.[14] As deontic *must* is highly discourse-oriented (Palmer [2]1990: 69–70), its particularly steep decline since 1961 may be due to its 'prototypically subjective and insistent, sometimes authoritarian-sounding' effect (Smith 2003a: 263).

As for the epistemic use of *must*, its partial decline could be due to contamination by the dramatic fall of deontic *must*. On the other hand, the

[14] Contrary to Myhill, however, *should* appears to be winning out against *ought to*: its deontic meaning is on the increase, whereas *ought to* is on a steep decline.

relatively shallow fall of epistemic *must* may be because neither *have to* nor any other form has become widely adopted as an alternative expression of strong epistemic necessity. In the past, the beneficiaries of this decline may have been semi-modals such as *have to* and *got to* (in Myhill's list – see also Krug 2000), which express obligation in a less authoritarian way. However, other verbal means of expressing obligation, such as *should* and the increasingly used *need to* (see section 5.1), could also be present-day beneficiaries of *must*'s decline. *Should*, as a modal comparable in frequency to *may* and *must*, has declined less than they have (12.1%, as contrasted with 24.6% and 31.2%) and it can be surmised that, in spite of a drastic loss in marginal uses of *should*, its flourishing deontic meaning has benefited as a more congenial, less face-threatening alternative to *must*.

Before concluding this section on the semantics of *may*, *should* and *must*, we will take a glance at the way these meanings are reflected in the spoken minicorpora of BrE, DSEU and DICE. The samples are too small for confident extrapolation, as we are dealing here with very small numbers. However, the general message is similar to that relating to the written corpora: the decline in modal usage is in virtually all semantic categories being analysed, and is overall more pronounced in the spoken data than in the written data of LOB and F-LOB (see Table A4.7). Two exceptional cases are these:

(a) *May* (= permission) has quite a high frequency in spoken BrE of the 1960s, but has lost virtually all of that by the 1990s. (On the other hand, permission is much less commonly expressed in the Brown family, outside of fictional dialogue, as the texts generally lack the level of interactivity, situational immediacy etc. of conversation.)
(b) The deontic meaning of *should* (weak obligation) has increased substantially between the 1960s and the 1990s. This gives some support to the hypothesis suggested above: that the decline of deontic *must* is linked to a rise (at least in BrE)[15] of deontic *should*.

4.6   Conclusion

To conclude: the purpose of section 4.5 has been to determine (using the cases of *may*, *should* and *must*) how far the loss of modal frequency identified in 4.1–4.4 could be linked to some kind of semantic loss: a restriction in the range of meaning covered by these modals. In fact, the evidence is ambiguous. To some extent, the evidence is of a diminution of frequency across the board, whatever the meaning. On the other hand, another trend, shown by *may* and *should*, is a tendency toward monosemy: toward the increasing prevalence of

---

[15] As Table A4.5 shows, for AmE the evidence is less compelling. Although the deontic sense of *should* has increased its proportion of the total usage of *should*, it has, along with other senses of *should*, suffered a decline.

one meaning over others – cf. the notion of specialization linked by Hopper (1991) and Hopper and Traugott (²2003: 116–18) to grammaticalization. That this trend is not followed by *must* could, indeed, be explained by socio-cultural factors leading to a particular unpopularity of the deontic meaning of strong obligation. The trend towards monosemy may therefore be a more general phenomenon, although this should not be assumed without a semantic study of other modals. Another possibly more general phenomenon, the negative side of the monosemy trend, is that minor or marginal usages decline more than others. This applies particularly to the quasi-subjunctive uses of *may* and *should*, and the backshifted-*shall* use of *should*. We might say, looking at both the modals in Figures 4.1–4.4 and the modal meanings in Figures 4.5–4.7, a general principle that 'losers lose out' (the infrequent suffer loss more than the frequent do) is at work.

5   The so-called semi-modals

The word 'semi-modals' is not a precise term.[1] It refers to a loose constellation of verb constructions which, according to many commentators (for example, Hopper and Traugott [2]2003, Bybee *et al.* 1994, Krug 2000), have been moving along the path of grammaticalization (see sections 1.2, 11.3) in recent centuries. The semi-modals are probably the most cited cases of grammaticalization in the ongoing history of English. Among these, in turn, the prototypical, most indubitable cases of semi-modal status are *BE going to* and *HAVE to*,[2] which are long-standing representatives of this evolving class, traceable back to the late ME or EModE period – see Krug (2000), Biber *et al.* (1999: 487), Danchev and Kytö (2002); also Mair (1997) on *BE going to*; Fischer (1992) on *HAVE to*. It is well known that in these two constructions, the lexically independent verbs *HAVE* and *GO* have, over the centuries, gradually acquired an auxiliary-like function in construction with the infinitive *to*.

This chapter is naturally to be seen as complementary to the previous chapter on the modals; and just as we did not refrain from referring to the semi-modals where relevant in Chapter 4, we will where relevant return to the modals in Chapter 5. To some degree, the boundary between these two chapters is artificial.

---

[1] See section 4.4 for a preliminary discussion of semi-modals. We have to contend with a plethora of terminology. For example, alongside 'semi-modals' (in Biber *et al.* 1999 and elsewhere), Hopper and Traugott ([2]2003) use 'quasi-modals' and Krug (2000) 'emergent modals'. Quirk *et al.* employ terms such as 'marginal modals' and 'semi-auxiliaries' in a more syntactically restricted way – see 5.1 below. In this chapter, as in the last, we confine our attention to (semi-)modals that convey modal meaning. It has to be borne in mind, even so, that the category of modality is a shifting category, appropriately described by Cort and Denison (2005) as a 'moving target'.

[2] For reasons of clarity, in this chapter, although not in most other chapters, we follow the practice of using italic capitals to indicate a form representing a lemma, rather than an individual word form. For example, *HAVE to* represents *have to, has to, had to* and *having to* used as a semi-modal, whereas *must* is not shown in capitals because it represents just a single form.

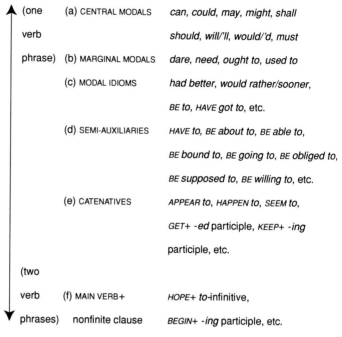

(one	(a) CENTRAL MODALS		*can, could, may, might, shall*
verb			*should, will/'ll, would/'d, must*
phrase)	(b) MARGINAL MODALS		*dare, need, ought to, used to*
	(c) MODAL IDIOMS		*had better, would rather/sooner,*
			BE to, HAVE got to, etc.
	(d) SEMI-AUXILIARIES		*HAVE to, BE about to, BE able to,*
			BE bound to, BE going to, BE obliged to,
			BE supposed to, BE willing to, etc.
	(e) CATENATIVES		*APPEAR to, HAPPEN to, SEEM to,*
			GET+ -ed participle, *KEEP+ -ing*
			participle, etc.
(two			
verb	(f) MAIN VERB+		*HOPE+ to-*infinitive,
phrases)	nonfinite clause		*BEGIN+ -ing* participle, etc.

Figure 5.1 The auxiliary–main verb gradient, from Quirk *et al.* (1985: 137)

5.1   Auxiliary–lexical verb gradience

Krug (2000: 3–5, *passim*) argues for a class of 'emergent modals', a small prototype category on the cline between auxiliary and main verb, including not only BE *going to* and HAVE *to*, but also HAVE *got to* and WANT *to*, as well as one or two more marginal candidates, such as *need (to)* and *ought to*. This is plausible, especially on the grounds of phonological reduction and the related factor of discourse frequency – witness the reduction of (HAVE) *got to* and WANT *to* to pronunciations popularly rendered in writing as *gotta* and *wanna*. However, there is a whole spectrum of possible candidates for semi-modal status. Quirk *et al.* (1985: 135–48) propose a gradient between auxiliaries and main verbs occupied by broadly defined intermediate categories as in Figure 5.1.[3]

The classes (a)–(f) are ordered according to their increasing remoteness from the auxiliary end of the scale, with central or core modals as the most 'extreme' case of auxiliary status. Core modals conform to the full set of

---

[3] See also Bolinger (1980) on the main verb–auxiliary gradient. Similar accounts of the cline between auxiliaries and main verbs are found in the grammaticalization literature, where they are linked to the diachronic progression towards auxiliary status: see, for example, Heine (1993). Krug's 'gravitational model' (2000: 214–39) places this cline on a more theoretical footing, while drawing on corpus linguistic methods.

auxiliary criteria in Quirk *et al.* (1985: 137) in terms of their use as operators in negation, inversion, emphatic positive and elliptical clauses, and other criteria such as negative contraction, the position of adverbs, postposition of quantifiers and independence of the subject (p. 137).[4] In addition, they conform to a further set of criteria peculiar to core modals: having (i) a following bare infinitive, (ii) no non-finite forms, (iii) no -*s* form and (iv) abnormal time reference, in particular in relation to the past tense. Most of the verbs in the intermediate classes (b)–(f) have meanings in the semantic domains of modality or aspect – see Coates (1983); Bybee *et al.* (1994: 176–81).

The term 'semi-modal' was not used by Quirk *et al.*, and we will not investigate the syntactic properties of these intermediate verbs in detail. However, a considerable number of verbs in Quirk *et al.*'s classes have a meaning falling within the domain of modality, and might be considered as *prima facie* candidates for semi-modal status. The following discussion draws on the list in Quirk *et al.* (1985: 236).

The **marginal modals** *ought to* and *need* (+ bare infinitive), have received enough attention in the last chapter.[5] They are members of a peripheral, infrequent, and somewhat anomalous groups of verbs, the main characteristic of which is their ability to adopt both auxiliary and main verb characteristics. *Ought to* in practice is constructed as a core modal with one non-modal characteristic: its infinitive marker *to*. If we place it at the bottom of the frequency table for core modals, as we do in Table A4.1, its sharp decline in frequency in the 1961–91 period fits in with that of other low-frequency modals, such as *shall*. *Need*, again, when constructed as a modal occurs as an invariant form with the bare infinitive, but as a main verb occurs (with regular inflections) before a *to*-infinitive. Thus *need* splits into two different verbs with similar, though not identical meanings,[6] and if we make this distinction

---

4 These criteria include the familiar 'NICE properties' (negation, inversion, code and emphatic affirmation) as syntactic auxiliary properties in English (cf. Huddleston 1980; Palmer ²1990: 4–5; Huddleston and Pullum 2002: 92–93; Facchinetti *et al.* 2003: vi). The 'independence of subject' criterion, to which we return later, means that, for example, semantic restrictions on the subject, which may limit the choice of lexical verb, do not apply to auxiliaries. Connected with this is the fact that semi-modals, like modals, lack agency, and cannot be used in the imperative: compare *Try to . . .* and *Dare to . . .*, which accept the imperative, with *Need to . . .* and *Want to . . .*, which do not.

5 As noted in section 4.1, *dare* and *used to* are not included in present study, as they are not modal in meaning. In any case, they are infrequent and anomalous compared with the core modals.

6 Unlike the NEED *to* construction, *need* + bare infinitive is not restricted to a deontic function. Historically, it has filled a slot in the system corresponding to *must* but with external negation (negation/interrogation of the auxiliary rather than the main verb):

'It could have been somebody else,' said Owen. 'It needn't have been the girl.' [F-LOB L09]

(Cf. *It must have been the girl*; *It can't have been the girl*.) The epistemic meaning of *need* in this example cannot in PDE be paralleled by NEED *to*. Also, with the perfect, *need* as modal conveys a counterfactual modality, like some other modals (*You needn't have washed*

it is very noticeable that NEED *to* is one of the semi-modals spectacularly increasing in frequency (see Figure 5.2, Table A5.1), whereas *need* + bare infinitive as a marginal modal is decreasing, and has only a residual status as a peripheral member of the core modal category (see Table A4.1).

We believe that Krug (2000: 238–9) was misled when he tentatively placed the verb *need (to)*, with *ought to*, on the periphery of the emergent modal category, bringing together the marginal modals (patterning largely like core modals) and the Verb + *to* emergent modal constructions. The evidence of frequency suggests that the peripheral modals *need(n't)* and *ought to*, like core modals, are declining sharply. Their virtual non-occurrence in present-day AmE conversation (see Table 5.2) is particularly persuasive in excluding them from the emergent modal or semi-modal category which is the subject of this chapter.

It is thus tempting to see the two verbs *need* as a classic case of layering in successive waves of grammaticalization. NEED *to* is not the variant of modal *need(n't)* that, synchronically, it may appear to be. Rather, it arose in relative independence as part of the more recent wave of grammaticalization which has given us new semi-modals such as WANT *to*. The motivation behind the rise of NEED *to* is thus not primarily a desire on the part of speakers to straighten out the irregular syntax of auxiliary *need*. Rather, it appears to be an independent development of grammaticalization based on the transitive main verb *need*, semantically helped by certain constructions involving the related noun *need* (as in, for example, *a need to do something*) – see sections 5.3.2, 5.4. Among other things, such an analysis would help to explain why, unlike auxiliary *need*, the newly grammaticalizing NEED *to* is not restricted to non-assertive contexts.

The modal idioms[7] are another small category, of which the most salient characteristics are that (a) they begin with an auxiliary, and (b) like core modals, they are restricted in having no non-finite forms and, in some cases, no tense contrast.[8] (*Had*) *better* and (HAVE) *got to* are notable in virtually being excluded from the written language, except in simulations of speech.

---

the glass bowl; cf. *You oughtn't to have washed the bowl. You shouldn't have washed the bowl.* With these examples, counterfactuality combines with negation to imply the truth of the proposition 'You *did* wash the bowl'.) In contrast, equivalent instances with NEED *to* are not counterfactual: for example, *You didn't* NEED *to wash the bowl* is consistent with the proposition that 'You didn't wash the bowl', as well as with 'You did wash the bowl'. Along with these arguments for the separation of *need(n't)* (modal) and NEED *to* (semi-modal), a further argument is that if treated as a single verb, NEED appears to go against the 'unidirectionality' hypothesis of grammaticalization (cf. Taeymans 2004: 108).

[7] The material of this paragraph is extensively treated by Denison (1998) from a longer-term diachronic standpoint.

[8] Lack of tense contrast is obvious in the case of *had better*, which lacks present tense forms **has/have better*. In the case of HAVE *got to*, in the Brown family there are only two examples of the past tense *had got to* – both occurring in LOB, with the special function of marking free indirect speech:

She *had got to* think of some way out [. . .]. [LOB N16]

HAVE got to, first attested after 1800 (*OED*; Krug 2000: 61–2), has already undergone habitual phonetic reduction, as the popular written forms such as *I gotta go* suggest. Forms of *had better* without the auxiliary *had* are also prevalent in speech: *Better go now*; *You better listen*. In the Brown family, both these semi-modals are infrequent and in BrE are even slightly declining in use: but their moderate frequency in conversational English (see Tables 5.2, 5.3) suggests that this unexpected pattern occurs largely because *had better* and *HAVE got to* are generally too colloquial to occur in printed texts. Another verb placed in this group, *BE to*, is again somewhat anomalous, and arguably could be moved into the semi-auxiliary category (d). What makes it belong here is the absence of non-finite forms: only the finite variants *am to*, *is to*, *are to*, *was to* and *were to* are found in recent English.[9] Especially in AmE, *BE to* shows itself atypical of semi-modals in declining sharply in frequency. It is particularly infrequent in speech (see Tables 5.2 and A5.2). Another member of this category, *would rather* or *'d rather*, is too infrequent for us to give it more than passing notice. In general, however, modal idioms are included in our 'semi-modal' category for the purposes of this chapter.

The semi-auxiliaries mostly begin with the primary auxiliary *BE*, and therefore enter into auxiliary criteria through the use of *BE* as operator: *BE going to*, most notably, belongs here. Thus the interrogative form of *They are going to leave* is *Are they going to leave?* rather than **Do they be going to leave?* In this respect semi-auxiliaries are auxiliary-like. In another respect, however, they are further removed from the core modals than the modal idioms are: they have tense variation, and can occur in non-finite forms, which gives them considerably more syntactic versatility than the core modals.

Although Quirk *et al.* (1985) place *HAVE to* in this category, this semi-modal is actually more main-verb-like in that it normally requires *DO* as an operator – cf. section 11.5, especially Table 11.3. Thus *Do they have to be boiled?* is the normal question form, nowadays, in both AmE and BrE, although it is still just possible in BrE to use the auxiliary *HAVE* as an operator – there is a handful of examples in the Brown family:

(1)   And she *hadn't to* doubt his sincerity any more … [LOB P06]
(2)   You'll meet lots of other girls. Why *has* it *to be* me? [LOB K18]

The remaining semi-auxiliaries listed by Quirk *et al.* (1985: 143) fit the template *BE* + participle/adjective/adverb + *to* infinitive:

---

[9] At an earlier stage of the language, however, *BE to* occurred with non-finite forms, as the following quotations from Jane Austen's novels attest:

   […] she would have felt almost sure of success if he had not *been to* leave Hertfordshire so very soon. (*Pride and Prejudice* [1813], Chapter 22)

   […] for this young lady, this same Miss Musgrove, instead of *being to* marry Frederick, *is to* marry James Benwick. (*Persuasion* [1818], Chapter 18)

BE *able to*	BE *bound to*	BE *likely to*	BE *supposed to*	BE *about to*
BE *due to*	BE *meant to*	BE *willing to*	BE *going to*	BE *obliged to*

The list is open: we could add a considerable number of additional items, antonymous to or roughly synonymous with items already in the list: BE *unable to*, BE *unwilling to*, BE *apt to*, BE *inclined to* (the last two, like BE *likely to*, having a meaning related to probability). But the relative infrequency of these and other candidates excuses their omission from our present survey. This group includes the 'canonical semi-modals' BE *going to* and HAVE *to*, but none of the other candidates in the above list come close to them in frequency, particularly in spoken English, and few show prominent grammaticalization traits such as coalescence and reduction. The closest to them are BE *able to* and BE *supposed to*, which can undergo reduction to something like /bjebltə/ and /spoustə/. Non-finite forms of BE *able to* also have a 'suppletive' syntactic function in relation to *can* similar to that of HAVE *to* in relation to *must*.

Main verb + non-finite clause: The distinction between the last two classes in Quirk *et al.*'s gradient – (e) catenative verb and (f) main verb + non-finite clause – is not significant for our study. In fact, the most convincing of the remaining candidates for semi-modal status are Verb + *to* constructions where the Verb has unquestionable credentials as a main verb: WANT *to* and NEED *to*. WANT and NEED have regular verb inflections, and can be followed by a direct object, as well as a *to*-infinitive:

(3) I *want* children, I *want* a home. I *want to be* a faithful woman. [Frown G35]
(4) . . . And I *need* some new shoes. [F-LOB K02]
(5) Ben, I *need to talk* to you in private. [F-LOB N07]

Indeed, a direct object can be interpolated between the main verb and the following *to*-infinitive:

(6) Bridget, I *want* you *to wash* these windows today. [Brown F31]
(7) We *need* you *to start* it. [Brown B09]

These verbs therefore fully qualify as main verbs both by morphological and syntactic criteria. Semantically, too, there is no immediately detectable discrepancy between the meanings of WANT and NEED as used as main verbs, and as used in the Verb + *to* construction, to tempt us to the conclusion that these verbs are moving towards auxiliary status. However, recalling the principle of co-existing layers associated with grammaticalization (Hopper and Traugott ²2003: 124–25), we are happy to accept that constructions already launched on the path towards auxiliary status can co-exist unproblematically with the persisting main verb constructions from which they derive. At one end of their evolving spectrum of usage that spans both inherent and externally oriented modality (see section 5.3.2 below; Quirk *et al.* 1985:

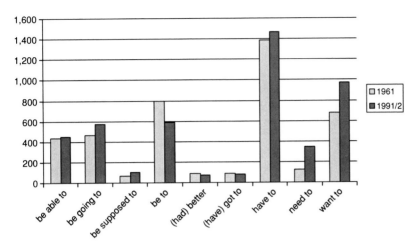

Figure 5.2 Change of frequency in the semi-modals in written English (the Brown family, AmE and BrE combined)

NOTE: The *x* axis represents number of occurrences in the combined corpora (approximately 2 million words each). The Figure above represents graphically the right-hand part of Table A5.1, p. 286 (revised from Leech & Smith 2006).

219–21), WANT and NEED + *to*-infinitive remain very close to the ordinary transitive use of the same verbs.

What, then, are the signs of grammaticalization that lead to the grouping of WANT *to* and NEED *to* with the semi-modals we have already referred to? WANT *to*, in particular, has clearly been undergoing phonetic reduction and coalescence to the pronunciation familiarly spelled *wanna*. Krug (2000: 131–5, 141–7) has also documented the change of meaning and increase in frequency of this verb since EModE. Although no similar obvious phonetic reduction has been taking place with NEED *to*, Krug (2000: 211, 286) mentions incipient reduction and coalescence in the pronunciation of this semi-modal as /niːtə/, /niːrə/. From the corpus angle, for both WANT *to* and NEED *to*, the most notable symptom related to grammaticalization is that these two constructions have greatly increased in frequency over the 1961–1991/2 period (see Figure 5.2, Table A5.1). For WANT *to*, an additional factor is semantic extension from the volitional meaning to the deontic meaning of obligation/necessity (see section 5.3.2). NEED *to*, as will be seen, also shows some tendency towards extension and generalization of meaning. There is one characteristic of auxiliaries (although not exclusively of auxiliaries) which applies to NEED *to* but not to WANT *to* – the ability to occur before the verb BE in existential constructions:[10]

---

[10] This traditional test for raising, for present purposes, is enlisted as a criterion of 'independence of subject' – i.e. the lack of selection restrictions between subject and auxiliary

(8)   [. . .] *there need to* be reasonable grounds for suspicion [. . .] [F-LOB
H10]

It is true that the argument for grammaticalization is weaker in the case of
NEED *to*, but our interest in investigating the main players in the evolving domain of obligation/necessity, together with this construction's recent
phenomenal increase in frequency, warrants its inclusion in this study.

The preceding discussion leads to the conclusion that the list of semi-
modals, for the purposes of this chapter, should include Krug's emergent
modals BE *going to*, HAVE *to*, *(HAVE) got to*, WANT *to* and NEED *to*,[11] with the
addition (using Quirk *et al.*'s terms) of the less commonly occurring modal
idioms and semi-auxiliaries BE *able to*, *(had) better*, BE *to* and BE *supposed to*.
Of these, the first six will be briefly examined individually in section 5.3.2,
after a survey of overall changes in semi-modal frequencies.

5.2   Overall changes in frequency of semi-modals

Figure 5.2 and Table A5.1 summarize the frequency changes of semi-modals
between 1961 and 1991/2 in the Brown family of corpora, presenting the list
of semi-modals given at the end of the last section in alphabetical order.

As might be expected from previous discussion, the chart and frequency
table indicate an overall significant increase in the use of semi-modals. This
increase in BrE (+9.0%) is smaller than the decline in frequency of (core)
modals (−9.8%). But the AmE increase is more dramatic, showing a rise in
the use of semi-modals of 18.2%. However, it is most important to notice
that in gross terms, modals, even when compared on the basis of 1991/2
frequencies, are more than five times as frequent as semi-modals (25,661 :
4,659). Clearly, in published written English, the semi-modals are far from
catching up with the declining frequency of the modals: there is little mileage,
from these figures, in the supposition that the decline of the modals is (solely
or mainly) due to the increasing competition of the semi-modals in the same
semantic space.

The only semi-modal that can plausibly be presented in support of the
competition theory is HAVE *to*, which has almost attained the frequency of
its 'rival' modal *must* by 1991/2 (see Table 5.1, especially the figures in bold).

---

verb – identified as one of the signs of auxiliary status in Quirk *et al.* (1985: 126–7). In
theory, the same construction attribute might be a possibility for WANT *to* (in its colloquial
deontic use, Krug 2000: 147–50): *There wants to be more weedkiller on that patch* [invented
example, where *want* would mean approximately 'ought to'], but a search of five corpora
(the Brown family plus the LCSAE) has failed to yield any examples.

[11]   Krug's (2000) list of emergent modals marginally includes *need(n't)* and *ought to*, which for
reasons already given we exclude from this chapter: they have been handled as (infrequent)
core modals in Chapter 4. Krug's list also includes DARE *(to)* – a marginal modal which
semantically is peripheral to the modal category, and which we exclude from both the
central modal list and the semi-modal list. Similarly, on semantic grounds we exclude *used
to*, which is an aspect marker rather than a modality marker.

Table 5.1. *Evolving rivalry between* must *and* HAVE *to in terms of frequency*

	Frequency in Brown and LOB (1961)	Frequency in Frown and F-LOB (1991/2)	Both periods
must	2,165 (1,072 pmw)	1,482 (737 pmw)	3,647 (905 pmw)
HAVE *to*	1,384 (685 pmw)	1,464 (728 pmw)	2,848 (707 pmw)

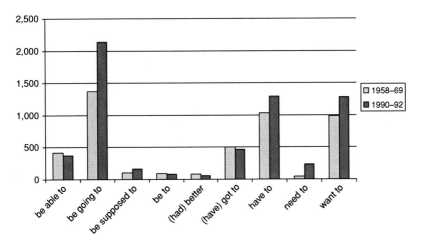

Figure 5.3 Frequency of semi-modals in spoken British English: increase in use based on the comparison of the DSEU and DICE mini-corpora

However, we will see later (in section 5.4) that this is not just a two-horse race: the situation in the domain of obligation/necessity is far more complex than this binary comparison suggests.

Turning to the DSEU and DICE mini-corpora used for comparing the 1960s and the 1990s in British spoken English (see section 2.4 D2), the picture shown in Figure 5.3 is remarkably different. As previously noted, we need to bear in mind the provisional nature of these results, based as they are on a small sample of c. 130,000 words per corpus. But the increase of 30% in the use of semi-modals between the 1960s and the 1990s found here is over twice the increase recorded for the Brown family as a whole (12.3%), and over four times the increase shown by the two written British corpora (9.0%).

However, we do not have to rely on this inconsiderable sample to recognize, in recent English, the enormous difference in the frequency of semi-modals

Table 5.2. *Approximate frequency count of modals and semi-modals in the LCSAE*

Modals (Numbers show combined rank-ordering)	approx. raw freq.[a]	estimated frequency pmw[b]	Semi-modals (Numbers show combined rank-ordering)	approx. raw freq.[a]	estimated frequency pmw[b]
can (1)	25,607	5,121	(BE) going to (4)	19,709	3,942
will (2)	25,312	5,062	HAVE to (5)	12,944	2,589
would (3)	24,848	4,970	WANT to (6)	11,548	2,300
could (7)	10,545	2,109	NEED to (9)	3,874	775
should (8)	5,946	1,189	(HAVE) got to (10)	3,244	649
might (11)	3,188	638	BE supposed to (13)	1,819	364
may (12)	1,981	396			
must (14)	1,485	297	BE able to (15)	1,357	271
ought (to) (16)	343	69	(HAD) better (18)	641	128
shall (17)	251	50	BE to (19)	166	33
need(n't) (20)	2	0			
TOTAL	99,508	19,901	TOTAL	55,302	11,060

[a] As the LCSAE corpus was untagged, and it was impracticable in most cases to undertake a manual count of occurrences, for most items it was necessary to estimate raw frequency by the 'thinning' procedure described in Chapter 2 (section 2.5 D3), whereby a representative subset of concordance examples was examined, and the resulting count scaled up.

[b] The frequency per million words is calculated on the rough estimate that the LCSAE is a corpus of five million words. The exact word count (as kindly supplied by Sebastian Hoffmann) is 5,082,382, but this is based on a tagged version of the corpus, POS tagged by the Helsinki tagger, and is therefore not directly comparable to corpus word counts used elsewhere in this book.

in informal speech as compared with writing. Table 5.2 gives the frequency of semi-modals and modals in the LCSAE, representing conversational American English of the 1990s (roughly contemporaneous with Frown, F-LOB and DICE). The numbers following the verb forms represent what would be their order of frequency if the modals and semi-modals were to be combined in a single list. This makes clear how far the semi-modals have been vying with the core modals in this 'advanced' variety of English.

From the bottom line of Table 5.2 it can be seen that in American speech the semi-modals as a group are more than four times as frequent as they are in the Brown family, and around twice as frequent as they are in the small samples of British speech from DICE we have used for comparison (11,060 pmw : 6,724 pmw). But even before this, the first thing to notice, perhaps, is that in speech both the modals and (even more so) the semi-modals are considerably more frequent than in writing. Compare the total frequency figures of 19,901 and 11,060 in Table 5.2 with the corresponding figures for the contemporary written corpus of AmE, Frown: 12,287 modals and 2,310 semi-modals (data from Table A4.2 and Table A5.1, respectively.)

Table 5.2, as the numbering after the modal forms shows, reveals the remarkable extent to which the semi-modals **in spontaneous AmE speech** have been catching up with the core modals. In gross terms, although there are only nine semi-modal types in the right-hand part of the table, in comparison with eleven modal types on the left, the overall frequency of semi-modals is more than 55 per cent of the frequency of modals; or, put otherwise, the ratio of modals to semi-modals is 1.8 to 1 – compared to more than 7 to 1 in the 1961 Brown corpus. Individually, *can*, *will* and *would* in AmE speech (all in the region of 5,000 pmw) hold their own as the most frequent verb forms for expressing modality, but the top three semi-modals BE *going to*, HAVE *to* and WANT *to* are not far behind them. Looking at the list of individual modals, we note some very marked divergences from the written (published) texts of Frown and F-LOB. For example, in the area of obligation/necessity, *must*, traditionally seen as the canonical modal for expressing this meaning, is a relatively infrequent item, rarer in US speech than the three obligation/necessity semi-modals HAVE *to*, NEED *to* and *(HAVE) got to* (see also Myhill 1996).

Unfortunately, the lack of any comparable corpus of US speech from the 1960s makes it impossible, at least at present, to estimate how far an AmE increase has taken place in the period of our study – from 1961 to 1991/2.

It is relevant here, though, to briefly compare the equivalent figures from spontaneous speech in BrE. We have BNCdemog – the demographically sampled spoken part of the BNC (of 4.206 million words) – to use as a parallel sample to the LCSAE.[12] The British equivalent of Table 5.2 can be seen in Table 5.3. Not surprisingly, BNCdemog as shown here occupies a middle ground between the comparable American conversational data and the Brown family. Although very significantly less frequent than in the American conversational corpus,[13] the semi-modals in the conversational corpus of BrE are nevertheless very significantly more frequent than they are in the Brown family, confirming in a more extreme form the tendency already observed in the DCPSE (DICE mini-corpus) data: more extreme, presumably because this conversational corpus represents impromptu private dialogue, at the 'spontaneous speech' extremity of the scale as far as the contrast between spoken and written language is concerned.[14]

---

[12] However, unfortunately the kind of comparison based on age groups illustrated by Figure 5.4 (p. 103) cannot yet (to our knowledge) be carried out on the LCSAE or any other sizeable present-day corpus of American speech.

[13] The chief exception to this is (HAVE) *got to*, which is much more frequent in BrE conversation than AmE conversation (see also Biber *et al.* 1999: 488). It has been supposed, by contrast, that the reduced form spelt *gotta* is more frequent in AmE conversation. However, this seems to be a misapprehension, as there are 2,714 *gotta*s in BNCdemog, whereas there are only 1,009 in the roughly comparable LCSAE, although the LCSAE is thought to be about 20% larger than BNCdemog.

[14] Biber's (1988: 104–5) first dimension of variation ('informational vs involved' focus) was shown by Lee (2000) to be the only stable and replicable dimension of the Biber model, and

Table 5.3. *Frequency of modals and semi-modals in the demographic subcorpus BNCdemog: the conversational part of the BNC*

Modals (full and reduced forms)			Semi-modals (full and reduced forms)		
	raw freq.	pmw		raw freq.	pmw
can	23,447	5,575	*(BE) going to*	10,145	2,412
will	28,301	6,729	*HAVE to*	6,796	1,616
would	15,712	3,736	*WANT to*	6,352	1,510
could	8,075	1,919	*NEED to*	880	209
should	4,396	1,045	*(HAVE) got to*	5,116	1,216
might	3,602	856	*BE suppose(d) to BE*	952	226
may	637	151	*able to*	883	210
must	3,014	717	*(HAD) better*	692	165
ought (to)	454	108	*BE to*	157	37
shall	1,652	393			
need(n't)	76	18			
TOTAL	89,366	21,247	TOTAL	31,973	7,601

In Table 5.3, the modals and semi-modals are listed in their order of frequency in the American corpus, and so it is easy to see where the frequency ordering in the two varieties differs. On the modal side, whereas in the American corpus, *can, will* and *would* are all roughly equivalently placed at the top of the list, in the British corpus they are spread out, with *will* at the top of the list, and *can, would* and *could* following at spaced-out intervals. The most unexpected finding is that *may* in the British conversational subcorpus has lost ground to the extent that *might* is roughly six times as frequent, and even *shall* is two-and-a-half times as frequent as *may*. Easy to write off as a 'lame duck' modal in the Brown family, *shall* is by no means so infrequent in BNCdemog: it is *may* that has suffered decline most of all.

On the semi-modal side, *(BE) going to*, *WANT to* and *NEED to* are far less frequent than in American conversation – while *(HAVE) got to*, *(had) better* and *BE to* are more frequent in BNCdemog. Whereas in both AmE and BrE writing, *BE to* is significantly declining, in AmE speech, it is becoming a rarity. Overall, however, the relative frequency of semi-modals in AmE is much greater (by 61%) than in BrE in conversation, while in BrE there is a contrasting (although less marked) tendency, in that the core modals are more frequent than in AmE by 9%.

Biber's more recent work (e.g. Biber 2003a) has tended to support this, giving precedence to a single 'literate'–'oral' dimension. In a related study, Rayson *et al.* (2002) compared word class frequencies across the four major subcorpora of the BNC (written informative, written imaginative, spoken context-governed and spoken demographic), and BNCdemog was at the 'spoken' end of the gradient, in opposition to informative writing, for all comparisons.

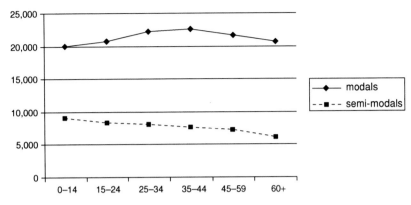

Figure 5.4 An 'apparent-time' study: comparison of age groups of speakers in the BNC demographic subcorpus (BNCdemog): distribution of modals and semi-modals according to age. (The sets of individual modals and semi-modals in Table 5.3 are aggregated here.) The *x* axis represents age groups of speakers, and the *y* axis occurrences per million words.

For spoken English, here as elsewhere, we have to lament a lack of sufficient data for recent diachronic comparison, but we can partially compensate for this by employing the technique of apparent-time comparison between the conversation of different age groups in BNCdemog.[15] There are naturally difficulties in trying to infer from the speech habits of different age groups the diachronic development of the language, especially in BNCdemog, where age groups are not strictly comparable (see below, footnote 16). However, the results shown in Figure 5.4 are suggestive of changes we have assumed to be taking place from other evidence. (The quantitative data of Figure 5.4 are spelt out in Table A5.3.)

Looking at the semi-modal line, we note that the apparent-time factor varies inversely with age: that is, increase of age is regularly correlated with a decrease in the use of semi-modals. In the lower age range, a contrasting trend is shown in the modal line, where in the first four age groups, the use of modals increases with age. A reversal of this trend, however, is observed in the eldest age groups, 45–59 and 60+, where despite the increase in age, modals are used less. Generally, then, the apparent-time factor in British conversation provides support for what has already been observed for real time in the Brown family comparisons, as well as the spoken mini-corpora comparisons. That is, the observed apparent-time changes in frequency

[15] The BNCdemog subcorpus is divisible into six categories according to age of speaker, as shown in Figure 5.4. BNCweb proved an excellent facility for tracking apparent time: the data in the figure were obtained using this software.

broadly confirm, for conversational data, the decreasing use of modals across real time, and more particularly the increasing use of semi-modals.[16]

In summary: the increase in use of semi-modals in the written corpora is paralleled, in a more dramatic form, in the spoken mini-corpora of the DCPSE. Even more dramatic evidence is provided by the large 1990s synchronic corpora of conversational English, indicating a much more frequent use of semi-modals, especially in AmE, than is manifest in any of the other corpora. The apparent-time analysis of the British demographic subcorpus BNCdemog gives, in addition, some extra support for the hypothesis that semi-modal usage has increased markedly in recent spoken English. The findings reported in this section, therefore, are consistent with the hypotheses that semi-modal use has increased dramatically in spoken language, and that this is reflected only to a subdued degree in the increase of semi-modals in the written corpora. Unsurprisingly American spoken English appears to be the most advanced variety in this study.

One puzzling aspect of the results in Table A5.1 is that, although written AmE shows a larger increase than written BrE, its starts from a lower point and ends at a lower point than BrE. (The raw frequencies are: Brown 1,904, Frown 2,237; LOB 2,225, F-LOB 2,422.) In other words, contrary to what is observed in the spoken data, overall these semi-modals are less used in written AmE than in written BrE. One conjectural explanation is that written AmE (as has been often suggested) is more subject than written BrE to prescriptive influence: Chapter 11 (section 11.6.2) provides some support for this. Although this tendency is not always observed,[17] its overall effect may be to make the 'prestige barrier' between spoken and (published) written language less permeable, so that colloquialization is resisted where spoken forms are felt to lack respectable credentials in the written language. Some

---

[16] Although their relevance to (semi-)modal distribution has yet to be demonstrated, it is worth bearing in mind here three factors that make the age distribution in BNCdemog less than ideal for the measurement of apparent time. First, there is an unevenness in the size of samples of different age groups, the two youngest age groups (0–14 and 15–24) particularly being under-represented. Second, there is no proportionate sampling of the other principal demographic factors (gender, social class and region) that might influence, along with age, the use of modality markers. There is a pronounced disparity in the 0–14 age group, where only 43% of the speech categorized for gender (according to the BNCweb word count) is produced by girls, whereas female speakers account for over 60% of the spoken words in all the other age groups (figures are again from BNCweb). Likewise, in the 0–14 age group, members of the lowest social class (DE) account for only 2% of the speech of that age group, whereas in other age groups they account for a range of higher proportions, varying from 9.5% to 25.5%. (Indeed, the DE social class is substantially under-represented in the demographic subcorpus as a whole.) A third concern, in view of the unexpectedly lower use of modals among the two oldest groups of speakers, is that age itself might disfavour the expression of certain kinds of modality, and that semantically determined tendencies to prefer or avoid types of modal expression might impinge on the overall pattern of increase or decrease. Perhaps further research on sociolinguistic or psycholinguistic factors connected with ageing will throw some light on this.

[17] Witness the use of *like* as a conjunction, more widely used and accepted in AmE than in BrE.

semi-modals, at least, fall into the low-prestige category – notably (*HAVE*) *got to*, perhaps because of the well-known taboo against the use of the verb *GET* in writing.[18]

The 'prestige barrier' mentioned above may also explain the particularly low frequency of the semi-modals (*HAVE*) *got to*, *had better* and *BE supposed to* in both the American and the British corpora of the Brown family. Compare the figures in BrE for the 1990s written corpus F-LOB with those for BNCdemog in Tables A5.1 and A5.3: *had better* and *BE supposed to* are more than **4 times as frequent** in the spoken subcorpus than in the written corpus, a figure that rises to approximately **45 times as frequent** in the case of (*HAVE*) *got to*! Other semi-modals, such as *NEED to*, *WANT to* and *HAVE to*, do not seem to suffer from the same degree of inhibition. A further explanatory factor might be that the semi-modals (*had*) *better*, (*HAVE*) *got to* and possibly *BE supposed to* occur rather rarely in the Brown family because they are associated with personal, emotive, interactive modal functions. These do not easily occur in published written sources except where speech is being imitated – as is incidentally illustrated in examples (9)–(18) below.

5.3   Further evidence for grammaticalization? Phonetics and semantics

In this section we turn our attention to evidence of two signs of grammaticalization: (a) phonetic reduction and coalescence, and (b) semantic shift to a more abstract and generalized meaning.

5.3.1   *Phonetic reduction and coalescence:* gonna, gotta *and* wanna

Generally the corpora we have used exist only in orthographic form, including orthographic transcriptions of speech. There can therefore be no direct evidence of phonetic reduction. The only evidence we have is indirect, and can be observed, for example, in non-standard spellings representing reduced pronunciation, especially *gonna* (for *BE going to*), *gotta* (for *HAVE got to*) and *wanna* (for *want to*). However, these are imperfect indicators, as we have no knowledge of the motivation of the authors or transcribers in opting for one of these spellings rather than the fuller form.[19]

Nevertheless, there is a remarkable consistency in the overall result of plotting reduced forms against age in the BNC. The diagram shown in Figure 5.5 uses data from Krug (2000: 175). The diagram reveals an almost

---

[18] As background to the diachronic development of (*HAVE*) *got to*, and its colloquial associations, see Johansson and Oksefjell (1996), Denison (1998) and Krug (2000).

[19] No doubt particular BNC transcribers, who were not trained phoneticians, were to some extent impressionistic and haphazard in their choice between the full and the reduced orthographic rendering (for fuller discussion, see Berglund 2000).

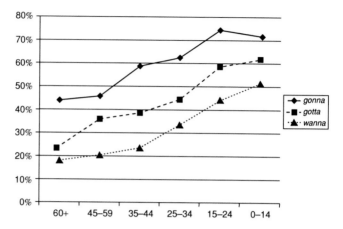

Figure 5.5 A study in apparent time: contracted forms *gonna*, *gotta* and *wanna*, as percentage of full and contracted forms, in the spoken BNC (based on Krug 2000: 175)

perfectly consistent progression: with one exception, each step down in age is a step up in the proportion of orthographically reduced forms. If we accept that the non-standard spellings are renderings of what were perceived to be colloquial, reduced pronunciations, then a reasonable conclusion is that, in general, the younger the speaker, the more likely the use of grammaticalized reduced forms.

There is a clear contrast here between the spoken (conversational) and written (published) corpora. In the former, the reduced, non-standard spellings form a sizeable proportion of all occurrences of the semi-modal: in the BNCdemog, *gonna* makes up 82%, *gotta* 48%, *wanna* 31.3%. In the latter, on the other hand, the non-standard spellings are a tiny minority: altogether, there are only 68 examples in the Brown family, or 2.5% of the combined occurrences of BE *going to*, *(HAVE) got to* and WANT *to*. Of these, 57 are from the American corpora, and only 11 from the British.

As positive declarative forms, and sometimes as interrogative forms, these three semi-modals illustrate another kind of phonetic reduction: the ellipsis of a whole word (the auxiliary BE, HAVE or DO, as the case may be):

(9)   So what is it, Lieutenant, you *gonna* read me my rights? [Frown L13]
(10)   We *gotta* go now. [BNC KB6]
(11)   Peter *wanna* come here? [BNC KB7]

Another case of auxiliary ellipsis is the common omission of *had* in the semi-modal *had better*. Like the other reduced variants, this is likely to occur in quoted speech in the written corpora:

(12) "She didn't mention bringing Myra", Mark said, maneuvering the car into the next lane. "She's probably getting old and – crotchety, I mean" – and we figured uh-uh, *better* not. [Brown K23]

(13) You shake your hands with that guy and you *better* count your fingers when you walk away. [Frown N10]

(14) Drewitt stood up and looked at his watch. '*Better* go.' [F-LOB L07]

It cannot escape notice that all three examples above are from quoted (fictional) speech. The ellipsis of the *had* of *had better* in spoken English is so prevalent as to be the rule rather than the exception in the conversational corpora. A further instance where phonetic reduction is reflected in non-standard spelling is the omission of the *d* at the end of BE *suppose(d) to*. This elision (occurring in 19% of the examples of this semi-modal in the LCSAE) is surely a sign that the passive construction of BE + *supposed* + *to* is no longer felt to be analysable into its grammatically individual parts.

5.3.2 *Signs of abstraction and generalization (semantic weakening)*

In view of the gradual and slow-moving nature of grammaticalization, one would hardly expect a period of thirty years to show much sign of semantic change. However, some indications of the abstraction and generalization predicted to be part of the grammaticalization process can be tentatively recognized in the Brown family of corpora. We briefly consider a number of semi-modals individually below. However, in view of the gradience of most of the distinctions being considered, judging semantic shifts from corpus evidence is difficult and largely subjective. Also, because of the limited numbers, in no case can we claim statistical significance.

BE going to
We concentrate on Brown and Frown here, because there is a highly significant increase in the use of BE *going to* (54%) in the American part of the Brown family, but (mysteriously) no such increase at all in the British. It is worthwhile mentioning here that the distribution of this semi-modal is heavily biased towards the Fictional dialogue part of the corpus, and against the Learned part.

The textbook definition (cf. Leech [3]2004: 58–9) of BE *going to* as an expression of future (or future in the past) time is that it refers to a future happening that in some sense is implicit in the present state of affairs – typically either an outcome of existing intentions as in (15), or of existing causes as in (16) – often with the implication that the future event will happen soon:

(15) 'Hell with it, I'*m going to* go out and have fun.' [Frown A28]

(16) By now she was sure she *was going to* have a baby [. . .]. [Brown G37]

However, it has also been recognized that in recent English BE *going to* has undergone a certain degree of semantic bleaching, in that the present causes of a future happening are sometimes vague and difficult to pin down. As a result it has been said that a more generalized future-referring function – akin to that of *will* – has been emerging, as seen in (17) and (18).

(17)   She has studied and observed and she is convinced that her young man *is going to* be endlessly enchanting. [Brown B08]

(18)   [. . .] you'll never know when there's *going to* be a mutation. [Frown R05]

A semantic coding of the examples in Brown and Frown did tentatively identify a trend towards a more generalized use of BE *going to*. Instances of all semantic varieties of BE *going to* have clearly increased, and those of present intention and present cause still account for a large majority of uses of BE *going to*. Yet instances like (17) and (18) that are judged to refer to the future in a general sense (including unclear cases) have more than doubled from 18 (8% of all BE *going to*s) to 39 (12%) – a larger than average increase.[20]

Specifically in the category of News reporting, there has been a very noticeable rise in BE *going to* (from 11 to 54 occurrences) and a corresponding decline in BE *to* (from 27 to 6), as if the press, in referring to a planned future event, has made a determined switch from one construction to another.[21] Compare these typical examples from Brown and Frown respectively:

(19)   The jail sentence *is to* begin the day after Sarkees graduates from Eastern High School in June. [Brown A21]

(20)   Rhode Island *is going to* examine its Sunday sales law. [Frown A05]

Although the two semi-modals are not precisely equivalent in meaning, this appears to be a rare case where the language of news reporting has increasingly avoided a shorter, more economical construction in favour of a longer one – perhaps because of the former's association with a somewhat 'stuffy' and more formal style.

---

[20]   As a further instantiation of this trend, Mair (1997: 1539–40) notes the occurrence, in the Press texts of Frown and F-LOB, of BE *going to* in the apodosis of *if*-clauses under conditions where *will*, but not BE *going to*, according to received grammatical wisdom (e.g. Quirk *et al.* 1985: 214–5) would normally be considered acceptable. For instance:

If we bring up Desert Storm, some wise guy Democrat *is going to* ask where the supplies came from [. . .] [Frown B14]

[21]   F-LOB also shows an increase in BrE in the use of *will be -ing* for future reference in Press texts (see section 6.7.2). Regarding BE *to*, preliminary analysis of the Lanc-31 (B-LOB) corpus shows that the decline of this construction has continued steadily since the early 1930s.

HAVE to, (HAVE) got to

In the case of *HAVE to*, the tendency to acquire a more abstract meaning has shown itself in the adoption of an unmarked sense of obligation/necessity, where the authoritative source of the obligation is presumed to be external to the 'obligatee', but is otherwise left vague:

(21)   The question *has to* be asked: Are we ready? [F-LOB R03]

The abstraction has also gone one stage further, in the emergence of an epistemic sense of both *HAVE to* and *(HAVE) got to*,[22] paraphrasable by 'It *BE* necessarily the case that . . . ':

(22)   "DID I hear a car?" Sally asked suddenly. [caps. sic]
        It was a car, but it was going in the wrong direction. It *had to* be Maria leaving. [F-LOB P29]
(23)   This *has got to* be some kind of local phenomenon. [Brown M04]

However, such instances are in short supply in the Brown family of corpora, no doubt because of the relative novelty of this usage. (Even in the conversational corpora instances are difficult to find: an inspection of 300 examples from 19 files in the American conversation corpus LCSAE revealed only 4 certain cases.) In Brown and Frown, examples of epistemic *HAVE to* increased from 14 to 26, while in LOB and F-LOB, frequencies were even lower, though moving up: they increased from 6 to 18.[23] Although the general picture was of an increase led by AmE, in every corpus the frequency of epistemic use was less than 5% of all *HAVE to*s. Examples of epistemic *(HAVE) got to* were an even rarer phenomenon (1 occurrence in Brown, and 3 in Frown; 4 in LOB, and 1 in F-LOB).

In the thirty-year period of our study, in gross frequency terms,[24] *HAVE to* overtook *must* as a verb of root obligation/necessity, while *must* remained as much as ten times as frequent as *HAVE to* in the epistemic sense.

NEED to

Although the semi-modal *NEED to* is less frequent than *BE able to* and *WANT to* (which will be briefly considered later), it comes in appositely at this point because of its position as a competitor for *HAVE to* in the domain of obligation/necessity. In its most basic sense, both as a semi-modal and as a transitive verb, *NEED* indicates some need pertaining to the subject referent,

---

[22] In historical studies of English, it is well known (see Traugott 1989) that epistemic meanings of modals developed out of earlier deontic meanings. The emerging epistemic use of *HAVE to* appears to show a similar pattern of development for semi-modals.
[23] These figures are a conservative revision of those given in Smith (2003a: 257). In fact, the boundary between epistemic and deontic use is often unclear. Including borderline cases increases the numbers to 12 (LOB) and 31 (F-LOB).
[24] This combines frequencies for both AmE and BrE, and for both finite and non-finite forms of *HAVE to*.

as in (24), the sense thus being one of inherent necessity (cf. Leech and Coates 1980: 83–4), rather than external or unmarked necessity, as in (25):

(24)   I've been out for a couple of weeks and I *need to* get used to the pace of the game again ... [F-LOB A32] (Here the constraint is internal to the speaker, who needs to improve his game.)

(25)   I *have to* get up early for church tomorrow,' she went on. [Brown P18] (Here the constraint is external to the speaker, determined presumably by the time of the church service.)

However, the link between the subject referent and the 'need' denoted by the verb can be loosened or severed in various ways. One way is to use a passive following *need to*, a common option whereby the subject referent is replaced by the agent referent, who usually remains implicit. The persons with the need, who would benefit from the action, are thus unspecified, and may be left vague:

(26)   My second revolutionary, Sigmund Freud, was an alien among Victorians, but he *needs to* be looked at as a vital contributor to Bloomsbury thought – [...] [Frown G21]

There are also other circumstances, for example where NEED *to* has an inanimate or non-referential subject, where the basic meaning of inherent necessity is obscured or lost:

(27)   If women are as likely as men to get into and through medical school, then efforts to understand why fewer women become physicians *need to* focus on gender differences in ambition rather than differences in opportunity. It *needs to* be determined why fewer women apply to medical school. [Frown J24]

In examples like this, it would be easy to substitute HAVE *to* for NEED *to*, without noticing anything amiss. Both would convey an 'unmarked' (neither internal nor external) necessity that could be paraphrased by the construction 'It is necessary (for NP) to VP'. Thus the last sentence in (27) could be paraphrased: 'It is necessary to determine why fewer women apply to medical school'.

Another possible reason for the increasing use of NEED *to* is its strategic value in 'camouflaging' an imposed obligation as being in the obligatee's best interest. This usage retains the connotation of internal obligation/necessity, and is best illustrated with a second-person subject:

(28)   I'm not a feminist, but I do think you *need to* hear a balanced view of matters. [F-LOB F13]

In (28), the mitigating implication 'I'm telling you this for your own good' would vanish if *need to* were replaced by *have to*, or even more, the quasi-imperative force of *must*. In the four corpora, the increase in *you need to* was from 0 occurrences in 1961 to 13 occurrences in 1991/2. Perhaps surprisingly, however, a more dramatic increase occurred in *we need to* – from 7 occurrences in 1961 to 33 occurrences in 1991/2. Here a double mitigation of imperative force occurs: not only is obligation represented as in the best interests of 'us', but by referring to 'we' rather than 'you' as the people with the need, the writer imposes a collective obligation on an often rather vague community of people including the addresser and the addressees:

(29)   The new Bishop of Hereford, the Rt Revd John Oliver, said in an enthronement sermon in his cathedral on 22 December that Christians ought not to be tempted, in an unfriendly environment, to pull up the drawbridge and hope for the best. 'We are in the business of celebrating and sharing our faith, of "singing the Lord's song"; we *need to* do it confidently, joyfully, expectantly [. . .]' [F-LOB D11]

Given the hugely increasing use of NEED *to* between the 1961 and 1991/2 corpora (from 122 to 348 adding both pairs of corpora), it is not surprising that all semantic varieties of NEED *to* are used with increasing frequency during that period. Again, however, there is tentative evidence that the more abstract (unmarked necessity) use of this semi-modal has made greater advances than the basic (inherent necessity) meaning. In a semantic coding of LOB and F-LOB, it was found, using admittedly impressionistically applied criteria, that the unmarked necessity category, combined with uncertain cases, increased from 23 to 109 (a more than a fourfold increase), whereas the 'inherent necessity' use increased from 22 to 54 (roughly half the rate of increase of the unmarked usage).

BE able to
BE *able to* occupies the same ability/possibility domain as *can* (see Facchinetti 2002), the only core modal which increased in frequency in the LOB/F-LOB–Brown/Frown comparison. Perhaps this is part of the reason why, in stark contrast to NEED *to*, use of BE *able to* did not increase more than 3% (see Table A5.1) in the thirty-year period: with no loss of *can*, there was no particular need to make more use of BE *able to*.

BE *able to* comes into its own in non-finite constructions, as a kind of 'suppletive' semi-modal where *can* cannot be employed: indeed, non-finite occurrences of this semi-modal outnumber finite ones. It is this that may be partly responsible for a semantic bleaching tendency where BE *able to* does show some similarity with NEED *to*.

Like NEED *to*, BE *able to* may be said to have a basic meaning of 'inherent modality', where a general notion of deontic modality (possibility for BE *able to*, obligation/necessity for NEED *to*) is oriented towards the subject referent(s), as the person(s) possessing a particular physical or mental ability or requirement. Our first example is of particular interest, because it shows

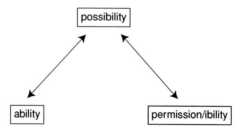

Figure 5.6 Meanings of *can* and BE *able to*

that the two semi-modals under discussion can combine in the same verb phrase:

(30)   You need to *be able to* use a circular saw and a jigsaw to build it [...] [Frown E17]
(31)   F. Scott Fitzgerald said it is a sign of genius to *be able to* entertain in the mind two mutually contradictory ideas without going insane. [Frown A12]

If we think of the semantic field of *can* as a triangle with three poles of 'ability,' 'possibility' and 'permission', as in Figure 5.6, then BE *able to* can be fitted to the same diagram.[25]

   The major semantic difference, however, is that (at least in the British corpora from the 1960s investigated by Coates 1983: 86) the most common meaning of *can* is the unmarked, abstract one of possibility, whereas the home ground of BE *able to*, and still its most common sense, is that of ability (i.e. capability, or possibility attributed to the inherent powers of the subject/agent referent). Nevertheless, like NEED *to*, BE *able to* has been extending its use into the externally constrained or 'unmarked' territory of deontic meaning.[26] Examples:

(32)   It is doubtful if Morgan *was able to* take home much money to his wife and children, for his pay [...] was $75 a month [...] [Brown G58]
(33)   Commissioner Donald Quigg stated that the Patent Office would not *be able to* act on animal patent applications before the end of the fiscal year on 30 September 1987. [Frown F48]

In (32), Morgan's action is constrained not by his own intrinsic ability, but by the external constraint of his salary. Similarly in (33), what prevented the Patent Office from taking immediate action no doubt included obstacles from outside itself, such as financial, legal or administrative constraints.

[25] Figure 5.6 is adapted from Leech and Coates (1980: 85).
[26] This is similar to what has previously been claimed for *can* – see Bybee *et al.* (1994: 191–3). The past/hypothetical modal *could* also has a similar semantic profile – and would be substitutable for *was able* and *would ... be able to* in examples (32) and (33), for instance.

Semantic coding of the concordances of BE *able* from Brown and Frown revealed that, as in the case of NEED *to*, the unmarked deontic meaning grew in frequency between 1961 and 1992 (from 68 to 87) more than the basic ability sense, which indeed declined. There was also an increase in the proportion of examples, such as (34), which could be labelled 'permissibility' or 'permission' (from 4 to 14), where the lack of constraint (unlike ability) comes from some external authority, such as a legal system:

(34)   Physiotherapists, architects and students will *be able to* practice or study anywhere in the Single Market on the basis of degrees they earned at home. [Frown A11]

Although the frequency of BE *able to* has apparently remained rather stable over the later twentieth century, there is tentative evidence, as we have seen, that it is paralleling NEED *to* and BE *going to* in gradually extending its semantic range to more abstract realms of meaning.

The arrows in Figure 5.6 represent gradience: it is not possible to draw a clear boundary between possibility and the two more specified meanings of ability and permission, a problem common to modal meanings in general. Hence our semantic findings are tentative, relying, as they have to, on impressionistic judgements, acknowledging uncertain cases.

WANT to *and other semi-modals*
For lack of space, we leave aside the semantics of other semi-modals, only noting that the remarkably increasing semi-modal WANT *to* will be the subject of further discussion in Chapter 9 (section 9.2.4).

WANT *to* does not, like the other increasingly common semi-modals, show a trend to more abstract or externally oriented meaning, since volition is necessarily a matter of internal modality (subsequent events being constrained by the internal state of the subject referent). However, Krug (2000: 141–51), after tracing the rise of WANT *to* as an emergent modal taking over some of the volitional range of *will*, points out a newer incipient extension into deontic meaning, potentially encroaching on the territory of NEED *to*.[27] Examples are rare in the four corpora, but can be found if one looks for second-person subjects:

(35)   "My, you're peaked. You *want to* watch out that you don't get burned to an ash, first sunny day." [Brown P23]

Want to here could be replaced by *need to* or *ought to*. The deontic shift is evident in that *want to* does not obey its normal speech-act restrictions as a volitional verb: we cannot felicitously inform our addressees of their wants,

---

[27] Krug (2000: 149–50) also cites one exceptional example of WANT *to* being used epistemically.

which are best known only to themselves. Hence *WANT to* is interpreted as deontic, and the whole speech act as an admonition.[28]

5.4   The ecology of obligation/necessity

This penultimate section of Chapter 5 takes up the topic of functional domains, i.e. the developing syntactic and semantic relations between modals and semi-modals in the same field of meaning. The term 'ecology' captures the idea that each form evolves its own niche in the expression of modality, expanding, contracting or maintaining its 'habitat' in relation to other, partially competing, forms. In this respect, the most interesting and complex field to examine is that of obligation/necessity. The traditional picture, in diachronic description, of two forms (say, *doth* and *does*, or *hath* and *has*) in mortal combat, such that by the familiar S-curve progression one finally yields the field to the other, is far from the truth in this case. Instead, there are four modals – *must*, *should*, *ought (to)* and *need(n't)* – to consider, and four semi-modals – *HAVE to*, *(HAVE) GOT to*, *NEED to* and *(had) better*.[29] In looking at the four written corpora, our attention, in practice, will be focused on the most common of these, *must*, *should*, *HAVE to* and *NEED to* (the laxer deontic modality of *should* being brought in as part of the backdrop for the other three).

Chapter 4 documented the extraordinarily steep fall in the frequency of *must*, and hypothesized that part of this might have been due to social factors – the democratization and individualization of society causing deontic *must*, with its overly authoritative tone, to decline in popularity.[30] A small piece of evidence supporting this is the exceptionally steep decline in frequency of deontic *must* with first- or second-person subjects (where the implication of personal imposition is likely to be uppermost) in comparison to *must* with third-person subjects. The decline with first- and second-person is steeper, especially in direct speech, and especially with second-person subjects (where it is as high as 50% – for details see Smith 2003a: 258):

(36)   [. . .] you *must* discuss the whole situation with your boy friend. [LOB
        F12]

---

[28] Like the comparable use of *NEED to* mentioned earlier, *you want to* therefore takes its place among the rich array of IFIDs (illocutionary force indicating devices) in English having a directive, or quasi-imperative function. See the similar notion of 'whimperative' discussed in Sadock (1974) and Green (1975).

[29] This set of alternatives could be considerably expanded. Though rare in the four corpora, *WANT to* in the colloquial deontic sense discussed in section 5.3.2 could be added to the list of semi-modals. Further, the mandative subjunctive (see Chapter 3) can be added to the set of alternatives for expressing obligation in subordinate clauses. Even this list oversimplifies the picture by disregarding, for example, adverbial and adjectival constructions (*It is necessary . . .*, *necessarily*, etc.).

[30] Compare a similar claim by Myhill (1995) regarding social factors changing the popularity of different verbs expressing deontic modality in nineteenth-century AmE.

(37) What is the remedy? Is it to spend more money on youth which we parents eventually have to pay? I do not think so. I think we *must* teach by example [. . .] [LOB A13]

In contrast to this, the more general (often externally oriented) root modality of *HAVE to* makes a less face-threatening impression, especially when combined with other (semi-)modals, which add further indirectness:

(38) 'Only the electric bill. It's up again. We'll *have to* go easy on the immersion heater next quarter.' [LOB R02]

Even more face-saving is the use of *NEED to* in situations where the speaker/writer may be construed as imposing on the addressee, as discussed in section 5.3.2 above:

(39) [. . .] hard questions *need to* be asked about the Government's record since 1981, and the Socialist Party leadership's current lack of direction. [F-LOB F18]

HAVE to has a history of increasing use for the last three hundred or so years (Krug 2000: 76–80), and the extent to which it is now challenging or outdoing *must* in frequency has in the past been fuelled by syntactic opportunities. The non-occurrence of *must* as a non-finite form, as a past tense form or with internal negation has left three important niches to be occupied by *HAVE to*:

(40) They may *have to* call up the reinforcement of the Common Market. [LOB B03]

(41) 'We *had to* leave him behind and he was picked up.' [LOB L21]

(42) 'And I *don't have to* stay here you know.' [LOB P29]

In none of these three examples can *HAVE to* be replaced by *must*. However, as shown by Smith (2003a: 255), the gain of *HAVE to* between LOB and F-LOB can only partly be explained in terms of syntax. There is reason to believe that both *HAVE to* and *NEED to* are benefiting from a narrowing social-semantic popularity of *must*.

Should, too, may be a beneficiary of the decline of deontic *must*. As was seen in the last chapter (section 4.5.2), *should* has maintained its 'weak' root modality surprisingly well, in contrast with the decline of epistemic *should*. There has even been a real increase of root *should* in spoken BrE according to the evidence of DCPSE (Table A4.7). This again fits the hypothesis that the decline of deontic *must* has benefited more muted or indirect expressions of root obligation/necessity.

(43) Renewed war could lead to drastic changes; the temptation to take this course *should* be resisted. [F-LOB B09]

Clearly the obligation expressed by *should* here is less dictatorial than the alternative *must*. (*Should* has also presumably benefited from the decline of its closest rival in expressing weak necessity, namely *ought to* – see also Myhill 1995.)

Nevertheless, *must* still has a dominant role in expressing epistemic necessity: one that in spite of declining frequency has not yet seriously been challenged by the epistemic variants of HAVE *to* and *(HAVE) got to*, let alone the declining epistemic use of *should*.

5.5   Conclusion

Reporting findings from the Brown family of corpora, Chapters 4 and 5 have shown, on the one hand, a substantial and significant decline in the frequency of the core modals, and on the other, a substantial and significant rise in the frequency of a representative set of semi-modals. However, the extent to which these two trends are interconnected has seemed problematic, because overall the core modals are several times more frequent in the four written corpora than the semi-modals. It can be observed, though, taking account of what evidence can be obtained from spoken corpora of the 1990s, that the semi-modals are indeed not far behind the core modals in their frequency in spoken English (especially AmE). It can be tentatively argued, then, that the competitive relation between core modals and grammaticalizing semi-modals in **spoken** English is an explanatory factor in accounting for the decline of the one and the ascendancy of the other in both **spoken and written** English. The balance of gain and loss in the spoken language, it seems, has a knock-on effect in the written language, even where that gain/loss equation does not (yet) materialize in the written language. Perhaps colloquialization is bringing these predominantly spoken forms into more extensive use in written English, but only after a time lag which has been keeping in check the full flood of increase observed in the spoken language.

The thirty-year window of time from 1961 to 1991/2 is too short to show dramatic grammaticalization effects in the semi-modals. But some signs of grammaticalization are detectable not only in their increase in frequency,[31] but also in tentative evidence (in the form of auxiliary ellipsis and non-standard spellings) of phonetic coalescence and reduction, and tentative evidence of semantic generalization of certain semi-modals.

The preceding section of this chapter looked at the 'ecology' of the domain of obligation/necessity, outlining how the competition between several modals and semi-modals is played out in our four corpora through

---

[31] Although increased frequency is not an inevitable concomitant of grammaticalization (see Lindquist and Mair 2004: 13), the cases discussed in the last two chapters appear to fit Bybee and Pagliuca's (1985) description, discussed by Krug (2000: 177): 'As the meaning generalizes and the range of uses widens, the frequency increases and this leads automatically to phonological reduction and perhaps fusion' (Bybee and Pagliuca 1985: 76).

changes of frequency not just of the verb forms themselves, but of their subtly differing functions. In conclusion, it should be mentioned, both for modality and other functional domains, that other factors such as genre and pragmatics are often more influential than diachrony in accounting for overall variation. For reasons of space, in this chapter we have placed such factors in the background, focusing on salient changes of overall frequency of semi-modals, modals and their semantic categories.

6   The progressive

6.1   Introduction

We now turn from mood and modality to a grammatical construction that is normally associated with the notion of aspect – that is, the manner in which the internal temporal constituency of a situation is represented.[1] We refer to this construction by its most popular title, the progressive.[2] It consists of a form of the verb BE followed by a participle ending in *-ing*.

(1)   I know where you*'re coming* from.

(2)   Have you *been waiting* long?

For a number of reasons the English progressive has been the subject of considerable scholarly interest. First, it is unclear how it originated. Second, over the last several centuries it has developed a rather complex meaning, or set of meanings, by comparison with progressive constructions in other languages (see Dahl 1985: 90, Bybee *et al.* 1994: 136). A third reason, probably resulting from the second, is that the progressive has enjoyed a meteoric increase in frequency in the Modern English period (see section 6.3).

So far, however, little empirical data has been adduced as to whether the trend of burgeoning growth has continued into the present period, and whether the two major varieties of English, AmE and BrE, have followed the same course in this respect.

This chapter focuses mainly on these last two questions. In doing so, it explores gross and genre-based frequencies in the Brown family and other contemporaneous corpora. It assesses the evidence for change in respect of, for example, the verb paradigm, different classes of verb and different uses of the construction. Our approach has been to target those parameters identified in previous research as potentially relevant to the development of

---

[1] The definition of aspect given here is adapted slightly from Comrie (1976: 3). Although numerous theories have been espoused on the aspectual systems of individual languages since Comrie's, his characterization of aspect in general has rarely been challenged.

[2] A host of other terms have been suggested for the progressive, such as the *continuous* (e.g. in English language teaching), and more theory-neutral labels such as the *Expanded Form* (see, e.g., Visser 1963–73), the *Expanded Tense* (e.g. Jespersen 1909–49), and BE + *-ing* (e.g. most French linguists).

the progressive in PDE. Once again we explore the hypothesis that observed grammatical developments are related to social/stylistic processes of change, in particular colloquialization (see sections 1.3, 11.3).

Before examining these questions, we first provide a brief background on the functions and history of the progressive.[3]

6.2 Basic and special uses of the progressive

There is a general consensus among linguists that aspect is an important cognitive category, and moreover that an important subcategory of aspect is the progressive aspect; that is, the representing of a situation from within, paying attention to its duration in time and to its ongoing or dynamic character.

However, it is sometimes disputed that the term 'progressive' adequately captures the meaning of the English construction. Opponents of the term cite numerous examples in which they allege that the notion of a situation in progress is absent; for example, where the situation being described is to be actualized in the future, and the realization is not (ostensibly) an ongoing event, as in (3) and (4); where the situation appears not to be bounded in time, cf. (5); and where the construction redescribes a situation that has already been described in the non-progressive, and might similarly be viewed as non-durative, cf. (6):

(3)   John *is leaving* town tomorrow.
(4)   I*'ll be having* my baby in June.
(5)   Come on, you*'re* always *whingeing*.
(6)   When she said that, she *was lying*.

We retain the term 'progressive' primarily because it is the most widely used and recognized label. Moreover, in our close readings of more than three thousand examples in a range of PDE corpora, the aspectual notion of situation 'in progress' is in evidence in the vast majority of cases. The situation as a whole appears to be represented as dynamic (involving an element of change) and as durative (extending over a period of time). Examples like (1) and (2) are considerably more frequent in corpus data than examples like (3) to (6). In this sense, then, we can call progressive aspect the prototypical meaning of the English progressive.

In our approach, examples such as (3) to (6) are treated as 'special' uses of the progressive, in that the meanings they convey amount to something beyond aspect.[4] Example (4), for instance, implies that the birth will

---

[3] We should also point out that, for reasons of time: (a) we do not examine rival constructions to the progressive in any depth, commenting only on the most obvious areas of competition; (b) our study concentrates significantly more on BrE than on AmE.

[4] Other scholars have used terms such as 'non-normal uses' (Lyons 1982), 'the experiential progressive' (Wright 1995), and 'not solely aspectual functions' (Smitterberg 2005). Their

happen routinely, as a 'matter of course' (Leech ^{3}2004: 67–8); (5) suggests a hyperbolic tone of disapproval.

There is a reasonable consensus that – with the exception of the progressive passive, and certain classes of predicate – the modern-day 'rules' for aspectual use of the progressive were more or less obligatory by around 1800 (see, e.g., Strang 1982, Nehls 1988, Fischer and van der Wurff 2006). It will be interesting to see, then, the extent to which special uses such as those illustrated above have played a part in expanding the functional range of the progressive still further in the twentieth century.

6.3   Historical background

The origins of the English progressive are as much a matter of debate as its modern-day meanings.[5] By most accounts, however, the main period in the development of the Modern English progressive was from the sixteenth to the eighteenth centuries, during which time it became more or less conventionalized as a marker of progressive aspect.

All the main parts of the paradigm were already attested by around 1700, with the exception of the progressive passive, as in (7), which emerged in the late eighteenth century in the present and past tenses, and has since established a foothold also in the more complex present perfect, past perfect, future and modal paradigms:[6]

(7)   I have received the speech and address of the House of Lords; probably, that of the House of Commons *was being debated* when the post went out. [1772. From a series of Letters of the First Earl of Malmesbury, cited in Warner (1995: 539)]

On the other hand, two structural realizations of the progressive have all but disappeared in Modern English: the participial progressive, as in (8),[7] and the 'passival' progressive (see section 7.1), a forerunner of the progressive passive,[8] as in (9).

---

categories partly overlap with our 'special uses', although views differ considerably as to whether aspect is involved at all in such uses.

[5] Two main theories as to its source have been espoused: (a) a construction of BE plus a present participle, e.g. *he wæs huntende*, widely called the Old English progressive; and (b) a locative construction containing BE plus a preposition and a gerund, e.g. *he wæs on huntunge*. Some have proposed further that the modern-day progressive is the result of a coalescence between the two constructions. For discussion see, for instance, Visser (1963–73), Scheffer (1975), Mitchell (1985), Fischer (1992), Denison (1993), Bybee *et al.* (1994) and Hübler (1998).

[6] Approximate dates of emergence of new parts of the paradigm can be found in Mustanoja (1960), Visser (1963–73), Fischer (1992), Denison (1993, 1998) and Rissanen (1999).

[7] In a one-million-word corpus of nineteenth-century British English, Smitterberg (2005: 143) found just two instances of this pattern.

[8] For discussion of the early development of the progressive passive, see, e.g., Denison (1998) and Hundt (2004a, 2004b).

(8)   John *being going* your way, I am willing to write [. . .] (1740, Richardson, *Pamela* I.8.32; cited in Visser (1963–73: 1955)

(9)   the whole *is* daily *accomplishing* all round us. (Macaulay, *Essays* 3.140, cited in Mossé 1938, section 237)

Thus in PDE, as Denison (1993: 394) states, '[t]here is now a systemic gap . . . which has actually opened up where previously the paradigm was complete'.

 Estimates of the frequency of the progressive since the start of the Modern English period almost universally present a picture of rapid ascendance. Elsness (1994: 11), for example, found an increase by more than a factor of three between the first and last sampling periods of the EModE part of the Helsinki diachronic corpus, i.e. between 1500–1570 and 1640–1710. Dennis (1940) sampled texts at five stylistic levels at regular intervals from the late fifteenth to the early twentieth centuries. Overall, she found an approximate doubling of occurrences in every century. In a study of the progressive in nineteenth-century BrE, Smitterberg (2005: 62) found a growth rate of between 71% and 81%, depending on the method of calculation. Smitterberg's study is, to date, also the most detailed empirical analysis of the progressive in the Late Modern period, and therefore provides valuable opportunities for comparison with our findings on the late twentieth-century corpora.

 Evidence for changes in frequency or use of the progressive *during* the twentieth century is more difficult to find, and based mainly on ad hoc collections of works of Press.[9] Mossé (1938: 2.271) gives normalized frequencies for various fictional works from the nineteenth and twentieth centuries, finding a higher rate of use for more recent writers. Strang (1982) produces similar findings in her surveys of novels from the eighteenth century to the twentieth century.

 Hundt's (2004a) study of ARCHER (see Figure 6.1) gives the first systematic coverage of corpus data up to the end of the twentieth century, including comparable material from BrE and AmE.[10] While the pattern of growth for the eighteenth to the end of the nineteenth centuries is, as expected, quite rapid, perhaps surprisingly it suggests that late twentieth-century usage of the progressive may have been higher and increasing at a faster rate in BrE than AmE.[11] There is clearly a need for a more detailed examination of twentieth-century trends.

---

[9] We exclude here our own publications (e.g. Mair and Hundt 1995; Smith 2002, 2003b) based on the Brown family corpora.
[10] At the time of Hundt's study, AmE data had not yet been assembled in all sampling periods of ARCHER.
[11] Cf. Dennis (1940) and Biber *et al.* (1999: 462), who find a higher rate of progressives in AmE than BrE.

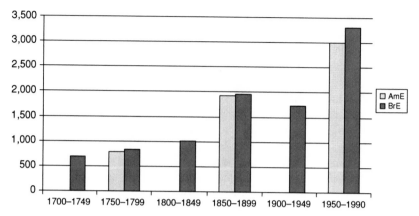

Figure 6.1 Distribution of the progressive in ARCHER (based on Hundt 2004a: 69): frequencies per million words

6.4   Overview of recent distribution patterns

6.4.1   Distribution in written BrE and AmE

We begin our survey of the recent distribution of the progressive with the Brown family corpora: see Figure 6.2 for BrE and Figure 6.3 for AmE. (More detailed quantitative results are shown in Tables A6.1–A6.4.)[12] Both national varieties present a picture of the progressive relentlessly marching on, much as it has been over the last several centuries. Overall, frequencies increase by about 10%, which is significant at p <0.001. The mean in the 1990s is just over 3,000 instances per million words in AmE, and slightly higher in BrE.

---

[12] We exclude from our analysis the following structures that are superficially similar to progressives: the BE going to construction, as in (a) (see sections 5.2–3 and also below, 6.7.2); equative constructions containing main verb BE and gerund, as in (b); and -ing forms used as predicative adjectives, as in (c).

    (a) It *was going to* be another hot day. [Brown L08]
    (b) Another difficulty *is ensuring* people leaving acute psychiatric care have somewhere to go. [F-LOB F33]
    (c) To hear him speak about music – about anything – *is hypnotizing* and *mystifying* and *moving*. [Frown E22]

Further, our analysis does not count clipped forms of the progressive, or coordinated cases that are not realized as full VPs (i.e. containing both BE and -ing).

    To retrieve instances of the progressive, each part of the paradigm was searched for individually using CQP, and the output manually edited. The queries allowed for a variety of optional adverbial or noun phrase patterns to appear between the form of BE and a present participle. For example, the query for the present progressive active was: [pos = "V.B[MRZ]"] [pos = "R.*|MD|XX"]{0,4} [pos = "AT|APPGE"]? [pos ="JJ.*"]? [pos = "PPH1|PP.*S.*|PPY|NP.*|D.*|NN.*"]? [pos = "R.*|MD|XX"]{0,4} [word=".*ing|.*in\'" & pos = "V.*G"]

    Additional checks were made for present participles being mistagged as adjectives or nouns, although some cases will have been missed where the material between the form of BE and the present participle was especially complex.

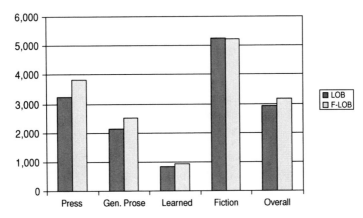

Figure 6.2 Progressives by subcorpora in LOB and F-LOB (1961–1991): changes in frequency pmw

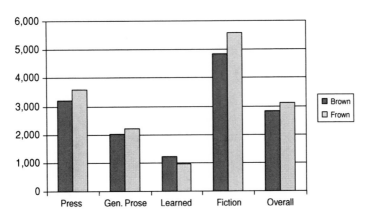

Figure 6.3 Progressives by subcorpora in Brown and Frown (1961–1992): frequencies pmw

Synchronically, the rankings of the broad genre categories (subcorpora) are the same across the regions, with Fiction ranked highest, followed by Press, General Prose, and Learned writing. Fiction attains a high level because it has frequent recourse to the progressive both in narrative (typically the past progressive) and in dialogue (typically the present progressive). We should add that the subcorpus categories used here conceal a fair amount of internal variation. In Press, for instance, the rate is 3,000 per million words on average, but in the reportage genre (category A) the figure rises to 4,000 per million. The latter figure is on a par with Biber *et al.*'s (1999) category of 'News'.

In both varieties, the progressive becomes more frequent in the Press and General Prose. Learned writing, which as we have seen tends to be the genre most resistant to change, shows no significant growth in BrE, and even decline in AmE. Puzzlingly, Fiction in AmE is expanding dramatically whereas in BrE it is apparently static.

Significantly, the corpora also reveal that the increase of the progressive is concentrated in specific forms rather than spread evenly across the paradigm (see Figures A6.1–A6.4). The main diachronic trends can be summarized as follows:

(a)   The advance of the progressive in written BrE and AmE is statistically most significant in the *present* tense.

(b)   The increase in present progressives occurs across both the *active* and *passive* voices in BrE, but only the active voice in AmE.

(c)   *Past progressives*, by contrast, have seemingly declined in use in the *active* in BrE and in the *passive* in AmE.

(d)   The only other significantly changing category is, in BrE only, the growth in progressives in combination with modal auxiliaries (*modal + progressive*).

(e)   In each corpus there are very few occurrences of the most complex parts of the paradigm, containing three or more auxiliaries, for example *will be being taken, must have been being considered.*

It is worth noting that the above trends (a) to (e) are generally supported if we change the method of calculation, measuring the frequency of progressives relative to their non-progressive equivalents (rather than normalized to a fixed text length); see Table A6.2.[13] Once again it is clear that present progressives are pre-eminent in raising the overall frequency of the construction.

We will focus shortly on the three clearest areas of change within the progressive paradigm – (a), (b) and (d) above – with a view to identifying contributory factors. First, however, we wish to broaden our outlook on register variation and change in the distribution of the progressive in BrE.

6.4.2   *Distribution in contemporaneous BrE speech and other registers*

We survey here: (a) frequencies of the progressive across the spoken and written registers of the ICE-GB corpus; and (b) frequencies of the progressive in spoken BrE, across our adapted version of the DCPSE (i.e. DSEU and DICE, comparing the 1960s with the 1990s – see section 2.5 D2). These additional resources help us to determine how far developments in the Brown

---

[13] For detailed discussion of the merits and drawbacks of different methods of calculating the frequency of the progressive, see Smitterberg (2005: 39–53).

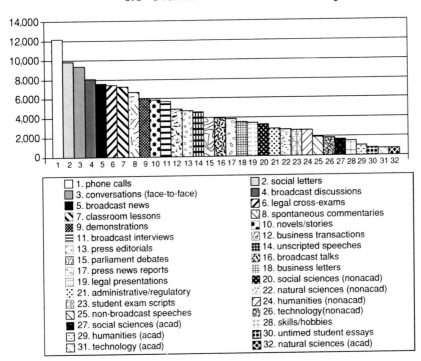

1. phone calls
2. social letters
3. conversations (face-to-face)
4. broadcast discussions
5. broadcast news
6. legal cross-exams
7. classroom lessons
8. spontaneous commentaries
9. demonstrations
10. novels/stories
11. broadcast interviews
12. business transactions
13. press editorials
14. unscripted speeches
15. parliament debates
16. broadcast talks
17. press news reports
18. business letters
19. legal presentations
20. social sciences (nonacad)
21. administrative/regulatory
22. natural sciences (nonacad)
23. student exam scripts
24. humanities (nonacad)
25. non-broadcast speeches
26. technology(nonacad)
27. social sciences (acad)
28. skills/hobbies
29. humanities (acad)
30. untimed student essays
31. technology (acad)
32. natural sciences (acad)

Figure 6.4 Distribution of the progressive in genres of the full ICE-GB corpus (1990–92): frequencies pmw

family corpora are mirrored in other registers, especially in spoken English (see Figure 6.4).

Even taking into account differences in word-counting methods between ICE-GB and the Brown family, it is clear that registers that are speech-based (or speech-like) and relatively informal in character show a much higher incidence of progressives than typical printed genres.[14] The highest-ranking genres in ICE-GB include, for example, telephone calls, social (i.e. private, informal) letters, face-to-face conversations and broadcast discussions. These registers are conducted in 'real-time', or at least – e.g. in the case of social letters – they are highly interactive in character. By far the dominant pattern is the present progressive (active), which is appropriate to describing situations as they unfold. Very often there is more than one instance of the progressive in a single utterance, as in the following:

---

[14] Similar findings on the higher rate of use in conversation are reported in Biber *et al.* (1999: 462), Mindt (2000: 248) and Römer (2005). The 'oral' character of the progressive has in fact been a trait across the history of English – see, e.g., Mossé (1938), Dennis (1940: 860) and Smitterberg (2005).

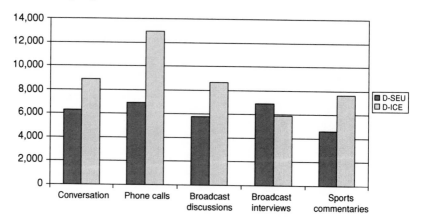

Figure 6.5 Progressives by broad genre category in the DSEU (1958–69) and DICE (1990–92): frequencies pmw

(10)   But they think they 're getting a good deal if they 're paying you know if they 're handing over the dosh [S1A-012#157:1:C, direct conversations]

(11)   Anyhow I'm having a good time so I'm not thinking about work. [W1B-009#27:1, social letters]

Because of a scarcity of suitable diachronic data, our survey of recent developments in spoken BrE is limited to five categories of the DSEU/DICE corpora: face-to-face conversations, telephone conversations, broadcast discussions, broadcast interviews and live commentaries (see Figure 6.5 and Table A6.4).

According to our limited corpus evidence, use of the progressive in spoken BrE has risen by more than 45%, i.e. even more sharply than in written BrE. Growth is significant ($p < 0.001$ or $p < 0.01$) in four of the five registers (face-to-face conversation, telephone conversation, broadcast discussions and sports commentaries). A lack of significant change in broadcast interviews may be attributable to the small number of words sampled (less than 6,000) in that genre.[15]

The still-changing frequency of the progressive in speech, especially in relatively unmonitored genres such as face-to-face conversation, may be a symptom of the construction continuing to grammaticalize, through an increase in its range of functions. Unfortunately the DSEU and DICE material became available to us too late to be able to conduct a detailed functional analysis of the progressives they contain. However, we do know that the present progressive, as in (10) and (11) above, is the realization *par excellence*

---

[15] At this stage we can only speculate as to the near doubling of instances in telephone conversations (from 68 cases in DSEU, 123 in DICE); for example, the relatively low cost of phone calls in the 1990s may have resulted in a less inhibited speech style.

in speech, and is becoming increasingly prevalent. It accounts for 85% and 90% of progressives in DSEU and DICE, respectively.

Since the corresponding figures in LOB and F-LOB are 36% and 43%, we may speculate that written BrE is increasingly shifting towards spoken norms of tense and aspect combination. One notable difference between our diachronic samples of spoken and written BrE is that in the former the progressive makes significant gains also in the past tense.[16] Past tense speech-reporting progressives such as the following are typical of narrative style in face-to-face and phone conversations, for instance, but as far as we are aware they are not yet widespread in printed BrE (other than reported speech):

(12) I *was talking* to this this guy at college and uhm he's really really really boring (DICE:C01:53)

See Biber *et al.* (1999: 1120–1) and McCarthy (1998: 159–62) on the prevalence of this construction in spoken English.

6.5 Present progressive active

Since the present progressive active is the most significantly changing part of the paradigm, we now examine it in more detail. Our investigation focuses on factors relating to the expansion of the present progressive in BrE primarily and (where time has permitted) AmE:

- quoted usage and contracted forms;
- stative verbs;
- subject type: generalized use of *you*, *we*, *they*;
- special uses: (i) attitudinal use with *always*, (ii) futurate use, (iii) interpretive use.

The selection of features is motivated by previous theories and empirical findings, as well as by the hypothesized process of colloquialization. One noteworthy category largely omitted is that of *Aktionsart*, which comprises features such as durative/non-durative, telic/atelic and stative/non-stative. For these features, vastly more problems of categorization arose in our corpus data than are to be found in textbook sentences. Indeed, the number of examples that defied satisfactory classification was too large for the results to be considered reliable (see further Smith 2005: 57–59). An exception was made in the case of stative/dynamic: many scholars (e.g. Aitchison 1991; Potter [2]1975) have commented on the growing importance of stative verbs with the progressive, and so an exploratory study in this area seemed justified.[17]

---

[16] Changes elsewhere in the paradigm in spoken BrE are statistically non-significant.

[17] Other features could have been examined, for example, animacy (Strang 1982; Hundt 2004a), agentivity (Ziegeler 1999; Hundt 2004a; Smitterberg 2005), clausal distribution (Nuñez

6.5.1   Quotations and contracted forms

As noted above, the situational characteristics of colloquial speech, whether genuine speech or speech represented in written form, are conducive to frequent use of the present progressive.[18] This begs the question of whether the recent frequency gains made by the progressive in written English are primarily the result of shifting modes of speech presentation.

Our analyses of the Brown family corpora indicate that the proportion of text within quotations (based on the presence of quotation marks) increased by a significant margin between the 1960s and 1990s (see section 11.3.6), and that most such quotations were of direct speech (rather than, for example, quoted writing). It is noteworthy, however, that use of the progressive outside speech quotations has increased at a faster rate than that within speech quotations, as Table A6.5 shows. The diachronic pattern is still overwhelmingly one of increased use. Thus, the spread of the progressive in written language is not simply an artefact of increasing use of quotations, but rather a reflection of a more general colloquializing tendency.

One salient feature of spoken and informal written language is the use of contracted forms. In the conversational part of the ICE-GB corpus, three-quarters of (active) present progressives occur with a contracted auxiliary or *not*. Yet in many types of published written text the use of contractions has – until recently – been largely proscribed, except in quotations in direct speech.

Table A6.6 gives the frequencies of present progressive contracted forms in BrE. They show a significant increase in Press and Fiction.[19] Only Learned writing remains resistant to their use.[20] These patterns become even more pronounced with the removal of instances in quotations (see Table A6.7).

When we compare these figures with contractions across *all* syntactic environments (Table A6.8), we find that rates of change are similarly high. In fact, the more general data shows that contractions of other auxiliaries (i.e. besides the progressive) are making a breakthrough even in Learned writing.[21] It appears that massive changes in the use of contractions in

---

Pertejo 2004; Wright 1995; Smitterberg 2005). Smith (2005) examines these categories in relation to BrE.

[18] For the rest of this chapter, 'present progressive' (without any further qualification) refers to the active form of present progressive only.

[19] Recent studies of British newspapers have shown a dramatic increase in frequency of contractions in all but the most conservative titles (such as *The Times*) in the late twentieth century (see, e.g., Krug 1996; Axelsson 1998; Westin 2002).

[20] The table conflates auxiliary contractions (e.g. *She's running*) with contractions of *not* (e.g. *She isn't running*), since the latter are very few in number. For further discussion of the increasing use of contractions, see section 11.3.1.

[21] Instances are mostly found in textbooks rather than scholarly articles (cf. Hundt and Mair 1999). For the general survey it has not been practicable to distinguish between quoted and non-quoted usage, or to provide a firm figure for potentially contractible forms that have not been contracted. LOB and F-LOB are not marked up in such a way as to enable automatic retrieval of quoted and non-quoted instances.

writing are a phenomenon in their own right, and have an automatic impact on any syntactic pattern involving auxiliaries – including the progressive.

6.5.2 Stative verbs

Strictly speaking, the progressive construction, which represents a situation as dynamic, cannot be used to describe a state, cf. *She is believing in God*. However, the distinction between static and dynamic situations is not sharply delimited, and in PDE there are a number of environments in which verbs that are normally stative can occur in the progressive. These include temporary states, as in (13); states changing by degrees, as in (14); and cases where the verb *BE* is used agentively, as in (15). In each case the situation no longer represents a pure state.

(13)   Mary's *living* in a flat in London.
(14)   The baby's *resembling* his father more and more every day. (Sag 1973: 88)
(15)   John's *being* silly.

Of all the factors suggested as contributing to expansion of the progressive in recent times, perhaps the leading contender is growing acceptability with stative verbs (see, e.g., Potter ²1975: 118–122; Aitchison 1991: 100). The comparative recency of the introduction of *BE* and *HAVE* as main verbs in the progressive – the first occurrences with *BE*, e.g. (16), occurring in the early nineteenth century – lends support to such intuitions.

(16)   You will be glad to hear . . . how diligent I have been, and *am being*. (Keats, *Letters* 137: p.357, July 1819; cited in Jespersen 1909–49: IV, 225)

Smitterberg's (2005) study of stative verbs in the progressive found a significant increase in their use across the nineteenth century. Our analysis follows previous proposals (notably Leech ³2004 and Huddleston and Pullum 2002) that divide verbs lending themselves to stative interpretation[22] into four semantic classes:[23]

(a) Perception and sensation (e.g. see, hear, smell, hurt, taste)
(17)   It's like she has been born again and we *are* now *seeing* the real Steffi. [F-LOB A22]
(18)   I think you*'re imagining* things. [F-LOB P06]

---

[22] The term 'stative verb' is largely a label of convenience, as many of the verbs in these categories allow both stative and dynamic interpretations.
[23] Verbs of bodily sensation (Leech ³2004: 27; Huddleston and Pullum 2002: 170) are omitted here, since the only member of this class to occur in the progressive in LOB/F-LOB is *feel* (as in *feel cold/ill*, etc.). This verb has been subsumed under the cognition/emotion/attitude category.

(b) Cognition, emotion, attitude (e.g. think, feel, forget, long, remember)

(19)   "And that will be much sooner than you*'re thinking.*" [LOB N28]

(20)   "Some secret part of me *is remembering* them." [Frown L07]

(c) Having and being (e.g. be, have, have to, cost, require)

(21)   They *are* now *having to* address issues some have avoided in the past. [F-LOB F14]

(22)   Nationalists [. . .] often think that the British Government *is being* deliberately slow and evasive. [LOB G73]

(d) Stance (e.g. sit, stand, lie, live, face)

(23)   And yet, accompanying our gratitude is the realization that we *are living* in a crucial time. [Brown H08]

(24)   Some trusts feel the campaign will not benefit them directly because they *are* already *standing* at a premium to net asset value. [F-LOB A25]

The total frequencies of verbs considered to lie around the border between stative and dynamic are presented in Table A6.9. Overall, the number of verb types and the frequency of tokens is slightly higher in the 1990s corpora, more so in AmE than in BrE. Despite slight increases among verbs of perception/sensation and having/being, however, the tokens are too few to enable firm conclusions to be drawn about diachronic change. Moreover, it is worth noting that, at least for BrE, the overall frequency of the same verbs in the present non-progressive has also increased.

Thus it seems that in printed English, use of the progressive with stative verbs did not contribute substantially to the growing use of the construction between the 1960s and 1990s, in either regional variety (see also Mair and Hundt 1995; Mair 2006b). This would appear to contradict the (largely intuitive) claims made by scholars such as Potter (²1975) and Aitchison (1991) cited above.

6.5.3   Subject type and reference

Pursuing the hypothesis of colloquialization further, we might expect the progressive to be increasingly used with first-person and second-person pronouns, since these are typical features of an involved, conversational style (see e.g. Chafe, 1982; Biber 1988). The LOB and F-LOB corpora show rather erratic fluctuations in pronoun usage with the progressive: first-person singular slightly increases (from 108 to 113 cases), and second person even decreases (from 111 to 105); see Table A6.10. Further, the distribution of first- and second-person pronouns as a whole across the BrE corpora roughly parallels their distribution in collocation with the progressive, and in the second person even shows a statistically significant decline: see section 11.3.6 for further discussion.

However, in terms of the reference of pronominal forms, there has been a noticeable increase in cases of present progressive where the subject pronoun has **generic reference**. Examples include:

(25) "The fun of portrait painting," she added, "is in trying to assess and understand the temperament of the people *you are painting*." [LOB C15]

(26) He said there had been previous vandal attacks but added: "When it gets to petrol bombing I think *you are talking* about a different category from breaking windows [. . .]" [F-LOB A34]

Generic *you* as subject increases from 19 instances (in LOB) to 35 (in F-LOB), while generic *we* increases from 31 cases in LOB to 80 in F-LOB. Although the numbers are small, they represent a significant proportional increase. Generic pronouns as subject can provide an equivalent, in informal usage, of the passive construction: compare (26) with . . . *a different category is being talked about*.

6.5.4   Special uses

We now turn to our category of 'special' uses of the progressive, i.e. where the meaning conveyed is not adequately covered by the aspectual notion of progressivity (see section 6.2). Included in the discussion are:

(a)   the **futurate use** of the progressive, i.e. present progressives with future time reference;

(b)   **expressive** or **attitudinal** functions of the progressive, i.e. those incorporating a high degree of subjective expression of the speaker/writer's attitude or evaluation of the situation (as opposed to the aspectual function of representing its temporal contour).

According to Killie (2004: 29), the only subjective (i.e. expressive or attitudinal) use of the progressive that can be identified with near certainty in corpus data is the *always*-type progressive.[24] As will be seen, our findings support this view. It seems nevertheless worthwhile to attempt an *approximation* to the frequency of less overt expressive uses, because these are another suspected growth area in the recent period (see, e.g., Charleston 1960; König 1995; Wright 1995; Hübler 1998; Kranich 2007). As a step in this direction

---

[24] Under the heading 'potentially experiential uses of the progressive' Smitterberg (2005) attempts to classify a much wider range of expressive uses than simply the *always*-type. Smitterberg readily admits, however, that his findings are provisional, because identifying such uses is highly subjective.

we present, besides the *always*-type progressive, an exploratory study of so-called *interpretive progressives* exemplified in (6) above.[25]

In describing these uses as 'special', we do not mean to imply that they are unconnected either synchronically or diachronically with progressive aspectuality (with its associated features of duration, situation in progress, temporariness, imperfectivity).

(a) Futurate use

English is rather untypical among the world's languages in having a 'futurate' progressive (cf. Bertinetto 2000: 588; Dahl 1985: 90), in which reference is made to a situation to be actualized in the future,[26] as in:

(27)   "Your Auntie Edie*'s coming in* for a cup of tea later." [LOB R02]

Because the actualization of the situation is in future rather than present time, this is sometimes treated as an anomalous, non-aspectual use of the progressive, i.e. lacking any connection with progressive aspect (see, for example, Huddleston and Pullum 2002: 171).

Information about the diachronic emergence of the futurate progressive is scant, although it was certainly available in EModE (Rissanen 1999: 223). Nesselhauf's (2007) recent study of the ARCHER corpus found a steady, significant increase in futurate progressives between the late eighteenth and the late twentieth centuries, with a more pronounced increase in AmE than in BrE. A less conclusive result – allowing even a possible decline – for futurate progressives in BrE in the nineteenth century is reported by Smitterberg (2005: 177). Differences of period and genre sampling in the respective corpora make it difficult to compare Nesselhauf's and Smitterberg's results directly, but there is agreement that the futurate progressive is consistently more frequent in informal, speech-based (or speech-like) genres.

We count as clearly futurate those cases where there is no evidence to suggest that the speaker views the actualization phase of an event as being (literally) under way at the time of utterance. In the clearest instances, the future time of the event's realization is specified by an adverbial expression, cf. (28) and (31), or it can be pragmatically inferred, cf. (29) and (30). In (29) Jed is unlikely to be sleeping at the time of speaking, and is almost certainly referring to plans or arrangements for sleeping in the coming evening.

---

[25] Smitterberg (2005) considers not only these two types but also those he calls 'potentially experiential' progressives, i.e. cases that have the *potential* to function experientially, based on the automated recognition of co-textual features. This approach seems promising, although it would seem necessary to combine it with close readings of the corpus data.

[26] A futurate use of the past progressive is also possible to indicate a past representation of a future event, as in the backshifted context of indirect speech and thought in (a):

(a) He stood watching the girl, wondering what *was coming* next. [Brown N05]

Such cases are considerably rarer than the futurate use of present progressives.

(28) "Your Auntie Edie's *coming in* for a cup of tea later." [LOB R02]

(29) The laughter sifted out of Jed's nostrils. "Where *am* I *sleeping?*" he said. [F-LOB K09]

(30) Finishing touches were this week being put to the programme for the visitors. Amersham estate agent and historian Mr. L. Elgar Pike, *is taking* the party on a history tour of the district by car. [LOB A42]

(31) "He's *coming* back tomorrow," she told him. [Frown L04]

In the Brown family corpora, clear-cut cases such as these are largely confined to news reportage and passages of direct speech in Fiction – see Tables A6.11 and A6.12.[27] Such cases are somewhat evenly balanced between the two BrE corpora, making it unlikely that the futurate use represents a source of continuing growth of the present progressive in BrE or AmE. Further evidence for this view is provided in a comparison of the futurate progressive with other expressions of future time – see Table A6.13 and Table A6.17, discussed in section 6.7.2 below.

There is, however, a sizeable number of present progressives – between 50 and 100 cases in each corpus – where it is difficult to say whether the speaker/writer envisages the event as already under way at the time of utterance. Such cases include characters in Fiction announcing their departure, cf. (32), or in media reporting, the actions of government agencies and other organizations, cf. (33) and (34).

(32) Frank straightened up his desk and went back out through the reception area. I'*m going* to the ranch, he said. [Frown K02]

(33) Timotei [. . .] *is introducing* a Facial Scrub to its skin care range. [F-LOB E34]

(34) However, for the present, this first Canadian Eskimo magazine is a wonderful accomplishment. To the continuing of it, the Department of Northern Affairs *is sparing* no effort or expense. [LOB F36]

A further source of confusion is suggested by linguists commenting on the conceptualization of the futurate use. Hirtle (1967: 95–96), Declerck (1991b: 67) and Williams (2002: 110), for instance, remark that the situations described by the verb can be construed as already 'in progress' at the time of utterance, in that part of the situation – plans, preparations, etc. – are already in train. On this interpretation, the futurate could be seen as a metonymic extension of the basic meaning of the progressive.

There is therefore some margin of error and/or ambiguity in the frequencies of futurate progressives, and their contribution to diachronic developments is difficult to estimate, although it is likely to be small.

---

[27] This probably reflects the extent to which news coverage includes events still to come, as well as events that have happened. The relatively high frequency of the futurate use in fictional dialogue is consistent with its distribution in ordinary spoken language: see section 6.7.

(b) Expressive use with always *and similar adverbials*
Where a clause in the progressive is modified by an adverbial such as *always,
continually, at all times, forever* or *constantly*, it usually functions hyberboli-
cally to convey an attitudinal nuance, such as condescension, annoyance or
amusement.

(35) "Husky young man", he said with mock distaste. "I imagine you*'re*
      always *battling* in school". [Brown Ko1]
(36) We *are* forever *being told* about increased competition from overseas
      once the Single market comes into being next year [. . .] [F-LOB B26]
(37) For starters, the stores *are* continually *wringing* excess costs out of
      the U.S. distribution system while squeezing price concessions out of
      suppliers. [Frown B10]

The *always*-type progressive dates back at least to Middle English (Jespersen 1909–49: IV, 191). Finding no significant change in the frequency of
the *always*-type progressive in his Corpus of Nineteenth-Century English
(CONCE), Smitterberg (2005: 214) concludes that it was already a mature,
highly 'integrated' feature of the language by Late Modern English.
    With respect to recent English, the Brown family corpora suggest a possi-
bly growing incidence of the *always*-type in published prose. The numbers
of clear occurrences found are: 10 in LOB, 19 in F-LOB, 5 in Brown and 9
in Frown. Although this represents a high rate of increase, the low number
of tokens suggests it would be unwise to attach much importance to it.

(c) Interpretive use
A growing number of linguists identify a use of the progressive they call
interpretive (or interpretative).[28] By this they mean that the clause containing
the progressive can be employed to interpret – or give meaning to – a
situation with which the addressee is assumed to be familiar, either because
it is mentioned explicitly, cf. (38) and (39), or inferrable from the context,
cf. (40).

(38) When Paul Gascoigne says he will not be happy until he stops playing
      football, he *is talking* rot.
(39) In joining the Euro we *might be giving away* our sovereignty.
(40) You*'re kidding*!

Some recent historical studies (e.g. König 1995; Wright 1995; Smitterberg
2005; Kranich 2007) suggest that the interpretive progressive has been growing in significance in Modern English. Smitterberg's (2005: 231) survey of
interpretive use in nineteenth-century BrE reports an increase from 3% to

[28] See, for example, König and Lutzeier (1973); König (1980, 1995); Ljung (1980); Wright
(1994, 1995); Fitzmaurice (2004); Bruyndonx (2001); Arnaud (2002); Huddleston and Pullum (2002); Kearns (2003); Smitterberg (2005).

5% of all progressives. Wright's analysis of EModE focuses on 'experiential' progressives, which are said to evoke the speaker's psychological stance and seem to largely overlap with the notion of interpretive use. Wright's study relates the functional development of the progressive directly to Traugott's (1989, 1995) influential theory on historical subjectification of meanings, i.e. that over time meanings of grammatical constructions become increasingly based in the speaker's subjective reasoning processes.[29]

Since the interpretive progressive is by no means universally recognized, it is worth pausing to examine how its proponents have characterized it. For convenience, we follow Ljung (1980) in calling the object of interpretation 'part A' (whether it is mentioned or simply understood) and the interpreting part (in the progressive) 'part B'. Between König (1980, 1995) and Ljung (1980), the following features have been proposed:

(a) the subjects in parts A and B are co-referential;
(b) A and B are construed as simultaneous: this and the previous feature together imply that the same underlying situation is being represented in both parts;[30]
(c) B redescribes A, giving it a deeper significance, e.g. by assigning illocutionary force;
(d) A and B appear in a syntactic frame, e.g. *In saying/doing A, X was (really) saying/doing B* (König 1980);
(e) the subjects of A and B are agentive: Ljung (1980) argues that it is generally only animate (human) behaviour that people are interested in and wish to interpret;
(f) B contains a speech-act (illocutionary) verb: this may help to identify the utterance as metalinguistic – a comment on another utterance.

Previous attempts (e.g. by König 1980 and Kearns 2003) to define interpretive progressives in terms of truth-conditions seem to be problematic. Treating (a) and (d), for instance, as essential conditions would rule out (41) and (42), respectively, which appear nevertheless to give the further-reaching significance of a given situation.

(41) "When it gets to petrol bombing I think you *are talking* about a different category from breaking windows [. . .]" [F-LOB A34]
(42) [. . .] anybody who believes that a reduction of £21 million will be achieved without loss of services and loss of jobs *is* clearly *living* in cloud cuckoo land. [F-LOB H18]

---

[29] In Wright's account there is no requirement for the clause in the progressive to interpret another (implicit or explicit) representation of a situation.
[30] There is some controversy among proponents of the interpretive progressive as to whether it is aspectual (conveying progressivity) or not. Buyssens (1968), König (1980) and Kearns (2003), for instance, argue that it is non-progressive, whereas Ljung (1980) deems otherwise.

It is probably more fruitful to consider interpretives in terms of prototypical characteristics than necessary and sufficient conditions. Even so, it is extremely difficult in a corpus analysis to apply these features in a consistent and non-arbitrary way. According to our most conservative estimate, based on cases clearly embodying these features, interpretive use of the present progressive has nearly doubled in frequency in BrE, from 52 cases in LOB to 97 in F-LOB (see Table A6.16).

However, it is important to point out two caveats. First, the number of cases in each corpus that defied clear classification was extremely high, far higher even than in the futurate use (approximately 200–300 in LOB and F-LOB). Second, it is unclear how far the notion of interpretation may be conveyed in clauses containing a *non*-progressive. Proponents of the interpretive progressive invariably reject or overlook such a possibility. Yet, some of the examples given so far could be considered to convey a similar force, albeit sounding archaic or formal: e.g. (38) above is recast as (43):

(43)   When Paul Gascoigne says he will not be happy until he stops playing football, he *talks* rot.

Thus despite some initial promise, it seems premature to conclude that interpretive progressives are a key factor in the spread of the present progressive. Clearly further research on the status of this alleged category is needed, taking both progressive and non-progressive forms into account on an equal basis.

6.6   The progressive passive

On the background to the progressive passive, the most recent innovation in the progressive paradigm, see section 6.3. At the level of overall frequencies, we have already identified significant differences between BrE and AmE usage of the progressive passive (see 6.4.1).[31] It is also noticeable that the *non*-progressive passive has declined significantly further in AmE than in BrE (see Chapter 7). This leads us to speculate that the diminishing use of progressive passives in that variety may be the result of a stronger prescriptive resistance in the United States to use of the passive in general.[32] Such a 'dampening effect' appears not to have been so powerful in BrE.

---

[31] Hundt (2004b) shows that this is not a recent divergence but a continuation of a development found in eighteenth- and nineteenth-century English.

[32] Hundt (2004b: 111) notes that usage guides in the United States do not single out the progressive passive for attack. On the other hand Elena Seoane (personal communication) comments that the strength of proscription against the passive in general is much higher in the US than in the UK.

Within BrE there is a clear difference between present tense usage – which has significantly expanded – and past tense usage – which has remained stable. More complex patterns, illustrated below, have remained extremely rare.

(44)   [. . .] for, if we first choose our time, a rare state in our stationary process will just as likely *be being approached* as *being departed from*. [LOB J18]

The relative scarcity of such combinations may be because they are perceived as cumbersome, particularly with the juxtaposition of *been* and *being* (see, e.g., Denison 1993; Fischer and van der Wurff 2006; and a similar case of *horror aequi* in section 9.2.1).

The present progressive passive in present-day BrE shows some interesting stylistic traits, which contrast with those of active present progressives in the preceding section. In the Brown family corpora, progressive passives rarely occur in contracted form or in quoted speech.[33] They are most prevalent in genres with an informational orientation, but particularly those pertaining to current affairs: for example, Press reportage and editorials, and trade or hobby magazines. A similar tendency can be seen in the BNC and ICE-GB corpora, where the highest-ranking genres include – besides news reportage and editorials – broadcast news, documentaries and discussions, press editorials, parliamentary debates and business letters. Examples include:

(45)   At the final party Amersham Inner Wheel will provide refreshments, and plans *are being made* for an exhibition of Scottish dancing. [LOB A42]

(46)   The importance of wind energy has been recognised by several governments and *is being* actively *encouraged* in Germany, the Netherlands and Denmark, where it now generates 2 per cent of electricity. [F-LOB B09]

(47)   I'm concerned that er people *are* not *being brought* to justice. [BNC HMG 37, spoken documentary]

The present-day distribution of the construction suggests a rather different picture from that of its beginnings. Most attestations in the eighteenth and nineteenth centuries are from informal rather than informational writings (see, e.g., Pratt and Denison 2000). Hundt's (2004b) data from ARCHER indicate that subsequently it became most prevalent in newspaper writing.

At the same time, the distribution of the main competitors of the progressive passive has also changed somewhat. We have already mentioned the dramatic decline of its chief (and still dominant) rival, the non-progressive passive. (Compare Figures 6.6 and 6.7 with Figures 6.8 and 6.9.) Up to the

---

[33] Fewer than 10 per cent of present progressive passives are in direct speech quotations; in the active, more than a third of cases are in quotations.

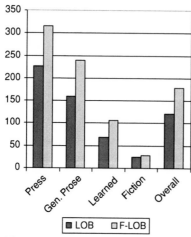

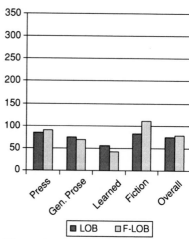

Figure 6.6 Present progressive passive in LOB and F-LOB: frequencies pmw

Figure 6.7 Past progressive passive in LOB and F-LOB: frequencies pmw

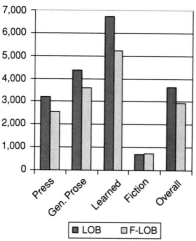

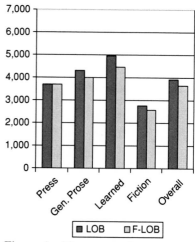

Figure 6.8 Non-progressive present passive in LOB and F-LOB: frequencies pmw

Figure 6.9 Non-progressive past passive in LOB and F-LOB: frequencies pmw

middle of the nineteenth century the passival construction (see sections 6.3, 7.1) was still strong, but since then the progressive passive has eclipsed it (see Hundt 2004b: 104; Smitterberg 2005: 128). In the late twentieth century the Brown family corpora yield not a single clear example of the passival. A more serious competitor nowadays is the active progressive with a generalized subject, which we observed in 6.5.3 to be gaining ground, especially in more colloquial usage.

6.7   The progressive in combination with modal auxiliaries

6.7.1   *Modal auxiliary* + be -ing

Patterns consisting of a modal + *be -ing* date back at least to Middle English (see Strang 1970: 208; Mustanoja 1960: 591; Fischer 1992: 255),[34] although frequent use with auxiliaries other than *will* and *shall* appears to have been a comparatively recent development. Smitterberg (2005: 134–5), for example, finds that the frequency of progressives with modal auxiliaries in CONCE is not only very low (65 occurrences in nearly one million words) but apparently in decline, most notably in the case of *will* + *be -ing*. Denison (1998: 145) meanwhile reports 'modest but inconclusive support' for expanding use of modal + progressive constructions in nineteenth-century writings.

Our findings for the late twentieth century suggest an expansion of modal + *be -ing* constructions in BrE, but relative stability in AmE. Taken *en masse*, these patterns in written BrE increase significantly ($p < 0.05$) between the 1960s and 1990s corpora (see Table A6.14), the most significant increase being in *will* + *be -ing* (see Tables A6.13 and A6.17). This general buoyancy is in contrast to a dramatic decline of almost all the modal auxiliaries in non-progressive environments (see Chapter 4). By contrast, the American data show barely any change in use of modal + *be -ing* (Table A6.15). The rate of use of *will* + *be -ing* is significantly lower in AmE than in BrE, and not significantly changing.

There is an interesting parallel between these findings and those of non-progressive and progressive forms of the passive construction (see section 6.6), which similarly show BrE 'trailing' AmE with respect to the former variant but developing independently with respect to the latter one. Once again it appears that in AmE declining use of a particular construction, in this case the modal auxiliary construction, has a 'dampening effect' on the frequency of its combination with the progressive.

6.7.2   Will be -ing

Will + *be -ing* in BrE merits closer investigation, because it has borne most of the recent increase of the pattern modal + *be -ing*. We shall compare its frequency profile with that of other expressions of future time, and also consider its semantic and pragmatic functions, which arguably could be added to the list of 'special' uses of the progressive discussed in section 6.5.4.

The frequency comparison in Table A6.13 indicates that *will* + *be -ing* is the only construction in BrE that has significantly increased out of the whole range of future expressions surveyed.[35] We have already reported (section

---

[34] Visser (1963–73: 2412) and Denison (1993: 383–4) argue that it is already attested in Old English.

[35] As mentioned above, futurate use of the simple present has not been included in the analysis.

6.5.4, (a) Futurate use) that the futurate use of the present progressive seems not to have advanced much in this period. In the last chapter (section 5.2) a similar observation was made on the progress of the BE *going to* future in written BrE. Meanwhile two other rival constructions, *shall* and BE *to*, have fared distinctly worse (see 4.1 and 5.2). *Shall* is now almost exclusively used with first-person subjects, and remains rare in construction with the progressive. Interestingly, the spread of *will* + *be -ing* is seemingly not due to its encroachment on the *will* + simple infinitive construction, as one might assume (cf. Declerck 1991a: 165). *Will* + simple infinitive not only dwarfs all other expressions, but remains very frequent in the same genres as *will* + *be -ing*, i.e. Press reportage and editorials.[36] One factor that may favour *will* + bare infinitive is a stylistic one. As Close (1988: 54) notes, it is often preferred where repetition of *will* + *be -ing* would sound jarring, cf. (48):

(48) He *will be taking part* in an international conference on the space project which *will* meet on January 30 in London. [LOB A03]

As to the uses of *will* + *be -ing*, two main types have been discussed in the literature:[37]

- Type 1: a regular use, as in (49), in which the speaker views the situation as being in progress at a reference time in the future;
- Type 2: a special use, as in (50), in which the future situation cannot be viewed as 'literally' in progress at reference time; it seems it must be viewed either as non-progressive, or as progressive only by a special interpretation.[38]

(49) When you reach the end of the bridge, I*'ll be waiting* there to show you the way. (Quirk *et al.* 1985: 216)

(50) "I*'ll be having* my baby in June!" (Adamczewski 1982: 175)

As well as being aspectually marked, Type 2 is often said to imply that the future event will happen independently of the will of anyone concerned (see, e.g., Samuels 1972: 57; Palmer [2]1990: 150; Leech [3]2004: 67; Huddleston and Pullum 2002: 172). Thus in (51), *I will not be taking part* is likely to come across as more tactful – less like a forthright refusal – than *I will not take part*, *I'm not going to take part*, etc.

---

[36] Presumably this can be attributed to a propensity in newspaper writing to refer to events in the future (as well as the past and the present).

[37] A third, much less common type is that of conveying epistemic judgements about situations in *present* time, as in '*Will* she still *be working* now?' [F-LOB N04]

[38] Scholars are divided on how to characterize the aspectual properties of what we call Type 2. Wekker (1976: 116), for example, describes this usage as 'progressive in form but non-progressive in meaning', Huddleston and Pullum (2002: 172) as 'perfective' and Leech ([3]2004: 67) as applying 'to a single happening viewed in its entirety'. Williams (2002) considers it to be an extended type of progressive, while Gachelin (1997) considers the whole construction to be aspectually neutralized. For discussion, see Smith (2003b).

(51)   WEDNESDAY, apparently, is National Vegetarian Day. I *will* not *be taking* part. [F-LOB B05]

Samuels (1972: 57), Declerck (1991a: 165) and Leech (³2004: 67) suggest this volition-disclaiming element has promoted the use of *will* + *be* -*ing* in PDE.

An analysis of *will* + *be* -*ing* in the BrE 1960s/1990s corpora suggests that Type 2 use is on the increase (see Table A6.17). Especially with first- and second-person subjects, as in (51), the motivation appears to be to disclaim volition. In other instances, however, notably with inanimate subjects, the future event is unlikely to be tinged with a volitional reading even if replaced by *will* + infinitive. The speaker's or writer's implication seems rather to be that the projected event will happen in the ordinary run of things, or that it has been determined in advance (Hirtle 1967: 109; Leech ³2004: 67; Huddleston and Pullum 2002: 172): see, for example, (52).

(52)   The bursary made all the difference and, since last summer, Lindsay's been the proud owner of a wooden clarinet. It *will be going* with her at Easter when she tours Germany with the Rutland Concert Band [. . .] And it *will be going* with her to Austria this year and to America in 1992. [F-LOB E23]

(53)   If Honda do provide me with a factory machine, I'*ll be competing* on a par with the top riders in the world. [F-LOB A41, reportage]

As with the futurate use of the progressive (section 6.5.4), the analysis is complicated by a high proportion of indeterminacy in the examples. It is difficult to assign a clear aspectual value to (53), for example, without the aid of a time specifier, such as *during the race*.

6.8   Summary and conclusion

The evidence from the Brown family points to a significant expansion of the progressive in BrE and AmE in the late twentieth century. The pattern of development is, however, highly variable across genres and across the paradigm. In both regional varieties shifts in frequency have been most conspicuous in the present progressive active. In two other parts of the paradigm there are signs of divergence between BrE and AmE, namely: (a) the progressive BE-passive; and (b) combinations of the progressive with a modal auxiliary, especially *will*. Only in BrE have these constructions expanded significantly. In AmE it seems that the general decline of modal auxiliaries and BE-passives (see Chapters 4 and 7, respectively) has been so overwhelming as to 'drag down' the usage of the progressive in combination with these structures. In their place AmE may be shifting towards alternatives such as active progressives with generalized subjects and the future with BE *going to*.

Closer examination of the present progressive active failed to identify any outstanding factor contributing to the increase. Contrary to what some scholars have supposed, stative verb use seems at best to be a minor player, especially in BrE. The same applies to the expressive uses with *always*, and to futurate progressives. A more promising growth area may be the so-called interpretive use. If we count only archetypal interpretives as described in previous literature, the frequency rises dramatically. However, this use is far from being well established, and unclear cases by far outnumber the clear ones.

The general patterns of development across AmE and BrE do not suggest one variety is exerting a clear influence on the other.[39] They do, however, provide partial support for the hypotheses of colloquialization and (to a limited extent) grammaticalization – for further discussion, see sections 11.2–3. Regarding colloquialization, the overall frequencies of the progressive in printed prose genres appear to be moving in the direction of speech-based or speech-like genres. The present progressive active, the key area of increase between LOB and F-LOB on the one hand, and Brown and Frown on the other, is the dominant pattern in conversational speech (see Figure A6.1 and Table A6.4; see also Biber *et al.* 1999: 462). Among present progressives, the growing incidence of contracted realizations across the Brown family further suggests a shift towards the norms of speech.

The spreading use of the progressive passive in BrE seems not to be connected to colloquialization.[40] This pattern does not have a close affinity with 'oral' or informal styles (witness its low rate of occurrence in quotations, in contracted forms and in genres such as conversation and letters). It is much more prominent in factually based, semi-formal genres such as newspaper editorials and broadcast discussions, which may suggest the media playing a role in its diffusion. In AmE on the other hand, a lack of growth of the progressive passive may be attributable to a more powerful decline of the passive in general – and this is arguably partly a result of a colloquializing 'anti-formal' tendency.

The short-term scope of our study makes it difficult to assess the extent of impact of grammaticalization. The expanding overall frequency of the progressive – whether calculated in terms of normalized text counts (per million words) or in relation to the non-progressive – suggests that it has been increasingly becoming conventionalized as a marker of aspectual and

[39] We have not considered here other contact varieties that may have influenced standard BrE. The fact that the progressive is generally more prevalent in the vernacular speech of western and northern parts of the British Isles – notably Ireland, Scotland and Wales (see e.g. Filppula 2002), as well as northern England – makes it plausible that migration and contact with speakers of these varieties has contributed to expanding use of the progressive in standard BrE. However, to provide evidence of such influence is beyond the scope of the present study.

[40] In its historical genesis, however, the progressive passive was a colloquial development (cf. Pratt and Denison 2000).

special functions. Although we have not witnessed new developments in the paradigm, it should be borne in mind that by the start of the twentieth century the English progressive already had a much more extensive paradigm than equivalent constructions in other languages.

The case for grammaticalization would probably be strengthened if we had observed frequency increases in the 'special' uses of the progressive. Each of these has a meaning beyond that of 'situation in progress' and arguably involves a more subjective assessment of the situation by the speaker (cf. Traugott 1989, 1995; Sweetser 1990). In the *always*-type, connotations of irritation, amusement and the like accompany the hyperbolic representation of a situation. In the case of the interpretive use, the progressive has apparently generalized its meaning range to express a subjectively based relational function (i.e. construing one representation of a situation in terms of another, thereby giving it added significance). The degree of subjectivity involved in the interpretive use is acknowledged in König's (1995: 164) comment: 'interlocutors may often be uncertain or even disagree about the truth or the appropriateness' of the interpretation. *Will + be -ing* has acquired the implication that the projected event is in keeping with what the speaker considers to be normal, and/or free of volition or intent. Yet, it is only with this last use that frequency gains between the 1960s and 1990s seem reasonably clear.

However, perhaps the most striking result of our enquiry into the reasons behind the increasing frequency of the progressive is a negative one: the syntactic and semantic factors which might have been expected to explain the expanding use of the progressive appear to account for only a small part of that overall increase. It is as if the use of the progressive is gaining strength under its own momentum, rather than being driven or dragged by other forces inherent in the language system. (For example, there are 300 more progressives in Frown than in Brown, and only a few of these are accountable in terms of 'special uses' and the like.) This is a matter to be further discussed in the last chapter – see section 11.7.

7   The passive voice

7.1   Introduction

This chapter focuses on passive and passive-like constructions, the central *be*-passive (1), the *get*-passive (2) and 'middles' or 'mediopassive constructions' (3):[1]

(1)   The book was sold.
(2)   The book got sold.
(3)   The book sold (well).

Another construction related to the *be*-passive is the passival, i.e. the active progressive use of a verb with passive meaning, as in *Thelonius Monk's ruminative 'Alone in San Francisco' is playing softly in the background* [BNC FBM 710]. The passival, however, is only a marginal construction in contemporary English, limited to a few verbs (like *do, play, ship, show*) and used slightly more frequently in AmE than in BrE (cf. Hundt 2004b). It is briefly discussed in connection with the progressive passive in the previous chapter.[2]

The passive is a gradient and prototypically structured category (cf. Svartvik 1966; Granger 1983: 106f.; Quirk *et al.* 1985: 167–71; Shibatani 1985: 821). This applies to *be* + V*ed* constructions on the one hand, but also on the other hand to the whole domain of 'passive voice' in English. In the following, we will very briefly define prototypical *be*-, *get*- and mediopassives, touching on a series of syntactic and semantic properties that have been discussed in more detail (and often controversially) elsewhere. References to these discussions are given in the frequent footnotes in this section.

---

[1]   On terminology used for the third type of voice alternation, see Hundt (2007: section 2.5). Occasionally, the term 'middle' is also used to refer to constructions like *we are agreed* or *you are mistaken* (cf. Jin 2002), which fall outside the scope of this chapter.
[2]   On the progressive passive in BrE and AmE, see further Smith and Rayson (2007); Hundt (2009b) surveys the use of the progressive passive in various inner- and outer-circle varieties of English. Other related (but non-passive) constructions are adjectival and verbal pseudo-passives (cf. Granger 1983: 109–113) – these will not be treated in this chapter. Statal passives are ambiguous between a passive and an adjectival reading (cf. Granger 1983: 114f.).

In the typical English *be*-passive, the affected (typically inanimate) patient of a corresponding active is moved to subject position (i.e. topicalized), the predicate is marked for voice and the agent is demoted to an optional *by*-phrase. *By*-agents are not an essential characteristic of *be*-passives. Text- or corpus-based analyses show that the majority of *be*-passives actually have no *by*-agent (cf. Jespersen 1924: 168; Svartvik 1966: 141; Givón 1993: 49; Kennedy 2001: 42f.; Biber *et al.* 1999: 477). Seoane (2006b: 372) provides evidence from the Helsinki corpus that the use of *by*-phrases in passives largely depends on the text types analysed (with informative texts having higher percentages of *by*-phrases than imaginative prose).

The *get*-passive and the mediopassive are less typical as passive constructions because they are both grammatically and semantically different from the *be*-passive. In the *get*-passive, a different copula-like verb[3] is used and more responsibility for the action expressed by the verb is assigned to the NP in subject position, as in *I ain't going to get caught like poor Mrs. Noah on the ark* [Frown K27].[4] Not surprisingly, therefore, *get*-passives have even fewer *by*-agents than *be*-passives (cf. Downing 1996: 193; Huddleston and Pullum 2002: 1441).[5] In mediopassives, voice is not marked in the verb phrase, as in *... a story that would not sell in America ...* [Frown G38];[6] instead, they usually require an additional element (adverb of manner, negation or modal modification). Even more responsibility for the action is assigned to the subject NP in mediopassives than in *get*-passives: a quality inherent in the subject either facilitates or hinders the process expressed in the verb. In other words, there is a cline of responsibility, ranging from the *be*-passive (with practically no responsibility for the process in the VP attributed to the subject NP) to the mediopassive (with even more responsibility attributed to the NP in subject position than in the *get*-passive).[7] Mediopassive constructions thus typically have modal meaning. Davidse and Heyvaert (2003:

---

3 Some grammarians refer to *get* as a passive auxiliary (cf. the section heading in Quirk *et al.* (1985: 160) which is qualified, however, by the following text). Strictly speaking, of course, *get* is not an auxiliary, as Jespersen (1909–49: IV, 110), Haegeman (1985) and Fleisher (2006: 227f.) point out. But it has developed into an alternative periphrastic option for the passive. In this chapter, the terminology introduced by Dixon (2005: 353) is used. For a discussion of the auxiliary(-like) status of passive *get*, see Denison (1998: 182).

4 On the responsibility of the subject in *get*-passives, see Chappell (1980), Collins (1996), Dixon (2005: 357), Downing (1996), Granger (1983: 192ff.), Lakoff (1971) and Sussex (1982). Dixon (2005: 359) points out that the semantics of the *get*-passive has been undergoing change and responsibility of the passive subject is no longer a requirement.

5 For a succint overview of the differences between the *be*- and the *get*-passive, see Meints (2003: 124f.).

6 This may also be the reason why the mediopassive is not always treated in the same chapter as the *be*- and the *get*-passive. Dixon (2005), for instance, has a separate chapter on 'promotion to subject' that deals with mediopassive constructions. This may make the range of phenomena covered under the heading more inclusive (see Yoshimura and Taylor 2004: 316). Unlike Yoshimura and Taylor, however, we would not extend the scope of the mediopassive construction to include examples without an implicit agent (such as *I don't travel well*).

7 For a more fine-grained analysis of the semantics of mediopassives into facility-, quality-, feasibility-, destiny- and result-oriented types, see Heyvaert (2003: 134–7).

71) also point out this inherently modal character of the mediopassive construction:

> What typifies this construction is the non-agentive *letting-function* of its Subject in the process... We have stressed that the letting notion is modal in nature... and arises from the constructional link between a non-agentive Subject and an active VP.

What all three constructions have in common is that they contribute to the detransitivization of the clause. They further allow writers/speakers to topicalize non-agent NPs.

As far as diachronic developments in the twentieth century are concerned, the *be*-passive has been said to be decreasing in both AmE and BrE (cf. Leech and Smith 2006: 194).[8] A curious exception to the hypothesis that the passive is decreasing can be found in *Webster's Dictionary of English Usage* (1989: 720): 'In spite of generations of textbooks, use of the passive has increased....'

The *get*-passive as an informal (colloquial) variant is likely to have increased, as Barber (1964: 135) suggests: '*get* is used for forming a passive, as *he got hurt* and *you'll get hurt* (not new usages, but ones which are spreading)'. Weiner and Labov (1983: 43) even claim that a shift to the *get*-passive appears to be one of the most active grammatical changes taking place in English. An increase in *get*-passives would be plausible both as part of the ongoing grammaticalization of the construction and also as a result of the increasing colloquialization of written English (cf. sections 1.2, 11.3). The mediopassive, though a much more marginal member of the passive domain, is also said to have increased (cf. Strang 1970: 153; Hundt 2006: 169; Fischer and van der Wurff 2006: 170). Indirect evidence of an increase in mediopassives comes from Visser's (1963–73: §168–9) list of attested mediopassive constructions. The frequency of examples in his data increases from one century to the next.

As far as diachronic developments are concerned, we can assume that the mediopassive construction has also increased in the course of the twentieth century and is now a productive syntactic pattern, probably more so in text types like advertising than in everyday spoken interaction (cf. Hundt 2006, 2007).

This brings us to previous findings and hypotheses on the distribution of the passive across different text types. *Be*-passives are most frequently used

---

[8] This can be seen as the reversal of an earlier spread of the passive from the fifteenth century onwards (cf. Taavitsainen and Pahta 2000). Oldireva Gustafsson (2006) shows that the nineteenth century is a period in the history of English when the use of the *be*-passive in scientific writing is stable.

in academic writing (25% of all finite verb phrases);[9] they are moderately frequent in journalistic writing and least frequent in conversation (2% of all finite verb phrases) (Biber et al. 1999: 476).[10] The authors attribute the relatively frequent use of the passive in academic prose to the Western scientific tradition that requires researchers to detach themselves objectively from their subject of observation. As Oldireva Gustafsson (2006: 133) puts it, 'scientific writings have generally been taken to constitute a semiotic space that is associated with a depersonalized tone of discourse' (cf. also Ding 2002; Seoane and Loureiro-Porto 2005: 107; Seoane and Williams 2006: 256f.). Dixon (2005: 355) criticizes this view and points out that passives are used 'to give an illusion of total objectivity, whereas in fact the particular personal skills and ideas of a scientist do play a role in his work, which would be honestly acknowledged by using active constructions with first person subject'. In press language, the passive is said to be used for economic reasons, e.g. if the agent is easy to infer from the context or uninteresting (see Biber et al. 1999: 477).

The reverse holds for the *get*-passive which, overall, is less frequently used than the *be*-passive, but more frequently in spoken than in written texts (Biber et al.: 476). 'Even in conversation, the *get* passive accounts for only about 0.1% of all verbs, and so is even less common than *be* passives' (p. 476), a finding that is corroborated by Johansson and Oksefjell (1996: 69), who found that the *be*-passive was used more frequently than the *get*-passive even in spoken data. Stubbs (2001: 164f.) attributes this to the non-neutral (adversative) semantics of the *get*-passive.[11]

From this short sketch of previous research, the following hypotheses emerge:

(i) *Overall frequencies:* we expect that the *be*-passive is decreasing whereas the *get*-passive and the mediopassive are being used more frequently.

---

[9] Ding (2002: 143) reports research that found between 53% and 75% passive constructions in scientific texts, depending on whether the count was based only on transitive verbs (higher relative frequency) or included intransitive and linking verbs (lower frequency). The higher frequency compared with Biber et al. (1999: 476) might be due to the inclusion of non-finite verb phrases. Seoane and Loureiro-Porto (2005: 108) found frequencies ranging from 66.4% in BrE scientific texts from the early twentieth century to 46.4% in AmE academic writing from the late twentieth century. They calculated the frequency of passive constructions on the basis of finite active and passive transitive VPs. Percentages of passives (in academic texts) thus vary greatly, depending both on the definition of the variable, the regional variety and the diachronic dimension.

[10] A similar propensity for academic texts to feature the passive voice emerges from Francis and Kučera (1982: 554). Corpus linguistics has thus been able to substantiate the view expressed in many style manuals (e.g. Burchfield 1996: 576; *Webster's Dictionary of English Usage*, 1989: 721) of the passive as a feature typical of scientific English.

[11] On the semantics of the *get*-passive, see also Chappell (1980), Collins (1996), Downing (1996), Granger (1983: 192ff.), Hübler (1992), Lakoff (1971) and Sussex (1982); on the possible connection between the semantics of the *get*-passive and its grammaticalization from an inchoative construction, see Fleisher (2006: 249f.).

(ii) *Variation across genres and styles:* we expect *be*-passives to occur particularly frequently in scientific texts and mediopassives in advertisements; *get*-passives are informal variants of the *be*-passive and therefore expected to occur more frequently in informal genres and spoken texts.

In the following, data from the Brown family of corpora will be used to test the hypotheses on the diachronic development and distribution across text types of the *be*- and the *get*-passive in the second half of the twentieth century. For the mediopassive, additional evidence comes from a manually analysed diachronic corpus of advertising copy. Additional hypotheses that apply to individual constructions (e.g. the frequency of *by*-agents in the *be*-passive or the semantics of the *get*-passive) will also be addressed in the relevant sections below.

7.2 The *be*-passive

Figure 7.1 gives a first approximation of the diachronic development of the passive in BrE and AmE. The core elements of the query are the verb *be* followed by a verbal past participle, with optional elements allowed in-between.[12]

The data in Figure 7.1 indicate a clear decline in the use of the passive voice, both in BrE (−14.0%) and AmE (−28.2%), but BrE is lagging behind AmE in this development, as the frequencies in the F-LOB corpus have now approximately reached those of the Brown corpus. This regional difference may well have to be attributed to the tradition of statements on the relative merit of active and passive voice in American style guides:

The active voice is usually more direct and vigorous than the passive ... This is true not only in narrative concerned principally with action but in writing of any kind. Many a tame sentence of description or exposition can be made

---

[12] The search strings for the finite be-passives were as follows: for the present simple: [pos="VAB[MRZ]"] [pos="R.*|MD|XX"]{0,4} [pos="AT.*|APPGE"]? [pos="JJ.*"]? [pos="PPH1|PP.*S.*|PPY|NP.*|D.*|NN.*"]? [pos="R.*|MD|XX"]{0,4} [pos="VVN| VVDN|VVHN"]; for the past simple: [pos="VABD[RZ]"] [pos="R.*|MD|XX"]{0,4} [pos="AT.*|APPGE"]? [pos="JJ.*"]? [pos="PPH1|PP.*S.*|PPY|NP.*|D.*|NN.*"]? [pos="R.*|MD|XX"]{0,4} [pos="VVN|VVDN|VVHN"]; for the present perfect: [pos="V.H[oZ]"] [pos="R.*|MD|XX"]{0,4} [pos="A.*"]? [pos="J.*"]? [pos="PPH1| PP.*S.*|PPY|NP.*|D.*|NN.*"]? [pos="R.*|MD|XX"]{0,4} [pos="V.BN"] [pos="R.*| MD|XX"]{0,4} [pos="VVN|VVDN|VVHN"]; for the past perfect: [pos="V.HD"] [pos="R.*|MD|XX"]{0,4} [pos="A.*"]? [pos="J.*"]? [pos="PPH1|PP.*S.*|PPY|NP.*| D.*|NN.*"]? [pos="R.*|MD|XX"]{0,4} [pos="V.BN"] [pos="R.*|MD|XX"]{0,4} [pos="VVN|VVDN|VVHN"]; for the modal: [pos!="TO"] [pos="V.BI"] [pos="R.*| MD|XX"]{0,4} [pos="VVN|VVDN|VVHN"]; for the modal perfect: [pos="VM"] [pos="R.*|MD|XX"]{0,4} [pos="A.*"]? [pos="J.*"]? [pos="PPH1|PP.*S.*|PPY|NP.*| D.*| NN.*"]? [pos="R.*| MD| XX"]{0,4} [pos="V.HI"] [pos="R.*| MD| XX"]{0,4} "been"%c [pos="R.*|XX|MD"]{0,4} [pos="VVN| VVDN|VVHN"]; for the subjunctive: [pos="V.Bo"] [pos="R.*|MD|XX"]{0,4} [pos="A.*"]? [pos="J.*"]? [pos="PPH1| PP.*S.*|NP.*|D.*|NN.*"]? [pos="R.*|MD|XX"]{0,4} [pos="VVN|VVDN|VVHN"].

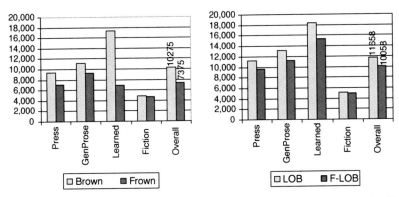

Figure 7.1 Finite non-progressive *be*-passives in the Brown family of corpora: frequencies per million words*

* Based on automatic tagging. For raw frequencies, see Table A7.1

[sic!] lively and emphatic by substituting a transitive in the active voice for some such perfunctory expression as *there is* or *could be heard*. (Strunk and White ³1979: 18)

The focus in this section is on non-progressive finite *be*-passives. In other words, non-finite passives of the type *The strength needed to pull a cart . . .* , *Left in a state of unrest, . . .* or *There is a lot to be said for . . .* were not included in our analysis.[13] These could easily be excluded by our definition of the search string. On closer analysis, however, some adjectival uses of participles were still included in the files. The following illustrate such patterns that would have to be manually excluded to obtain more accurate figures:

(4) Unlike many commercial articles, this chair *is* solidly *built* and capable of withstanding the heavy handling of the most destructive youngster. [LOB E04]
(5) The place *was deserted*. [F-LOB N13]
(6) But investors might have other ideas and may, like BAe, choose to take what *is left* of their money and run. [F-LOB A25]

Other non-passive uses included fixed phrases, such as *as far as x is concerned* (7) or *be* + past participle constructions that replace reflexive constructions (8):

(7) . . . the water supplied by the board was of 100 per cent purity so far as this test *was concerned*. [LOB E28]
(8) . . . in fact, this is a matter with which he *is* not directly *concerned*. [LOB G57]

---

[13] The first (without *be*) are 'bare' passives in the terminology of Huddleston and Pullum (2002: 1430).

As a rule, however, POS tagging (which distinguishes verbal and adjectival participles) generally ensured that passives were separated from non-passives by our search string. This can be illustrated with identical lexical strings that have different functions. In (9), *devoted* is used as a passive participle, whereas in (10) its function is clearly adjectival.

(9)   ... if resources *were* not *devoted* to purposes like the exhibitions, the money spent on the school would simply save the ratepayers from the education rate, ... [F-LOB J37]

(10)   Rose's friends believed that she *was devoted* to Grace, [...] [F-LOB G23]

Only (9), but not (10), was retrieved by our search routine for passive constructions in the tagged F-LOB corpus. While a comprehensive qualitative analysis of the *be* + verbal participle strings would have been beyond the scope of this study, the analysis of subsets of data (every fortieth instance) revealed that the precision of the search string for retrieving passives was well above 80% (around 85% in F-LOB and 83% in LOB). The data in Figure 7.1 can therefore reliably be taken to indicate the general development.

In terms of qualitative changes, a look at agentless *be*-passives and those with an agent *by*-phrase is of interest. One function of the passive is, after all, to defocus the agent role (cf. Shibatani 1985). If there is pressure to use the passive less frequently because of stylistic reasons (see below), those instances where the agent is known and made explicit are more likely to be rephrased in the active voice. We might therefore expect a decrease (in relative terms) of *by*-agents in *be*-passives. To test this hypothesis, we analysed subsets of passives from the Brown family of corpora.[14] Surprisingly, the relative frequency of passives with an overt agent increased from 11.8% in LOB to 13.4% in F-LOB. In Brown, the proportion of passives with an overt agent is higher than in both LOB and F-LOB at 18.6%, but in Frown it has dropped to 14.7%. The decline of the *be*-passives thus has different effects in BrE and AmE. In AmE, the proportion of *by*-agents declines with the overall recession of finite *be*-passives. In BrE, it leads to a relative increase of passives with *by*-agents over time. The relative increase in *by*-agents in our British data might be explained in terms of the text linguistic function of passives. They are one of the devices in English that can be used to rearrange the linear order of constituents (i.e. promoting non-agent roles to topic/theme position). In that case, the *by*-agents occur as comments/rhemes. A decrease of stylistically motivated *be*-passives may thus have had an increase of commenting *by*-agents as an indirect spin-off (in

---

[14] These were obtained from an analysis of every twentieth concordance line of the data summarized in Figure 7.1. The raw frequencies were as follows: LOB – 295 constructions, 246 passives (29 with *by*-agents); F-LOB – 253 constructions, 217 passives (29 *by*-agents); Brown – 260 constructions, 236 passives (44 with *by*-agents); Frown – 210 constructions, 190 passives (28 with *by*-agents).

absolute terms, the frequency of *by*-agents has remained stable from LOB to F-LOB). The question is, however, whether the defocusing of the agent is really the reason why the relative frequency of overt *by*-agents increases at the same time that the overall use of the passive declines. Alternatively, what might be at work here is the fact that in passives with agents, the agent is given focal salience (the motivation for the agentful passive being largely to assign rhematic prominence, i.e. end-focus and end-weight, to the agent). In this case, the replacement of the agentful passive by a corresponding active would hardly ever be a realistic option. This is also what the following examples from our corpora suggest:

(11) The girls are kept booked and moving *by several agents, notably voluble, black-bearded Murat Somay, a Manhattan Turk who is the Sol Hurok of the central abdomen.* [Brown B24]

(12) [. . .] AIDS was put in Africa *by whites in the World Health Organization to attempt genocide.* [Frown B09]

(13) The Jurassic rocks within the Vale of Wardour are affected *by a series of gentle rolls, trending north-west to south-east, which disappear under the transgressive lower Greensand and Gault without affecting them.* [LOB J11]

(14) Within minutes, however, the happy family idyll is shattered *by a forest fire in which the wife and children, plus the family dog, die . . .* [F-LOB C06]

In other words, the relative frequency of passives with *by*-agents increases because there is no competing structure they could be changed into.

With respect to distribution across genres, the data in Figure 7.1 show that the decline is more substantial in academic prose (where it starts off from the highest level) than in Fiction (which has the lowest figures in the 1960s corpora). On the basis of evidence from the early twentieth century (including academic texts), Seoane and Williams (2006) have shown that passives were still more frequent in scientific writing than active transitive VPs at the beginning of the century in both BrE and AmE. The decrease of passives in academic writing in their data occurs in the second half of the century, the period also covered by the Brown family of corpora. They define the variable slightly differently from the way it has been defined in this study: the frequency of central *be*-passives is compared to the frequency of active transitive constructions with overt objects rather than simply measuring the *be*-passives in relation to corpus size. Their results show that in AmE academic prose, active transitive VPs are now more frequent than passive VPs (see also Seoane 2006b: 193).

One explanation of this change might be that we are seeing the effect in language change of a sustained attack in usage manuals on the passive as a clumsy and awkward construction. The construction has also been part of the crusade of the plain English movements in both Great Britain and the US (cf. McArthur 1992: 785ff.). Peters (2004: 411) points out the usefulness of the passive in (objective) academic writing but also mentions that 'the Council of Biology Editors in the US has pushed for more direct, active reporting of scientific observations since the 1960s, encouraging their members to counter the ingrained habit of using passive verbs'.[15] Seoane and Williams (2006: 260f., 267) found that there was a shift in scientific style manuals around the 1980s which started attacking superfluous passives; this may have contributed to the ongoing decline of the passive. The impact of style manuals is likely to have been reinforced most recently by automated grammar checkers in word processing software, especially in AmE (though, obviously, this is probably not something that has had an immediate effect on the texts of our corpora).

A related factor that might have contributed to the marked decline of *be*-passives in academic prose could be a change in writing traditions that attempt to make the scientist more visible; supporting evidence of such a process would come from an increased use of first-person pronouns like *I* and *we*. Hundt and Mair (1999) have observed an increase in first-person pronouns and relate it to the ongoing colloquialization that can, to a certain extent, even be observed in academic writing. It is thus not surprising that a grammatical construction that is associated with the written mode is losing ground as written genres (foremost among them newspaper writing) are developing towards a more oral style. However, Seoane and Loureiro-Porto's (2005) more detailed study of ongoing colloquialization in scientific English did not produce evidence of an overall trend towards more colloquial patterns in this particular genre in the second half of the twentieth century.

We have shown that the dramatic decrease in the use of passives does not seem to be a symptom of the increasing colloquialization of scientific English, since other features typical of the oral varieties of English do not increase in frequency in similar proportions, nor do literate features seem to decrease to yield a more colloquial style. (Seoane and Loureiro-Porto 2005: 115)

Leech (2004: 73), in contrast, refers to the decline in the passive construction as a 'negative manifestation of colloquialization' but still an aspect of collo-quialization. Instead, the change can be seen as part of a movement towards more democratic (or more personal) writing, particularly in academic circles: '... the decay in the use of the passives also seems to derive from a reaction against the detached and alienating style characteristic of nineteenth-century and early-twentieth-century scientific discourse' (Seoane and Williams 2006: 268). An extremely dense use of passive VPs is attested in a text from category D (religious writing):

[15] For the discussion about indirect and direct, 'active' styles of writing in scientific discourse, see Mair (2006b: 191f.).

(15)   Lest it *should be thought* that what *has been said is intended* to belittle or
diminish the divinity of Jesus, [...]. [F-LOB D04]

But *be*-passives are obviously not restricted to formal usage; they may combine with informal verbs, as the following example from F-LOB shows,
where *nick* is used in the sense 'arrest':

(16)   [...] racially harassing Golliwog, the woman policeperson told him.
Golly! Noddy exclaimed. Right. You*'re nicked* as well. [F-LOB R05]

Seoane and Williams (2006: 262) observed an increase in passives in prescriptive legal texts (laws, directives and regulations) in their corpora. A change
like this would be obscured by the presentation of data in Figure 7.1 which
gives the combined figures for General Prose (including, among other genres,
legal writing). However, even a look at category H (miscellaneous) which –
among other texts – also contains government reports and legal writing,
would not be suitable to verify Seoane and Williams' results as only two text
units in category H would fall under the heading of 'prescriptive legal texts'
(H13 and H14).[16]

In the early seventeenth and eighteenth century, a combination of the
be-passive with the perfect was still avoided (Denison 1998: 183). In our
twentieth-century data, the proportion of *be*-passives that combine with the
present perfect or past perfect has remained stable at around 10% (10.7%
and 10.6%, respectively, in LOB and F-LOB). The earlier avoidance of a
combined perfect passive most likely has to be attributed to the fact that
auxiliary *be* at the time served the double duty of forming both passives
and perfect constructions with certain verbs (mainly verbs of motion). In
the twentieth century, this is no longer an issue, which may account for the
stability observed in the LOB and F-LOB data.

We noted above that the decline of the *be*-passive was least marked in
Fiction, the genre with the lowest figures in the 1960s corpora. One possible
explanation for this finding might be the fact that this subsection of our
corpora contains a fair amount of fictional dialogue. We therefore suspected
that the frequency of passive constructions in spontaneous speech was already
low in the 1960s and has remained that way. Thus, the decline of the *be*-
passive is likely to be a change that is exclusively encountered in formal
written English. For verification of this hypothesis in spoken BrE, we turned
to the evidence available in the DCPSE. To keep the amount of data within
manageable bounds, only parts of the DCPSE were searched (a total of
approximately 60,000 words each for the early 1960s and 1990s).[17] The
results confirm our hypothesis: at 40.2 (1960s) and 44.2 (1990s) per 10,000

[16] What is more, there is a decrease from 1,013 cases of *be* + verbal participle in category H of
LOB to 880 in F-LOB.
[17] For a table with information on the composition of this subcorpus, see Table A7.2.

words (246 and 255 occurrences, respectively), the use of finite *be*-passives is stable in spontaneous spoken English.

7.3   The *get*-passive

The passive with *get* is a relatively recent innovation. The earliest attestation in the ARCHER corpus is, in fact, from the end of the seventeenth century,[18] but the pattern only becomes more frequent by the end of the eighteenth century (cf. Hundt 2001).

Though a relative newcomer, the passive with *get* is fully grammaticalized; some web-based examples (Mair 2006a: 361) show that it can now even combine with lexical *get* (a usage that remains unattested in our small corpora and even the BNC):

(17)   Its one of those deals where its either going to be the dragon that *gets got* ... (quoted from Mair 2006a: 361)
(18)   There's no sense of suspension of disbelief, no suspense of any kind and so it's just a case of who *gets got* next. (p. 361)
(19)   The most entertaining moments in his docos are when he *gets got* back. (p. 361)

As was the case with *be* + Ved-constructions, not all combinations of *get* and a past participle are instances of the passive.[19] In some instances, the participle clearly functions as an adjective (e.g. *He got so confused that he no longer knew what to do*). This type of construction is also referred to as an inchoative *get*-construction. But the difference between the verbal and the adjectival interpretation of the participle is not always clear-cut.[20] A sentence like *The channel got blocked* could be analysed as a passive with *block* as the lexical verb. Alternatively, it could be given a relational reading with *get* as a copular verb and the past participle functioning as an adjective (i.e. 'the channel *became* blocked').[21] We therefore distinguished between these three possibilities: passive constructions (20), relational constructions with a participial adjective (21) and ambiguous cases (22):

---

[18] On possible earlier attestations, see Fleisher (2006: 227).
[19] Potter (²1975: 133), who points out an increase in the use of *get* + past participle, does not, however, distinguish between passive and other uses of the construction. His main concern seems to be with a general increase of *get* rather than the *get*-passive.
[20] Historically, *get*-passives developed from inchoative *get*-constructions, as Fleisher (2006) convincingly shows.
[21] See Huddleston and Pullum (2002: 1441) on the disambiguation of verbal and adjectival interpretations, or Fleisher (2006: 229).

(20) a. [...] they'll promptly *get snapped up* by another industry, [...] [LOB A12]

  b. Charles Burke *got turned down* by Dartmouth [...] [Brown A30]

  c. [...] slightly fewer women drivers, agreed with the statement that if they drove carefully after drinking they were not likely to *get caught* by the police. [F-LOB H10]

  d. The WIC (Women, Infants and Children) program that provides vital nutrition to poor pregnant women and their babies would *get zapped* by Bush. [Frown B19]

(21) a. So he started instead what he called a Country Club [...] where they could go and *get drunk* when they *got tired* of looking at the wild animals. [LOB K29]

  b. *Get pig-drunk*, that's what he wants. [Brown K24]

  c. "You can *get* so *wrapped up* in making films, he laments [...] [F-LOB E35]

  d. [...] "he got savage and I *got scared*." [Frown P27]

(22) a. Depends on whether I *get bored* or not. [LOB P07]

  b. The counters rode through the pasture countin' each bunch of grazin' cattle, and drifted it back so that it didn't *get mixed* with the uncounted cattle ahead. [Brown F35]

  c. Worst of all it was totally, impractical for cooking and no one could use it without *getting burnt*, least of all Amy. [F-LOB N06]

  d. Shorenstein said the meetings Monday were designed to "*get acquainted*" with Shinn and determine the extent of his commitment to the Giants. [Frown A17]

Passives typically have eventive interpretations, may be accompanied by a prepositional *by*-phrase denoting the agent role (all examples in 20)[22] and typically do not denote lasting states (unlike 22c and 22d, for instance). Instances with a degree adverb (21c) or some other kind of premodification (21b), on the other hand, are clearly adjectival. Coordination with another adjective makes the adjectival reading more likely for (21d). An incipient change of state, as in (23), also favours the interpretation as a relational (non-passive) construction.

(23) My sister and I were alone for so long I began to *get frightened*. [Frown L22]

In a lot of grammar books and style manuals, *get married* is treated as a passive construction (cf. Biber *et al.* 1999: 481;[23] Peters 2004: 229). We

---

22 An external agent may also be implied in the context, as in the following example, which is also clearly a passive: *If the people whom we were trying to 'civilize' didn't want to get 'civilized', we went out and 'civilized' them anyway!* [Frown F12]

23 Some other participles that are said to frequently occur in the *get*-passive are *involved* and *stuck*, again forms that are more likely to be used with an adjectival than a verbal function.

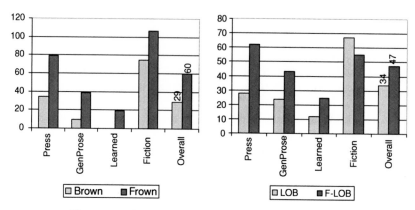

Figure 7.2 *Get*-passives (all forms) in the Brown family of corpora: frequencies per million words*

* For raw frequencies, see Table A7.3 in Appendix III

followed Huddleston and Pullum (2002: 1441) in classifying it as adjectival when used without a *by*-phrase.[24] Instances of idiomatic patterns like *get used to*, *get rid of*, *get fed up with* or *get started* were not included in the counts.

A search in the Brown family of corpora for all instances of *get* followed by a past participle, and rigorous post-editing of the concordances, produced the results shown in Figure 7.2.[25] The data in the figure suggest that the *get*-passive is an extremely rare option (the *be*-passive is about 400 times as frequent as the *get*-passive). Despite its overall *in*frequency compared with the *be*-passive, the data in Figure 7.2 verify that the *get*-passive is being used slightly more frequently in the 1990s than in the 1960s – clearly in AmE, and probably in BrE.[26] In AmE, the frequency of *get*-passives has even doubled from the 1960s to the 1990s. In other words, AmE is again in the lead of an ongoing change. Fiction writing is the genre that is the most innovative one, academic prose the most conservative, with Press and General Prose occupying the middle ground.

As far as the semantics of the *get*-passive is concerned, the slight increase from the 1960s to the 1990s has not resulted in a marked shift towards a more neutral meaning. The majority of *get*-passives are still adversative (see Figure 7.3). On the contrary, the relative frequency of adversative *get*-passives has even increased slightly.

[24] *Married* in *They are getting married at the weekend* is considered adjectival rather than verbal because it denotes a change of state and thus is similar to *get dressed*, *get changed*, *get shaved*, which are also adjectival (though non-gradable) if used without a *by*-phrase. Huddleston and Pullum (2002: 1441) also note the close similarity of *married* and *engaged*, which is always adjectival.

[25] Different definitions of the variable account for differences between the results reported here and in previous research (cf. Hundt 2001: 87; or Mair 2006b: 357). A much wider definition of the *get*-passive was used, for instance, in Smith and Rayson (2007).

[26] The change in BrE is below the level of statistical significance.

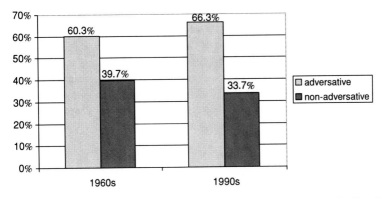

Figure 7.3 Semantics of the *get*-passive in the Brown family of corpora (based on pooled frequencies for the two subperiods)

The following examples from our corpora illustrate the typical adversative semantics of the *get*-passive:

(24)   Did they know how wealth from over-large estates *gets misused*? [LOB G11]
(25)   This time last year it was evident that the Scottish football team would *get gubbed* in the World Cup, having qualified and been gubbed in the first round of the finals many times before. [F-LOB F29][27]
(26)   . . . a sailor returns, unrecognized, and *gets done in* by his wife. [Brown C07]
(27)   We've been through too much together to *get killed* now [Frown N17]

The *get*-passive may also have non-adversative, neutral semantics (28) and can even be used with positive (29) connotations, but these are not beginning to make a major contribution to the neutralization of the semantics of the *get*-passive.

(28)   . . . if people are to learn to live together and *get trained* to do things well, . . . [LOB G60]
(29)   [. . .] those who deserve rewards *get rewarded* appropriately [F-LOB E25]

The non-neutral semantics of the *get*-passive is one of the reasons why it is not likely to replace the *be*-passive in the near future. In writing, the *get*-passive additionally still encounters prescriptive resistance (cf. Johansson and Oksefjell 1996; Smith and Rayson 2007).

ICE-GB yields a total of 55 *get*-passives, of which the large majority (46) are from the spoken part. In spoken BrE, the *get*-passive is used with a

---

[27] Note that adversative meaning may also combine with the *be*-passive (in the second part of the sentence, the same verb is construed with a non-finite auxiliary *be*).

frequency of approximately 72 instances per million words (compared with 34 and 47 instances in LOB and F-LOB, respectively). Further evidence that the *get*-passive is still a colloquial variant that is largely restricted to informal face-to-face conversations comes from the DCPSE. The 1960s sample does not yield a single instance of a *get*-passive in informal conversations.[28] The 1990s sample yields a total of 68 *get*-passives.[29] A restriction to formal face-to-face conversations, however, yields only one prototypical example of the passive construction:

(30)   I can't see much point in doing it at the moment because you don't *get paid* for it [DI A14]

The remaining 14 occurrences were instances of the participle *married* (12) and *engaged* (2) (these were not included in our definition of the *get*-passive as none of these were followed by an overt agent phrase and thus counted as examples of the change-of-state, adjectival use rather than the passive use).

Overall, then, the passive with *get* is still a very infrequent alternative to the *be*-passive, both in written and (formal) spoken English.[30] For individual verbs (such as *caught, paid, smashed, hit*), the *get*-passive in spontaneous spoken English is more frequent than or almost as frequent as the *be*-passive (see Mair 2006b: 115–17, for relevant BNC data); but this applies to individual verbs rather than the construction as a whole.

7.4   The mediopassive

Mediopassive constructions are slippery customers for a study that makes use of machine-readable corpora. They are a phenomenon at the interface of grammar and lexis. Tagged corpora do not allow for the automatic retrieval of all mediopassive constructions either, as the most common type of tagging is usually by part of speech rather than syntactic categories such as 'intransitive' and 'transitive'. But a corpus like ICE-GB, which is tagged for such syntactic categories, is not the solution to the problem. For the correct interpretation of a mediopassive construction, the human parser has access to the kind of

---

[28] This rather extreme finding probably has to be attributed to the sampling of the LLC which is the basis of the 1960s part of the DCPSE. In the LLC, the speakers are all educated to university level. Of the 144 speakers listed for individual texts, 66 are male or female academics and 18 more are involved in academic life (as lecturer, research worker, undergraduate, etc.; cf. Svartvik and Quirk 1980: 26–31). The 'informal' spoken English in the 1960s part of the DCPSE might thus, on the whole, be rather more formal than that sampled for the 1990s, which comes from the spoken component of ICE-GB and is socially more stratified.

[29] The search involved all forms of GET (*get, gets, getting, got*) as passive auxiliaries (this is the tag assigned to them in DCPSE). Four instances (e.g. *get involved, get dressed*) had to be removed manually from the concordance files as they were not true passives.

[30] Interestingly, the *get*-passive is used more frequently in outer-circle varieties of English like Singapore English and Philippine English than in the inner circle (see Hundt forthcoming b).

information that no kind of tagging will be able to provide in the near future. This store of information includes syntactic knowledge of the semantics of individual verbs and semantico-syntactic frames (i.e. the fact that the construction typically involves the intransitive use of an inherently transitive verb) as well as encyclopaedic knowledge (cf. Yoshimura and Taylor 2004: 305ff.; Hundt 2007: 44). The characteristic pattern meaning associated with the mediopassive, i.e. the fact that these constructions focus on inherent properties of the patient subject that facilitate or hinder the process expressed by the verb, will always pose problems for the automatic annotation of a machine-readable corpus. A verb like *reverse*, for instance, may occur in a mediopassive if the construction highlights design features of the subject, as in *This car reverses easily*. In the following sentence, however, inherent properties of the subject are not responsible for the reversability, and (31) can therefore not be (easily) rephrased as a mediopassive:

(31)   This was a revolution which could not *easily be reversed* since, in fact, it had little to do with the state and everything to do with society. [F-LOB Fo1]

(31′)   *?This was a revolution which could not reverse easily [...]

According to Yoshimura and Taylor (2004: 310), the attribution of properties to the subject (in connection with the verb) also accounts for the fact that a mediopassive construction is an option for *sell* but not for *buy*:

In the case of buying, responsibility lies very much with the Agent. A buyer not only has to want to buy the merchandise, he has to be prepared to pay for it. The buyer's role cannot therefore be easily suppressed. In the case of a selling activity, the seller ... has to decide to sell the merchandise. A crucial factor in his success, however, is the quality of the merchandise; in order for the selling event to take place, the merchandise has to attract a buyer.

In the following example, the passive of *buy* could be replaced by mediopassive *sell* since the property of the merchandise (i.e. its ability to fetch a certain price) is also highlighted in the second part of the sentence:[31]

(32)   Wax dolls could *be bought* quite cheaply a few years ago, but are now fetching higher prices. [F-LOB E03]

(32′)   Wax dolls *sold* quite cheaply a few years ago, but are now fetching higher prices.

The reason why, in this particular example, a *be*-passive with *buy* is used instead of the mediopassive might be that, in the following sentence, the buyer is mentioned (... *If you buy an old doll, or own one, don't be tempted to refurbish it* ...).

---

[31] Note that the modal *could* is not carried over to the mediopassive – because the mediopassive itself has inherent modality, as noted earlier.

Matters are further complicated by the possibility that the pattern meaning of the mediopassive can be extended to marginal cases, as in the following example from Frown which was discovered serendipitously, in the process of compiling and proof-reading the corpus:

(33)   [. . .] the routes are designed *to bicycle* in a few hours. [Frown F41]

This use of the mediopassive is marginal because the NP in subject position is not the patient of the related active construction but a locative. Furthermore, it is a 'bare' mediopassive, i.e. there is no modification (in the form of a manner adverbial, modal auxiliary or negation)[32] that is said to be typical or even required in mediopassives. Do these problems make mediopassive constructions inaccessible for a corpus-based investigation? The solution, it seems, is to take a two-pronged approach to the empirical study of mediopassive constructions and to combine evidence available from machine-readable corpora (by searching for specific, potentially mediopassive lexical verbs) with information available from close manual reading of a non-computerized corpus.

In a verb-based approach, for instance, it is possible to search for verbs that are likely to be used in the mediopassive construction. The following typical examples of the mediopassive were amongst those retrieved from the Brown family of corpora in a verb-based approach:

(34)   It [the film script] *reads* like a demented kind of litany [. . .]. [LOB C06]
(35)   Business was bad; the fluffy dressing-gowns *weren't selling* [. . .]. [F-LOB P27]
(36)   Oilcloth only costs about 79c a yard for the very best. Tougher than plastic, it *wears well.* [Brown E14]

But even a systematic search of 30 such verbs produced no clear diachronic trends in the Brown family of corpora. A verb like *wear*, for instance, occurs with a frequency of 507 in the four corpora taken together; only 3 of the occurrences are mediopassive constructions (0.6%). The proportion of mediopassives for *read* and *reduce* were slightly higher at 1.3% and 1.5%, respectively. *Sell* is even more likely to be used in a mediopassive, but with 40 mediopassives out of 521 occurrences, the relative frequency (7.7%) is still rather low (see Hundt 2007: 88).

One reason that we do not find a significant increase in mediopassives in the Brown family of corpora might have to do with corpus size. But it might also be the case that an increase occurred earlier in the twentieth century and that the development has slowed down again. Hundt's (2007) study – based

---

[32] Emphatic *do*, prepositional phrases – as in *Harry Potter and the Deathly Hallows releases on July 21, 2007* (an announcement on the internet) – or the price of merchandise may also be used as modification devices in a mediopassive. One could thus argue that the temporal adverbial in (33) serves as the modification device and it is therefore not a bare passive.

on the manual analysis of four mail-order catalogues – has shown that the main increase in mediopassives (in that particular register) occurs between the late 1920s and late 1950s.[33] The fact that 425 different verbs make up the total of 4,719 mediopassive constructions in her corpus confirms that the mediopassive construction is a productive syntactic pattern in modern advertising language.

Unlike the *be*-passive, the mediopassive is not restricted to particular semantic verb classes. Möhlig and Klages (2002: 251) mention CONTACT verbs as one possible exception (e.g. *?The ball hits easily* or *?The drum beats well*). But mediopassive *kick* is attested in the following example from a 1957 catalogue:

(37)   Mitered corners hold sheet firmly in place [. . .] won't *kick off.* (*Sears & Roebuck*, 1957: 457)

The fact that mediopassives construe readily from denominal verbs like *flange, hinge* or *ink*, and compound verbs like *wall mount* provides further evidence of the productivity of the pattern:

(38)   [pump] *Flanges* for direct mounting. (*Sears & Roebuck*, 1986: 737)
(39)   [storm screen] *Hinges* either left or right. (*Sears & Roebuck*, 1986: 747)
(40)   [typewriter ribbon] *re-inks* as it rewinds. (*Sears & Roebuck*, 1957: 709)
(41)   [air cleaner] does not *wall mount.* (*Sears & Roebuck*, 1986: 730)

While the mediopassive has become obsolete with some verbs (e.g. *make up*),[34] others have become available for the construction. Sometimes, extra-linguistic reasons are responsible for the introduction of a new mediopassive. Mediopassive *zip*, for example, only became possible with the invention of zips at the beginning of the twentieth century.[35] The first attested example in the mail-order catalogue corpus is from 1957:

(42)   Corduroy Slacks [. . .] *zip* to fit each side of waist. (*Sears & Roebuck*, 1957: 87)

Bare mediopassives, i.e. constructions without any kind of modification, are particularly frequent in advertising language (Hundt 2007: 114). In addition to examples (33), (34), (35) and (37), the bare mediopassive is illustrated in the following examples from the mail-order catalogues:

---

[33] For a description of the corpus, see Hundt (2007: Appendix 2).
[34] The mediopassive of this verb is frequently used to describe a fabric that 'makes up pretty in tailor-made skirts' (*Sears & Roebuck*, 1897: 255); this pattern is still attested in the 1920s but no longer used by the 1950s (cf. Hundt 2007: 161).
[35] According to the *OED* on CD-ROM, *zipper* was registered as a trade mark in 1925, but with the meaning of 'boots made of rubber and fabric'. Verbs are derived both from the full form *zipper* and from the clipping *zip*. The first attestation of *zip* (noun) in the *OED* is from 1928, and the first recorded use of the verb *zip* is from 1932. The *OED* also quotes an early mediopassive use of *zip* from an advertisement in *Time* magazine (23 February 1942, p. 78): 'Zips flawlessly'. Interestingly, only *zip* is used in the mediopassive construction, not the slightly longer verb *zipper*.

(43)   [. . .] Spandex *adapts* to your figure [. . .]. (*Sears & Roebuck*, 1986: 198)

(44)   Leveling glides *adjust*. (*Sears & Roebuck*, 1986: 806)

(45)   [pump] *Disassembles* for cleaning. (*Sears & Roebuck*, 1986: 713)

(46)   [high chair] *Converts* to youth chair. (*Sears & Roebuck*, 1986: 266)

(47)   Barrier can be used in hatchback cars where back seat *folds* forward. (*Sears & Roebuck*, 1986: 697)

In the data from the mail-order catalogues, the proportion of bare mediopassives increases steadily from the end of the nineteenth to the end of the twentieth century (Hundt forthcoming a). Modal verbs show the most drastic decrease as modifiers in mediopassive constructions from 29% in the 1897 catalogue to 0.7% in the 1986 catalogue. A look at some examples shows why:

(48)   [husking pin] [. . .] can *adjust* to any size hand. (*Sears & Roebuck*, 1897: 229)

(49)   [Handy lamps] Will *clamp* to almost anything . . . (*Sears & Roebuck*, 1927: 655)

(50)   [Screwdriver] Can *convert* to manual return (*Sears & Roebuck*, 1957: 1403)

Mediopassive constructions in advertising copy are used to verbally display important design features of the merchandise. The modal verbs do not add essentially to this function, as the modified examples in (49′)–(51′) illustrate:

(48′)   [husking pin] adjusts to any size hand.

(49′)   [Handy lamps] Clamp to almost anything

(50′)   [Screwdriver] Converts to manual return

The goods advertised are still *adjustable, clampable* and *convertible*; leaving out the modal therefore does not result in a semantically impoverished expression. It just makes for snappier advertising copy that reads better and takes up less space on the page. In other words, as modal modification does not add substantially to the semantics in a core mediopassive construction,[36] it is not surprising that modal modification decreases as bare mediopassives become more frequent in the course of the twentieth century.

Generally, mediopassives also replace modal adjectives in *-able* (such as *adjustable, removable, reversable*) over time in the data from the advertising corpus (Hundt 2007: 157). Exceptions to this general trend are *washable* (which increases at the expense of the related mediopassive *wash*) and *detachable* (with a brief decrease in the 1950s catalogue).

---

[36] Note that this holds mainly for mediopassives in the generic present tense (and thus typically for the advertising examples). But if the examples have a more specific (non-generic) meaning (as in example 35), there is no built-in modality. Compare 'The stains wash off easily' (generic, iterative or modalized) with 'The stains washed off easily' (referring to a specific event, not modalized).

In the data from the mail-order catalogues, the mediopassive increases at the expense of the *be*-passive (and other alternative patterns). Even a cursory glance at examples in the F-LOB and Frown corpora shows, however, that the *be*-passive is still used in contexts where it may be replaced by a mediopassive:

(51) Ideal for use on the face and body, this light moisturising lotion *is easily absorbed* and offers both UVA and UVB protection. [F-LOB E34]

(52) But such things *are not erased* so easily. [F-LOB B09]

(53) There's no need to peel them and they *are easily sliced* if you have a processor, or use a mandolin (a specially made wooden board with a sharp blade). [F-LOB E20]

(54) High frequency words *are processed* faster and more easily than words at low frequencies. [Frown J32]

(55) Your router base will slide easily and this material *is easily repaired* with epoxy if you accidentally damage the surfaces with the router cutter. [Frown E20]

In example (53), a *be*-passive is probably used because the implied agent (reader, as putative cook) is made explicit in the following *if*-clause, despite the fact that the potatoes are inherently 'easily sliceable'. Not all *be*-passives with facilitative adverbs would make good mediopassive constructions, however, as the following examples illustrate:

(56) This relationship *is easily observed* in English monosyllables, which are all syllabically heavy and all inherently stressed . . . [F-LOB J35]

(57) I gather that *is not easily done*, even by the likes of Gaynor. [F-LOB M02]

The demoted semantic roles in the *be*-passives above (experiencer in (56) and agent in (57)) bear the sole responsibility for the process expressed in the VP and the semantics of the mediopassive does not apply. In another instance (58), the combination with a present perfect is one of the factors that make the mediopassive an unlikely option, since it combines typically with generic statements (whereas the present perfect makes it into a non-generic, single event); additionally, mediopassive *absorb* is more likely to take concrete than abstract entities as patient subjects:

(58) So far, most of the cash calls *have been easily absorbed*. [F-LOB A16]

Similarly, mental process verbs (59) do not usually make good mediopassives; additionally, mediopassives are extremely unlikely to co-occur with a *by*-phrase:

(59) . . . show the teachings of the Buddha in a way that *could be easily understood by the masses*, just as cathedral carvings served to instruct the illiterate in the West. [F-LOB E01]

Facilitative adverbs in *be*-passives are therefore not the central property that accounts for the variation between *be*-passive and mediopassive constructions. In other words, while mediopassive constructions appear to be spreading, they have a very special constructional meaning and are subject to a number of constraints which hinder their treatment as straightforward competitors of the *be*-passive.

7.5   Summary and conclusion

The data in the Brown family of corpora support the hypothesis of an ongoing decline in passive constructions in written English. The trend pointed out by Dixon (2005: 354), that 'everything else being equal, a speaker of English will prefer to use a verb with two or more core roles (a transitive verb) in an active construction, with subject and object stated', rather than a passive, has become even more marked in the second half of the twentieth century. AmE, as in so many instances, is leading this change that, most likely, has to be attributed to the sustained attack on the passive in usage guides. This, in turn, is motivated by the association of the passive with a less direct, less vivid, mode of presenting a situation. In both AmE and BrE, the development away from the *be*-passive is most marked in academic writing. However, in this decline we see colloquialization working not in its usual positive manner (i.e. making writing more speech-like), but rather negatively, in the sense of decreasing use of a markedly 'written' feature.[37]

While there is a clear trend away from the use of the *be*-passive, there is only a slight increase in the use of the *get*-passive from around 30 instances per million words in LOB and Brown to around 50 instances per million words in F-LOB and Frown. The *be*-passive, on the other hand, is used with a frequency of approximately 10,000 and 8,300 per one million words in F-LOB and Frown, respectively. The increase of the *get*-passive is thus far from compensating the decrease of the *be*-passive in written English.[38] Contrary to Weiner and Labov's (1983: 43) claim, there is little sign of shift to the *get*-passive; this even holds for spoken English, as the data from the DCSPE and the BNC show. Why should this be the case? Most likely because the *get*-passive has not yet become a stylistically and semantically neutral alternative for the *be*-passive in either BrE or AmE. The *be*-passive is still the prototypical passive construction in contemporary English. Its main competitors in conversation are active forms with a generalized subject pronoun (see section 6.5.3).

---

[37] Data from the DCPSE show that the locus of this change is definitely the written medium: *be*-passives occur with a stable frequency in spontaneous speech of the early 1960s and 1990s.

[38] The gap between *be*- and *get*-passives would be even greater if non-finite passives had been included for *be*-passives (as they were for the *get*-passive).

While the *get*-passive remains a marked alternative to the neutral and prototypical *be*-passive, this holds even more for the mediopassive. It is a highly specialized construction, both with respect to its meaning and text type specific usage. In fact, it turned out to be so infrequent in the Brown family of corpora that we had to draw on a different source of evidence. The results from the corpus of mail-order catalogues show, however, that within its functional niche, the use of the mediopassive construction has increased in the course of the twentieth century.

8 *Take* or *have* a look at a corpus? Expanded predicates in British and American English

In place of simple verbs like *look*, *bite* or *hug*, speakers of English can use constructions that combine a semantically reduced or 'light' verb like *have*, *take* or *give* with the indefinite article and a deverbal noun, as in:

(1) a. "I'd just like you to *have a look* at one of the patients – I'm a bit worried." [F-LOB P24]
   b. She *took a sip* now and eyed him over the rim of her glass. [F-LOB P23]
   c. [...] he grabbed hold of her and *gave* her such *a hug* the goldfish slopped out of the bowl [...]. [F-LOB K10]

The verb *have* combines with deverbal nouns such as *chat, drag, drink, escape, fall, glance, glimpse, laugh, look, nap, puff, shower, stroll, talk, taste* and *walk*, to give but a few examples. This variety of possible combinations suggests that we are dealing with a fairly productive constructional type. The fact that deverbal nouns like *neglect, eat, jump, open, close* or *shut* cannot be used in the construction indicates that the productivity is limited to a certain extent by collocational restrictions. In other words, the topic of this chapter is a phenomenon at the borderline between syntax and the lexicon.[1] This may be one reason why linguists have not paid much attention to verb–noun combinations of the *have a look* type. Those interested in the construction will find that any attempt to get an overview of existing research on the topic is complicated by the fact that linguists apparently cannot agree on a term for *have-a-look* constructions. Poutsma (1926) refers to them as 'group verbs', others (Renský 1966; Hoffmann 1972; Akimoto 1989; Stein 1991; Stein and Quirk 1991; Quirk 1995; Labuhn 2001) as 'verbo–nominal phrases' or 'constructions' and Live (1973) simply calls them '*take-have*-phrasals'. Alternative terms are 'periphrastic' or 'complex verbal structures' (Wierzbicka 1982 and Nickel 1968, respectively), 'eventive object constructions' (Quirk *et al.* 1985) or, more recently, 'stretched verb constructions' (Allerton 2002, based

---

[1] Lexico-grammatical phenomena will also be dealt with in section 9.2 (complementation of verbs like *help* and *start*). Lexico-grammatical aspects were also relevant for the mediopassive (see section 7.4).

166

on Heringer 1989) and 'support verb constructions' (Krenn 2000). Huddle-ston and Pullum (2002) treat the construction under the heading of 'light verbs'. In generative grammar, the pattern has been labelled as 'complex predicate' (a subtype of 'composite predicates' in Cattell 1984) or 'object idiom chunks' (a more widely used generative term).[2] The terminological variation also reflects a problem with the definition of the phenomenon. On closer inspection, most of the terms include other phenomena than just the *have a look* or *take a bite* construction; Renský (1966: 290) – to mention just one example – includes idioms such as *to become master, to be head of, to cut with a lathe* in his category of 'verbo-nominal phrases'. We decided to focus on constructions that combine a semantically reduced or 'light' verb with a deverbal noun. Furthermore, we opted to use Algeo's (1995) term 'expanded predicate' because it is more restricted and more clearly defined than some of the other terms. It is because of their problematic status that we devote more discussion to the nature of expanded predicates than to other constructions covered in this book.

8.1   The state of the art

A look at previous research shows that expanded predicates have been treated within very different theoretical frameworks. Nickel (1968) and Prince (1972), for instance, are early transformational approaches. Interestingly, Nickel (1968: 17) combines the generative with a pragmatic approach; he draws on the notion of 'functional sentence perspective' to explain why expanded predicates might be used instead of simple verbs:

. . . complex verbal structures . . . are to be regarded as the structural means which allow the actional content of the underlying verb to become focussed in the sense of the theory of functional sentence perspective in connected discourse.

Many studies focus on semantic aspects. Some attempt to list semantic classes of verbs that have corresponding expanded predicates: Makkai (1977) is one of those people who addresses the semantics of the deverbal noun. But the semantics of the so-called 'light' or 'reduced' verb have also been studied. Dixon (2005), Wierzbicka (1982), Stein (1991) and Labuhn (2001) focus on differences between constructions that allow both *have* and *take* as a light verb, as in *have a look* vs *take a look* or *have a walk* vs *take a walk*. These semantic differences are fairly subtle. According to Dixon (2005: 469ff.), expanded predicates with *have* are used whenever a human agent does something for pleasure or relief; constructions with *take* also typically have human agents but they foreground the fact that some physical effort on the part of the agent is involved. He also claims that, unlike expanded

---

[2] For a generative account, see Radford (1988: 422).

predicates with *have*, those with *take* tend to refer to a single activity rather than one that lasts for a while (pp. 474ff.). Typical deverbal nouns that combine with *take* are *bite* and *swallow* (*he took a quick bite of his sandwich*).

Stein (1991: 21) points out that the semantic difference between expanded predicates with *have* and *take* is not absolute. According to Stein, constructions with *give* differ from those with *have* and *take* in that the human agent does not act willingly.[3] An example would be *to have a cough* and *to give a cough*. If one *has* or *takes* a look at corpus examples, one soon finds that these semantic differences are not absolute. In example (2), *give* is used as a light verb, but in this case the context suggests that the agent is, indeed, acting willingly:

(2)   He judged that she had been sufficiently dazzled and *gave a* long raucous *cough*. [LOB R03]

Wierzbicka's study is the most rigorous attempt to explain the semantics of expanded predicates with *have*. The basis is her natural semantic metalanguage. According to her, *have-a-look* constructions always refer to repeatable actions. This, apparently, also explains why constructions like **have an eat* are impossible:

In contrast to *have a V*, the *take a V* frame suggests a definite MOMENT of time as the starting point of the action. The action itself need not be momentary . . . ; on the contrary, it is *extended in time*, though it lasts only a short time. But there must be a definite *initial impulse* – momentary, *deliberate*, and apparently *involving physical motion* . . . Semi-voluntary actions like yawning or crying do not lend themselves to description in the *take a V* frame. (Wierzbicka 1982: 794; emphasis original)

For example, the contrast of *have a bite* or *a lick* or *a taste* vs **have an eat* may result at least partly from the contrast in repeatability of the actions in question. One could bite John's sandwich, or lick his ice cream, or taste his soup – not once but twice, or more – but one could eat his sandwich only once. But stylistic factors also play a role in the formation of expanded predicates: colloquial or non-technical verbs like *pee*, *chat* and *think* have corresponding constructions with *have*, whereas more technical terms like *urinate*, *converse* and *contemplate* do not.

Most linguists agree that there is an aspectual difference between a simple verb like *look* and an expanded predicate like *have a look*.[4] Stein (1991: 18), for example, remarks that *walk* does not imply a temporal restriction, whereas the expanded predicate *have a walk* refers to a temporally bounded activity. The same idea is expressed in Brinton and Akimoto (1999: 6):[5]

---

[3] See also Jespersen (1984: 118) and Quirk *et al.* (1985: 752).
[4] See, for instance, Live (1973: 34), Renský (1966: 294), Prince (1972: 412), Hoffmann (1972: 175) or Labuhn (2001: 79ff.).
[5] See also Müller (1978: 214ff.).

. . . it seems that the complex verb is an important means of making situations telic, that is, of converting activities into accomplishments or achievements, yet without the necessity of stating an explicit goal (e.g. *dream/ have a dream, nibble/ have a nibble, move/ make a move . . .*).

Syntactic features may also help to explain why expanded predicates are used instead of the simple verbs. Expanded predicates allow for a wide range of modification patterns.[6] Deverbal nouns can be modified not only by a simple adjective (as in example 3a), but also by post-modifying relative clauses (as in example 3b). While admittedly rare, examples (c) and (d) illustrate even more complex clausal modification patterns.

(3) a. She *gave* me *a* coquettish *look*.
    b. She *gave* me *a look* that was coquettish in a naive sort of way. (Nickel 1968: 15)
    c. Mary *gave* John her 'I told you so' *look*. (Müller 1978: 155)
    d. He *gave* what in stage directions is sometimes called *a* "dark *laugh*" and snuffed once [. . .]. (Müller 1978: 152)

Unlike simple verbs, expanded predicates allow for multiple modification.

(4) a. John gave a *short* laugh of *royal scorn*.
    b. *John laughed *shortly, royally, scornfully*. (Renský 1966: 296)

But even a single adjective cannot always be replaced by an adverb in a corresponding simple verb construction:

(5) a. [. . .] Wilson had a *good* look at him. [Brown No5]
    b. *Wilson looked *well* at him.

The adverb *finally* in (6b) is not the equivalent of the adjective *final* in (6a).

(6) a. He [. . .] went to give himself a *final* glance in the looking glass. [F-LOB R08]
    b. # He went to *finally* glance at himself in the looking glass.[7]
    c. ?He went to glance at himself in the looking glass for the last time.

Adjectives like *little*, *unruffled* and *pained* in (7) lack corresponding adverbs altogether.

(7) a. Esther jumped up, ran to him and gave him a *little* hug. [Brown G47]
    b. Oso gave me an *unruffled* look. [Brown No4]
    c. Sandra gave a *pained* cry. [LOB Po6]

Live (1973: 35), Müller (1978: 209) and Stein (1991: 21) point out that attributive adjectives co-occur particularly frequently with expanded

---

[6] For a more detailed treatment, see Labuhn (2001: Chapter 6).
[7] The #-sign is used to indicate that the second sentence is grammatical but not semantically equivalent to the first sentence.

predicates with *give*. Live (1973: 34) and Stein (1991: 26) further point out that expanded predicates with *have* are more polite than constructions with a simple verb. Stein attributes this to the overlap with offers/suggestions of the type *have a coffee*.[8]

More recently, expanded verbs have also been studied historically. According to the articles published in Brinton and Akimoto (1999), complex predicates can be found as early as Old English.[9] They only start being used with a higher text frequency in Late Modern English, however (cf. Jespersen 1909–49: VI, 117; Visser 1963–73: §148; Bailey 1996: 228f.; Brinton 1996: 200; Brinton and Akimoto 1999: 1). Both Hiltunen (1999) and Claridge (2000) found that the construction with the indefinite article emerged relatively late; in EModE, 'the majority of types seem to prefer the zero-article form' (Claridge 2000: 137). Direct comparisons between Present-Day English and usage in and before the Early Modern period are therefore problematic because we are, in a way, comparing different kinds of apples (cf. Claridge 2000: 173ff.).

8.2 Hypotheses

Previous studies on expanded predicates suggest a number of hypotheses that merit an empirical evaluation in the light of corpus data.

- Hypothesis 1: Expanded predicates are stylistically marked. Their frequency of use therefore depends on text type.

Numerous linguists have claimed that the use and frequency of expanded predicates depends on text type. Some say that they are particularly frequent in scientific texts (e.g. Renský 1966: 297; Brinton 1996: 189), while others (e.g. Wierzbicka 1982: 766; Rohdenburg 1990: 137) suppose that they are typical of colloquial language use. This apparent contradiction can be explained by the varying definitions of the phenomenon that have been used from one study to another. Renský and Brinton include constructions with abstract deverbal nouns in their definition. While constructions like *give consideration* or *make a decision* are admittedly more frequent in specialized discourse, it is also clear that deverbal nouns like *chat, cuddle, drink, guess, laugh* and *look* are more characteristic of everyday colloquial speech. Allerton (2002: 29) is probably right in claiming that some constructions are typical of scientific, others of colloquial language. Similarly, Dixon (2005: 483) suggests that

---

[8] Slightly less convincing is the connection she makes between this pragmatic function of expanded verb constructions and stylistic connotations: 'One might therefore question the informal (or "highly colloquial" (Wierzbicka)) character attributed to the $V + N$ construction where $V +$ [sic] *have*' (Stein 1991: 26).

[9] Note, however, that some of these studies also include constructions like *to give way* and *to do harm*, and are thus not directly comparable.

different types of expanded predicates may be used as markers of a formal or informal style:

It would surely be instructive to study the occurrence of HAVE A, TAKE A, and GIVE A across a variety of speech styles. Indeed, these constructions might well prove to be an indexical feature for the sociolinguistic classification of different formal and informal speech styles.

- Hypothesis 2: Expanded predicates have become more frequent over the last thirty years.

Expanded predicates are attested in Old and Middle English but only start spreading in Modern English. This probably has to do with the fact that conversion has become a very productive word formation process in Modern English. Various linguists assume that expanded predicates are being used more and more frequently in Present-Day English (cf. Barber 1964: 141; Nickel 1968; Strang 1970: 59; Hoffmann 1972; Rohdenburg 1990; Algeo 1995). According to Dixon (2005: 461), the spread is closely related to the issue of regional variation:

In British (and Australian) English HAVE A VERB has increased in popularity while TAKE A VERB may actually have dropped in frequency; in American English the TAKE A construction has become more common and HAVE A appears to have contracted. This would account for the fact that Americans prefer to say *take a run/kick/swim/look* where an Englishman would use *have a run/kick/swim/look* . . . .

Trudgill, Nevalainen and Wischer (2002: 9–11), on the basis of evidence from the *Chadwyck-Healey* literary databases of BrE, attribute the regional difference between AmE and BrE to the fact that AmE lagged behind BrE in the development of dynamic uses of the verb *have*.

It seems very likely then that North American English represents an earlier stage of development as far as these idioms are concerned, as compared to British English. That is, *have*-avoidance in these restricted collocations in North America is the result of the fact that North American English *have* never acquired as much dynamism as British English *have*. (p. 11)

According to their evidence, *have* starts taking over from *take* in expanded verbs after 1800 in BrE. In the nineteenth-century fiction database, constructions with *have* show an increase from the previous level of 24% to 48% (p. 10).[10]

- Hypothesis 3: Expanded predicates are more typical of British than American English.

---

[10] Note that Trudgill *et al.* searched for expanded predicates 'in sequences where the verb (in any person or tense) was immediately followed by the noun' (2002: 10), i.e. they excluded examples with modifying elements.

The hypothesis concerning regional variation is probably the most widespread one. Most linguists seem to agree that BrE not only prefers expanded predicates with *have* and *give* but that expanded predicates generally are used more frequently in BrE than in AmE. This is interesting because AmE is typically regarded as the more informal variety.

All three hypotheses touch on the aspect of frequency, but so far none of the existing studies allows us to verify the hypotheses empirically. One reason is that the definition of the phenomenon often includes more than just the *have* or *take a* + verb pattern. Another reason is that the few existing empirical studies tend to be based on only one text type; Stein (1991), for instance, is based on the analysis of fifteen novels.[11] As far as diachronic variation is concerned, quantitative studies only cover the period up to EModE but do not include the possible spread of the construction in ModE and PDE. Most surprisingly, perhaps, the aspect of regional variation has been sorely neglected in corpus-based research, despite the fact that so many studies comment on the difference between British and American English. Algeo (1995) is the first to approach this aspect empirically in a comparison of data from LOB and Brown. Biber *et al.* (1999) also include frequency information in their grammar, but only for the use of *have* and *take a look* in British and American English.

Initially, Algeo's study seemed like a good starting point for the analysis of the diachronic aspect. But on closer inspection, his results turned out to be an unsuitable basis for comparison with results from our more recent F-LOB and Frown corpora. Algeo includes patterns like *have a ballot* and *have a scrimmage*, even though the verbs *to ballot* and *to scrimmage* are derived from the noun and not vice versa. The following examples are therefore not instances of expanded predicates:

(8)   a. There is little doubt if they *had a secret ballot*, they would vote for food for their family [. . .]. [Brown C04]
   b. "We'll work hard Tuesday, Wednesday and Thursday", Meek said, "and probably will *have a good scrimmage* Friday." [Brown E11]

Similarly, the following instances of *have a bounce*, *have a crackle* and *have an answer* are not examples of expanded predicates because *have* is used in the lexical sense of 'possess':

(9)   a. "Where the Boys Are" also *has a* juvenile *bounce* [. . .]. [Brown C04]
   b. [. . .] the apples that grow there *have a* wintry *crackle*. [Brown E11]
   c. Larkin *has an answer* to all that. [Brown C01]

In the appendix to his article, Algeo gives an alphabetical list of all the expanded predicates with *have*, *take* and *give* that he included in his analysis. Among them we find *have a study* as an AmE construction. The only instance

---

[11] The same data are discussed in Stein and Quirk (1991) and Quirk (1995).

of *have a study* in the Brown corpus is clearly not an example of an expanded predicate but a causative construction:

(10)   The resolution urges the governor to *have a* complete *study* of the Sunday sales laws made with an eye to their revision at the next session of the legislature. [Brown A05]

It might be the case that the context Algeo looked at was not sufficient to exclude examples such as the one quoted under (10). These and other examples cast some doubt on the reliability of his results.

A study on the frequency of expanded predicates cries out for a corpus-based approach. All three aspects – stylistic, diachronic and regional variation – can best be studied on the basis of the Brown family of corpora. However, because expanded predicates are a phenomenon at the borderline between syntax and the lexicon, a study based on one-million-word corpora is likely to indicate trends in the use of the construction but might not yield conclusive evidence. Additional information will therefore come from two corpora of spoken British and American English, namely the spontaneous conversations in the BNC (BNCdemog) and the LCSAE. The BNC contains about 4.2 million words in the spoken demographic part and the LCSAE about 5 million words of spontaneous spoken discourse.

8.3   Defining the variable

The following study is restricted to expanded predicates with the verbs *have*, *take* and *give*. Using WordSmith, all instances of the verbs immediately followed by the indefinite article were collected from our set of corpora. Another restriction imposed on the definition of the variable concerns the nominal element in the construction: only deverbal nouns derived by conversion were included, i.e. patterns such as *have a thought* or *have an argument* were excluded. This means that, theoretically, a construction like *have a bath* would have had to be left out because the verb *to bathe* and the noun *bath* are not isomorphic. But on closer inspection, this clear-cut distinction breaks down. The corpus-based *Collins COBUILD Dictionary* (1987: 106) lists *bath* as a transitive verb. The following examples illustrate that *bath* is used both transitively and intransitively:

(11)   a. "If we *bath* in mineral water," Samantha said, "I'd like to try the fizzy sort." [BNC FB9 2193]
        b. Great-gran knows that I *bath* her. [BNC HWE 1098]
        c. You can *bath* in it, drink it, spill it down your dress and it won't leave a mark. [LOB P22; quoted from Algeo 1995: 213].

Similarly, the form *bathe* is also attested as a noun. An example would be:

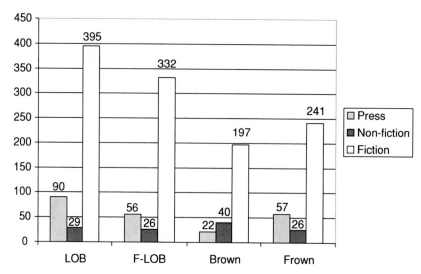

Figure 8.1 Expanded predicates across different text types (frequencies pmw)*
* For absolute figures, see Table A8.2 in Appendix III.

(12) a. She did not flinch when he suggested a *bathe*. [BNC CDE 2164]
     b. And often we would lie together in the sun after a *bathe* [. . .]. [BNC FEE 908]

Collins COBUILD Dictionary (1987: 106) lists the noun *bathe* only in the context of expanded predicates. In the BNC, however, the ordinary use of the noun is more frequent than its use as part of an expanded predicate. Instances of *to have* or *take a bath(e)* were therefore included in the analysis. The initial results were quite heavily edited manually, eliminating, for instance, idiomatic uses such as *have a word with someone* or *have a say in something*. For each corpus in the Brown family, a list of the verb + noun combinations that were eventually included in the counts can be found in Table A8.1.

8.4   Results

8.4.1   Stylistic variation

With respect to the variable 'text type', the Brown family corpora indicate a clear preference for fictional texts across the whole family (see Figure 8.1). Expanded predicates occur most frequently in the text type that also turned out to be very open to colloquial patterns in other studies; they decrease somewhat in British and increase in American Fiction, but fictional writing still remains the genre that expanded predicates favour across regional and diachronic variation. A closer look at the use of expanded predicates in the Fiction sections shows that they occur more often in narrative passages (73.6% of all occurrences) than in fictional dialogue (24.4%);[12] in other words, their high frequency in this genre cannot be attributed to a written–spoken divide.[13]

The hypothesis that expanded predicates are frequently used in scientific discourse is not verified: in Learned writing, Brown yields only 4 examples (out of a total of 77), and Frown 1 occurrence (out of a total of 86). Not a single instance was attested in the Learned categories of either LOB or F-LOB. This result probably reflects our fairly narrow definition of the linguistic variable that excludes patterns such as *give consideration to something*.

8.4.2 Diachronic variation

The overall comparison of the 1960s and 1990s British and American corpora does not yield evidence of a clear diachronic trend: expanded predicates are used slightly more frequently in Frown than in Brown (86 and 77 instances, respectively), but F-LOB yields fewer such constructions (109) than LOB (133). If the frequencies of the 1960s and 1990s corpora are pooled together, however, the change from 104 to 97 expanded predicates per million words in the 1960s and 1990s, respectively, is obviously not significant.

An interesting detail emerges from the comparison of the different light verbs. The results from Brown and Frown confirm Dixon's (2005: 461) hypothesis that a shift in preference has taken place in AmE: the significant decrease of expanded predicates with *have* is paralleled by a significant increase in constructions with *take* (see Figure 8.2).

Dixon (2005: 461) also supposes that *have-a-look* constructions have become more popular in BrE; this is not supported by the corpus data. On the contrary: the frequency of expanded predicates with *have* has decreased, but, unlike in AmE, this decrease is not paralleled by an increase of constructions with *take*. In the long run, this trend may be another instance of AmE setting the model for a global development. This brings us to the topic of regional variation.

8.4.3 Regional variation

Even relatively small one-million-word corpora of the Brown and LOB type produce enough evidence to verify hypotheses on regional variation.

---

[12] In the sampling of the corpora, fictional texts that contained more than 50% dialogue were excluded. In the British corpora, the proportion of quoted to non-quoted material is more or less stable at 26% (rising to 27.2% in F-LOB), so the density of expanded predicates is even slightly greater in narrative than in dialogue passages.

[13] Labuhn (2001: 253) also found that expanded predicates with *give* occurred more frequently in narrative passages than in fictional dialogue.

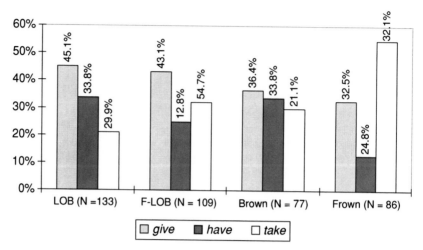

Figure 8.2 Diachronic development of light verbs in expanded predicates (proportion of light verbs per number of expanded predicates)

Expanded predicates have increased slightly from Brown to Frown and decreased from LOB to F-LOB, but they are still used more frequently in British than in American English in the 1990s.[14] As far as the preference for individual light verbs in the expanded predicates is concerned, the absolute frequency of constructions with *have* in the British corpora is consistently higher than that in Brown and Frown. In terms of relative frequencies, constructions with *give* are the dominant pattern in BrE. We now turn to evidence from spoken corpora.

A comparison of the spoken component of the BNC with the LCSAE confirms that expanded predicates, overall, are used far more frequently in British than in American English. If anything, this regional difference is more pronounced in the spoken medium (see also Figure 8.5 below): the frequencies per million words amount to 543 and 105 in the spoken demographic part of the BNC and the LCSAE, respectively. The much larger spoken corpora further indicate that *have* is clearly the preferred light verb in BrE whereas *take* dominates in AmE (see Figure 8.3).

The trend towards more frequent use of *take* from LOB to F-LOB is not supported by spoken BrE data, where *have* is firmly established as a light verb in expanded predicates. *Give* is also used more frequently in British than in American English, but it is not used quite as frequently in spoken as in written BrE. The almost complementary distribution of *have* and *take* in British and American usage becomes even more evident if we limit the analysis to those patterns that allow for variation, as for example *have* or

---

[14] The difference between LOB and Brown proved significant at $p < 0.001$, whereas the difference between F-LOB and Frown is only significant at $p < 0.01$.

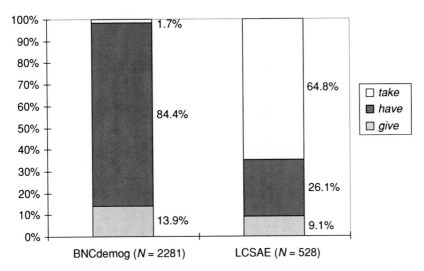

Figure 8.3 Expanded predicates in spoken British and American English

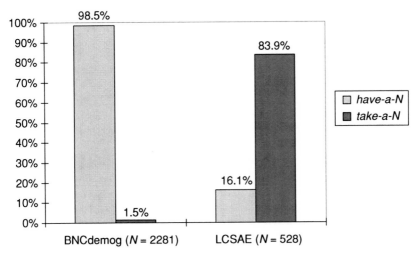

Figure 8.4 Expanded predicates with variable use of *have* and *take* in spoken British and American English (relative frequencies)

take a bath (see Figure 8.4). The difference proved highly significant in a chi-square test at $p \leq 0.001$.

The absolute figures (Table 8.1) show that AmE only prefers *have* over *take* in the construction *have a drink*. Initially, we suspected that this might have to be attributed to the fact that *have a drink* might be used more frequently in offers or requests such as *Would you like to have a drink?* or *Could I have*

Table 8.1. *Expanded predicates with variable use of* have *and* take *in spoken British and American English (raw frequencies)*

	BNCdemog	LCSAE
have a bath	93	2
take a bath	0	34
have a shower	34	5
take a shower	1	70
have a drink	105	17
take a drink	0	3
have a look	959	15
take a look	13	100
have a walk	31	3
take a walk	5	12

a drink, please? But only six of the occurrences of *have a drink* were from such contexts (e.g. *Why don't you come and uh have a have a birthday drink on us*, LCSAE 133902 1691). Note, however, that occurrences of *have a drink* can be ambiguous between the expanded verb construction, illustrated in example (13a), and a simple verb–noun combination where *have* is not a light verb, as in (13b):

(13)   a.   He *had a* quick *drink* of the   (He drank the whiskey quickly.)
              whiskey.
        b.   He had an ice-cold drink.   (*He drank ice-coldly.)

This may account for the results obtained on *have a drink* in the American corpus.

Wierzbicka (1982: 777) points out that expanded predicates can be followed by an *of*-phrase in British and Australian English, but not in American English. The BNC provides us with two examples of this option:

(14)   a.   No he hasn't *had a lend* of your tie! [BNC KCA 2630]
        b.   She said oh well let's *have a try* of one. [BNC KBE 2125]

The question is whether this observation has to be attributed to a higher overall discourse frequency of expanded predicates in BrE rather than a regional difference. This is an area of variation where elicitation data might be more useful than corpus data: for infrequent but acceptable collocations 'statistical comparisons of British and American English are not meaningful, and speaker intuition is the only feasible way of distinguishing them nationally' (Algeo 1995: 209).

Finally, the data from spoken corpora confirm that the expanded predicates investigated in this study are typical of informal, colloquial usage. The

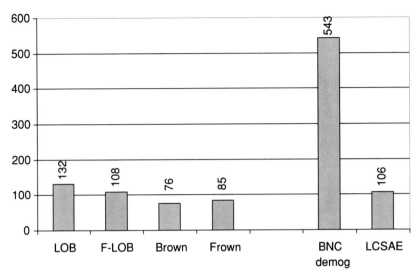

Figure 8.5 Expanded predicates in written and spoken English (pmw)

results for all corpora in Figure 8.5 have been normalized to occurrences per one million words in order to facilitate a direct comparison between the written and spoken medium. Figure 8.5 reveals a further interesting regional difference: namely that spoken and written usage in this area of lexico-grammar are much further apart in British than in American English. This has to be attributed to the fact that, even in spoken AmE, the use of expanded predicates only approximately reaches the proportions that we find in written BrE of the 1990s. Our data thus prove expanded predicates to be a feature typical of informal, spoken BrE.

8.5 Summary

Standard one-million-word corpora of British and American English substantiate the hypothesis that expanded predicates with *have*, *take* and *give* are used more frequently in fictional than in non-fictional texts. The spoken British and American corpora confirm that expanded predicates are typical of colloquial language use: spontaneous spoken texts yield much higher overall frequencies than written texts. This trend is especially pronounced in the British data.

   With respect to regional variation, corpus evidence shows that expanded predicates are used more frequently in British than in American English. Corpus evidence also confirms the hypothesis that BrE prefers *have* as a light verb in expanded predicates whereas AmE prefers *take*. These regional differences are more pronounced in the spoken than in the written data.

Regional variation in the use of light verbs may also account for the fact that semantic differences between expanded predicates with *have*, *take* and *give* are not absolute.

As far as diachronic developments are concerned, the corpora do not provide conclusive evidence that expanded predicates have become more frequent in the recent past. If the data from our British and American corpora are pooled together, the resulting picture is one of stable diachronic variation rather than change. In other words, regional differences are neutralized in a strictly diachronic comparison of our data. The story of the expanded predicate in written (published) English, then, is a good example of purported change that is not corroborated by data. This chapter has shown that it is definitely worthwhile to *take* or *have a look* at the Brown family of corpora, even if it turns out that the story they have to tell is one of regional and variety-internal variation rather than ongoing diachronic change.

9 Non-finite clauses

Having explored a wide range of phenomena in the grammar of the finite verb phrase in Chapters 2 to 8, we will now turn to developments in the field of non-finite verb forms. As in the discussion of the subjunctive, the focus will be on subordinate clauses in complex sentences. A particular problem facing the analysis is the degree of abstractness and generality aimed at in the description. If we decide to focus on a specific non-finite complement structure – such as, say, the *to*-infinitival clause or the gerund with possessive/genitive modifier – we will find these structures serving a large variety of functions, with most of them not being involved in current diachronic change. If, on the other hand, we decide to focus on more specific constructions – combinations of particular superordinate predicates and particular patterns of complementation (such as, for example, variation between infinitives and gerunds with *accustomed to*) – we can easily home in on areas of ongoing diachronic change, without, however, being able to correlate individual shifts in usage preferences with general trends in the evolution of the system of English non-finite verbal forms.

To provide a balanced account of developments, the present chapter will draw on both perspectives. Section 9.1 presents the long-term historical background to ongoing changes, pointing out that in the history of English, non-finite subordinate clauses have emerged as strengthened grammatical categories. Section 9.2 follows this up with four detailed case studies. They show how general trends of long historical standing are manifesting themselves in specific contexts in the present. Sections 9.3 and 9.4 represent an attempt to bring the two perspectives together for an integrated picture.

9.1 Introduction: long-term trends in the evolution of English non-finite clauses

Present-Day English is characterized by a complex system of non-finite clauses – infinitival, gerundial and participial – which sets it apart both from older stages of the language such as Old and Middle English and from most other European languages. For most of the recorded history of English, this system has been subject to change and restructuring. While some of these changes have been minor, others have been systematic long-term drifts active for periods of up to a thousand years. One such long-term development, for example, is the spread of infinitival subordinate clauses at the expense of finite ones.[1] Consider, for example, the following two finite object clauses depending on the verb *tell*:

(1)   China has been through a period of isolation. It needs people going in and telling it *what the world thinks*. [F-LOB A06]
(2)   Lewis told him *what clothes he should bring along*, and enjoined him not to buy anything that he did not already own, they would do that in New York. [Brown G67]

An important difference between the two examples is that in (1) the object of the verb *tell* is not co-referential with the subject of the finite *wh*-complement clause, whereas in (2) it is. Example (2) thus allows a reduced variant in which the finite clause is replaced by an infinitive:

(3)   Lewis told him *what clothes to bring along*.

This reduced variant is the normal one today when two conditions are met: the object of *tell* needs to be co-referential with the subject of the subordinate clause, and the subordinate clause needs to have a 'suasive' modal semantic orientation. The Brown family corpora contain numerous similar examples, not only involving *tell*, but a large number of other verbs and even nominal expressions which can be combined with the full range of interrogative pronouns and adverbs – as is shown by the three typical specimens given below:

(4)   HARRIET BOWERS didn't know *what to think* when she heard Chrissie had turned Charles down. [F-LOB P20]
(5)   I don't know *where to put my face*. [Frown K22]
(6)   Lacking good judgment, or the ability to detect through deliberation *what action to perform, and how and when to perform it*, the slavish, who lack the ability to deliberate, cannot have prudence either [. . .]. [Frown J63]

Note that in examples (4) and (5) it is the **subjects** (rather than the objects) of the main clauses that are co-referential with the understood subjects of the subordinate clause, whereas in (6) the understood subject of the infinitival clause is not specified grammatically, but needs to be inferred from the

---

[1]   Aspects of this development have been covered in several studies. Los (2005) shows how *to*-infinitives spread at the expense of finite *that* + subjunctive clauses in Old and Middle English; Rohdenburg (1995) carries the story forward to c. 1800.

context. Regardless of these differences in 'control',[2] though, the suasive modal semantics is present in all infinitival clauses.

The emergence and spread of infinitival *wh*-complement clauses is one of those innovations in English syntax which is measured in centuries rather than decades, and no dramatic shifts in preference can therefore be detected in the mere thirty years separating Brown and LOB from their successors. The following, however, are the major steps which have led to the present situation in the course of almost a thousand years of linguistic evolution. In Old English, with very few exceptions, finite complement clauses were the norm. From around the thirteenth century, the infinitival variants emerged and started spreading, though not immediately in the ditransitive environment represented by *tell*. In those cases in which there is a choice between finite and infinitival clauses (i.e. when the complement clause has a forward-looking 'prospective' or 'suasive' orientation), finite *wh*-complement clauses remained common well into the nineteenth century,[3] but – judging from the evidence of the Brown family of corpora – have become rare today. In fact, example (2) above is the only relevant case involving the superordinate verb *tell* in which there can be said to be free variation between a finite and an infinitival complement clause.[4] In the three remaining[5] examples there is always some extra motivation which justifies the use of the by now rare finite clause:

(7) [. . .] if everyone does what gives him the greatest pleasure and cannot do anything else, what is wrong and why is the moralist needed to tell us *what we ought to do*? [LOB D09]

---

[2] Government and Binding Theory has popularized this convenient term to refer to the relation which exists between the understood agent or notional subject of the infinitive and some constituent of the higher clause. In *Lewis told him what clothes to bring along*, it is thus understood that the object of the higher clause (*him*) is the 'performer' of the action expressed in the infinitive (*bring along*).

[3] For a typical instance, compare the following *OED* quotation from a letter to Jonathan Swift written in 1731 (s.v. *principal*): 'At the same time tell me what I shall do with the principal sum'; or Emmeline's desperate appeal to Cassy from Chapter 36 of Harriet Beecher-Stowe's 1852 bestseller *Uncle Tom's Cabin*: '"Horrid!" said Emmeline, every drop of blood receding from her cheeks. "O, Cassy, do tell me what I shall do!"'

[4] If the temporal orientation of the complement clause is neutral/simultaneous or retrospective or if a suasive orientation is absent, finite complement clauses continue to be frequent, of course. Compare, for example, 'I think by this age I know what I want' [F-LOB A10].

[5] Two straightforward ones are discussed as (7) and (8) below. The third one is:

"Remember, when the little hand is straight up that's negative. Positive results start when it goes towards the hand you use to make your mark". "But I'm ambidextrous". Ryan told him *what he could do then*. Ekstrohm smiled, and followed the captain through the airlock with only a glance at the lapel gauge on his coverall. [Brown M04]

Coming from a science-fiction text, this example is difficult to contextualize. Taken at face value, it looks like a theoretical exposition intended to instruct the ambidextrous character 'Nogol' about possible courses of future action (and would thus be comparable to the two regular cases discussed below). However, as the wider context of the passage shows, 'Nogol' is a creature who is rather slow on the uptake, so that an ironic–sarcastic reading is also possible.

(8)   At this moment, throughout the world, there are hundreds of thousands of people ruined because politicians have told them *what they have got to think and say and do.* [LOB D16]

In (7) and (8), the context suggests that we are not just talking about 'telling people what to do', but asking them to consciously consider a proposition about their possible future course of action – for example in the context of a philosophical debate. This means that the structurally more elaborate finite clause is a marked choice, prompting the reader to infer more than the note of suggestion or advice expressed by the infinitive clause. It is, of course, tempting to propose a functional explanation for the rise of the reduced infinitival complement clause as the unmarked or 'default' option in such cases. In comparison to its finite alternative it is more information-efficient because it saves the speaker the trouble of redundantly repeating a constituent of the main clause.

Moving from complementation to adverbial subordination, we easily find further instances of variation between finite and infinitival clauses in Present-day English, for example in the area of clauses of purpose and result. There is, for example, a choice between *in order that* and *in order to.* With 101, 92, 88 and 97 instances in Brown, LOB, Frown and F-LOB, respectively, the latter form is fairly evenly distributed throughout the corpora. *In order that*, by contrast, was rare in 1961 and has been marginalized to the point of extinction in the material from the 1990s. There are a single instance in Frown (down from seven in Brown) and three in F-LOB (down from eight in LOB).[6]

Another striking decrease in frequency can be noted for the finite subordinator *so that*, particularly drastically in AmE, where it decreases from 229 instances in Brown to 137 in Frown. The trend is parallel, though somewhat more moderate, in BrE, with 230 examples attested in LOB and 173 remaining in F-LOB. Of course, this must not be read as a sign of imminent structural change (in the sense that *so that* might be removed from the inventory of relevant subordinators), but could be taken as a sign that contemporary writing prefers the shorter and generally more informal infinitives when encoding the notions of purpose. However, precise correlations between this clear decline in one strategy of finite subordination and a potential increase in functionally equivalent infinitival clauses are difficult to establish in this case, because: (i) several important uses of *so that* do not allow paraphrases by means of infinitival clauses; and (ii) the number of infinitival clauses in the corpora which would need to be checked as possible replacements for a *so that*-clause runs into several thousands.

---

[6] Variability between infinitives and finite clauses after *in order* is, however, a somewhat untypical case in its long-term development because the infinitive (1609) rather than the finite clause (1671) was attested first (cf. *OED*, s.v. *order* (n.)). As a consequence, *in order that* has never been the statistically dominant variant.

If the spread of infinitival complement clauses at the expense of finite ones is a phenomenon which, in one form or another, can be observed throughout the whole recorded history of English, the rise of the gerund is a more recent phenomenon, dating back to the seventeenth century when the deverbal nouns ending in -*ing* began to take on verbal and clausal properties. The gerund thus emerged as an additional competitor in the domain of clausal subordination and started spreading in its turn, both at the expense of finite clauses and infinitival ones (cf., e.g., Fanego 1996a, 1996b). Again, it is not difficult to find evidence of this in the corpora. For example, there is variation in F-LOB between (old and established) infinitival complements (examples 9 and 10) and (more recent and spreading) gerunds (examples 11 and 12) after *accustomed to*:[7]

(9) "But I am sure no Eton boy, and certainly no Harrow boy of my day," – Churchill was at Harrow from 1888 to 1892 – "ever received such a cruel flogging as this Headmaster was *accustomed to inflict* upon the little boys who were in his care and power." [F-LOB G04]

(10) This small borough, of which Blenheim was a part, had scarcely more than a thousand electors; it had long been *accustomed to send* members of the Ducal family, or their nominees, to Westminster. [F-LOB G04]

(11) However, they all have a useful function, and you will be amazed at how quickly you become *accustomed to using* the right ones to tune in and hold the signal. [F-LOB E26]

(12) "We may conclude that the best-educated men in England at the end of the sixteenth century would have held that the correct way of reading Latin verse was with prose stresses, but that even they would be *accustomed to using* the stressed-ictus method for learning by heart or for scanning" (Attridge 1974: 40; see also Pulgram 1975: 192). [F-LOB J35]

Note that both examples of the older construction are from one and the same text, and one of them is 'out of date' in F-LOB, because it represents a verbatim quotation from Sir Winston Churchill (1874–1965). The frequency of either constructional option, however, is too low to allow any statistical generalizations on the basis of the Brown quartet of corpora.

Seen in the long historical term, however, the situation is clear. The infinitives were there first, and the gerund came later, and this clearly shows up in investigations of larger databases. For example, both the BNC and the *OED* quotations allow robust statistical generalizations and additionally show that the reversal of preferences in favour of the gerund is of very recent origin, in fact an entirely twentieth-century phenomenon. At 219 against 78 instances, gerundial complements clearly outnumber infinitival ones in the

---

7 For a study of changes in the complementation of *accustomed to* from the eighteenth century to the present, see Rudanko (2006).

BNC. In the *OED* material, on the other hand, the very first instances of *accustomed to* + gerund do not go back further than 1775,[8] and a survey of the 157 instances of *accustomed to* in the *OED* quotations of the second half of the nineteenth century (1851–1900) revealed 50 instances of complementation by means of a noun phrase, 100 infinitival clauses and a mere 7 gerunds.[9]

Cases such as this one, and many others,[10] show that the considerable diachronic dynamic which has been in evidence in this component of the grammar for practically the whole history of English has by no means abated in the recent past. Change is, in fact, so pervasive, that a recent publication has referred to developments since c. 1600 in the following terms:

Over the past few centuries, English has experienced a massive restructuring of its system of sentential complementation, which may be referred to as the Great Complement Shift. (Rohdenburg 2006: 143)

Clearly, this makes non-finite subordinate clauses potentially very rewarding subjects to study on the basis of the Brown family of corpora.

9.2   Changes in non-finite clauses I: case studies of individual matrix verbs

One useful way of identifying specific constructions involving non-finite complement clauses is through concordancing for specific superordinate (or 'matrix') verbs, such as, for example, *begin, start, help, prevent* or *remember*. This strategy guarantees high recall among the selected verbs, as no relevant instances are likely to be missed in the search, but has two disadvantages. It occasionally involves a lot of weeding out of irrelevant data and, more importantly, it is bound to miss marginal but potentially very interesting patterns of complementation – such as, for example, unorthodox uses of a pattern with matrix verbs with which it does not traditionally associate.

However, within the limitations described, previous corpus-based research on non-finite clauses in present-day English carried out along these lines (e.g. Mair 2002, 2006b; Rohdenburg 2006) has revealed considerable regional variability between national varieties of English and even more pronounced diachronic developments. The two cases considered here are:

---

[8] 'An experienced trawlman, accustomed to sweeping [dragging the sea-bottom]' (*OED*, s.v. *trawl*). A further early attestation is from 1802: 'I do not know whether the dancing at Poona is particularly good, or whether I am getting accustomed to nautching; but I have liked it better since I came to Poona.' – cf. *OED*, s.v. *nautching*). Note that the phrase *the dancing* in the preceding sentence suggests a verbal noun rather than a clausal analysis here.

[9] Including several which merely consisted of one word, such as *kangaroo-shooting* or *travelling*, and were thus ambiguous in status between noun phrase and gerundial clause.

[10] Cf., e.g., recent studies by Rudanko (1999, 2000, 2006), Rohdenburg (2006) and Vosberg (2003a, 2003b, 2006a, 2006b).

(i)   parallel diachronic developments in British and American English (with AmE possibly in the lead); and

(ii) divergent developments in the two varieties.

The latter present the more interesting case, as such divergence between the major international reference standards of Present-day English is not usually suspected, given the prevailing opinion among scholars and lay observers alike that the grammar and vocabulary of standard English have been thoroughly Americanized over the past century.[11] Owing to the limited availability of suitable corpora of spoken English, previous work has tended to focus on developments in the written language. To redress this imbalance, care will be taken in the following case studies also to include spoken data.

9.2.1   Help + *infinitive*

As an example of the first constellation – parallel diachronic development – consider the complementation of *help* with either a bare infinitive or a *to*-infinitive, as illustrated in the following examples:

(13) Let us see how our efficiency wage model *helps to provide* an understanding of the existence of wage differentials for labour of homogenous potentiality. [F-LOB J45]

(14) Underlining *helps provide* the sculptured look that these garments call for. It helps reduce wrinkling and provides a foundation so that interfacings, facings, boning and hems can be sewn without stitches or ridges [. . .]. [F-LOB E04]

(15) She said the training programme's case studies and problem-solving tasks would *help* social workers *to recognise* the experience of families. [F-LOB F08]

(16) But he does mention a man called Noel Smith, the road manager with Pink Floyd, who *helped* him *get* hold of The Beatles' drumskin at least. [F-LOB A44]

Many attempts have been made to account for this instance of variability in present-day English. In a small number of cases, use of one or the other variant seems to be largely conditioned by structural factors. For example, a negated infinitive seems to favour the use of *to*. While the BNC contains a

---

[11] Cf., e.g., Sidney Greenbaum on the grammatical changes he noted in BrE on returning in 1983 after fifteen years' absence in the United States: "What about grammatical changes in those fifteen years? The only one that I have noticed affects an individual word: the word *nonsense*. I repeatedly heard it being used with the indefinite article: *That's a nonsense*, whereas I could only say *That's nonsense*. Many British speakers now treat *nonsense* in this respect like its near-synonym *absurdity*: *That's an absurdity/ That's a nonsense*. My impressions of other differences from the BrE I remembered involve differences in relative frequency. They all bring BrE closer to the English I had grown used to in the States, and perhaps they reflect American influence" (1986: 7).

small number of negated *to*-infinitives after *help* (cf. 17), bare infinitives are not attested:[12]

(17)   The teacher's job is not to correct mistakes the pupil has already made, but to *help* him *not to make* that mistake next time. [BNC EVB 220]

Conversely, the bare infinitive is the more likely choice if the verb *help* itself occurs in the *to*-infinitive:

(18)   *To help meet* these objectives the Home Secretary appointed a Civil Emergencies Adviser (Mr David Brook CB CBE). [F-LOB H24]

Sequences of two *to*-infinitives tend to be avoided for reasons of euphony, which is an instance of Rohdenburg's (1995) postulated *horror aequi* principle. As instances of *to help to* are not at all rare, however, the effect is statistical rather than categorical–structural.[13]

More often, the choice between the two variants is motivated stylistically, with the more explicit *to* variants being preferred in formal styles[14] and the bare infinitives being preferred in informal styles. Apart from these structural and stylistic factors, grammarians have explored the possible iconic and semantic motivations for structural variation. Dixon, for example, has argued that the *to*-infinitive represents more indirect causation or support than the bare infinitive, claiming that *John helped Mary to eat the pudding* suggests that he did so indirectly, for example 'by guiding the spoon to her mouth', while *John helped Mary eat the pudding* actually means that he himself ate part of it (2005: 201).

The most common assumption found in the literature, however, is that this particular instance of grammatical variability in present-day English reflects diverging preferences in British and American usage, with the bare infinitives being the preferred option in AmE (cf., e.g., Trudgill and Hannah [4]2002: 67).

A previous analysis of the use of *help* in the Brown family of corpora was published in Mair (2002). With the B-LOB ('Before LOB') corpus documenting 1930s British usage now being complete, we can place the findings of this study in a wider diachronic context. As Figure 9.1 (based on

---

[12] However, rare as they may be, negated bare infinitives with *help* are not ungrammatical. A recent study (McEnery and Xiao 2005: 177) reports an example from the Corpus of Spoken Professional American English which – in its full context – has the following form:

when I started thinking of what the draft would look like that would be helpful, it would be helpful in the draft if you had things, like, in bold or italics, things like more elaboration will be added here, or more detail will be added, so people can see that we're talking about the topic, that we have some initial ideas on it, but more is coming. So, *to help people not jump* all over it as soon as they see it and say, oh, my God, they didn't say enough about it.

[13] In other words, the effect is not of the same order as the well-known double-*ing* constraint, which rules out forms such as *being working hard, we hoped for a pay-rise*.

[14] Or cognitively more complex processing environments – on which see Rohdenburg (1996, 2006).

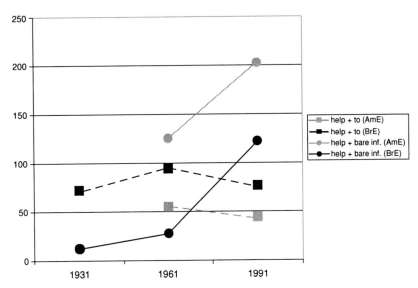

Figure 9.1 *To-* vs bare infinitives with *help* (all construction types) in five corpora – diachronic trends (Broken lines indicate the *to* construction)

Table A9.1) shows, there is (diminishing) regional variation between British and American English, but these regional contrasts are obviously overlaid by an even more pronounced parallel diachronic trend, namely the steep rise of bare-infinitival constructions in both varieties.

Throughout the greater part of the twentieth century until at least the 1960s, BrE tended to favour the *to*-infinitive, and AmE the bare infinitive. A synchronic comparison of LOB and Brown (1961) still shows a fairly clear regional contrast in usage, even if it was not categorical but manifested itself as a strong statistical tendency. Thirty years later, in F-LOB and Frown (1991/92), the bare infinitive has become the preferred option in both varieties (compare the cross-over in the relevant trend-lines between LOB and F-LOB in Figure 9.1). British and American English now merely differ in the degree of statistical preference they display for the same option. If current trends in BrE continue, the gap between the two varieties will narrow even further, and even today we may well ask whether a different degree of preference for the **same** option should be considered a salient regional contrast.

However, convergence between the two varieties is clearly not all there is to this particular development. Diachronically, the variation observed between the two types of infinitive is not a zero-sum game, in which one variant gains to the extent that the other one loses. What we are seeing is something else: a slight decline in the use of the explicit form with the *to*-infinitive, coupled with a dramatic increase in number of bare infinitival complements, the latter going far beyond what would be needed merely to compensate for the decrease of *to*. Note also that this increase builds up slowly from the 1930s (B-LOB) to the 1960s (LOB), and then takes off at a much faster rate. Mair (2002 and 2006b: 136–140) has argued that this should best be seen as a sign of an incipient process of grammaticalization, in which the lexical verb *help* is undergoing semantic bleaching and starting to take on grammatical properties. This is seen in examples such as (19) and (20), which – because it is such a clear instance of the development at issue – was added from BNC data:

(19)   He made important contributions to a number of periodicals such as Il Leonardo, Regno, La Voce, Lacerba and L'Anima which *helped establish* the respectability of anti-socialist, anti-liberal and ultra-nationalist ideas in pre-war Italy. [F-LOB J40]

(20)   The right person may just happen to come along, or it may be necessary to take certain steps to *help this happen*. [BNC B3G]

Here, the core trivalent meaning of the verb *help* ('A helps B to do C') has been bleached considerably – to result in a notion of generalized causation, which is ideally expressed in example (20), with its inanimate–abstract object *this*. If, as in (19), there is no object of *help*, the main function of the verb is to highlight one of several causal or contributory factors involved. Contributions which 'help establish' respectability are one factor among others. If *help* is followed by an object (example (20)), the notion expressed is a similar one of weak causation, which can impressionistically be described as being about half-way on a scale between *enable such a thing to happen* and *make such a thing happen*.[15]

What previous studies on the subject and the analysis so far have failed to investigate are recent developments in spoken English – a gap which needs to be filled particularly with a phenomenon suspected to involve grammaticalization. Table 9.1 surveys the use of *help* + infinitive in the spoken-demographic portions of the BNC (c. 4.2 million words) and the 'Switchboard' section of the American National Corpus (ANC), which comprises c. 3 million words of unscripted telephone conversations among American speakers of diverse regional and social backgrounds and is thus a reasonable match for its British counterpart in size and composition.

The results present an interesting mix of the expected and the thought-provoking. Among the expectations confirmed is that – at 126 as against 66 instances – the bare infinitive is now the statistically normal form in spoken BrE, as well. As in the written data, the preference for the bare infinitive is even greater in AmE (227 bare against 40 *to*-infinitives). Beyond that, however, there is little in common between the spoken and the written

---

[15] Note that the semantics of grammaticalization is also found in examples involving *to*-infinitives: *How can a worksheet help this to happen?* [BNC FUA].

Table 9.1. Help + *infinitive in spoken American and British English*

	ANC Switchboard	BNCdemog
help + NP + *to*-inf.	23	44
help + NP + bare inf.	130	92
help + *to*-inf.	17	22
help + bare inf.	97	34
help **with** object NP	153	136
help **without** object NP	114	56
all *help* + *to*-inf.	40	66
all *help* + bare inf.	227	126
TOTAL	267	192

data. First, the frequency of infinitival constructions as a whole is far lower with *help* in speech than in writing; absolute numbers are comparable in the various corpora but, in the case of the spoken ones, taken from a much bigger amount of data. The second contrast between speech and writing concerns the presence or absence of an object after the verb *help*. In spoken English, *help* is more often used with an object when complemented by infinitives than without one (136:56 in the BNC; 153:114 in the ANC), whereas the opposite preference can be observed in practically all samples of contemporary written English. For example, from the 199 relevant instances in F-LOB, 121 do not have an object after *help*, whereas only 78 do. In a typical BNC press sample of roughly 2.7 million words,[16] however, the objectless forms dominate, as well – at 111 to 35.

The picture which thus emerges is that of a binary but partly overlapping diachronic development in which the bare infinitive becomes more frequent across the board, in all varieties and across genres and style, but the grammaticalization processes discussed and illustrated above seem largely to be confined to written English. This is unusual, though not without precedent in the history of English.[17]

The Diachronic Corpus of Present-Day Spoken English (DCPSE) was made available to the scholarly community only in the year 2005 and offers a fascinating opportunity to study the evolution of spoken BrE, based on real-time evidence, over roughly the same period of time covered by the LOB and F-LOB corpora. Owing to size limitations, the findings for *help* are scant, but in sum they corroborate the picture which has been sketched above. The

[16] To be precise, texts classed as reportage in national broadsheet newspapers (and coded as W_newsp_brdsht_nat_report) in David Lee's genre classification of the BNC World Edition.

[17] Compare, for example, the grammaticalization of complex prepositions such as *with regard to* or *notwithstanding*. For a comprehensive corpus-based treatment of the history of complex prepositions in English, see Hoffmann (2005).

Table 9.2. Help *in the Diachronic Corpus of Present-Day Spoken English*

	DCPSE old[a]		DCPSE new[b]	
	face-to-face	prepared	face-to-face	prepared
help + NP + *to*-inf.	3	4	2	1
help + NP + bare inf.	2	1	5	4
help + *to*-inf.	1	0	0	3
help + bare inf.	1	1	0	2
all *to*-infinitives	8		6	
all bare infinitives	5		11	

[a] The 'old' DCPSE is the material recorded for the Survey of English Usage between 1958 and 1977.
[b] 'New' refers to the texts recorded between 1991 and 1993 for the ICE-GB corpus.
NOTE: The 'DCPSE old' and 'DCPSE new' subcorpora differ in size from the subcorpora DSEU and DICE, which represent more limited and more strictly comparable samples from DCPSE, as discussed in section 2.5 D2. In the present case, sparsity of tokens recommends the use of the whole DCPSE, subdivided into 'old' and 'new' material.

face-to-face conversations of the DCPSE (c. half a million words) contain 85 uses of the verb *help*, of which only 14 govern infinitival complement clauses, which is a frequency much below that found in the written corpora. For purposes of comparison, the prepared-speech section of DCPSE (c. 64,000 words) was investigated as well. Although only an eighth of the amount of text, the material actually yielded more cases of *help* followed by infinitives (16 instances) than the face-to-face portions. While 14 and 16 instances, respectively, are insufficient in order to draw far-reaching statistical conclusions, Table 9.2 nevertheless reveals some interesting clusterings and diachronic developments. On a statistical basis which is admittedly weak, Table 9.2 confirms in real time what the apparent-time data from the spoken BNC have suggested, namely that the reversal of preferences in favour of the bare infinitive has recently taken place also in spoken BrE. Equally interesting is another finding, namely the increase in frequency of those constructions in which *help* appears without an object in the 'prepared speech' genre. A look at the relevant examples reveals that they are very similar in structure to those obtained from the written corpora (see examples 19 and 20 above):

(21) This will *help identify* where racial disadvantage exists so it can be tackled. [DI-J15]
(22) For the first time the nineteen ninety-one census will include a question about long-term illness to *help plan* services and facilities for long-term sick and elderly [DI-J15]

To conclude, we can see that the overall trend observable in the corpora, namely increasing use of bare infinitives, seems to be the result of two parallel developments which, however, differ somewhat in scope, speed and volatility. There is a slow but general groundswell in favour of the bare infinitive which affects all varieties of English (written and spoken, British and American) and both constructions (*help* with object, *help* without object). Superimposed on this, and largely confined to writing and formal and elaborate speech, there is a more specialized development, namely the spread of the specific constructional type *(to) help* + bare infinitive (as illustrated in examples 19–22 above). This latter development accounts for the additional boost to the frequency of the bare infinitive that we have noted in formal speech and writing.

9.2.2 Prevent/stop + NP + (from) + *gerund*

While the development of *help* shows convergence between British and American usage in the late twentieth century, the opposite is the case for *prevent* and *stop*. These verbs can be used with *from* + gerund in all varieties of English:

(23) Has overmanning *prevented* resources *from being* channelled towards essential maintenance work? [F-LOB F14]

(24) But the questions she raises, unlike Lee's, come from the perspective of a woman who must deal not only with racism but with pregnancy, miscarriage, and the experience of being an intellectual whose academic husband was able to do the things her pregnancies *prevented* her *from doing*. [Frown G29]

An alternative, *from*-less, pattern was current in eighteenth- and nineteenth-century British and American English.[18] In the course of the twentieth century, however, the two varieties seem to have parted ways, and while constructions such as (25) and (26) would not have been regionally specific in 1900, they have become clear syntactic Briticisms today.

(25) His alleged motive was *preventing them leaving* their £250,000 estate to his eight-year-old son instead of him. [F-LOB A11]

(26) Michael Heseltine was much better known than the man who *prevented him reaching* 10 Downing Street. [F-LOB B12]

Tables 9.3 (*prevent*) and 9.4 (*stop*) present the relevant statistical shifts in the Brown family of corpora and the 1930s British B-LOB corpus, which – given the time it usually takes for grammatical changes to run their course – are fairly drastic. The *from*-less constructions have made great headway in

---

[18] Among major reference works on American English, it is still recorded – mistakenly as contemporary usage – in *Webster's Third* of 1961 (s.v. *prevent*).

Table 9.3. *Prevent NP* from *V-ing vs* prevent *NP V-ing in five corpora*[i]

	AmE	BrE
1930s	no data	54 : 13
1961	47 : 0	34 : 7
1991/92	36 : 1	24 : 24

(BrE diachr. $p < 0.01$; all other contrasts not significant.)

[i] One of the seven instances of *prevent* NP *V-ing* in LOB has *her* as the notional subject of the gerund and could thus have been excluded as representing the 'archaic' type (*prevent my leaving*) disregarded here. The sole American attestation of the 'British' pattern (in Frown) is from a work of military history dealing with the Battle of Britain. Not unexpectedly, the 'archaic' variant is attested best in B-LOB, with three unambiguous instances and two more involving ambiguous *her*.

Table 9.4. Stop *NP* from *V-ing vs* stop *NP V-ing in four corpora*

	AmE	BrE
1930s	no data	1 : 1[i]
1961	6 : 0	7 : 4
1991/92	7 : 0	3 : 17

[i] Interestingly, the example without *from* has *stop* in the passive, which is unusual even today. 'And old Farre, being not at all the fool he had seemed, had seen that Gronard could not be *stopped getting* away with those secrets – save in one way.' (B-LOB K26)

written BrE in the course of the past few decades, whereas nothing has changed in AmE.

In view of the results obtained in the analysis of the written corpora, it is, of course, tempting to consult the DCPSE material in order to see whether there has been a parallel recent development in spoken BrE. As for *prevent*, the problem is that this fairly formal verb seems to be rather rare in speech. Constructions with the preposition outnumber those without *from* at a rate of 7:4 in the older (1959–1977) material, whereas the preference is reversed (3:5) in the recent (1991–1993) data. In other words, we can observe the same trend as in the written data, though, of course, the numbers are too low for reliable statistical conclusions.

The frequency of *stop* NP *(from) doing something* is roughly comparable in speech and writing. The *from*-less variant already outnumbers the one with *from* by 6 to 3 in the older DCPSE texts, and this distribution is reproduced in the more recent data, although the absolute frequencies have risen to 14 and 7, respectively. Whether this conspicuous rise in frequency is significant is difficult to assess. It is probably best to interpret it in connection with a noticeable general increase in the frequency of 'catenative' uses of *stop* and *start* which will be the subject of the next section. We shall provisionally conclude the discussion by drawing attention to one example from DCPSE which hints at an ongoing restructuring in this fragment of the grammar because it violates a traditional constraint on the passivization of *from*-less *stop*.

(27)   but if your tongue is denervated if the nerve to your tongue is cut then *the taste buds are stopped being renewed* all the time [DCPSE DI-B79]

9.2.3   Start *and* stop *in catenative uses*

Present-Day English has a number of catenative[19] verbs which may be used to indicate the beginning, continuation or end of an activity or state, the most important among them being *begin, start, continue, go on, finish, cease* and *stop*. They differ considerably with regard to the complementation patterns they occur in. *Stop* (in the relevant sense) and *finish*, for example, require a gerund and do not allow infinitives. *Cease*, by contrast, allows both types of complementation, as do *go on, continue, start* and *begin* (though the statistical preferences and semantic constraints on the use of the two options are far from comparable for these verbs).

   In view of such variability, some ongoing diachronic change is only to be expected. Corpus-based studies with a synchronic orientation (e.g. Biber *et al.* 1999: 746f.) have found that with *begin* the infinitive is the statistically normal form and the gerund a minor additional option, whereas with *start* there is more of an even distribution of the two variants. Diachronic studies have noted a tendency towards increasing use of gerunds in the recent past, which seems to continue a long-term general trend towards the use of more gerundial complements (see, e.g., Mair 2002; Fanego 1996a). Thereby, the increase in gerunds takes off from a higher level and is more pronounced for *start*, whereas it is as yet largely restricted to certain types of written AmE in the case of *begin*.

---

[19] In some recent grammatical descriptions of English, e.g. Huddleston and Pullum (2005: 214–222), this term is used to cover almost all constructions in which a non-finite clause is an internal complement of a verb, that is both *I arranged to leave early* and *I arranged for them to leave early*. Here we restrict it (as in Quirk *et al.* 1985: 146–7) to those cases in which no noun phrase intervenes between the higher verb and the non-finite clause (the 'simple' catenative construction in Huddleston and Pullum's terminology), and particularly to those cases in which the finite verb shows signs of incipient grammaticalization as a semi-auxiliary. In this sense, *start/stop doing something* are better exemplars of the catenative construction than *endeavour to do something* or *suggest doing something*. Note that in the latter case the subject of the main verb and the understood agent of the gerundial clause are not even identical.

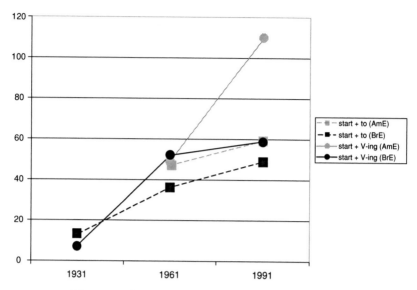

Figure 9.2 Infinitival and gerundial complements with *start* in five corpora – diachronic trends

Whereas previous studies have thus concentrated on the relative frequency of gerunds and infinitives with *begin* and *start*, we would like to shift the focus here on to a different but related phenomenon, namely the increasing frequency of catenative uses of these verbs as a whole. With catenative uses conveying very general actional concepts such as the inception or termination of activities, we are looking at a process of ongoing grammaticalization not entirely unrelated to the one discussed for *help* above. To assess the speed and extent of the development, consider the following figures from the four corpora and B-LOB for catenative uses of *start* (see Figure 9.2). As can be seen, in addition to the pronounced rise of gerunds in the American material, there is an overall increase in the total frequency of the relevant construction (from 88 and 96 cases respectively in 1961 to 108 and 169 in 1991/92). What we are to make of the extremely small total of 20 relevant constructions in the 1930s British material is a question difficult to answer in the absence of corresponding American material. The likeliest explanation is that this informal synonym of *begin* was not fully established yet in formal and written English at the beginning of the century.

Figure 9.3 (see also Table A9.4) focuses specifically on gerundial complements, providing the results from the five corpora for both *start* and its antonym *stop* (for which the infinitive is not an option in the relevant sense, as it would be interpreted as an infinitive of purpose: cf. *I stopped to have a look* = 'I stopped in order to have a look'). How can we account for the diachronic semantic development giving rise to these catenative uses? The

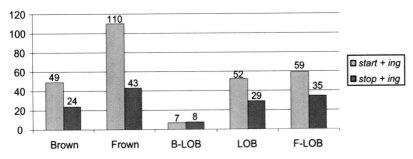

Figure 9.3 Gerundial complements with *start* and *stop* in five corpora –
diachronic trends

earliest attested meanings of *stop* and *start* in English were narrowly lexical:
'block, plug' and 'leap, jump', respectively. These meanings are generally not
compatible with any type of non-finite clausal complement. *Stop* developed
its currently dominant meaning of abstract cessation (which is compatible with clausal complements) slowly from the late Middle English period
onwards; *start* in the sense of 'begin' emerged even later, in the eighteenth
century.

As gerundial complements generally increased in frequency from the
eighteenth century onwards, it is not surprising that an antonymic pattern
of the type *start/stop* + gerund should have emerged as a candidate for rapid
grammaticalization, all the more so as this pattern could be extended to
include transitive uses of the two verbs, so that in present-day English there
is a well-balanced four-way set of options:

(28) a. We started walking up the street, MacCready still holding my arm.
          [F-LOB K11]
      b. We started them walking up the street.
      c. We stopped walking up the street.
      d. We stopped them walking up the street.

As it is likely that this particular process of grammaticalization is driven by
spoken rather than written use, it is useful to study spoken corpora, as well. A
first rough comparison of the spoken-demographic component of the BNC
and spoken texts of the ANC shows that the grammatical asymmetry between
begin and *start* – the former preferring the infinitive while the latter equally
clearly prefers the gerund – is even more sharply pronounced in speech than
in writing. The minor regional contrasts in usage evident from the Brown
corpora, on the other hand, disappear, as the results show the gerund to be at
least as firmly entrenched with *start* in spoken BrE as it is in AmE (see Figure
9.4).[20] While these figures illustrate present-day usage in spoken English,

[20] It will be remembered that *help* + infinitive constructions were shown to occur more commonly in writing than in speech. There is a similar distribution for *begin* + gerund/infinitive.

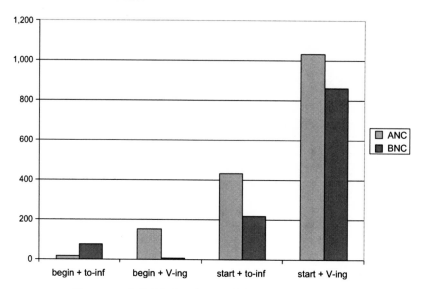

Figure 9.4 Infinitival and gerundial complements with *begin* and *start* in two spoken corpora – regional comparison between British (BNC-demog) and American English (ANC)

they say little about possible diachronic trends. A more detailed analysis of the BNC material on the 'apparent-time' pattern, however, reveals a clearly directed diachronic trend, with a perfect age gradient for *stop* + gerund, and a tolerably convincing one for the corresponding structure with *start* (see Table 9.5).

Interestingly enough, there is no corresponding apparent-time patterning (or diachronic increase in the frequency) of the long-established infinitival construction – either after *begin* or after *start* (see Table A9.2). This is further evidence that it is indeed the historically younger *stop/start* + gerund option which is currently undergoing grammaticalization.

Fortunately, *start* and *stop* in the DCPSE are just common enough to make possible a real-time study of developments on the basis of the DCPSE. Tables 9.6 and 9.7 present the frequencies – absolute and normalized – of gerundial complements after these verbs. We note an overall increase parallel in extent to what we observe in the written data of LOB and F-LOB. As for the infinitive after *start*, the figures from DCPSE similarly show an

Whereas the frequency of this type is 283, 283, 224 and 297 in LOB, Brown, F-LOB and Frown, respectively, the spoken corpora, which are several times the size of a Brown corpus, contain only 84 (BNC) and 170 (ANC). The reverse is true for *start*, for which the total frequency (gerunds plus infinitives) reaches 169 in Frown and hovers around a hundred instances in the other three corpora. As Table A9.5 shows, the roughly 4.2 million words of the spoken-demographic sample of the BNC contain more than a thousand instances, and the similarly sized spoken ANC contains almost 1,500. *Start* + *-ing* is thus a construction whose development seems clearly speech-driven.

Table 9.5. Stop/start + *gerund by speaker age in the spoken-demographic BNC*

	stop		start	
Age	raw freq.	pmw	raw freq.	pmw
0–14	61	172	91	257
15–24	50	101	123	247
25–34	68	99	134	195
35–44	67	96	171	244
45–59	52	71	102	140
60+	33	49	107	160

Table 9.6. Start + *gerund in DCPSE*

DCPSE old		DCPSE new	
raw freq.	pmw	raw freq.	pmw
63	136	63	150

Table 9.7. Stop + *gerund in DCPSE*

DCPSE old		DCPSE new	
raw freq.	pmw	raw freq.	pmw
15	32	22	52

increase – from 26 instances in the old (1958–77) to 41 in the new (1991–93) material, which corresponds to normalized frequencies (per million words) of 56 and 97, respectively – a trend which, however, is not corroborated by the apparent-time data from the much bigger BNC (cf. Table A9.3).

9.2.4   Want to

The grammaticalization processes assumed for *help* and *stop/start* in the discussion above are still in their incipient stages, and their outcome is uncertain. This is different for the construction *want + to*-infinitive, which is a much discussed textbook example of ongoing grammaticalization in English (see, e.g., Krug 2000: 117–166, for an analysis and review of the literature). The earliest attested meaning of the lexical verb *want* in English was 'lack' – preserved today in fossilized uses such as *he was found wanting*.

Table 9.8. Want *in five corpora*

	Brown	Frown	B-LOB	LOB	F-LOB
want/wants/wanting/wanted	647	912	591	697	776
want/wants/wanting/wanted + *to*-inf.	323	553	258	361	421
wanna	5	2	–	3	1

The verb subsequently developed an additional meaning, 'desire', which through semantic bleaching soon expressed a general notion of volition, thus effectively entering the grammatical domain of modality. In the course of the past century, further and more clearly modal functions have been added, such as weak obligation, and the relevant uses of *want to* are becoming distinct from the lexical verb use also in a number of formal properties. The following are good examples of such 'advanced' uses of *want to*:

(29) "You don't *want to* look at the eclipse," the Sioux man said. "It will make you blind." [Frown N18]
(30) "You know the first question Peterson's goin' to ask, don't you, Marshal? He's goin' to *want to* know who's payin' for the buryin'." [Frown N03]

In (29) *don't want to* clearly means *shouldn't* – and not *don't wish*. Note that this use shares an important grammatical property with true modals, namely a defective tense system. If we transform the sentence into the past tense (*you didn't want to look at the eclipse*), the modal meaning disappears, and only the non-modal meaning of 'desire/wish' remains. In (30), which carries a meaning of volition rather than weak obligation, the context strongly suggests a phonetically reduced pronunciation *he's gonna wanna know* (with phonetic reduction being an important formal correlate of ongoing grammaticalization).

In view of the advanced stage which has been reached in the process of grammaticalization, *want to* has been treated in Chapter 5 of the present book, together with related developments in the area of mood and modality, such as the pronounced increase in the use of *need to*. What remains to be done here is to point out a puzzling discrepancy between the frequency of the most clearly modal uses of *want to* ('weak obligation', as illustrated in (22)), which is still very low at least in the written corpora of the Brown family,[21] and the massive short-term increase in the frequency of the *want* + *to*-infinitive construction as a whole. Table 9.8 recapitulates the relevant figures.

---

[21] Even on a generous count, the number of instances of the 'weak obligation' use does not exceed 20.

The table shows that practically all of the total increase in the frequency of *want* (line 1) is due to an increase of the *want* + infinitive construction, i.e. the starting point of the grammaticalization process (line 2). At least in the written corpora investigated here, however, it is not the clearly grammaticalized uses which predominate but those in the transition zone between the standard lexical meaning 'desire' and the partly modal 'volition'. The following is a typical example:

(31) That's one of the main problems with 'God's Hands,' a semiauto-biographical new musical by Douglas J. Cohen that opened Theatre-Works' Stage II season at Palo Alto's Cubberley Theatre Saturday. You *want to* like these people. You *want to* believe that their story has significance beyond its particulars. You certainly sympathize with them at times. But the whole thing feels like an exercise in self-indulgence. [Frown C01]

9.2.5 *Assessing the speed of changes*

With the B-LOB corpus complementing LOB and F-LOB it is now possible to make statements about the relative speed of the changes observed in BrE over a period of sixty years. In this regard it is interesting to note that none of the four changes surveyed seems to have progressed at a constant speed. The catenative uses of *stop* and *start* developed most dynamically from B-LOB to LOB, whereas for the other three variables investigated – spread of bare infinitives with *help*, spread of *from*-less gerunds with *prevent* and a general increase in the frequency of *want (to)* – the 'hot' phase of dynamic change was the period separating LOB and F-LOB.

While too much should not be made of the results of a study of merely four variables, the potential benefits of an extension of the Brown family of corpora are great. Once a larger and representative number of morpho-syntactic variables has been investigated, it may become possible to distinguish between phases of dynamism and stability in the development of written English in the twentieth century.

9.3 Changes in non-finite clauses II: statistical trends in the tagged corpora

As has been seen in the above case studies, lexical searches for individual matrix verbs and their patterns of complementation allow us to chart the development of specific constructions at close range and in great detail. Nevertheless, this approach clearly has its limitations – the most obvious one being that the Brown corpora do not contain enough material to study many further interesting instances of possible change, such as, for example, the variable use of infinitives and gerunds after *intend* or *propose*. In this section

Table 9.9. To-*infinitives in four corpora*

	Brown	Frown	LOB	F-LOB
Press	2,591	2,904	2,688	3,106
Gen. Prose	6,392	6,330	6,641	6,686
Learned	2,153	2,145	2,150	2,370
Fiction	3,919	4,022	4,354	4,206
All genres	15,055	15,401	15,833	16,368

(AmE automatic)

Table 9.10. To-*infinitives as percentages of all verbal tags in four corpora*

	Brown	Frown	LOB	F-LOB
Press	9.0%	9.4%	9.1%	10.2%
Gen. Prose	9.3%	9.4%	9.6%	10.0%
Learned	8.4%	8.8%	8.6%	9.3%
Fiction	7.3%	7.3%	7.7%	7.6%
All genres	8.5%	8.7%	8.8%	9.2%

(AmE automatic)

we shall return to a topic discussed in section 9.1 above and investigate whether the known long-term increases in the overall frequency of infinitival and gerundial clauses are reflected in the short temporal range documented by the Brown corpora. Table 9.9 gives the frequencies, overall and by major genre (Press, General Prose, Learned, Fiction), of *to*-infinitives (tag 'TO'). The table reveals the expected mild increase in frequency for the infinitive. Developments in the individual genres are less consistent, ranging from near diachronic stasis in 'General Prose' to pronounced increases in 'Press'.

Of course, infinitives are obviously not independent variables; their frequency can be expected to co-vary with the overall frequency of verbs. Table 9.10 thus gives the frequency of *to*-infinitives as a percentage of all verbal tags. These figures support and expand the picture first sketched in Smith (2002) on the basis of the then available portions of the tagged LOB and F-LOB corpora.[22] This measure broadly confirms the picture obtained in the direct counts, namely that there is a mild general increase, more pronounced in

---

[22] Smith produced figures for the ratio of *to*-infinitive to finite verbs. Between LOB and F-LOB the proportion of infinitives thus calculated increased by 5% across the entire corpora, which is significant. The ratio for Press showed the biggest increase (15%), which is fully corroborated by the current findings.

Table 9.11. *Prepositional gerunds in four corpora*

	Brown	Frown	LOB	F-LOB
Press	616	646	623	670
Gen. Prose	1,683	1,494	1,523	1,541
Learned	760	589	610	637
Fiction	548	565	630	516
All genres	3,607	3,294	3,386	3,364

(AmE automatic)

AmE and largely driven by one genre, namely 'Press'. This can be interpreted as further evidence of the fact that the press represents an 'agile' genre in the sense outlined in Hundt and Mair (1999).

Whether they function as noun clauses, adverbial clauses or relative clauses, infinitival constructions are often in variation with structurally more elaborate finite clauses and thus serve as a convenient device to compress information into fewer words. Over and above the general grammatical drift in favour of complementation by non-finite clauses in the history of English, it may be this functional advantage which makes them particularly suitable for use in journalistic writing, where space is at a premium. Like the nominal chains, which (cf. sections 10.2–3) have increased even more dramatically in the press in the period under review, they increase the information density of texts, thus partly counteracting the trend towards more colloquial writing which is evidenced in the growing frequencies of contracted forms and direct quotations.[23]

Of more recent historical origin than the spread of infinitival clauses is the spread of gerundial clauses. In contrast to the *to*-infinitives surveyed above, the gerunds in the corpora are impossible to access directly as the tag 'VVG' (and the corresponding tags in the 'VA' category) are ambiguous between verbal and nominal uses of the *ing*-form. A search for 'I* V*G', however, targets sequences of preposition + V-*ing* with a high degree of precision and thus represents a reasonable way of accessing one statistically important subtype of gerundial clauses (the other two being the more difficult to retrieve gerundial clauses functioning as subjects and objects). The relevant figures are presented in Table 9.11.

For anyone hoping for confirmation of a continuing across-the-board expansion of the gerund (i.e. the long-term trend since the seventeenth century), this is a sobering picture. Figures in Press go up, but in all three other major genres they go down in at least one of the two varieties, and so do

---

[23] These general observations must not blind us to the fact that there are individual counter-examples: it can be more economical to say (or write) 'I hope I can' rather than 'I hope to be able to'.

the totals, particularly in AmE. What the Brown corpora reflect is diachronic changes in the status of specific constructions involving the gerund (such as *start/stop* + V-*ing* discussed above), but not changes in the grammatical status of the form itself. It has too many functions, and genre conventions, stylistic fashions and plain statistical 'noise' intervene as additional distorting factors.

9.4   Conclusion

The present chapter opened with a brief survey of long-term trends in the history of English non-finite clauses, providing the backdrop for the corpus-based study of the very recent diachronic developments discussed in the following sections. Two long-term trends were identified:

- Infinitival clauses have been gaining ground at the expense of finite clauses since the late Old English period.
- From the Early Modern period onwards, gerundial clauses have emerged as an additional structural option, extending their territory both at the expense of finite and infinitival clauses.

Non-finite clauses thus represent a strengthened grammatical category in Present-Day English – displaying more structural diversity, greater functional range and higher discourse frequencies than in earlier stages of the language. In addition, many of the relevant changes are still going on, which makes the phenomenon eminently suitable for studies based on the Brown family of corpora.

In a small number of cases the analysis of the Brown family of corpora has brought to light instances of rapidly proceeding structural change in the system of Present-Day English clausal complementation (e.g. *prevent, help, stop, start*). Rather more often, though, results from the four one-million-word corpora remained inconclusive if seen by themselves. This is partly due to: (i) the relatively small size of the corpora, which restricts searches to only the most frequent matrix verbs; (ii) the fact that the thirty-year period separating Brown and LOB from Frown and F-LOB, or even the sixty-year period covered by B-LOB, LOB and F-LOB, are far too short to present more than a brief episode in the development of changes which usually take several centuries to complete; and (iii) of course also the fact that these corpora contain no spoken language – the site in which many important grammatical changes first take shape and unfold more rapidly than in the generally more conservative written registers. These limitations were partly overcome by the use of the *OED* quotation base, which added time-depth, of the spoken portions of the BNC and ANC, which provided large quantities of current British and American spoken English, and finally the DCPSE, which – though small in size – afforded the unique opportunity to carry out real-time studies of change in spoken BrE.

In all, the diachronic trends in the field of non-finite clauses which the present investigation has brought to light probably fall short of representing the 'Great Complement Shift' which was recently posited (not without an element of facetious hyperbole?) by Rohdenburg (2006) and Vosberg (2006a). Nevertheless, they are still among the more substantial and noteworthy changes currently going on in the language. Some of them deserve attention because they have remained relatively under-researched in the past (e.g. the rapid spread of *stop/start* + gerund), and others are worth further study because they challenge widely held assumptions about the supposedly inevitable Americanization of British English (e.g. the spread of *from*-less gerunds with *prevent* and *stop* in British English).

10   The noun phrase

Most of our chapters so far have focused on verb constructions, and this might have given the impression that other aspects of English grammar have remained relatively stable. Not so, however. In this chapter we concentrate on the noun phrase, and show that much of interest is happening to this major structure. However, we cannot cover all aspects of the noun phrase in any detail, and so the focus will be on three main topics: parts of speech (especially nouns and noun sequences), the *s*-genitive versus the *of*-genitive, and relative clauses. Other topics, such as premodification, will be touched on in passing.

These topics emerged from a combination of bottom-up and top-down thinking. First, the POS tagging of the Brown family of corpora allowed us to compare word class frequencies across the 1961 and 1991/2 corpora, and we were surprised to note an increase in the occurrence of nouns as a very highly significant trend. This led us to narrow down our focus on increasing frequency to particular subclasses and combinations of nouns, hoping thereby to find some pointers to explanation. The high increase of frequency of certain noun classes – especially proper nouns – together with a spectacular increase in *s*-genitives, noun–noun sequences and acronyms – pointed to an overall pattern of condensation of information in the noun phrase, to which we gave the label 'densification'. Other corpus-based work – for example by Johansson (1980) on plural attributive nouns, by Rosenbach (2002, 2003, 2006) on genitives and by Biber and Clark (2002) and Biber (2003a) on compression and complexity in noun phrases – motivated us to investigate particular areas of noun phrase compactness of structure in greater depth.

The last major topic in this chapter, relative clauses, was partly chosen through serendipity. Given that the Brown corpora were POS tagged but not parsed, many aspects of phrasal and clausal post-modifying structure in the noun phrase were difficult to investigate; but in the case of relativization, the *wh*- relatives and *that*-relatives, on the basis of POS tagging, could be identified with reasonable accuracy. The subsequent manual post-editing was considerable, especially for zero relative clauses. However, initial results showed some startling changes – in particular, in the rise of *that*-relatives and

Table 10.1. *Percentage changes in the frequency of part-of-speech categories*

	AmE (Brown → Frown)	BrE (LOB → F-LOB)
Nouns	*** +4.8%	*** +4.7%
Adjectives	*** +2.0%	*** +6.2%
Pronouns	*** +1.0%	*** −6.5%
Determiners	*** −9.3%	*** −7.5%
Articles	*** −7.3%	*** −3.1%
Prepositions	*** −5.2%	*** −2.8%

NOTE: The figure for pronouns excludes relative *that*; the figure for articles includes possessive determiners *my*, etc. (AmE automatic)

the decline of *which*-relatives in American English. One obvious explanatory factor here was prescriptive influence in the US (see section 10.5.2). However, the more general changes in frequency among relativization types seemed likely to conform to the pattern of colloquialization. These issues naturally invited a more detailed study of relative clauses.

10.1   Parts of speech: an overall survey

Changes in the frequency of occurrence of parts of speech (see Mair *et al.* 2002) are rather easy to measure in the Brown corpus family once the POS tagging has been completed.[1] However, it is much more difficult to give an explanation of why these changes have taken place. Measured in terms of statistical significance, some of these changes relating to the noun phrase have been phenomenally large, and suggest that something important is happening to the distribution of part of speech categories in written English. In particular, they suggest overall that the noun phrase in written English has been becoming more densely packed with information. Table 10.1 gives percentage changes in the major parts of speech featured in the noun phrase (see Tables A10.1a and A10.1b for a fuller frequency list of word classes 1961–1991/2). In Table 10.1, if we ignore the pronoun category, where there is a puzzling disparity, the American and British corpora show closely similar tendencies. The open-class parts of speech at the top (nouns and

[1] It should be recalled, however, that the version of the Brown Corpus which is used here has been automatically tagged without hand-editing, and to that extent the automatic frequency counts for this corpus are less reliable than those for the other three corpora. A corrective coefficient, based on observed individual tag error rates, has been used (see Chapter 2, footnote 27 and Mair *et al.* 2002: 262–4 for the method) to adjust the Brown count and arrive at an estimated 'correct' count. In this chapter the warning flag '(automatic)' will appear where we are using error-adjusted automatic counts for the Brown Corpus.

adjectives) show an increase, varying from 2.0% to 6.2%, while the closed-class categories at the bottom (determiners,[2] articles and prepositions) show diminution, varying from 2.8% to 9.3%. The open-class categories are, of course, often referred to as 'content words', as they are the chief carriers of information content, whereas the closed-class words are often known as 'function words', suggesting that their role is not so much to express referential content as to realize grammatical functions. The change in part-of-speech frequencies therefore strongly indicates an increase in *lexical density* – an increase in the proportion of content words to function words, which in turn indicates a tendency to condense more information about the world into a smaller number of words.[3]

Lexical density will be treated as a factor in its own right in section 11.4, and at this stage we are content to address some issues that on the one hand highlight the significance of this change, and on the other hand warn against too facile conclusions.

First, as to the matter of significance, there should be no temptation to dismiss these 'small' percentages as trivial. Because of the great frequency of occurrence of part-of-speech categories, an increase of a few percentage points reflects a statistically highly significant result. As the asterisk markings show, all the figures in Table 10.1 are highly significant (whether measured by the log likelihood or chi-square test), with a probability in all cases of $p <$ 0.0001 in chi-square terms. For BrE (switching to log likelihood) nouns show a soaringly high significance score: as high as $G^2 = 349.7$ as compared with the critical value of $G^2 = 15.13$ corresponding to the chi-square $p < 0.0001$. Since the noun is by far the highest-frequency part of speech (accounting for more than a quarter of the words in all four corpora), the increase of four or five per cent in the occurrence of nouns is indeed more significant than the higher percentage decrease of determiners (7.5%), which is itself of extremely high significance ($p < 0.0001$).[4] Results are similar for AmE.

Turning to less confidently interpretable aspects of Table 10.1, the adjective and preposition percentages cannot be entirely attributed to noun phrase structure. Naturally, adjectives can be predicative (outside the noun phrase)

---

[2] The 'determiner' category is defined here according to its use in the CLAWS tagset (see Appendix II): all tags beginning with D are counted as determiners. This excludes articles, but (contrary to some versions of grammar – e.g. Quirk *et al.* 1985: 245–331) includes indefinites such as *some*, *any* and demonstratives such as *this*, *these* even when they occur 'pronominally' as the head of a noun phrase. The analysis we follow here corresponds closely to that of determinatives in Huddleston and Pullum (2002: 54–6).

[3] A previous study by Biber and Clark (2002) has shown that this trend towards greater density of information in the noun phrase took place over a longer-term historical period, and applied to both BrE and AmE. A similar trend can also be found in Biber and Finegan's (1997) finding, in a diachronic multidimensional study, that learned, technical varieties of written English – medical, scientific and legal writing – moved away from the more general colloquializing tendency found in other varieties.

[4] According to our most accurate estimate, there are 24,233 more nouns in the two 1991/2 corpora than the 1961 corpora.

as well as as attributive or absolute (acting as modifier or head of a noun phrase). In fact, however, a large majority of adjectives in written texts are attributive (see Biber *et al.* 1999: 506),[5] and Smith (2005: 223) finds that attributive adjectives in F-LOB are significantly more numerous than in LOB.

Similarly, although the loss of prepositions cannot necessarily be connected with the noun phrase (since the prepositional phrases they introduce can function adverbially as well as as modifiers in the NP), a larger number of them are in noun phrases than are adverbial in function,[6] so the decline in prepositions may indeed reflect the tendency to make noun phrases more compact. Certainly this is an obvious interpretation of the declining use of the most frequent preposition, *of*, which characteristically functions in the post-modification of noun phrases. *Of*[7] shows a very clear downward trend in the four corpora, declining by 11.3% in AmE and by 4.7% in BrE. If we use N to represent the nouns or noun phrases linked by *of*, then it is frequently possible to recognize a synonymous relationship between N_1 *of* N_2 and either N_2 N_1 (juxtaposition in a noun sequence)[8] or N_2's N_1 (the *s*-genitive construction), as in:

(1) a. the fruit of the coconut palm [Brown F34] $- N^1$ of N^2
     b. the coconut palm's fruit $- N^2$'s N^1
     c. coconut palm fruit $- N^2 N^1$
(2) a. the behaviour of the patient $- N^1$ of N^2
     b. the patient's behavior [Brown J34] $- N^2$'s N^1
     c. patient behavior $- N^2 N^1$

It is noticeable that the loss of the preposition *of* in the (b) or (c) variants goes with a loss also of the definite article[9] – an indication of how compression of information in the noun phrase can help explain the frequency loss in two closed-class categories: not only prepositions, but also articles.

---

[5] In conversation, on the other hand, the incidence of attributive and predicative adjectives is roughly equal (Biber *et al.* 1999: 506).

[6] Again, the source of this comparison is Biber *et al.* (1999). Although no precise counts are provided, their Table 10.1, p. 768, gives the overall frequency of adverbial prepositional phrases as 25,000 pmw, whereas their Figure 8.12, p. 606, gives the frequency per register as roughly 16,000 pmw (conversation), 33,000 pmw (fiction), 62,000 pmw (news) and 69,000 pmw (academic writing). Other syntactic functions of prepositional phrases (e.g. adjective complement) are comparatively infrequent, and may be disregarded here.

[7] We exclude from the count here occurrences of *of* in fixed expressions such as *in spite of*.

[8] Rosenbach (2006) shows that Noun + Noun sequences, like *s*-genitives, have increased dramatically in LModE, and that whereas the *s*-genitive has tended to move *down* the animacy scale, increasingly taking in non-human nouns, attributive nouns have tended to move *up* the animacy scale, increasingly taking in human nouns such as *patient* in *patient behavior* (2c). Hence there is increasing overlap in the range of choice of these two constructions, as illustrated by (1b, c) and (2b, c).

[9] In the four corpora, the definite article declines by 11.1% between Brown and Frown, and by 5.4% between LOB and F-LOB. One particular case of article loss is in noun phrase name appositions – see section 10.3.

At this point a caveat is in order: it is important to avoid overemphasis on diachronic development at the expense of synchronic variation. At any given point of time, the frequency of nouns and the complexity of noun phrases vary enormously between one genre and another (Biber *et al.* 1999: 65–6, 578–9, 589, 606). High noun frequency is a characteristic heavily associated with information-oriented written language. In diametric contrast to this, high frequency of pronouns is strongly associated with spoken language (see Biber *et al.* 1999: 235; Rayson *et al.* 2000; Leech *et al.* 2001: 298–300). On Biber's Dimension 1 (Biber 1988: 112–8) – informational vs involved, closely aligned with the written–spoken or learned–colloquial gradient – the frequencies of nouns and of pronouns are polar opposites.[10] Hence a diachronic change of 5% – massive though it is in significance terms – could be compared to a less-than-seismic synchronic shift towards a more involved or more informational style on this scale. However, the surprising thing (see further sections 10.2, 11.3–4) is that this shift is in the opposite direction from colloquialization. In the composition of the noun phrase, it appears that an anti-colloquial trend – a 'densification' that packs more information content into a given number of words – has been at work.

Here the question naturally arises: does this anti-colloquial trend apply also to speech, or is there a widening gulf, in this respect, between written and spoken English? From initial counts made of the approximately matching mini-corpora of speech from DCPSE (DSEU and DICE – see section 2.5 D2), the finding was that, although, as is to be expected, nouns are very much less frequent in the spoken than in the written corpora, there has been an 11.1% growth in the frequency of nouns between DSEU (1960s) and DICE (1990s). This is significant at $p < 0.001$.

Another surprising finding is that the subcorpus category that has the greatest proportion of nouns – Press – has increased its quota of nouns hardly at all in the thirty years (see Table 10.2). It is as if, having spearheaded the increase of noun frequency,[11] it is reaching a 'noun saturation point'. On the other hand, the Learned subcorpus and the General Prose subcorpus – the latter being a rather heterogeneous collection of expository text types less noun-loaded than news writing and academic writing – appear to have been making headway towards catching up with the Press. A less surprising observation is that this trend towards 'nouniness' (as with so many other trends we have noted) is further advanced in AmE than in BrE: there are actually fewer nouns in the BrE corpus of 1991 than in the AmE corpus of 1961. In F-LOB 26.5% of the words are nouns; in Brown 27.8% (automatic).

---

[10] Also revealing of these trends is a multivariate analysis of the POS tags in the LOB corpus by Nakamura (1991). The thesis that the sum of nouns and pronouns in a text is a constant, argued by Hudson (1994) is not too far from the truth, as can be seen from Figure 4.1 in Biber *et al.* (1999: 235).

[11] As Rosenbach (2006: Figure 2) has shown using the ARCHER corpus, the proportion of nouns in news texts has increased steadily since 1650.

Table 10.2. *Frequency of nouns in the LOB and F-LOB corpora, showing major genre subdivisions of the corpora*

Genre	LOB raw freq.	pmw	F-LOB raw freq.	pmw	Change %
Press	52,661	297,124	53,222	300,375	+1.1%
Gen. Prose	107,732	259,478	114,280	275,786	*** +6.3%
Learned	42,067	260,905	44,222	274,795	*** +5.3%
Fiction	51,371	202,884	53,732	212,188	*** +4.6%
TOTAL	253,831	252,101	265,456	263,946	*** +4.7%

A familiar theory is that nouns and verbs are in a mutually contrastive relation – that a more *nominal* style is likely to mean a less *verbal* style, and vice versa. This relationship is confirmed through corpus-based register variation studies by Biber *et al.* (1999 – see especially Figure 2.2, p. 65), who explain it as follows:

Altogether, the relative proportion of nouns v. lexical verbs reflects the density of information packaging and the complexity of phrases and clauses in the registers. A high ratio of nouns to verbs corresponds to longer clauses and more complex phrases embedded in clauses. (p. 66)

In Biber *et al.*'s study, conversation is the most 'verbal' register, and academic writing the most 'nominal' register. However, this nominal–verbal cline cannot account for the changing frequencies of parts of speech in the Brown family. Contrary to expectation, the increase of nouns is not at the expense of verbs: the verb category shows only a small loss of 1.0% in LOB/F-LOB and even a small gain of 0.1% in Brown/Frown (see Tables A10.1a, A10.1b). Rather, the increased concentration of nouns in the 1991/2 corpora appears to be mainly at the expense of the closed-category words in the noun phrase itself – that is, the main change is in the parts-of-speech make-up of noun phrases.[12]

10.2 Nouns and noun sequences

To investigate the increase of nouns further, we look first at the frequency of various noun subcategories, and then at the frequency of nouns in juxtaposition, that is, at noun + noun sequences (section 10.3) and genitive constructions (10.4). A considerable part of the increase of nouns is found in

[12] Ideally this should be measured by calculating frequencies of parts of speech per noun phrase; but lacking parsed versions of the corpora, we have had to rely on overall changes in part-of-speech frequency.

Table 10.3. *Increasing frequency of various subcategories of noun in AmE and BrE*

	singular common nouns	plural common nouns	proper nouns	(proper nouns which are acronyms)
AmE (Brown → Frown)	** +0.9%	*** +15.5%	*** +15.5%	(***+178.5%)
BrE (LOB → F-LOB)	*** +2.5%	*** +9.4%	*** +11.4%	(*** +235.3%)

(AmE automatic)

two subcategories: plural common nouns and proper nouns. (Among proper nouns, acronyms have shown a particularly large increase.) See Table 10.3 (and for further detail, particularly regarding changes in subcorpora, see Table A10.2).

10.2.1   Common nouns

By far the most numerous category of nouns represented in Table 10.3 is that of singular common nouns,[13] and yet in percentage terms they have increased relatively little. Proportionately, a bigger increase has come from plural common nouns and proper nouns.

The size of the increase in plural common nouns is puzzling, and detailed research would be needed to investigate it. But one small part of the increase is due to the rising frequency of noun + noun sequences in which the attributive noun is plural, as in *sports car* [F-LOB C04] and *women artists* [Frown G56], a topic we return to in section 10.3.2.

10.2.2   Proper nouns, including proper nouns as acronyms[14]

The increasing use of proper nouns is worth considering in its own terms. The class of acronyms such as *UNESCO, FIFA, WHO*, which are usually organization names, is easily recognizable as undergoing expansion. The right-hand column of Table 10.3 represents a subclass of acronyms as proper nouns[15] – printed all in capitals – which, if one combines the American and

---

[13] For example, in LOB there are more than three times as many singular common nouns as plural common nouns. For details, see Table A10.2.

[14] We do not distinguish here between acronyms narrowly defined (e.g. *UNESCO* pronounced as a single word /juːˈneskəʊ/) and alphabetisms (such as *WHO*, where the letters are spelt out individually). This section does not take cognizance of acronyms functioning as common nouns (e.g. *AIDS, CPU*), where it seems likely that significant increases have also been taking place.

[15] We excluded from the count of acronyms place-names (such as *UK, USA*) and personal names (such as *FDR* for *Franklin D. Roosevelt*, and *JFK* for *John F. Kennedy*). If acronymic place-names had been included with acronyms, the count of acronyms in the American corpora would have increased even more considerably, because of the abbreviations for states such as *NC* for *North Carolina*.

Table 10.4. *Change in relative frequency of subcategories of proper noun in AmE and BrE, based on 2% randomized samples of the four corpora*

	American English			British English		
	Brown raw freq.	Frown raw freq.	Change % 1961–92	LOB raw freq.	F-LOB raw freq.	Change % 1961–91
personal names	476	542	* +13.9%	453	527	* +16.3%
place-names	205	210	+2.4%	228	245	+7.5%
other names	79	116	** +46.8%	94	98	+4.3%
TOTAL	760	868	** +14.2%	775	870	** +12.3%

British corpora, has almost trebled in frequency between 1961 and 1991/2. It appears that the increase in proper nouns is at least partly due to an increase in these names whose whole *raison d'être* is to compress the information spelt out in a sequence of words into a single word. Yet the number of acronyms in LOB and F-LOB represents only 1 in 5 of proper names in general and accounts for only about a quarter of the overall increase in proper nouns. Other reasons needed to be explored (see p. 261, footnote 25 on the increased use of personal names).

Undertaking a semantic count of a randomized sample of 2% of proper nouns in the Brown family (see Table 10.4), we observed that while the frequency of place names increased only moderately, there was a large increase in personal names, amounting to 13.9% in the American corpora and 16.3% in BrE.[16] The increase applied almost equally to surnames and to given names. (We counted initials like the *D.* in *Franklin D. Roosevelt* as personal names, but not as given names: these were the only category of names to decline sharply in frequency.) It seems likely, then, that apart from the increase in the use of acronyms (and more generally of institutional names), the increase in proper nouns can be attributed substantially to names of people. Especially in Press, where they are approximately twice as frequent as in General Prose and Fiction, proper nouns themselves are tools for condensing information. A single name can compress a highly specified meaning into a small amount of space:[17] consider the informational 'punch' of a word like *Madonna*, the *Pentagon* or *Iraq*. Such words will summon up a whole uniquely identifiable rich information schema in the mind of the reader. One would expect this role of proper nouns as conveyors of condensed information to be particularly important in Press. Acronyms, too, are increasingly

[16] There was also a significant increase, as Table 10.4 shows, in 'other names' between Brown and Frown. This is a mixed ad hoc category including names of months and days of the week, tradenames, names of racehorses and sports teams. There was no obvious reason why this category increased so much in the AmE comparison, but not in BrE.
[17] Cf. Marmaridou's (1991: 102–132) cognitive account of proper names.

Table 10.5. *Expressions referring to the President of the United States in Brown and Frown*

Types of expression	1961: Brown Corpus	1992: Frown Corpus
(a) Surname only	*Eisenhower, Kennedy*: 85	*Bush*: 253
(b) Forename(s)[a] + surname	*Dwight (D.) Eisenhower,*	*George Bush*: 36
	John F. Kennedy: 11	
(c) *Mr* + surname	*Mr. Eisenhower, Mr. Kennedy*: 42	*Mr Bush*: 15
(d) *President*[b] + surname	*President Eisenhower/Kennedy*: 48	*President Bush*: 44
(e) *the/Mr President*[c]	*the President*: 203	*the/Mr President*: 73
TOTAL	389	421

[a] In 1961, first forename + initial (*John F.*) are always used for Kennedy. There is no such usage in the case of George Bush.
[b] Two instances are of *President-elect Kennedy*.
[c] Examples of *Mr President* are found only in the 1992 corpus, always in a vocative context.

useful, in the era of ever-expanding information sources, as they typically link an explicit descriptive phrase (e.g. *the World Health Organization*) to a brief name (*WHO*).

Why should references to named people increase so greatly? Without further study, one can only speculate; but one obvious suggestion is that modern Western societies place increasing emphasis on the identity and personhood of the individual. In the public sphere, this trend towards individualization manifests itself, for example, in *ad hominem* party politics and the cult of personality.

One sidelight on this increase of personal names is provided by the data for expressions referring to the president of the United States in the two American corpora. In 1992, President George Bush (Senior) held office throughout, but in 1961 President Eisenhower gave place to President Kennedy, so both presidents' names will be considered. In Table 10.5, the interest lies mainly in row (a), where the plain proper name *Bush* in 1992 is far more frequent than its equivalent in 1961, and row (e), where the honorific title alone (*the President*), counted as a common noun, is far more frequent in 1961. Another factor that boosts the frequency of proper names in the more recent corpus is the greater use of forename + surname – both proper nouns – in row (b), in contrast to the diminishing use of *Mr* + surname – where there is only one proper noun – in row (c). What we appear to observe is a lowering of the honorific status of presidential references (see section 11.6.1 on 'democratization'). The consequence of all this is that the 1961 data yield only 208 proper nouns that identify the incumbent president, whereas the 1992 data yield 384.

10.3   Noun sequences and other juxtapositions

We now pursue another train of thought on the textual density of nouns. If there is an increasing use of nouns in the noun phrase, part of the reason for this is that nouns, or more extended nominal expressions, are tending to occur with larger numbers of noun + noun (henceforth N+N)[18] sequences. The N+N sequence, an ancient Germanic resource for noun compounding, has been reasserting itself in recent centuries.[19] It is normal that the first or attributive noun of a sequence will be singular, and it is on this 'normal' type that we focus initially. There has been a strong assumption that the habit of using such combinations, and creating new ones, grew during the twentieth century – and recent corpus studies (especially Biber 2003a and Rosenbach 2006) bring confirmation of this. The trend has been particularly attributed to the press (where it has been glaringly prevalent in headlines such as *PIG TRANSPORT OFFENCES MAN FINED* [F-LOB A35]) and to the language of specialist discourse such as that of technology or social science, where the requirement of deriving new concepts from existing ones is an ever-present need: *fission products, household size, illiteracy rates, fiber coupler* are examples picked at random from Frown. These considerations lead to a reasonable expectation that the Press and Learned subcorpora will show a particular tendency to increase N+N sequences. In fact, we will show that the growth in noun sequences, though steep in these subcorpora, has been even steeper in General Prose.

First, however, we need to contextualize the phenomenon of noun sequencing more carefully. We restrict attention here to juxtaposed nouns which are orthographically separated by a space, as in *treasure hunt*, rather than being spelt as part of the same compound word, as in *windpipe* or *place-name*.[20] It is easy to find examples in the corpora not only of N+N but of longer sequences (within a single noun phrase) in which N+N sequences are multiply combined:

(3) boat manufacturers and real estate tax shelter sales people [Frown A02]
(4) San Francisco Redevelopment Agency Executive Director Edward Helfeld [Frown A02]
(5) Black Country car sales group West Midland Motors [F-LOB A38]

---

[18] In the remainder of this chapter, we will use the following abbreviations for word sequences:
N+N = noun + noun
N+CN = noun + common noun
PN+PN = proper noun + proper noun
[19] Leonard (1968), cited in Leonard (1984: 4), reports a corpus study showing a 'great increase in the occurrences of noun sequences in prose fiction from 1750 to the present day'. See also more recent studies: Biber and Clark (2002) discover a rise in N+N sequences in news texts in the ARCHER Corpus, detectable in the nineteenth century and increasing through the twentieth century. Rosenbach (2006), arguing for a discontinuity between N+N compounding, as manifest in OE, and N+N constructions where the first noun is a modifier, claims that the latter was a new development in ME, taking further Biber and Clark's results, and establishes an accelerating increase in the use of the construction from the nineteenth century up to the present day.
[20] Inevitably this restriction is adopted as a matter of convenience, although the distinction between the two ways of combining nouns is surely a matter of gradience rather than a clear category distinction as implied by Rosenbach (2006).

Strings like these often contain bracketed structures, and may have an admixture of other parts of speech, such as adjectives. In (6), for example, each pair of words forms a bracketed constituent:

(6) [[[San Francisco] [Redevelopment Agency]] [Executive Director]] [Edward Helfeld]

In (7), two of the modifiers in those constituents (*black* and *west*) are adjectival, although they each form part of a compound place-name:

(7) [[*Black* Country] [car sales group]] [[*West* Midland] Motors]

It can be seen, from examples like these, that N+N sequences are not an isolated phenomenon. The increasing use of attributive adjectives contributes, like that of nouns, to the more compact packaging of information in the noun phrase. We will not analyse the use of adjectives in the noun phrase in depth here, but will demonstrate briefly that noun sequences are not the only manifestation of the increased bunching together of content words in the noun phrase. The sequence Adjective + Noun, which is the most common building block of complex noun phrases, has increased unevenly in the Brown family: by 1.09% in AmE and by 7.3% in BrE. However, the sequence Adjective + Adjective, another manifestation of noun phrase complexity, has risen more sharply, by 9.8% in AmE and by 20.2% in BrE.

These increases can be linked to other trends in premodification involving the juxtaposition of open-class words, and the condensation of information. Rydén (1975) documents an emerging construction in the twentieth-century press where the article is omitted before two nominals in apposition, as in *midnight bather Brian Best*. Although primarily an American innovation, this construction has made its way into British journalism, and has been studied in depth by Jucker (1992: 207–249). It competes with a more traditional construction with appositional post-modification (*Brian Best, the midnight bather*) and is part of more general developments in complex noun phrase premodification in newspaper English (see Mazaud 2004).

10.3.1 Noun + common noun sequences

To provide further quantitative evidence of this 'densification' tendency, we focus henceforth on nouns, in particular looking for sequences where the attributive word is a noun of any kind, and the following head word is a common noun (singular or plural), for example *car door*, *research teams*, *Disney characters*. For these we can use the formula N+CN ('noun + common noun'). (The exclusion of proper nouns from the final position makes sense, in that sequences ending in a proper noun are typically compound names, such as *John Betjeman*, *New York*, *King John*, *Glenda Jackson*, having a rather different function.) The following sentences, from the Learned part

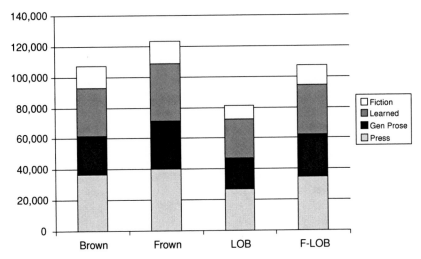

Figure 10.1 Increase of noun + common noun sequences in AmE (Brown to Frown) and BrE (LOB to F-LOB). Frequencies normalized to pmw.
(AmE automatic, adjusted using error coefficient as described in note 27, p. 34)

of Frown, give a brief illustration of how such noun sequences tend to cluster densely in texts with a technical content:

(8)   PEXlib uses the existing X mechanisms: the *communication channel, protocol requests* and replies, the *event queue*, and *error events*. [Frown J69]

(9)   At a *county tour* held during the fall of 1989, *county commissioners, conservation district supervisors*, and other local *agency personnel* saw first-hand what it takes to successfully establish *CRP cover*. [Frown J70]

In theory the sequence of nouns may be indefinitely long, but in the present four corpora no more than eight nouns occur in sequence. The general picture of frequencies in relation to length of sequence (2 nouns, 3 nouns, 4 nouns . . .) is given in Tables A10.3a and A10.3b, specifying frequencies in the two most relevant subcorpora: Press and Learned. However, we concentrate here on combinations of two nouns only, on the grounds that longer sequences are simply (for quantitative purposes) combinations of overlapping two-noun sequences. For example, a sequence of four common nouns in a row will count as three overlapping N+CN sequences. Figure 10.1 shows the very remarkable increase of N+CN sequences of 33.8% between LOB and F-LOB, and a somewhat less remarkable increase of 15.9% between Brown and Frown. (A more detailed picture, both of AmE and BrE, is given in Tables A10.4a and A10.4b.) The N+CN rise is found in every text category A–R, not just the four subcorpora shown in the tables. Strikingly, Table A10.4a reveals that the main growth in N+CN sequences is in registers where such sequences are far less common than in the Press and Learned registers. In other words, we appear to have once again a catch-up phenomenon: the habit of noun–noun sequencing which had already become highly prevalent in these registers in the previous hundred years or so (Biber and Clark 2002; Rosenbach 2006) was in 1961–1991/2 becoming increasingly established in General Prose and Fiction.

As a comparison of Tables A10.4a and A10.4b indicates, the construction is generally much more frequent in AmE than in BrE (31.9% more frequent in 1961 and 14.3% more frequent in 1991/2). In other respects, the picture for AmE is similar to that for BrE. Overall, N+CN sequences have been increasing, although not so dramatically as in BrE (17.2%, instead of 33.6%). BrE appears to be 'playing catch-up', narrowing the lead of AmE in this trend by more than 50% in thirty years. In LOB and F-LOB, the Press and Learned categories (like those of Brown and Frown) have the highest frequencies of these sequences, whereas General Prose and Fiction show the greatest increases.

In this respect, Press as the most 'agile', innovative genre and Learned as the most 'uptight', conformist genre (see Hundt and Mair 1999) seem to be behaving in a similar way, as if moving towards a saturation point in the use of N+CN sequences. But how can this idea of 'saturation' be given a rational interpretation? To answer this, we refer again to Biber (2003a), who argues from corpus evidence that 'popularization' and 'economy' have made competing demands on the Press. Popularization is associated linguistically with colloquialization – using the kind of language that is most accessible to a mass readership. Economy means condensing news into a small linguistic compass – another kind of pressure that affects newspaper language, not only in headlines, but also in running text. Both popular appeal and information density being desiderata for the language of the press, there is a potential conflict between them: too much information density in this area would come at a cost to accessibility[21] – and presumably, in turn, popular appeal – a price which editors and writers are apparently unwilling to pay.

However, this is not a conflict of interest restricted to the Press. In another paper, Biber and Clark (2002) more generally relate the increasing 'nouniness' of written English to the information explosion which comes from technological advance, increasing social complexity and the growth of information needs in our present-day world. If this is reflected in the increase of

[21] It is well known that the semantic relation between the two nouns in N+N sequences is extremely variable (see, for example, Leonard 1984; Biber et al. 1999: 589–94). As Biber et al. (1999: 590) put it: 'On the one hand, they bring about an extremely dense packaging of referential information; on the other hand, they result in an extreme reliance on implicit meaning, requiring addressees to infer the intended logical relationship between the modifying noun and the head noun'. Such being the case, it is understandable that beyond a certain 'saturation point', frequency of N+N sequences causes processing difficulties.

Table 10.6. *Additional noun + common noun sequences as a percentage of additional nouns in the 1991/2 corpora*

Brown → Frown increase			LOB → F-LOB increase		
A extra N+CNs	B extra nouns	A as a %age of B	C extra N+CNs	D extra nouns	C as a %age of D
4,145	10,420	+39.8%	6,488	11,625	55.8%

NOTE: N+CNs = noun + common noun sequences
(AmE automatic)

noun–noun sequences and other signs of information compression we have observed, then it is found not only in the Press, but also in the Learned and General Prose varieties, and even Fiction.[22] But the Press and Learned registers, being those that have led this trend in the past, may now (we suggest) be reaching a point where rising information density no longer pays its way. Similarly, AmE, which led the trend for N+CN sequences and which had built up a much greater frequency of these by 1961, lost more than half of its lead over BrE in the 1961–1991/2 period – as already noted, another apparent example of 'catch-up'.

Returning to the density of nouns with which this chapter started, it might be wondered how far the observed sharp rise of N+CN sequences accounts for the increasing use of nouns in general. A rough indication of this can be obtained if the number of additional noun sequences in the 1991/2 corpora is expressed as a percentage of the number of additional nouns in general – see Table 10.6. As a rough-and-ready measure, if we suppose that each extra N+CN leads to an increase of 1 in the tally of nouns, then N+CN sequences account for a substantial proportion (40% in AmE and 56% in BrE) of the increase of nouns.

10.3.2 *Noun sequences with plural attributive nouns*

N+CN sequences in which the former (i.e. attributive) noun is plural have been considered exceptional, since the traditional practice in English, both in N+N compounds and N+N sequences, has been to omit the plural inflection of the first noun, even if it is semantically appropriate. Consider such examples as *bookshelves* ('shelves for books'), *place-names* ('names of places'), and

---

[22] Furthermore, the growth in 'nouniness' is not restricted to the written language. From initial counts we have made of DSEU and DICE, these spoken mini-corpora show a highly significant increase in the use of nouns in combinations of N+N, especially when the nouns are common nouns. The increasing use of combinations like *blood sports*, *career woman*, and *brass hats* (examples from DSEU and DICE) suggests that whatever pressures are causing densification in the written language are also influencing speech.

animal rights ('rights of animals'). Yet studies of recent English (Johansson 1980; Biber *et al.* 1999: 594–6) have noted the apparently increasing variety of formations with a plural attributive noun, suggesting factors which are favourable to their occurrence.[23] One of these factors, borne out by the evidence of the Brown family of corpora, is that plural attributive nouns are particularly likely to occur if they are morphologically irregular in having no -*s* inflection. *Women*, for example, is particularly prolific in this function, as in: *women candidates, women leaders, women students*. Another observation amply illustrated by the four corpora is the tendency for plurals in -*s* to be used where singular forms would indicate a different and inappropriate meaning. Words such as *rights* and *arts* are well established as attributive nouns, in combinations such as *animal rights campaign* and *Arts Faculty*, whereas their meaning would become unclear or misleading if the singular were substituted.

It is also noted that the -*s* plural is common in names of organizations, committees and the like: *Veterinary Products Committee, Voluntary Services Unit*. These examples illustrate a further characteristic: that the plural noun tends to take a medial position in a longer sequence of nouns (see Johansson 1980: 56–8). In *animal rights campaign*, for example, *rights* is a head with respect to *animal*, as well as attributive with respect to *campaign*. Some examples of this type are semantically akin to genitives, but lack the apostrophe and are inclined to be indeterminate as to whether the -*s* signifies a possessive meaning, a plural meaning, or both:

Ramblers Association	[F-LOB]
Citizens Advice Bureau	[F-LOB]
dolls clothes	[F-LOB]
masters degree	[F-LOB]
Concord Veterans Assistance Center	[Frown]
Texas Bankers Association	[Brown]

The Brown family of corpora shows that the frequency of plural attributive nouns increased in the late twentieth century, particularly in BrE. Although in this respect AmE was in the lead in 1961, by the 1990s BrE seems to have leap-frogged over AmE with an extraordinary increase of 70.4%: see Figure 10.2 (and for quantitative detail, Table A10.5). The increase of plural attributive nouns may well have been brought on by the general increase in noun sequences, bearing in mind that the implicit link between two adjacent nouns has to be inferred, putting a burden on the cognitive processing abilities of the reader. In such circumstances an -*s* at the end of a word may be a handy clue to interpretation. Thus the generic meaning of the plural in

---

[23] In his detailed corpus-based study of plural attributive nouns, Johansson (1980: 1–2, 117–18) briefly traces the history of studies of plural attributive nouns back to 1911, and notes how the construction appears to have extended its range over the intervening period, although quantitative data have been lacking.

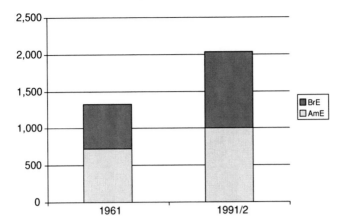

Figure 10.2 Increase in plural attributive nouns in N+N sequences (AmE automatic)

weapons purchases or *fisheries protection* is helpful in eliminating the possibility of a singular interpretation (that *one* weapon is to be purchased, or that *one* fishery is to be protected) and in capturing the intended generic meaning of the whole.[24]

10.3.3 Sequences of proper nouns

The more than 11% increase of proper nouns in Table 10.3 invites explanation, and part of the explanation is that proper nouns, like common nouns, tend increasingly to occur in sequences. The frequencies of proper noun + proper noun (henceforth PN+PN) sequences (in effect, compound names) in the corpora are as in Figure 10.3 (quantitatively presented in Table A10.6). Again we note a general increase in frequency, but the difference between the two regional varieties is very striking. The increase in BrE is three times that in AmE, and once again, a 'catch-up' phenomenon is observed. In the thirty-year period, BrE has been closing the gap, so that the difference between higher frequency in AmE and lower frequency in BrE has been diminishing.[25]

---

[24] At the end of his monograph, Johansson (1980: 116) summarizes a number of factors that may have played a role in the spread of plural attributive nouns.

[25] Before leaving N+N sequences, one remaining category should be incidentally mentioned: one in which the first noun is a common noun and the second noun a proper noun: N+PN. This category, in sharp contrast to the others, has been dwindling (by 9.7% in AmE, and by 13.4% in BrE). One reason appears to be that courtesy and respect titles such as *Mrs, Mr, Miss, Dr, Colonel, President*, which generally precede proper nouns and which are given common-noun tags in the tagged version of the corpora, showed a very considerable decline between the 1961 and 1991/2 corpora (see the discussion of democratization in section 11.6.1).

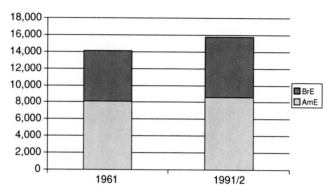

Figure 10.3 Increase in frequency of proper noun + proper noun sequences 1961–1991/2 in Brown, Frown, LOB and F-LOB (AmE automatic)

This increase appears to reflect a change in habits of personal reference – the honorific conventions of 1961 giving way to more casual informal habits, even in referring to the President, in 1992.[26] Similar trends are no doubt to be found in BrE.

10.4   The *s*-genitive and the *of*-genitive

Many commentators on language change in progress in present-day English assume that the clitic *s*-genitive has been spreading at the expense of the analytic *of*-genitive in recent times, mainly because a supposed constraint on the use of the *s*-marker with inanimate nouns has been weakened. Among the first to suspect such a trend was Otto Jespersen in the earlier twentieth century:

During the last few decades the genitive of lifeless things has been gaining ground in writing (especially among journalists); in instances like the following the *of*-construction would be more natural and colloquially the only one possible. (1909–49: VII, 327f.)

As examples he cites expressions such as *the sea's rage*, *the rapidity of the heart's action*, or *the room's atmosphere*. Jespersen's views have been echoed in further treatments of change in progress in twentieth-century English such as Barber (1964: 132–3) or Potter (²1975: 105). However, the issue has remained controversial. Strang, for example, argues: 'we lack figures to confirm these trends; in any case it is not wholly clear how far the special varieties of English favouring these tendencies (newspaper writing...) are simply becoming

---

[26]   See Table 10.5. The growing influence in American society of 'camaraderie' as opposed to more traditional respectful forms of personal reference is discussed by Lakoff (1990: 38).

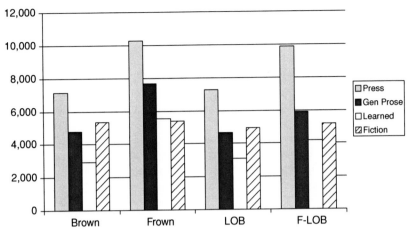

Figure 10.4 Increase in frequency of s-genitives 1961–1991/2 in Brown, Frown, LOB and F-LOB (frequencies pmw) (AmE automatic)

more preponderant, and how far their preponderance is influencing standard British usage' (1970: 58). Denison also reserves judgement on the issue in the *Cambridge History of the English Language*: 'The ranges and relative frequencies of the competing constructions have varied over the course of time, with genitives of inanimates perhaps on the increase' (Denison 1998: 119). Indeed, available evidence from corpora (e.g. Raab-Fischer 1995; Hinrichs and Szmrecsanyi 2007) shows that any expansion due to the use of genitives with inanimate nouns is difficult to demonstrate. For Hinrichs and Szmrecsanyi, working on categories A and B of the four corpora, the effect is found in AmE, but not in BrE. Clearly, as we shall see in sections 10.4.1–2, there is dramatic change, but no single factor can account for it.[27]

10.4.1 The s-genitive

Our analysis of the Brown family confirms Rosenbach's finding that 'the s-genitive is currently increasing, . . . and this increase is more advanced in American than in British English' (2002: 3). Figure 10.4 shows the climbing frequency of the s-genitive in the four corpora (and Tables A10.7a and A10.7b give further detail). This rise is of c. 43% in AmE and of c. 25% in BrE, far in excess of the 3.9% and 4.7% increases in the overall frequencies of nouns

---

[27] Another factor playing a significant role in both AmE and BrE is the relative length (in words) of the possessor and the possessum (i.e. *X* and *Y* in *X's Y*). Rosenbach (2002: 154–70), using an experimental method based on questionnaires, and investigating variation according to apparent time (see our section 5.2, especially Figure 5.4), concludes that the increase in the s-genitive is partly due to the increasing use of this construction with inanimate nouns.

from Brown to Frown and from LOB to F-LOB, respectively, so the general increase in numbers of nouns can only account for a small proportion of the increasing numbers of *s*-genitives.[28]

In view of the clear link between the use of the genitive and information density, as discussed in section 10.1, it is not surprising that the greatest changes in usage are found in the information-oriented Press and Learned subcorpora, showing remarkable rises of 44% and 91% in AmE and 36% and 35% in BrE, respectively. Moreover, as assumed by many observers, Press writing particularly favours the *s*-genitive, and the increase (unlike that of N+N sequences) shows no sign of approaching a 'saturation point'. Fiction writing, on the other hand, shows the lowest increase of genitives (virtually nil in AmE), in keeping with the overall low incidence and low increase of nouns in Fiction (see Table 10.2).

10.4.2 The of-*genitive*

We distinguish between the terms *of-phrase* (which refers to all prepositional phrases introduced by *of*) and *of-genitive* (which applies to *of*-phrases sharing the genitive function with the *s*-genitive, i.e. as an alternative way of expressing the same meanings).

Both the *s*-genitive and the N+N construction have an effect of concentrating information density in the noun phrase. In this respect, their increased use, especially in Press, is a further manifestation of a modern trend already noted (Hundt, 1998a: 47, in this connection points out the 'more snappy' quality of genitives). In a historical perspective, however, their growing popularity can be seen as a continuation of a trend centuries old.[29] The *of*-construction, rarely attested in OE, underwent a vast extension of its range in ME, but could be expected to suffer decline with the resurgence of the *s*-genitive in Modern English. This pattern is indeed what we find from the limited data[30] displayed in Table A10.8, which presents the hand-checked set of *of*-genitives (that is, all *of*-phrases which are judged semantically and formally interchangeable with *s*-genitives) from a 2% sample from each corpus.

---

[28] However, perhaps the steeper increase in proper nouns (11%, 12%) is more relevant in explaining the increasing use of the genitive, since, as pointed out by Raab-Fischer (1995), the genitive is particularly frequent with personal names, and F-LOB shows an increasing use of personal names as compared with LOB.

[29] In the historical account argued by Rosenbach (2002: 177–234), the OE genitive inflection underwent a decline in ME up to c. 1400, when it took on a new lease of life as a clitic. The revived and expanding use of the *s*-genitive from EModE onward has presumably been continuing up to the present day. Altenberg (1982) provides a detailed account of the variation between the *s*-genitive and *of*-genitive in EModE. With regard to the comparable increase of N+N sequences in ModE, see footnote 19, p. 215.

[30] An exhaustive analysis would have been impractical, as it would have involved inspecting and categorizing over 130,000 instances.

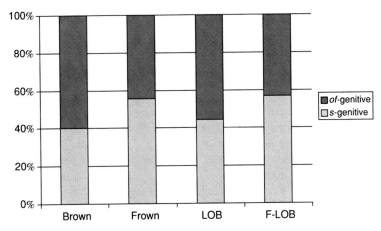

Figure 10.5 Change of frequency of the *of*-genitive in relation to the *s*-genitive between 1961 and 1991/2, expressed as a percentage of all 'genitives'
(Note that the frequencies for the *of*-genitive are scaled up from a small 2% sample, and cannot therefore be regarded as more than approximations.) (AmE automatic)

AmE and BrE show a very similar decline of c. 24%, and it is reasonable to assume that the close parallel, in BrE, between the upward trend of *s*-genitives and the downward trend of *of*-genitives is more than coincidental. However, detailed empirical studies of the genitive (e.g. Altenberg 1982; Leech *et al.* 1994; Rosenbach 2002, 2003; Hinrichs and Szmrecsanyi, 2007) have demonstrated that a number of factors, syntactic, semantic, pragmatic, even phonological, have a role in determining the preference for one construction or the other. By no means can the *s*-genitive and the *of*-genitive be considered in free variation. For example, Rosenbach (2002: 33–74) surveys a range of factors, finally focusing on three, listed here in order of importance: animacy, topicality, and the possessive relation. Hinrichs and Szmrecsanyi (2007) submit the following factors to a multivariate analysis of genitives in Press categories A and B of the Brown family of corpora: animacy of possessor, thematic status, information status, final sibilant on the possessor, end-weight, persistence (i.e. repetition), nested structure, type-token ratio, and the 'nouniness' of the text/passage.

Nevertheless, the data from the four corpora in Figure 10.5 suggest that, by 1991, the *s*-genitive had overtaken the *of*-genitive in frequency in both AmE and BrE. British English is in the often-noted position of following the American lead in increasing use of *s*-genitives (which are more frequent in Brown, and even more frequent in Frown, than the British equivalents). However, unexpectedly, BrE is itself in the lead in the decline of *of*-genitives. The fact that both constructions are more frequent in AmE than in BrE is

difficult to reconcile with any claim that the *s*-genitive and the *of*-genitive
are in a simple competitive 'either X or Y' relation.[31]

10.5   Relative clauses

Like other structures considered in sections 10.3 and 10.4, relative clauses are
a means of introducing complexity of structure and meaning into the noun
phrase.[32] However, they are the most fully explicit form of noun modification,
and do not compress meaning in the way that N+N sequences and *s*-genitives
do. This may be the reason why, overall, relative clauses have not increased –
at least in BrE, where there is a modest decrease of c. 3% between LOB
and F-LOB.[33] The interest of this section lies rather in the choice between
three different devices of relativization: (a) *wh*- pronouns (*which, who, whom*
and *whose*), (b) the relativizer *that* and (c) zero relativization, which are
stylistically associated with different text types ((a) being more formal in
distribution, and (b) and (c) more colloquial – see Biber *et al.* 1999: 609–
618). Attention will also be given to the choice between relativization by
preposition + *wh*- pronoun (pied-piping) and by preposition stranding, the
former being restricted to type (a) (see section 10.5.4).

The history of English relative clauses is somewhat complex,[34] as is also
the present-day set of conditions (such as animacy of the antecedent and
syntactic function of the relative pronoun or relative 'gap') that determine
the choice of one relativization device rather than another. As far as possible
here, our focus will be on stylistic choices a writer can make between one
relativization type and another. Biber *et al.* (1999: 609–12) show that, in
conversation, *that* is the most frequent relativizer, followed by zero, whereas
in the more formal and information-packed registers of Press and Academic
Writing, the *wh*- relatives are by far the most common type.

This distribution, however, has to be seen against the background of a
greatly varying frequency for relative clauses as a whole. The most formal
written registers, with their much greater noun phrase complexity, have a far
higher incidence of relative clauses than conversation. As regards the choice
of relativizer, *wh*- relative pronouns are predominant in written registers,

[31] As is discussed in detail by Rosenbach (2002: 23–41), the variationist model whereby two
variants are in an 'either–or' competitive relation, such that a gain in one implies a loss in the
other, is problematic when applied to syntactic alternatives such as the *s*-genitive and the
of-genitive. For this reason, we go no further here in attempting to specify the parameters
of a shift of preference from the *of*-genitive to the *s*-genitive. All we can say is that the
frequency changes between 1961 and 1991/2 are persuasive in suggesting that such a shift
of preference has been taking place.
[32] We will restrict attention to adnominal relative clauses, including both restrictive and
non-restrictive clauses, but leaving out of account sentential relative clauses.
[33] Overall figures for AmE have not been calculated, because of the amount of hand-editing
required for zero relatives.
[34] For longer-term corpus-based or corpus-informed historical studies of relative clauses, see
Nevalainen and Raumolin-Brunberg (2002), Rissanen (1986) and Rissanen (1999: 292–99).

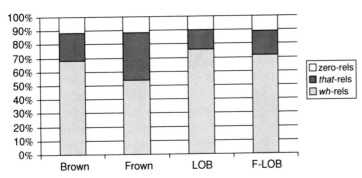

Figure 10.6 Change of frequency of the three types of relativization 1961–1991/2: decline of the *wh-* relatives, and increasing frequency of the *that-* and zero relatives. Expressed as a percentage of all (finite) relative clauses apart from those with an adverbial gap.

while *that* and zero relativizers take a bigger share in more colloquial styles. Stylistically, then, there is a division between the *wh-* relatives, which are more literate in their affinity, and *that* and zero relatives, which are more oral. Overall, however, *wh-* relative clauses are more frequent than *that-*relatives, which are in turn more frequent than zero relatives (see Figure 10.6).[35] However, this is not merely a matter of stylistic preference: the *wh-*pronouns have a virtual monopoly in non-restrictive relative clauses, and the *wh-* pronoun *who* is very strongly preferred over *that* for human antecedents (Biber *et al.* 1999: 613–14). Moreover, the informational registers have by far the greatest complexity of noun phrase structure, and the *wh-* pronouns are useful here because they can bear a heavier functional load than *that* and zero, and can give a stronger, more unambiguous signal of the beginning of a relative clause, thus mitigating the structural ambiguities and processing difficulties associated with syntactically more complex NPs.[36] In PDE, zero is by definition the most reduced form of relativization. *That* is also less salient, as a structural signal, than the *wh-* pronouns, because its vowel is habitually reduced to schwa, and *that* as a word form is not only one of the commonest items in the language, but also multiply ambiguous as to its grammatical function. Overall, moreover, *wh-* relatives are the most versatile in that they can be used with the greatest variety of syntactic functions.

---

[35] This order of frequency (*wh-*, *that*, zero) even applies to the general spoken corpus DCPSE (including a considerable range of spoken genres), according to a small-scale investigation we made of a random 5% sample taken from the whole corpus. The proportions were: *wh-*relatives 166; *that-*relatives 107; zero relatives 76; or, in percentage terms, 48% : 31% : 22%.

[36] Rissanen (1999: 295) speculates on the role played by functional load in the rise of *wh-*relatives in EModE. See also Rohdenburg (1996) on the relation between grammatical explicitness and cognitive complexity.

In the Brown family of corpora, the *wh-* relatives are predominant throughout. Overall, in Brown the frequencies of *wh-*, *that* and zero relatives are in the proportion 68% : 21% : 11% (changing to 54% : 35% : 12% in Frown). In LOB, the proportions are 74% : 14% : 12% (changing to 70% : 17% : 13% in F-LOB). The predominance is huge in the LOB Learned texts, where the ratios are 84% : 11% : 5%. In LOB Fiction, however, types (a)–(c) are more evenly spread, with the proportions 53% : 22% : 25%, while the *wh-* relatives still remain in the majority.[37] Comparing Learned, as the most formally informative variety, with Fiction, the variety closest to speech, we note in the above comparisons that (a) (*wh-* relatives) have a distribution contrasting with both (b) and (c) (*that* and zero relatives), which have their strongest representation in Fiction writing. The difference between (b) and (c) is more subtle, but it is clear, from the percentages above, that zero relatives have a slightly more pronounced association with more 'colloquial' writing, and are correspondingly more strongly avoided in expository–informative writing.[38]

Turning to the changing use of these three types of relative clause, we now examine the frequency data from the four corpora of the Brown family.

10.5.1   Wh- *relative clauses*

From Figure 10.6 (and from Tables A10.9a and A10.9b) we note that *wh-* relative clauses are (i) considerably less common in AmE than in BrE, and (ii) declining fairly steeply in both varieties. Because of the stronger association of *wh-* relatives with formal written text types, the latter is a change strongly suggestive of colloquialization (see sections 1.3, 11.3).

A further striking finding is that the decline is more than twice as steep in AmE as in BrE. There is thus a widening of the frequency gap between the two varieties: in 1961 *wh-* relatives were 15.5% more frequent in BrE than in AmE; by 1991/2 this difference had almost doubled, to 30.0%. This is

---

[37] This result might be felt unsurprising, because of the monopoly *wh-* relatives have of non-restrictive clauses, and if we subtracted these and limited our calculation to restrictive clauses, a more equal distribution of the three types would result. This is true, yet the proportion of restrictives to non-restrictives is roughly 70% to 30%, so restrictive *wh-* relatives are still more common than the other types of restrictive relative clause.

[38] Compare Sigley's (1997: 229) analysis of the distribution of *wh-*, *that* and zero relatives in corpus data from New Zealand English, including the Wellington Corpus of Written New Zealand English, compiled on the Brown model, as well as spoken corpus data. Using Principal Components analysis, Sigley defined 'a crude formality index', which he then applied to the choice of the three relative clause strategies in a context where all three strategies were available. Looking at the plot in Sigley's Figure 4.3 (p. 229), his findings for written English confirm our results above, *which* being associated with formality, and *that* and zero with informality. In speech, however, he reports that *that* is favoured over zero in spontaneous dialogue.

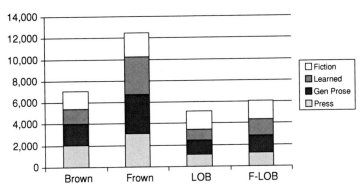

Figure 10.7 Increasing use of *that*-relative clauses 1961–1991/2 in AmE
(Brown → Frown) and BrE (LOB → F-LOB): frequencies pmw

a case where the two varieties have notably diverged during the thirty-year
period.

Looking at the data more carefully, however, we discover (see Table
A10.10) that the decline in AmE is entirely due to one relative pronoun, *which*.
This has lost frequency to the extraordinary extent of 34.4% (compared with
a decline of 9.4% in BrE). Of the other *wh-* relative pronouns (*who, whom* and
whose), *who* has slightly increased in AmE, whereas the relatively infrequent
whom, surprisingly, has risen from 144 to 166 instances (see the discussion
in section 1.1). In BrE, on the other hand, there has been a more moderate
decline of *wh-* pronouns across the board: *which* has lost 9.5%, *who* 4.2%,
whom 20.0% and *whose* 17.0%.

The disparate results for *wh-* relatives in AmE will require some explanation. Although no reason for the small rise in frequency for *who* and *whom*
suggests itself, the astonishing loss of frequency in the case of *which* needs
to be considered alongside the even more astonishing growth in the use of
that-relatives, to which we now turn.

10.5.2   That *relative clauses*

In Figure 10.7 (see further Tables A10.11a and A10.11b) we find an increase
of *that*-relative clauses of 73.1% in written AmE, and of 15.3% in written
BrE. The increase in BrE can be reasonably explained in terms of the trend of
colloquialization, and mirrors the (somewhat less dramatic) fall in the use of
relative *which*. In AmE, however, the immense increase in the use of relative
that calls for special scrutiny. Of all relativizers, *which* and *that* are closest to
being in a competitive relation, such that they can replace one another in a
majority of cases. In examples (10) and (11), but not (12) and (13), *that* and
which can felicitously replace one another:

(10)   Visual works *that* do not meet this standard are taken to be craft, 'motel art,' commercial art, or anything considered to be less than art. [Frown G56]

(11)   [. . .] anxious to develop something *which* could carry an atomic warhead of their own manufacture. [LOB A03]

(12)   The last doorman *that* saw me do that should calm himself. [Brown A32]

(13)   We live in an age in *which* it is no longer acceptable even for churchmen to talk in terms of right or wrong [. . .] [F-LOB B07]

The lack of precise interchangeability between the two types is due to a number of factors, of which these are the most important:

(i)   *Which*, but not *that*, can be used for non-restrictive relative clauses.[39]
(ii)   *Which* is virtually restricted to non-personal antecedents, whereas *that* can be used (albeit rarely) with personal antecedents.
(iii)   *Which*, but not *that*, can be used with a preceding preposition in the 'pied-piping' construction (while both *which* and *that* can be used with preposition stranding).

In spite of these factors, it is highly likely that the gain in frequency of *that* in AmE is largely at the expense of *which*. This would fit in with the way these relativizers are often contrasted in usage handbooks, style guides, and the like. The decline of *which*, and the corresponding increase of *that*, is no doubt influenced by a strong prescriptive tradition in the US[40] of rejecting *which* as an introducer of restrictive relative clauses. Such a tradition has not been prevalent in usage guides in the UK, although since the early 1990s it has influenced countries throughout the world, including the UK, through its incorporation in internationally marketed word processors and grammar checkers. We suspect that if a comparable corpus analysis were undertaken today, there would be an even bigger rise in relative *that* and fall in relative *which*. However, the American avoidance of *which* in restrictive relative clauses is not a new phenomenon: the difference between AmE and BrE in this respect was clear even at the beginning of our period, in 1961 (see Table A10.10).

---

[39]   There are rare exceptions, e.g.:

These thoughts occupied him as the lift, that was to take him to the mail-order department on the fourth floor above the bookshop where he worked, stalled obstinately on the ground floor. [F-LOB N22]

[40]   'Usage authorities' in this context are not confined to authors of usage guides and manuals of style, but can include influential educators writing textbooks for Freshman English courses, editors enforcing the editorial policy of newspapers, magazines and books, and the like. See discussion of the 'sacred That rule' (the ironical terminology of Arnold Zwicky's Language Log) in section 1.1.

10.5.3   Zero relative clauses

Like *that*-relative clauses, zero relative clauses (clauses with no overt relativization device) showed an increase between 1961 and 1991/2. In this
case, however, there was a more moderate rising trend, of 6.1% in written
AmE and 8.2% in written BrE: a trend that may again be attributed to
colloquialization. (See Table A10.12a and A10.12b for details.)

However, the change varies greatly among the different subcorpora: most
of the increase in AmE is found in Press, and in BrE is found in General
Prose. As the pmw columns in the tables show, the frequency of zero relatives
in Fiction is roughly double their frequency in other registers, and roughly
four times their frequency in the Learned register. In the context of written
English, this confirms the zero relative's status as a marker of colloquial
style. Hence relative clauses of types (a)–(c) all show a clear diachronic trend
that invites the label 'colloquialization': the decline of *wh*- relatives between
1961 and 1991/2 is countered by the rise in the use of *that*-relatives and
zero relatives. On the other hand, the more moderate rise for zero relative
clauses throws into greater prominence the competition between *that* and
wh- pronouns (particularly *which*) as relativizers, the one taking frequency
from the other.

The tables for zero relative clauses exclude clauses with an adverbial gap,
as in the following examples from Frown, text category P:

The minute *she walked into the house*	(cf. . . . *when she walked into the house*)
a place *you'd rather not be*	(cf. . . . *where you'd rather not be*)
the way *he acts*	(cf. . . . *in which he acts.*)
the reason *he was a successful actor*	(cf. . . . *why he was a successful actor*)

These were omitted from our counts because of incomparability with the
counts for *wh*- relatives, which did not include the *wh*- adverbs *where*, *when*
and *why* functioning as relativizers. However, it is worth mentioning that
these zero adverbial-gap relatives are rather common (Brown: 201; Frown:
318; LOB: 208; F-LOB: 253), and that their frequency has been increasing
faster than the other zero relatives – by over 20% in BrE and by over 50%
in AmE. In the Brown family, over half of them occur in Fiction texts.

10.5.4   Pied-piping vs preposition stranding

We now consider another case where, as with *that* and *which*, there is typically a stylistic choice between two alternatives: the case where the relative
clause gap functions as a prepositional complement. The two alternatives[41]
we consider now are the pied-piping construction illustrated by (14a) and the

---

[41] Here we disregard other alternatives which occur for particular variants of the pied-piping
construction: viz. (a) the choice between *whose* and *of which*, and (b) the choice between
at / on / in which and a relative adverb *when* or *where*.

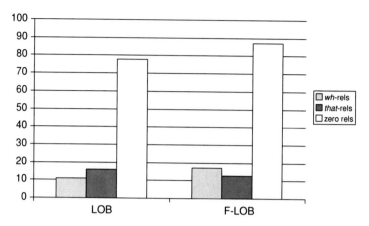

Figure 10.8 A small increase in preposition stranding in relative clauses in the three varieties of relative clause between 1961 and 1991 in written BrE.

The figures for zero relatives are a low approximation; see note 41.

preposition-stranding construction illustrated by (15a). The corpus examples below are followed, in each case, by the non-attested but acceptable alternative constructions in (14b) and (15b).

(14) a. a town *for which he had a great affection.*   (pied-piping)
          [LOB A30]
      b. a town *he had a great affection for.*   (stranding)
(15) a. the people *they live with* [Frown R06]   (stranding)
      b. the people *with whom they live*   (pied-piping)

Figure 10.8 and Table A10.13 show the changing frequency of pied-piping and stranding in relative clauses. In the pied-piping construction, the preposition normally takes initial position in the clause in front of a *wh-* pronoun, whereas in the stranding construction, it typically (though by no means always) takes final position. Of course, preposition stranding is a general phenomenon which occurs in a number of different English clause types; but here we restrict our attention to stranding in relative clauses, and more particularly, in zero relative clauses.

Although in both the examples above the alternative constructions (14b) and (15b) strike one as normal and acceptable, there are many other cases where one construction or another is scarcely acceptable, as in (16b) and (17b).

(16) a. the awkward interval *during which the United States policy tends to mark time for want of leadership* [LOB G76]
      b. ?the awkward interval *(that) the United States policy tends to mark time for want of leadership during*

(17) a. things *we could perfectly well do without* [LOB B10]
      b. ?things *without which we could perfectly well do*

Example (16b) is difficult to process because the clause is too long, and disrupts the relation between the preposition (*during*) and the antecedent (*the awkward interval*). Example (17b) is difficult to interpret because pied-piping separates the preposition from the verb to which it is idiomatically tied, in the prepositional verb *do without*. The problem of length mentioned in connection with (16b) in practice limits the length of relative clauses with stranding: characteristically brief examples are: *(people) they lived with*; *(building) I was looking for*; *(goods) we know of*. However, there is nothing to prevent clause embedding occurring in the clause with stranding, and this sometimes results in clauses of unusual length as in (18):

(18) His wife was wearing a hat *I was glad I wasn't sitting behind*. [LOB L19]

The choice between pied-piping and stranding is another case where there is a formal/colloquial contrast between the options. The distribution of examples across the four subcorpora (see Table A10.13) is heavily biased in favour of the more expository or formal registers (Learned and General Prose) in the case of pied-piping, and heavily biased towards the less academic registers (Fiction and, to a lesser extent, Press) in the case of stranding. Of the 87 examples of stranding in F-LOB in Figure 10.8, only 4 occur in Learned, whereas 43 occur in Fiction. Again, in this case, as in the case of relativizers, the change between 1961 and 1991/2 is in the direction of the less formal option, that is, in the direction of colloquialization. There is a highly significant decline in pied-piping (16.9% in BrE), and a considerable rise in stranding (11.4% in BrE). We do not have general figures for pied-piping and stranding in AmE, but the increase of stranding in zero relative clauses is over 50%. However, it is evident that pied-piping is still much more common than stranding in written texts such as we find in the Brown family of corpora. Even in Fiction writing, where stranding has been comparatively common, pied-piping is by far the more common strategy to use.

10.6 Summary and conclusion

This survey of some aspects of noun phrase structure has revealed very striking changes of frequency, which in many areas are of higher significance than changes in the verb phrase studied in earlier chapters. Unfortunately, it has been necessary to investigate these noun phrase phenomena in less detail than they deserve.

In the main, the changes studied seem to have been caused by two different and somewhat conflicting impulses: the impulse towards a more speech-like style of writing (colloquialization) and the impulse towards greater information density (densification). Colloquialization has been observed strikingly in the changes in frequency of relativization devices. *Wh-* relatives on the whole have been markedly declining, and *that*-relatives and zero relatives have been increasing. It is also a sign of colloquialization in relative clauses that the stranded preposition construction has been gaining some ground at the expense of the pied-piping construction.

The other changes we have studied in the noun phrase appear to indicate an impetus towards greater information density in the noun phrase. This is seen in the greater frequency of nouns and adjectives (particularly of proper nouns and attributive adjectives), and also of N+N sequences of various kinds and *s*-genitives (in contrast to the loss of frequency of prepositions, and especially of the *of*-genitive). These changes move in the opposite direction to colloquialization:[42] nouns are most frequent in the informational varieties of written text, and least frequent in Fiction, which in other respects has been shown to be closer to the spoken language.

Constructions where nouns are juxtaposed, whether in *s*-genitive constructions (N's N) or in straightforward noun sequences (N+N), most obviously contribute to the condensation of information into a smaller space. The evidence is that newspaper writing, showing a greater frequency of these constructions, had a major role in promoting this trend. However, in the 1961–1991/2 period, the gap between the Press and other varieties of informational English (General Prose and Learned) diminished somewhat, as the latter subcorpora increased their use of N's N and N+N more conspicuously.

What interpretation we put on these findings must remain somewhat speculative, but evidence from earlier research and older corpora suggests that before the mid-twentieth century, AmE and particularly the Press variety (both in the US and in the UK) were innovative in spearheading this tendency towards more compact noun phrase structure with greater density of information, and that this tendency was then passed on to other varieties of written English, where a 'catching-up' phase has been under way during the thirty years covered by our corpora.

Although this chapter has not highlighted developments in speech, it is worth mentioning that, although densification has been characterized as a phenomenon of written English, there are also signs (see footnote 22) that the same trend is taking place in spoken English. We are by now familiar with the spectacle of written English following (albeit slowly and belatedly) a trend set by the spoken medium – e.g. in the growing use of semi-modals.

---

[42] The increase in the *s*-genitive also runs counter to the long-term diachronic trend towards more analytic structures (such as *of*-genitives rather than *s*-genitives), a trend of great importance in earlier phases of the history of the language. The characterization of the *s*-genitive as an enclitic form, rather than an inflectional suffix (Rosenbach 2002), however, means that we can no longer regard its resurgence as a countertrend in favour of inflectional morphology. Indeed, it is doubtful whether this 'analyticization' trend is still active, but for some small evidence in its favour, see the discussion of adjective comparison in section 11.6.3.

But what we seem to see here is spoken English following a trend set by written English. This somewhat puzzling (and still tentative) finding awaits further research.

The themes of colloquialization and densification will come to the fore again in the next (and final) chapter, where we discuss linguistic, social and other determinants of grammatical change.

11 Linguistic and other determinants of change

This final chapter will reverse the procedure we have normally followed so far: the 'bottom up' methodology outlined in Chapter 2 (section 2.3). According to that methodology, the natural way for corpus linguistics to operate is to work from the identification and quantification of formal phenomena in texts towards the functional interpretation of the resulting findings. Our method in this chapter, however, is to begin with types of functional explanation, and to consider them in relation to the various formal phenomena they might explain. This will include gathering together the functional explanations we have (tentatively) offered here and there in various chapters, to see how far they lend support to one another. But focusing on function rather than form will also give us the opportunity to go beyond the limited set of grammatical topics covered up to now – verb categories and their constructions, plus one chapter on the noun phrase – and to touch on extra topics, such as negation, and extra levels of language, such as morphology and punctuation. Ultimately, of course, wherever possible, we would like to identify common motivations – rooted in discourse conventions, the sociolinguistic dynamic or even the general socio-cultural context of the late twentieth century – which may reveal unexpected relations between changes which we have so far discussed largely in isolation. This reflects our conviction that – viewed at close range – structural change is a process which is mediated through register and text type, with developments unfolding at differing speeds in spoken and written English, vernacular and standard usage, informal and formal registers and, of course, also across various regional and social varieties of the language.

11.1 The functional and social processes of change

Formally, we have shown that changes of frequency, often highly significant, have been taking place during the period 1961–92. Functionally, we have suggested as tentative explanations certain processes which bring about change of frequency. As support for such explanations, we have often linked one change to another: thus, a growth of frequency of feature A may be weighed against a loss of frequency of another feature B with a similar meaning or function. It is rare, however, for there to be a simple 'A versus B' rivalry, and there could be a number of functional determinants for the same change of frequency. Rarely can any single causative explanation be offered for a given change, yet explanations can be given substance by seeing how far they can account for diverse linguistic changes, rather than one or two changes here and there.

With the above caveats in mind, we will consider in this chapter the following explanatory processes we have postulated in preceding chapters:[1]

(a) grammaticalization
(b) colloquialization
(c) densification of content
(d) changes induced by contact among regional varieties of standard English (notably 'Americanization')
(e) other processes (e.g. prescription and language planning)

With (a), we are focusing on a largely language-internal (though psychologically motivated) process at the interface between the lexicon and the grammar. Processes (b) and (c) are essentially discourse-based phenomena, two partly conflicting trends shaping the expectations we have about styles, genres and text types. While grammaticalization usually results in the straightforward addition and subsequent entrenchment of new structural options in the grammar, changes at the discourse level more often reflect the shifting preferences in the choice between already existing options. Processes of type (d) finally take us more squarely into sociolinguistics, as we are dealing with competing norms and changes in the linguistic prestige accorded to them. Towards the end of the chapter we will consider some further minor influences, such as prescriptive influences, that might help to shape frequency change. The processes we have listed are far from unconnected with one another, and from time to time, in the chapter, we will bring out interrelations between them.

11.2 Grammaticalization

Of the processes listed in (a)–(d) above, the first, grammaticalization, stands out as a process internal to the language system, albeit spurred on by forces, such as the psychological drive for economy of means, external to the language system.

---

[1] We find it difficult to avoid contributing to the fashionable proliferation of abstract nouns ending in (*iz*)*ation* referring to diachronic processes. This appears to be a current hazard of functionally oriented historical linguistics: note the proliferation of terms like 'auxiliarization', 'conventionalization', 'decategorialization', 'de-iconicization', 'fossilization', 'idiomatization', 'paradigmaticization', 'subjectification' and 'univerbation', all to be found in the index of Krug (2000).

Grammaticalization has had a relatively limited part in our armoury of explanations, not because it is unimportant in itself, but because it is generally a gradual, slow-moving process which casts a very long language-historical shadow. Therefore, the 'time window' of thirty years which is opened by the Brown family of corpora does not usually capture more than a short episode in such processes. As an example: the *to*-infinitive still proliferating today (see Chapter 9) ultimately goes back to a grammaticalization process begun in the pre-Old English period (see Los 2005). But of course the picture is complicated by many further ramifications which have taken place in the shadow of this overarching drift. Individual infinitival constructions, for example – most conspicuously, the 'new modals' *going to* and *want to* – have taken grammaticalization much further in their specific functional domains. Conversely, the move from the *to*-infinitive towards the bare infinitive after *help* has led to a local decrease in the frequency of *to*-infinitives, which – however – can be seen as a stage in a different process of grammaticalization. It is clear that, given the time-frame of the present study, we are in a better position to chart individual episodes in the general development rather than any large-scale language-historical 'drift' (Sapir 1921: 147–70) in its entirety.

Similarly, other increases of frequency – of the progressive aspect and of the semi-modals – appear to be continuations of a grammaticalization-actuated growth trend hundreds of years old. Little difference, apart from increase of frequency, can be observed as a reflex of grammaticalization in the four corpora. However, in Chapter 5 we detected some indications of increasing coalescence (*wanna* instead of *want to*, *gotta* instead of (*have*) *got to*, etc.) and semantic bleaching (e.g. *be going to* taking small steps towards a 'pure future') – both well-known aspects of grammaticalization.

It seems that grammaticalization leads to a growth trend, often termed 'generalization', as the new grammaticalized form expands its contexts of use. This raises an obvious question: What happens to the existing forms with which the grammaticalized form is in functional competition? The phenomenon of layering allows for more than one layer of semantically competing forms (such as modals and semi-modals) to co-exist in the same *état de langue*. The modals, however, have been significantly declining in frequency, and a natural explanation would be that they are being somehow encroached upon by these relative newcomers, the semi-modals. The evidence of the Brown family of corpora (see section 4.4), where modals are several times more frequent than semi-modals, does not bear this out, but the 'encroachment hypothesis' becomes far more credible when spoken corpora are examined: in AmE conversation, semi-modals are in some respects overtaking core modals (e.g. *have to*, *need to* and *have got to* have all overtaken *must*). However, there needs to be some theory of linguistic decline explaining a long-drawn-out process of losing frequency, apparent in the case of the modals. Towards the assumed atrophic end of this process, observable symptoms of decline include paradigmatic atrophy (e.g. the restriction of *need(n't)* to negative contexts and *shall* largely to first-person subjects), as well as restrictions of genre and context (in section 4.5 termed 'distributional fragmentation'). This can be seen almost as a mirror image of what happens in grammaticalization.

A major contribution of the corpus-based study of grammaticalization at close historical range is to make us aware once again of the role of style and genre in the spread of innovation. The different results obtained from spoken and written corpora show that layering is a stylistically sensitive phenomenon. Older forms usually hold out longer and newly grammaticalized forms are accepted more slowly in written English than in spoken English. In other words, the time which elapses between the creation of a new form through grammaticalization and a noticeable statistical increase is expected to be rather short in the spoken language but may easily extend to a couple of hundreds of years in formal writing (cf. Mair 2004: 127–9 on *be going to*; and Hundt 2001: 59 on the *get*-passive).

11.3   Colloquialization

This brings us to colloquialization, or the shift to a more speech-like style (cf. Mair 1997; Hundt and Mair 1999), which has been hypothesized to explain changes in frequency in more than one chapter of this book. For example, it is a plausible factor in the continuing rise of certain semi-modals (section 5.2) and the progressive (Chapter 6), also in the decline of *wh-* relatives (10.5.1). It also appears to be clearly capable of definition and investigation as 'writing becoming more like speech'.[2]

The processes we now consider may be termed 'discourse-pragmatic', in that they point to social influences in language change. Informalization and colloquialization have been well documented in the language of the media. In news reportage, for example, the past three decades have seen a definite trend away from the cool distancing of traditional written style and towards a kind of spontaneous directness which (though often contrived) is clearly supposed to inject into journalistic discourse some of the immediacy of oral communication. Such developments have been quantified in textual analysis: for instance, a recent corpus-based study of editorials in the British 'quality' press in the twentieth century (Westin 2002) shows informalization as a trend persisting through the twentieth century, and accelerating towards its end. As Biber has argued, this development is part of a much broader long-term drift in the evolution of English writing styles:

---

[2] There is, however, a distinction (in principle) between *informalization* and *colloquialization*. Informality of style, which is a matter of the absence of distance between addresser and addressee, is strongly associated with speech, but can also have characteristics specific to the written language. Consider the article-free apposition of *Supermum Sue* (as contrasted with *Susan, a perfect mother*) – a decidedly informal construction which is nevertheless absent from speech. On the other hand, colloquialization (as seen, for example, in the increasing use of contractions) is more evidently a matter of adopting speech-like habits.

Written registers in English have undergone extensive stylistic change over the past four centuries. Written prose registers in the seventeenth century were already quite different from conversational registers, and those registers evolve to become even more distinct from speech over the course of the eighteenth century . . .

However, in the course of the nineteenth and twentieth centuries, popular written registers like letters, fiction, and essays have reversed their direction of change and evolved to become more similar to spoken registers, often becoming even more oral in the modern period than in the seventeenth century. These shifts result in a dispreference for certain stereotypically literate features, such as passive verbs, relative clause constructions and elaborated noun phrases generally. (Biber 2003a: 169)

With the burgeoning mass media of the late nineteenth and early twentieth centuries, one notable trend was the evolution of a 'public-colloquial' style (Leech 1966: 75–6, 166) through which the spoken language had great influence on writing in the popular press and in advertising.

Although the above factors give *prima facie* credence to colloquialization, it is not an observable trend across the board. There appear to be numerous exceptions to it, and its apparently simple definition is not unproblematic. We now consider these points both positive and negative, focusing initially on findings favourable to the colloquialization hypothesis,[3] and moving on in the next section to the countervailing influence we term *densification*.

11.3.1   Contracted negatives and verb forms

Contractions both of negatives (*not* to -*n't*) and of verb forms (*it's*, *we'll*, etc.), as we have mentioned in Chapters 1 and 2, have increased enormously over thirty years in the four corpora. This might be considered the paradigm case of colloquialization: it is so easy to count contractions automatically and calculate their frequency.

It is instructive here to look at a further case of contraction: the first-person plural imperative *let's*. Both the full form *let us* and the contracted form *let's* can be easily tracked in the four corpora, providing a neat illustration of colloquialization, with increase of the contraction *let's* measured against the decrease of the full form *let us* (that is, *let us* as a first-person imperative for which *let's* can be substituted), particularly in the US. The full form declines from 58 to 15 in the AmE corpora, whereas it remains steady in BrE (LOB 39, F-LOB 43). In both pairs of corpora, however, *let's* has increased – from 68 to 85 in AmE, and from 34 to 58 in BrE. Within each individual corpus, Fiction, as the most speech-influenced variety, contains the vast majority of occurrences of *let's*. In sharp contrast, in AmE, *let us* is almost totally absent

---

Many of the topics considered in the remainder of this section are treated in more detail in Smith (2005: 206–30); see also Seoane and Loureiro-Porto (2005) and Seoane (2006a).

from Fiction, with no examples in Brown and only one in Frown. Looking at all four corpora, the *contraction ratio* (that is, the proportion of contracted forms *let's* against the possible contexts where they might have occurred), has risen from 102/199 (51.3%) in 1961 to 143/201 (71.1%) in 1991/2.

The movement from *let us* to *let's* provides a nice object lesson in colloquialization; but *let's* is also well known in the grammaticalization literature. In fact, it is worth pointing out the link between these two processes, probably best thought of in sequential terms. That is, at the risk of oversimplification, we can say that grammaticalization brings about some change in the spoken language, which then through colloquialization invades the written language.[4]

11.3.2 Not-*negation vs* no-*negation*

Often these two kinds of negation are incapable of mutual substitution; but where they are (as in the three examples below), the *no*-negation alternative tends to be more favoured in written registers than in spoken registers (see Tottie 1991: 140).

(1) NOT NEGATION: He didn't know anything about the problems we face today. [Brown D07]
(NO NEGATION would be: *He knew nothing about the problems we face today.*)

(2) NOT NEGATION: She would not take any unnecessary chances. [Frown P29]
(NO NEGATION would be: *She would take no unnecessary chances.*)

(3) NO NEGATION: Once again, I say that there will be no reduction. [F-LOB H17]
(NOT NEGATION would be: *Once again, I say that there won't be any reduction.*)

According to Biber *et al.* (1999: 170), 'in the written registers, about three out of ten negative forms are of the *no*-type; the corresponding figure for conversation is only about one in ten'. This is therefore a case rather like the *be*-passive (see section 7.2), where colloquialization predicts a choice strongly associated with written texts to be on the retreat.

Table 11.1 fulfils this prediction. Whereas in the Brown family *not*-negation has remained buoyant (with a gain of 8.3% in AmE and a loss of 0.4% in BrE), the table shows a marked decline in the use of *no*-negation

---

[4] In the grammaticalization literature, it has been pointed out that *let's*, particularly in AmE speech, is diverging from the full form, and cannot (at least in all cases) be considered a contraction of *let us*: for example, it can be argued that *Let's you and me talk* has no corresponding full form *?Let us you and me talk*. However, no such blended forms occur with *let's* in the four written corpora. Cf. Hopper and Traugott (²2003: 11–13) on adhortative *lets* (spelt thus).

242 Linguistic and other determinants of change

Table 11.1. Not-*negation and* no-*negation in AmE (Brown, Frown) and BrE (LOB, F-LOB)*

	AmE			BrE		
	Brown raw freq.	Frown raw freq.	Change (% of Brown)	LOB raw freq.	F-LOB raw freq.	Change (% of LOB)
Not-negation	6,958	7,469	*** +8.3%	7,427	7,392	−0.4%
No-negation	3,055	2,584	*** −14.7%	3,169	2,599	*** −17.9%

(AmE estimated)

(a loss of 14.7% in AmE and 17.9% in BrE). These figures are based on all occurrences of *not* and *n't* tagged as a negative particle, and all occurrences of the negative items *no* (article/determiner), *nobody, nothing, none, no one, never, nowhere,* rather than on counts of cases where *not*-negation and *no*-negation can be interchanged.[5]

11.3.3 *Questions*

In contrast to *no*-negation, **questions**[6] are obviously more characteristic of speech than of writing, and it therefore seems to be a positive sign of colloquialization that they have increased significantly between LOB and F-LOB. Overall questions have increased by 9.5%, although in two subcorpora (Press and General Prose) they have in fact decreased. The increase is mainly due to Fiction, where numbers have risen by 17.5%. A considerable part of this will have come from a 9% increase in the amount of quoted speech (dialogue) in that variety – see further discussion in 11.3.6 – but there is still an excess rise in frequency of questions to account for.

Table 11.2 compares the overall increase of questions in AmE and BrE with the increase of particular varieties of questions – non-sentential questions and tag questions – which in BrE show very high and very low increases respectively. (Non-sentential questions are deemed to be those which contain no finite verb, such as *Philip?, Here?, Why?, So what?*) Both of these non-canonical types of question are concentrated heavily in Fiction texts (in

---

[5] The inventory of negative items included in *no*-negation follows that of Tottie (1991: 106), except that one rare case is excluded: the use of *neither... nor* as an alternant of *not either... or.* The spellings *no one* and *no-one* are both included. *No place* in AmE is counted where it is a colloquial equivalent of *nowhere.* As the query has been expressed with POS tags, dialectal variants such as *nae, na'* and *no'* are automatically included.

[6] Occurrences of questions in the Brown family of corpora are simply recognized by the final punctuation '?'. Unsurprisingly, Biber *et al.* (1999: 211) find that questions are many times more frequent in conversation than in written texts. In fiction texts, of course, questions are exceptionally frequent as compared with the other written subcorpora, but only one third as frequent as questions are in spoken conversation.

Table 11.2. *Questions in AmE and BrE*

	AmE			BrE		
	Brown raw freq.	Frown raw freq.	Change (% of Brown)	LOB raw freq.	F-LOB raw freq.	Change (% of LOB)
Non-sentential questions	349	449	*** +28.8%	407	529	***+30.1%
Tag questions	67	101	** +50.9%	119	121	+1.8%
Questions (all)	2,349	2,867	*** +22.2%	2,584	2,827	*** +9.5%

LOB, 73% of non-sentential questions and 90% of tag questions are in Fiction). The generally low frequency of tag questions in these written corpora may be because they are a little *too* colloquial – too dependent on shared immediate context between speaker and hearer – to be adapted to monologic written language. But the gaping difference in BrE between the increases of 30% for non-sentential questions and 2% for tag questions is puzzling, both being highly characteristic of interactive spoken language. Perhaps American influence might have some role in this: Tottie and Hoffmann (2006) report that tag questions are as much as nine times as frequent in conversational spoken BrE as in conversational spoken AmE, so Americanization might take the form of a relative reluctance to use tag questions, even in the spoken medium.[7] In contrast, the exceptionally high increase in non-sentential questions, which tend to be more colloquial in style than canonical questions, is on the face of it a further strengthening of the case for colloquialization.

In AmE, the picture is somewhat different and easier to explain. Tag questions have been increasing by as much as 51%, though in 1991/2 they still fall short of the frequency in BrE. This means that all three rows of Table 11.2 for AmE show a steep increase – again, apparently supporting the case for colloquialization.[8]

11.3.4 Other plausible grammatical signs of colloquialization

To further exemplify the colloquializing tendency, we return to plausible cases we have noted in earlier chapters on the verb. **Semi-modals** such as *have to* and *want to*, as we saw in Chapter 5, are closely associated with spoken language, and their overall increase in the Brown family (by 18.5%

---

[7] On the other hand, since Tottie and Hoffmann (2006) investigated only canonical tag questions with subject–operator inversion, the relative infrequency of tag questions in AmE in their count must be partly due to American speakers' penchant for the single-syllable invariant tags *huh?* and *right?*, both of which are common in AmE. Examples from the LCSAE are: *It's pretty easy, huh?, You guys know Inez, right?*

[8] The alternative explanation that there has been a Britishization of AmE in this respect seems, on the face of it, implausible.

in AmE and 9.0% in BrE) encourages us to see this as another example of colloquialization, which here, as with *let's*, may be seen as working in tandem with grammaticalization. Similarly **progressives** – especially present progressives – (Chapter 6) have increased substantially. Because of their stronger showing in spoken than written English, there is again a case for saying that here colloquialization builds on grammaticalization. This is also arguably the case in AmE for the *get*-passive (see section 7.3) which has increased in AmE in the written corpora, though not in BrE. The far more frequent *be*-passives (7.2), however, are heavily concentrated in the more academic written genres, and are little used in speech or in Fiction – the most speech-related subcorpus of the Brown family. Hence their decline may be another negative manifestation of colloquialization, although other factors (especially prescriptivism) are certainly involved.

Turning to the noun phrase, we have observed the decline of *wh-* **relative clauses** (section 10.5.1), a further grammatical category strongly associated with the written language. Here, as with the passive, prescriptivism plays a role, but at least in BrE, colloquialization appears to be the main driving force for this change. *That-* and **zero relative clauses** (10.5.2–3), on the other hand, being to some degree the more colloquial counterparts of *wh-* relative clauses, have increased. Especially in AmE, *that* can be seen as a positive beneficiary of the decline of *which*. Since these relative clause types have a stronger representation in speech relative to writing, their growing frequency appears to be another positive mark of colloquialization.[9]

Still with reference to relative clauses, **preposition stranding**[10] (section 10.5.4) is another colloquial feature that has increased in frequency. **Pied-piping**, on the other hand, being in partial competition with stranding and particularly common in Learned and General Prose subcorpora, declined substantially between 1961 and 1991/2, showing again how grammatical markers of formal styles retreat under the influence of colloquialization.

11.3.5 Punctuation

Punctuation features cannot strictly reflect the spoken language, but some aspects of punctuation more closely related to spoken production and delivery tend to be associated with more informal styles of writing. (Changes in punctuation frequency are given in Table A11.2a, where the data for AmE, being based on automatic counts, must be considered approximate only.) Although some changes may be aligned with colloquialization, others might be more

---

[9] Oddly in this case, colloquialization (contrary to expected practice) is aided by prescriptivism (see sections 1.1, 11.6.2), which elsewhere commonly supports the retention of entrenched written forms.

[10] We have not been able to investigate preposition stranding and pied-piping in other constructions such as direct and reported *wh-* questions, although these might be expected to show similar trends.

realistically associated with a closely related trend of **popularization** – making written texts more engaging, accessible and easy to process for the reader. One obvious example of speech-like habits in writing, the question mark (as we saw in discussing questions) has increased. The full stop or period has also increased by 4.9% in Brown/Frown but declined by 4.7% in LOB/F-LOB, while, strangely, the exclamation mark, although judged to be one of the most 'colloquial' of punctuation marks, has declined by 13.2% (in Brown/Frown) and as much as 20.0% (in LOB/F-LOB).

While there are no clear positive signs of increased informality in punctuation, apart from increasing use of question marks, we can point to one negative sign: a very significant decline in the occurrence of the semi-colon (22.7% in Brown/Frown; 17.3% in LOB/F-LOB). This punctuation mark is densely concentrated in the more formally oriented subcorpora of Learned and General Prose, where it remains entrenched in the 1991/2 corpora. Elsewhere, there is apparently less need for the semi-colon's role in helping to segment complex sentences into more easily digestible chunks for the reader. In AmE its incidence falls by 47.9% in Fiction, but only by 1.3% in Learned.

11.3.6   Problems and issues concerning colloquialization

Despite many plausible cases such as those listed above, the colloquialization hypothesis cannot be adopted wholesale. First, contrary to colloquialization, there are facets of grammar where *anti*-colloquialization – a movement further away from spoken English norms – appears to be in the ascendant. We discussed in Chapter 10 a notable set of cases where structural and semantic **densification** has taken place (sections 10.2, 10.4): for example, an increased frequency of nouns, noun sequences and *s*-genitives, whereas colloquialization would lead us to expect fewer nouns and more pronouns. We will return to densification as a separate factor in the next section. Like many of the findings mentioned in this chapter, these phenomena have not yet been studied in detail, and therefore invite further research, using both the Brown family and other corpora.

Anti-colloquial tendencies appear also in punctuation use (see Table A11.2a). In discussing punctuation above, we briefly postulated the increasing use of the question mark as a positive marker of colloquialization, and decreasing use of the semi-colon as a negative one. However, if we look at other punctuation marks, the trend is the opposite of these. Whereas semi-colons have decreased, colons have increased (in BrE, by as much as 25.7%). This is puzzling, since both semi-colons and colons are devices for splitting up complex sentences into major subunits. Part of the explanation may lie in writers' switching from the semi-colon to the colon in certain contexts. In the following example, the normal expectation that the post-colon part of the sentence will explain the pre-colon part is absent. A semi-colon would have done equally well.

(4)   One US commanding officer in Germany recently threatened to court-
martial a GI if he filed for CO status: the soldier didn't know this threat
was illegal. [F-LOB F15]

Another punctuation mark which, as already mentioned, bucks the colloquialization trend is the exclamation mark. Like the question mark, this
is typically sentence-final, and is particularly likely to occur in speech-like
contexts. Yet, in contrast to the question mark, the exclamation mark has
declined (approximately by 13.2% in AmE, and by as much as 20% in BrE).[11]
Similarly, brackets have increased immensely, whereas dashes in BrE have
declined. Brackets (both round and square) generally have a parenthetical function, being considered more typical of serious written style, while
dashes, also parenthetical, have an air of informality. (Commas, which can
also have a parenthetical function, have remained relatively stable, though
slightly declining.)

The decreasing frequency of full stops by 4.7% in BrE is seemingly
another trend contrary to colloquialization, in that fewer full stops would
appear to mean longer sentences, and hence more complex syntax. In this
connection, it is interesting to look at Table A11.2b, which shows changes
in frequency of some punctuation marks between the Lanc-1931 (B-LOB)
corpus and F-LOB, over the period 1931–91. Here it is evident that the
changes between LOB and F-LOB reflect longer term trends, except for the
full-stop decrease, which goes against a highly significant trend of increasing
full stops between 1931 and 1991 (and in AmE between 1961 and 1992). It
is strange that the apparently pronounced tendency for BrE to use shorter
sentences between 1931 and 1961 is reversed between 1961 and 1991.

Another area, that of pronouns, has some puzzling anomalies. As mentioned in Chapter 10, Brown and Frown show a pronoun *increase* of 1.0%,
whereas LOB and F-LOB show a pronoun *decrease* of 6.5% (see Tables
A10.1a and A10.1b). As personal pronouns account for a large majority of pronouns, this loss actually includes a notable decrease of personal pronouns –
no less than 7.1%. This, in turn, is partly due to a very significant decrease in
the use of first-person pronouns in BrE (of 9.7%), as opposed to an extraordinary increase of 25.1% in the use of first-person pronouns in AmE. Here we
have a further leap-frog phenomenon, whereby AmE, which used fewer first-
person pronouns than BrE in 1961, has ended up using more such pronouns
in 1991/2. Something similar has happened with second-person pronouns:
AmE shows an increase of 18.0%, whereas BrE remains virtually unchanged,
with an increase of 0.3%. As first-person and second-person pronouns are
much more common in speech than in writing, the conclusion is that AmE

---

[11]   There may be an element of prescriptive influence here, as it is commonly maintained that
exclamation marks are signs of weakness in written style, and that one should write in a way
that makes them superfluous: 'Excessive use of exclamation marks is . . . one of the things
that betray the uneducated or unpractised writer' (Fowler [2]1965: 590).

has shown a very strong colloquializing pattern – whereas BrE (in the use of *I/me/my/mine/myself*) shows a mysterious anti-colloquial trend. Further research is needed to determine the likely reasons for this.

However – if one may speculate – such anomalies may be due in part to a failure of our definition of colloquialization ('writing becoming more like speech') to take into account the multifarious and scalar nature of the difference between 'oral' and 'literary' style. This view was famously put forward by Chafe (1982), confirmed through multi-factorial statistical modelling by Biber (1988) and expanded on in Biber *et al.* (1999: 1041–51), who refer to several interlinked functional factors distinguishing conversation from written varieties of the language, including:

(a)   its avoidance of elaboration or specification of content;
(b)   its shared addresser–addressee context;
(c)   its interactive nature;
(d)   its informal style.

Of these, (a) does not easily penetrate the written medium, where, on the contrary, information density is often at a premium. Hence the anti-colloquial trend we have called densification (see section 11.4) has flourished alongside colloquialization. Characteristics (a) and (b) explain the high frequency of pronouns and other pro-forms in speech, but in written texts, where there is little shared context between the addresser and addressee, their role is minimized. With (c), we can also explain how speakers are inclined to take meanings as understood, reducing communicative explicitness by such time-and-effort saving devices as ellipses and contractions. As we saw from the increasing use of non-clausal questions and contractions, these characteristics can be advantageously transferred to writing. However, factor (d) is probably the one that is most centrally involved in colloquialization. Informal style implies that the interlocutors are in a casual, close and personal, rather than distant and impersonal social relationship.[12]

One of the texts in the F-LOB corpus, an amateur photography magazine, is suggestive of a growing enthusiasm for a colloquial style of writing, and conscious awareness of what this involves. The writer is giving advice to would-be photographers on how to get their work published in magazines. He advises them to use a speech-like style, and in doing so gives a good example of that style himself:

(5)   Don't worry. Editors don't want school *compositions* or *essays*. All you need do is *tell it like it is*, write as though you were talking to your neighbour over the garden fence. The more simply you write, the better it is.

---

[12] Fairclough (1992: 98, 204) discusses this from the viewpoint of critical discourse analysis. For a sociological perspective on informalization, see Misztal (2000: 43).

[...] The basic rule is to write concisely and simply. Don't waste words; don't use a long word where a short one will do and don't try to be "literary". Write the way you talk. Use varied, but fairly short, sentence-lengths: and keep the paragraphs short – maybe 50–60 words, three or four sentences only. [F-LOB E10, emphasis original]

The first- and second-person pronouns have more to do with interactiveness: the frequent use of *I* and (especially) *you* in (5) indicates that the writer is setting up a personal rapport with the reader. Hence it is possible for a first- and second-person interactive style to be avoided by a writer who nevertheless cultivates a more colloquial style in other respects. It is significant that the loss of first-person pronoun frequency in BrE is restricted to the expository genres of General Prose and Learned writing. The persistence of established habits of impersonal exposition could partly explain why BrE uses fewer first-person pronouns in 1991 than in 1961, although this is not the whole story.

A further instance of colloquialization failing to take place, in our corpora, is the case of semi-modals such as *(have) got to* – even more so, in its reduced form *gotta* (see section 3.1) – or, less conspicuously, *(had) better*. Although frequent in the spoken parts of the BNC, *(have) got to* is rare in the Brown corpus family, perhaps because it is *too* colloquial, as yet, to be acceptable in written texts. Here there has been no significant rise in frequency, and once again, it pays to think of colloquialization as a scale, such that more extreme forms of colloquial usage can scarcely find their way into written usage. In the 1990s, it seems, there is still a 'prestige barrier' resisting the more extreme forms of colloquialism in print.

In addition to its immediate grammatical symptoms, colloquialization also manifests itself at the discourse level, for example in a notable increase in passages of direct speech, quotations or pseudo-quotations in the Press texts, a strategy obviously intended to make reportage more spontaneous, immediate and dramatic.[13] This means that some of the increase in colloquial features noted in the written corpora of the Brown family will be genuine – that is, informal/colloquial forms being used directly in a written context – but some of it will be indirect, due to the fact that the amount of direct speech, an environment traditionally appropriate for colloquial forms, has increased. This situation requires some analytical caution in interpreting the statistics but does not change the overall diagnosis presented above.

The increase of quoted speech in the later corpora of the Brown family is found both in fiction and non-fiction. This seems to be part of a general change towards a more 'oral' culture. In LOB and F-LOB, the admixture of quoted speech has increased in all four subcorpora, varying considerably, however, from Learned (where quotations – including quotations from

---

[13] The use of quotations or pseudo-quotations is also linked to 'evidentiality', as discussed by Garretson and Ädel (2005).

written texts – constitute only 4.0% of all textual material) to Fiction (where direct speech quotations constitute 27.6% – quoted speech in this case being, of course, a fictional simulation). This means that corpus-based measures of colloquialization reflect not just *writing becoming more like speech* but *writing containing more speech*. However, by no means can the trend we have called colloquialization be dismissed as an epiphenomenon of the increase in speech quotation. For example, given that 11.6% of the LOB corpus represents speech, F-LOB raises that figure to 12.7% – an increase of only 1.1% of the whole corpus, or an addition of 9.3% to the 'quoted speech' part of the corpus as it was in 1961.[14]

All in all, we conclude that the colloquialization of written English is a real linguistic trend, although the reasons why it shows up in some cases but not others remain debatable.

11.4 Densification of content

Chapter 10 (sections 10.1, 10.3.1, 10.4.1) has already made the case for **densification** (compacting meaning into a smaller number of words) as a countervailing influence in the noun phrase, alongside colloquialization. We revisit the topic here in order to show that it is not restricted to noun phrases, but a more general trend. This can be done by using the measure of lexical density on the corpora as a whole: that is, calculating the number of open-class or lexical word tokens (chiefly nouns, verbs, adjectives and adverbs)[15] as a proportion of the total number of word tokens in the corpus (Ure 1971; Stubbs 1996) – see Table A11.1.[16] Not unexpectedly lexical density (as shown in Biber *et al.* 1999: 65, Figure 2.2) is lower in conversation (at c. 35%) than in written registers, and reaches its peak in News writing, at c. 54%. The observation of increasing lexical density in Table A11.1 (overall 4.4% in AmE and 2.6% in BrE) is therefore clearly contrary to colloquialization, and in line with densification.

It is curious that the subcorpora that have the highest and lowest lexical density in 1961 (Press and Fiction, respectively) increase by a relatively small

---

[14] In a small-scale study of how far a particular measure of colloquialization (increasing use of contractions) in AmE is attributable to increase of quotation, we counted examples of the contracted form *it's* in quoted speech in Brown and Frown, and compared them with the overall increase in *it's*. The increase of *it's* in quoted speech (from 188 in Brown to 420 in Frown) accounts for only part of the overall increase of the same contraction (from 299 in Brown to 767 in Frown). Of the 468 additional examples of *it's* in the later corpus, less than half – 232 – can be attributed to increased quotation of speech.

[15] In the CQP query for this corpus search (see section 2.4 C), we defined lexical words as any words tagged as adjective, noun, lexical verb, adverb, number, letter of the alphabet or other formulaic expression. Thus, adverb particles (such as *up, out, off*) and lexical uses of *be, do, have* were excluded.

[16] Alternatively, Halliday and Matthiessen ([3]2004) define lexical density as lexical words per finite clause, a measure that produces a more varied result than lexical words as a percentage of all words. See Smith (2005: 208–9).

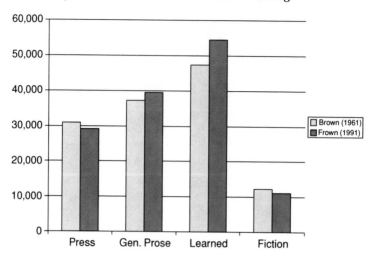

Figure 11.1 Abstract nominalizations in AmE: frequencies pmw

amount – 3% or less in every case, whereas the subcorpora of intermediate lexical density increase the most: General Prose increases by 5.3% (in AmE) and 3.1% (in BrE), while Learned, showing the most intense densification, increases by 7.7% (in AmE) and 4.9% (in BrE). Although these percentages of increase appear to be small, it must be remembered that the increase takes place across all four subcorpora, and applies to both AmE and BrE. In fact, the results for the corpora as a whole, and for most subcorpora, are statistically highly significant.

In Chapter 10, densification in the noun phrase seemed mainly to show up syntactically, in changing structural habits leading to higher frequency of Noun+Noun and *s*-genitive constructions. However, compactness of meaning can also be achieved by morphology and processes of word-formation. We noted this in section 10.2.2, in the marked growth of the use of acronyms. Turning to more traditional morphological processes, consider the word *densification* itself. In working on this and the last chapter, we were reluctant to introduce yet another term alongside *colloquialization* and the like, but we found it awkward to use more than one word (such as 'becoming more semantically compact') to express a meaning for which we had recurrent need. The single word *densification*, despite its ugly grandiloquence, satisfied our need much better. Three necessary elements of meaning 'dense' + '[dens]-ify' + '[densif]-ication' were condensed into one abstract noun meaning 'the *process* of *causing* [something] to become *denser*'. Figures 11.1 and 11.2 show the increasing use in AmE and BrE of abstract nouns with one of the suffixes *-tion, -sion, -ment, -ness, -ity, -ance, -ncy, -acy, -ism, -ship, -archy* (see also Tables A11.3, A11.4).

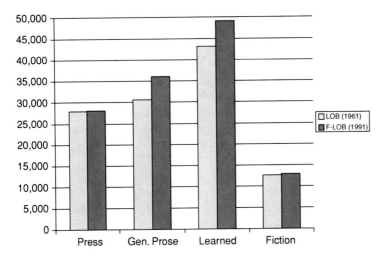

Figure 11.2 Abstract nominalizations in BrE: frequencies pmw

It is noticeable that the growth rate of abstract nominalizations is much higher in BrE than in AmE: the British level in the 1990s approximating to the American level in the 1960s. Again, this could be a case of BrE catching up with AmE in the adoption of a change. The following passage from F-LOB text J62 shows how prevalent such nominalizations can be, something indeed illustrated by our own vocabulary in this chapter.

(6) *Symbolization*, the reader's initial response, can be defined as a peremptory *perception* and *evaluation* of the text. It is an imaginative *interiorization* which is differentiated from a purely sensorimotor response. *Interpretation* of the text is referred to as motivated *"resymbolization"*, where *resymbolization* is defined as the *mentation* involved in a conscious response to the *symbolization*. It is a reframing of the *symbolization* which occurs when the present adaptive needs of the individual demand an act of *explanation* or *interpretation*. [F-LOB J62, emphasis added to highlight the words ending in *-tion*.]

It is not surprising that the varieties where such abstract nouns are most closely packed are Learned and, to a lesser extent, General Prose: the non-fiction subcorpora containing expository writing. A more telling observation, however, is that these same subcorpora are the ones that have increased their representation of nominalizations most strongly: by 13.7% and 17.6% respectively in BrE, and by 14.9% and 6.0% in AmE. The implication is that the tendency towards more abstract and dense writing, already characteristic of Learned prose, is increasing substantially, and is spreading to the General

Prose subcorpus. This trend towards densification and abstraction is probably linked to a greater specialization of topic and audience. The writing in these genres is likely to be increasingly addressed to a restricted specialist readership, rather than a lay public.[17] One symptom of this is more highly specialized writing on social science topics, as exemplified in (6) above. This trend was already under way in 1961, but if we go back a further thirty years, to the B-LOB corpus (see Leech and Smith 2005: 89) we find that social science topics such as sociology carried a style more in tune with the tradition of humanistic and philosophical scholarship than with specialized scientific writing.

The result of this trend as seen in F-LOB and Frown is that the 'more specialized' subcorpora (Learned and General Prose) and the 'less specialized' ones (Press and Fiction) are on somewhat divergent paths, separated by increasing differences of frequency. Yet, it is surprising, from the colloquialization point of view, that in F-LOB the latter pair of genres appears not to have moved away from abstraction and density of content. With respect to this particular measure, they are clearly not following the advice of the author of (5), in writing 'as though you were talking to your neighbour over the garden fence'.

Reverting to Biber's (2003a) drama of 'competing demands', we often find cases where colloquialization and densification compete with one another in the same text. Putting it flippantly, one could argue that the current trend in written English is to pack ever more information into a given length of text and then to 'sell' this fairly heavy intellectual diet in a somewhat more informal/colloquial style than used to be the case. An interesting question which takes us beyond the realm of the merely linguistic is, of course, what the motivation is behind this mostly external and tactical 'audience design' (Bell 1984; see also Fairclough 1992: 98, 204).

11.5   Americanization?

As far as written English is concerned, the Brown family provides an excellent testing ground for claims about the differential patterns of change in AmE and BrE, as we have seen in previous chapters. Although it has not been feasible to compare AmE and BrE in all the areas of language we have studied, we have come across instances of the broadly defined kinds of patterns of change mentioned in section 2.5.4, as illustrated in (a)–(e) below. Note, however, that these types are not mutually exclusive: more than one can be combined, and

---

[17] We should point out, however, that the sampling of the corpora of the Brown family did not stratify publications in categories D to J according to level of specialist knowledge assumed. On the other hand, Frown and F-LOB did follow the sampling of Brown and LOB by matching individual publications as far as possible, so that a similar distribution of samples according to level of specialization can be assumed in these genres between the 1961 and the 1991/2 corpora.

moreover, since we are dealing with quantitative differences, the contrasts between them are often gradual, rather than absolute.

(a) *Regionally specific change*, where one variety changes in a certain respect but the other does not, is illustrated by the *prevent NP V-ing* construction without *from* (9.2.2), which has spread further in BrE but is still absent from AmE.

(b) *Convergent change*, where AmE and BrE show convergent frequencies, is illustrated by the choice between mandative subjunctive and mandative *should* (Figure 3.1, section 3.2.1), where BrE has changed in the direction of AmE, whereas AmE has changed only trivially.[18] This is also, therefore, a case of region-specific change (and also of follow-my-leader change, as in (e) below).

(b') *Divergent change*, as the opposite of (b), is notable in the case of the progressive passive (6.6), which increases in frequency in BrE, but declines in AmE.

(c) *Parallel change*, where the two varieties change in the same direction and to a similar extent, is best illustrated by the increasing frequency of the present progressive (AmE by 33.5%; BrE by 29.4% – see Table A6.1).

(d) *Different rates of change* are illustrated by Noun + Common Noun sequences (10.3.1–2), where AmE, starting from a higher frequency in 1961, increases less than BrE in the thirty-year period, so that BrE partially 'catches up' with AmE. In contrast, (c) (present progressive) shows an example of similar rates of change. Changes of type (d) often combine with those of type (e) below.

(e) *Follow-my-leader*, the pattern where one variety, moving in the same direction as the other, takes the lead, which the other follows, is illustrated by the decline of the core modal auxiliaries (4.1), which may be pictured as in Figure 11.3.

Pattern (e) often recurs in our data, so that it begins to look like the 'normal' pattern. Sometimes AmE takes the lead in declining frequency – as in the case of the modals (4.1), the *be*-passive (7.2) and *wh-* relatives (10.5.1). In other cases AmE takes the lead in increasing frequency – as in the case of epistemic *have to*, the *to*-infinitive (9.3), the *help* + (to) V construction (9.2.1), nouniness (10.2) and the *s*-genitive (10.4.1). In rare cases, we see BrE taking the lead, and AmE following. This pattern occurs in the semi-modals as a group, as well as for *have to* as an individual semi-modal.

From instances such as these, the evidence is cumulatively persuasive in indicating American 'leadership' being one of the major moving forces on

---

[18] This finding is, to a degree, something that is 'created' by focusing on our thirty-year timespan: AmE *has* changed in the twentieth century, but much earlier, so in a longer view this is really a change of types (d) and (e).

more frequent --> less frequent

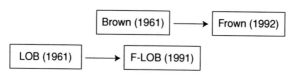

Figure 11.3 A follow-my-leader pattern: declining frequency of the core modals in AmE and in BrE

[NOTE: Figure 11.3 is not to scale.]

BrE. As with colloquialization, however, we have caveats regarding the too easy assumption of 'Americanization' in the sense that direct dialect contact is the reason for change.

First, it is true that we have often observed the follow-my-leader pattern, where AmE is ahead or is changing more quickly than BrE. But this does not necessarily signal direct transatlantic influence through dialect contact, but could merely show that a trend common to AmE and BrE (as well as other regional varieties) is somewhat more advanced in one variety than another.

Second, there are other patterns of change apart from 'follow-my-leader', as we illustrated above. We have observed cases where AmE and BrE follow opposite paths – one declining while the other increases. This may lead to an increasing divergence between the two varieties (as with the progressive passive), or less commonly, to a convergence – where a decline in one variety and an increase in the other have resulted in less difference in 1991 than existed in 1961. (For example, in the frequency of the first-person singular pronoun (see section 11.3.6), the increase in AmE (5,825 → 7,632) and the decrease in BrE (7,600 → 6,848) result in less difference.) There are also rare cases where BrE shows a more extreme tendency than AmE – for example, the increasing use of Adjective + Noun and Adjective +Adjective in the noun phrase (10.3). Perhaps the most surprising case of this is the increase in semi-modals (5.2), which, although more pronounced in AmE, starts and ends at a higher point in BrE – we return to this below.

The pattern most clearly suggestive of transatlantic influence from AmE to BrE is one where there is a convergence – the change being smaller or virtually non-existent in AmE. One such pattern that seems likely to show direct transatlantic influence is the increase in the mandative subjunctive in BrE, which together with a slight (non-significant) decline in AmE, brings the two varieties appreciably closer in 1991/2 than they were in 1961. In this case, since colloquialization does not fit the bill (as the mandative subjunctive is not colloquial – see Table 3.1, section 3.2.2), and since the BrE increase seems to run counter to the decline of the mandative subjunctive in earlier decades, the only convincing explanation for a revival of a form previously

Table 11.3. *Decreasing use of main verb* have *constructed as an auxiliary, and increasing use of* do-*support with* have *in negation and inversion*

	AmE		BrE		
	Brown (1961)	Frown (1992)	Lanc-31 (1931±3)	LOB (1961)	F-LOB (1991)
Aux. construction	17	17	66	60	21
do support	131	175	17	53	126

NOTE: The raw frequencies here are (somewhat underestimated) approximations, based on a hand-editing of a concordance search for *do* followed by *have* with one or two words intervening.

considered moribund (see 3.1) seems to be American influence (for further evidence, see Övergaard 1995).

We now briefly examine another case of possible American influence: one of the changes noted in anecdotal treatments of recent grammatical change – see 1.3. This is the decline of *have* used as a finite main verb with the characteristics of *have* as an auxiliary. We examine two variants of this construction:

(a)   *Have* with a following *not* or *n't*:
      He hadn't a chance. [LOB N08]
(b)   *Have* with a following subject in inversion:
      Have you time to help me? [F-LOB P24]

These have increasingly given way to the equivalent 'American'[19] construction, with *do*-support: *He didn't have a chance*; *Do you have time to help me?* A further option, of course, is to use the semi-modal *have got* (as in *I haven't got a clue*), which, as we have already pointed out (5.2), is rarely used in the Brown family of corpora, and which we will not investigate further here.[20]

Table 11.3 presents the results of the comparison of AmE and BrE in the four corpora regarding the use of *have* or *do* in negation and inversion constructions. For BrE, to give additional historical evidence, we have included a fifth corpus, the Lanc-31 (B-LOB) corpus from the early 1930s, demonstrating that the *do*-support construction has been increasing remarkably over the sixty-year period. At the beginning of this period, the rare uses

---

[19]   Calling *do*-support the 'American' option is more than a loose form of words. See Biber *et al.* (1999: 161–2, 215–17) for the predominance of *do*-support in AmE, as compared with its minority status in BrE.
[20]   Regarding the negation of main verb *have*, an in-depth corpus study of all three variants is provided by Varela Pérez (2007), demonstrating the growth of *do*-support and the decline of *have* + *not/n't* in recent English. See also Hundt (1998a: 55–6).

of *do*-support with *have* were mostly cases where the meaning of *have* was dynamic, rather than stative, as in *Well, did you have a nice walk?* (for which **Well, had you a nice walk?* was not a possible alternative). At the end of the period, in F-LOB, *do* + *have* with stative meaning was not unusual, as in *We just don't have the time.*

The pattern of change here combines the (b) convergent and (e) follow-my-leader types. On the one hand, convergence is what one would predict assuming American influence. In BrE, from 1961 to 1991/2, the 'British' construction with *have* drastically declined by 65% towards an American 'norm' of rarity (21 occurrences compared with 17 in AmE), while the 'American' construction with *do* more than doubled its frequency, considerably closing the gap between AmE and BrE.[21] On the other hand, AmE itself had increased its use of *do* + *have* in the intervening years, so it is still possible to treat this as a continuation of a long-term parallel change dating from EModE, with *have* belatedly coming into line with other lexical verbs in accepting *do*-periphrasis (cf. the similar cases of *dare* and *need*), and with BrE tardily catching up AmE in the familiar follow-my-leader pattern.

11.5.1 'Americanization' in relation to other trends

We now briefly consider the interrelations between colloquialization and American 'leadership' in change. To some extent, these two forces appear to cooperate with each other. As a textbook example of colloquialization, contractions, for example, have invaded the written language more thoroughly in AmE (see Figure 11.4). From roughly the same starting point, AmE has raced ahead of BrE.

Other cases where colloquialization takes the lead in AmE are semi-modals such as *want to* and *going to* (5.2), and the *get*-passive (7.3). Indeed, if we look at the relative frequency of the semi-modals as a group in AmE conversation, as compared with BrE conversation (see Tables 5.2 and 5.3, section 5.2), as regards frequency, AmE is way ahead of BrE in this of grammaticalization. However, this finding is curiously at odds with the findings for the Brown family, where BrE is ahead of AmE in the use of semi-modals, although AmE is catching up. The most plausible reason for this discrepancy

---

[21] Arguably another aspect of the decline of main verb *have* with auxiliary characteristics is a decrease in the frequency of the main verb use of the contractions *'s*, *'ve* and *'d*, as in *You've only yourself to blame.* Clearly contractions of main verb *have* are only likely to occur in texts (especially those in Fiction) where there is use of contracted forms in general. However, an approximate count of these cases reveals a decline from 41 to 18 in BrE (LOB to F-LOB), whereas the change from Brown to Frown is, bizarrely, one of increase from 1 to 10. The numbers are too small to derive any firm conclusions, but the general pattern is consistent with the prediction that BrE is declining towards the very infrequent occurrence of contracted main verb *have* found in AmE. This is a case where we can point to an apparently moribund grammatical feature of the standard spoken language.

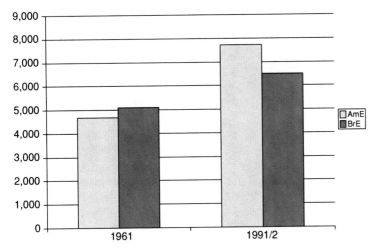

Figure 11.4 Increasing use of contractions in AmE and BrE: summary (frequencies pmw)

is that the 'prestige barrier' causing writers to shun semi-modals in 1961 was stronger in AmE in 1961 than in BrE – although things were changing considerably by 1991/2. One notable exception to this, however, is the semi-modal *be going to* (Table A5.1), for which the 'prestige barrier' (if that explanation is accepted) was more robust in BrE, persisting strongly up to the 1990s.

In using terms like 'prestige barrier,' we touch on one of the limitations of this study: the corpus linguistic paradigm gives no access to the attitudes to usage that may influence the changes of frequency we observe. Ideally, then, corpus research should be complemented by experiments or questionnaires eliciting informants' judgements and attitudes. The power of attitudes to influence usage is more overtly discussed in 11.6.2 below.

AmE has also taken a lead, as we noted in section 10.1, in the anti-colloquial trend we have labelled densification. The increase in nouns, in Noun + Common Noun sequences, and s-genitives, all factors contributing to the compression of information within the noun phrase, have each had a more pronounced effect in AmE, although there are signs, especially in Noun + Common Noun sequences, that BrE in the 1960s–1990s was catching up with this densification trend (10.3.1–2). The American mass print media from the early twentieth century, which gave us the condensed apposition construction illustrated by *bearded Cuban revolutionary leader Fidel Castro*,[22] probably provided the original driving force for this change.

---

[22] Example from Mair (2006b: 118).

11.5.2   'Americanization' and sociolinguistic globalization

Our perspective on American 'leadership' of change has been largely restricted (a) to the US and the UK, (b) to the standard written language and (c) to a particular period: from the 1960s to 1990s. It is worth while finally placing the evidence of the four corpora in a wider 'global sociolinguistic' perspective, taking into account spoken English, including vernacular Englishes, worldwide.

On such a broader view, it becomes clear immediately that the worldwide presence of American English and the resulting spread of its usages into other varieties will not inevitably lead to the linguistic homogenization of the English language and global convergence on American norms. As recent sociolinguistic research on the globalization of vernacular features has shown (e.g. Meyerhoff and Niedzielski 2003), 'Americanisms' such as the emphatic negative *no way* or the new quotative *be like* may well be taken over as linguistic forms, but their function in the new sociolinguistic environment may be very different from the one they performed in the source variety.

Given the limitation of Brown corpora to written English, it is, of course, not surprising that they should not contain a single instance of quotative *be like*, one of the most prominent recent innovations in English worldwide. First identified as innovations in American English by Butters (1980, 1982),[23] the new quotatives *go* and *be like* are among the fastest-spreading grammatical constructions in varieties of English today. In particular, *be like* is not only spreading in the variety in which it originated, American English, but has been reported as an innovation in Australian English, Canadian English and Newfoundland English, British (= English) English, Scottish English and Jamaican English (see Barbieri 2005: 223 and Buchstaller 2006: 363, for a review of pertinent research). As the following Jamaican example (from ICE-Jamaica) shows, however, it is used in contexts which do not suggest the suppression of local features and wholesale Americanization:

(7)   You know she knows nothing about these people. Me fraid you know the man a call her she run gon go go take picture So *I'm like* where's the picture we thought it was a instant thing. *She's like* no him have it. The man go Okay

Buchstaller makes the point that these quotatives are no passive borrowings from AmE, but are active appropriations by regionally diverse language communities, where they are acquiring their own habits of usage (in Jamaican English, for example, *be like* is common but *go* is rare), and their own attitudinal characteristics – such as those of socially attractive solidarity traits.

---

[23] For important follow-up studies on the phenomenon in American English see Blyth *et al.* (1990), Romaine and Lange (1991) or Barbieri (2005).

This picture of English combining globalization with diversity goes beyond traditional models of borrowing through language contact and dialect contact, and may equally well be applied to the written language. 'Americanization', whether we put it in quotation marks or not, is not a passive process, and happens differently in different English-speaking communities. We have come across many examples in this book where the generality of American influence on British English cannot easily be denied, but where it is far from eclipsing the independent developments found in this and other national standards.[24]

11.6   Other trends

The forces for change we have dealt with in some detail (grammaticalization, colloquialization, densification, 'Americanization') are not the only ones that count. In the remainder of this chapter we take a brief look at some other trends that should not be overlooked, and indeed deserve more attention than we can give them.

11.6.1   Democratization: ironing out differences

From a critical discourse analysis viewpoint, Fairclough (1992: 98) used the term democratization to refer to 'reduction of overt markers of power asymmetry'. He meant the term in a broad sense, covering a range of linguistic behaviours including 'a tendency towards informality of language' leading to 'a shift in the relationship between spoken and written language' (p. 204). In short, in his eyes democratization can subsume what we have called colloquialization.

However closely related to colloquialization it may be, in this section we distinguish democratization as a reflection, through language, of changing norms in personal relations. The tendency has been to phase out markers of distance, respect, superiority or inferiority, and to aim at the expression of greater equality and familiarity. We have already seen a likely manifestation of this: the decline of *must* (see section 4.1) and the rise of *need to* – as well as *have to* – may have been partly motivated by avoidance of an authoritarian stance in utterances with directive implications.

Another example is the decline in the use of titular nouns used as a prefix to names. *Mr, Mrs* and *Miss* are the most common (see Figures 11.5 and 11.6). Two kinds of bias persist from the 1960s into the 1990s: one is a heavy preponderance of male rather than female titles; the other is a weaker partiality for these titles in AmE, where titular nouns are approximately 45%

---

[24] Incidentally, 'Americanization' is neither a new word nor a new trend. The LOB Corpus contains a quotation from George Bernard Shaw using the word as follows in 1912: *For what has been happening in my lifetime* [. . .] *is the Americanization of the whole world.* [LOB G13].

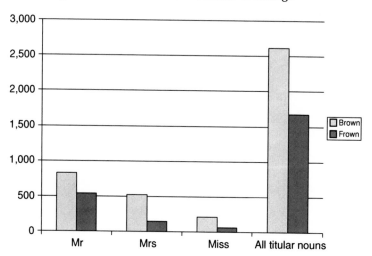

Figure 11.5 Decline of titular nouns preceding personal names in AmE
(frequencies pmw)

(AmE estimated)

*All titular nouns (both with and without the abbreviatory full stop) preceding
personal names were counted.

NOTE: The new titular noun *Ms.* occurs occasionally in the 1991/2 corpora:
there are 44 occurrences in Frown, and 13 in F-LOB.

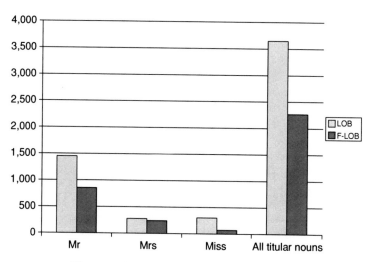

Figure 11.6 Decline of titular nouns preceding personal names in BrE
(frequencies pmw)

less frequent than in BrE in both 1961 and 1991/2. Although both of these contrasts invite obvious socio-cultural comment, more relevant here is the trend common to both AmE and BrE: a very marked decline in the use of titular nouns, phasing out the expression of social distinctions that these nouns encode (see Table A11.5). If we ask what has replaced these titular nouns, the answer is 'nothing'. The name alone (*Susan, Shakespeare*) or the given name with a following surname (*Susan Smith*) have become the normal way to address or refer to a person.[25]

It is reasonable to include, as part of the same trend, the effect of the women's movement during the late decades of the twentieth century in seeking to eliminate gender bias in the language. The most salient example of this, of course, is the avoidance of the gender-neutral use of the masculine pronoun *he*[26] (i.e. *he* with male and/or female referent(s)). The Brown family of corpora shows what is expected here. Although it was impractical to conduct an exhaustive search of many thousands of instances of *he* in the four corpora, a randomized 3% sample of approximately 500 examples of *he* from each yielded the results shown in Table 11.4.[27] Examples of pronominal types (x), (y) and (z) as represented in the table are:

(x)   Require each employee to work *his* last shift before and after the holiday to be eligible for pay. This cuts the absentee rate. [Brown E30]

(y)   Utilitarianism asks the individual to aggregate the consequences of *his or her* actions for the promotion of pleasure and avoidance of pain, and demands that *she or he* should morally only follow that course which causes more pleasure than it does pain. [F-LOB J27]

---

[25] We undertook a small-scale frequency study of personal names from 2% of proper nouns in each of the four corpora, to see if they reflected a 'democratization' trend towards given names in the period 1961–1991/2. In total, a randomized set of 2,000 personal names was classified. We expected an increase of given names, and a decrease of surnames. However, the most significant finding was a general increase (of personal proper nouns) of 13.9% in AmE and 13.7% in BrE. Clear cases of given names rose by 25.1% (in AmE) and 19.2% (in BrE), whereas clear cases of surnames increased by 20.3% (in AmE) and 18.0% (in BrE). Although given names showed the bigger increase, perhaps the most surprising result is that surnames, as well as given names, increased steeply. Very few of these were used vocatively in direct address, however, so the implications for the 'democratization' hypothesis are not clear. On the general increase in proper nouns, see Table 10.3, section 10.2; Table 10.4, section 10.2.2.

[26] *He* in this discussion includes *he, him, his* and *himself*.

[27] It is regrettable that time prevented us from inspecting larger samples, and examining larger contexts where the concordance lines did not provide enough contextual information. Furthermore, the numbers of examples inspected in the 3% samples varied from 473 (for *he* in Frown) and 600 (for *he* in Brown). The rarity of gender-neutral *he* compared with the generally high frequency of these pronouns also resulted in small counts. The trend towards gender neutrality represented by these counts, however, is fairly obvious. If corroborative evidence is needed, Holmes (2001: 307–8) reports that the *New Zealand Women's Weekly* 'used four times fewer generic forms in 1984 than in 1964,' and that a 'dramatic drop in the use of generic forms from twelve to four per 5000 words' took place in a wide range of American magazines between 1971 and 1979. See also Pauwels (1998).

Table 11.4. *Decline of gender-neutral* he *and rise of alternative pronominal expressions*

		AmE		BrE	
		Brown	Frown	LOB	F-LOB
	(x) Gender-neutral HE (*he, him, his*, etc.) in the 3% sample	20	7	32	4
		(9)	(4)	(18)	(2)
ALTERNATIVES	(y) *he or she, his or her*, etc. (numbers in the whole corpus)	***9	***53	**11	**34
	Alternatives (y') *she or he, her or his*, etc. (numbers in the whole corpus)	*0	*3	*0	*3
	(z) *they* (*they, them, their*, etc.) with singular reference in the 6% sample	7	9	**0	**9
		(9)	(11)	(1)	(1)
	Occurrences of HE in the 3% sample	600	473	543	487
	Occurrences of THEY in the 6% sample	510	511	508	511

NOTE: It is important to note that the quantities in different rows of this table are not comparable. The numbers in parentheses in rows (x) and (z) represent uncertain cases. Asterisks, as elsewhere, indicate significance levels (log likelihood).

(z)   "You have to consider that everybody lies about *their* age by about five years [. . .]" [Frown A40]

Notice that example (y) exemplifies both variants of the coordinative pattern: *he or she*, and *she or he*.

The change is striking enough, despite the small numbers. Supposedly 'generic' *he* is eight times as frequent in the LOB sample as in the F-LOB sample. Conversely, singular *they*, often considered colloquial and 'incorrect',[28] is absent from a 6%[29] LOB sample entirely, but occurs nine times in the corresponding 6% F-LOB sample. Contrary to expectation, the gender-neutral use of *he* is less frequent in the AmE corpus sample than in the BrE corpus sample in 1961, and declines less sharply than in the BrE corpus in 1991/2. The *he or she* device, as an alternative to the generic use of *he*, increases more than threefold in the BrE corpora between 1961 and 1991. The corresponding change is even more dramatic in AmE: more than a fivefold increase. The *she or he* device does not occur at all in the 1961 corpora, and makes a very infrequent appearance in the 1991/2 corpora (three occurrences each in F-LOB and Frown). Even relying on these small samples, we see in these corpora a precipitous decline in the gender-neutral

---

[28] As is well known, however, singular *they* has been current in the colloquial language for centuries, and is even used by Shakespeare – see Bodine (1975).

[29] As the pronoun *he* is more than twice as frequent, in the Brown family of corpora, than the plural pronoun *they*, a 6% sample from occurrences of *they* was taken as approximately comparable with the 3% sample of *he*.

use of *he*, and a tentative move in favour of singular *they*.[30] Ironically, the newly popular coordinative pattern Pronoun-*or*-Pronoun still preserves a kind of gender bias, in that the masculine pronoun nearly always precedes the feminine. The written option *s/he* does not occur at all in the Brown family.

11.6.2   Language prescriptions

The term 'prescriptive' has negative connotations for most linguists, who are likely to think that any attempt to prescribe correct usage (or proscribe incorrect usage) is a throwback to earlier generations, when doctrinaire linguistic attitudes (often ill-informed) were rife, and understanding of language and language change was obscured by bigotry. However, in choosing the fairly neutral term 'language prescription' we wish to encompass any conscious efforts to change the language habits of English speakers (or more often, writers), whether bigoted or not.

Such consciously motivated influences on language are typically supposed to be conservative attempts to preserve and maintain 'standards'. They are also considered to be ineffective – as Samuel Johnson wrote in the Preface to his *Dictionary* (1755): 'sounds are too volatile and subtile for legal restraints; to enchain syllables, and to lash the winds, are equally the undertakings of pride, unwilling to measure its desires by its strength.' However, the movement towards gender-neutrality just discussed is an example where advocacy of 'acceptable standards' of usage (a) has been influential in initiating and popularizing change, and (b) has embraced innovation rather than conservatism.

As for the more long-standing prescriptive tradition, Crystal (2004: 523) claims: 'Institutional prescriptivism began to come to an end in the later decades of the twentieth century.' One example that might illustrate this is the rising use in print of singular *they*, shown in a small way in Table 11.4. Another example is the familiar shibboleth of splitting infinitives: *to really live*, *to unwittingly give*, etc. These 'solecisms' increased nearly threefold (from 12 to 35) from LOB to F-LOB, and more than doubled between Brown and Frown, from 33 to 85.[31] It seems that the split infinitive has been losing its power to shock, though it still seems to cause more of a stir in BrE than in AmE.[32]

---

[30] One symptom is the often-noted occasional appearance in current English of the hybrid singular–plural reflexive pronoun *themself*, which Huddleston and Pullum (2002: 494) date from the 1970s. However, no instances of this 'monstrosity' were found in the four corpora.

[31] The search was limited to cases where a single word (normally an adverb) intervenes between the *to* and the infinitive of the verb. Increasing the gap to two words yielded no further examples.

[32] Another prescriptive shibboleth, the use of *shall* rather than *will* or *'ll* after a first-person pronoun, has also kept its hold over British writers more than over American writers. As a proportion of all three variants *I/we shall/will/'ll*, *I/we shall* declined from 19% to 13%

It is much too early, however, to write off the traditional prescriptivist. Crystal, in support of his decline-of-prescriptivism thesis, cites the educational reforms in the teaching of English in the UK, as well as in Australia and Canada (2004: 523). But in the USA, there are notable negative cases of prescriptivism that have not only maintained, but increased their hold on usage since the 1960s. These are condemnations of the passive (see sections 7.1–2) and of relative *which* in restrictive relative clauses (see 10.5.1). Prescriptivism maintains it hold over written AmE through channels which are absent from the UK, such as handbooks for obligatory freshman English courses,[33] and the pronouncements of 'language mavens' in the press. Moreover, through modern media, such prohibitions can achieve their ends by more covert means than the traditional usage handbooks or style guides. They can be effected by the invisible hand of editorial rule books of publishing houses, newspapers and journals. (For a relevant discussion of the 'That rule' that [or which!] proscribes *which* in restrictive relative clauses, see 1.1.) More recently, the impact of grammar checking tools on users of American-based software has no doubt spread the inhibition against using the passive and relative *which* worldwide. It is not unlikely that frequency of these two grammatical constructions will show an even steeper further decline from 1991, when successors to the Frown and F-LOB corpora are available for the current language.[34]

On the other hand, it cannot be overlooked that the medium of print represented by the Brown family of corpora is now in competition with electronic media such as email and the web, whose influence has been growing vigorously since the 1990s. This, together with the increasing power of spoken mass media, gives dominance to relatively spontaneous uses of language that show signs of evolving beyond the reach of prescriptivism.[35]

11.6.3   Analyticization?

This section concerns a process of change which, to all appearances, has been taking place only marginally in recent decades. It has been a powerful idea that the movement from synthetic to analytic structure (**analyticization**), which transformed the language between OE and EModE, is still at work in the latest decades of English. In the chapter on 'drift' in his book *Language* (1921: 156–70), Sapir envisaged that the future language would lose further

---

between Brown and Frown. In LOB and F-LOB there was a smaller decline from a higher starting point: from 30% to 27%.

[33] For example, Hommerberg and Tottie (2007: 46, 61), discussing the low frequency of the *try and V* construction in AmE as compared with BrE, cite the influence of American college writing handbooks, 'which still strongly advocate the use of *try to* instead of *try and*'.

[34] Such a corpus (a twenty-first century matching sequel to F-LOB) is currently being compiled from Web sources by Paul Baker at Lancaster University.

[35] On the Web, however, split infinitives remain a persistent talking point: consult, for example, http://itre.cis.upenn.edu/~myl/languagelog/archives/000901.html.

Table 11.5. *Periphrastic and inflectional comparison in AmE*

	Brown (1961)		Frown (1992)		Change: periphrastic relative to all comparatives
	Periphrastic	Inflectional	Periphrastic	Inflectional	
Press	136	323	133	309	+1.6%
Gen. Prose	378	864	370	807	+3.3%
Learned	180	459	201	420	+15.0%
Fiction	117	389	93	361	−11.5%
TOTAL	811	2,035	797	1,897	+3.9%

(estimated)

Table 11.6. *Periphrastic and inflectional comparison in BrE*

	LOB (1961)		F-LOB (1991)		Change: periphrastic relative to all comparatives
	Periphrastic	Inflectional	Periphrastic	Inflectional	
Press	139	306	111	305	−14.6%
Gen. Prose	371	914	426	1,001	+3.4%
Learned	137	404	199	494	+13.4%
Fiction	110	335	124	360	+3.6%
TOTAL	757	1,959	860	2,160	+2.2%

remnants of its inflectional past: *whom* would ultimately disappear, and the inflectional *s*-genitive would become restricted to animate nouns. As we have seen, on both these counts, up to now Sapir's prediction has failed to come true: *whom* is showing no particular signs of decline (see section 1.1), and the *s*-genitive, increasing its frequency, has been expanding, rather than restricting, its range of possessor nouns (10.4.1).

A third area where the inflectional remnants of English have seemed under pressure is in the comparison of adjectives, where inflectional and periphrastic comparatives co-exist. Our findings are not conclusive, but taken in conjunction with previous research (cf. Bauer 1994; Kytö and Romaine 1997; Leech and Culpeper 1997; Kytö and Romaine 2000; Lindquist 2000; Peters 2000; Mondorf 2007) they provide evidence that mild incremental changes in the system of comparison-formation have been taking place.

Interestingly, in terms of overall usage of comparative forms (that is, combining the two main types), BrE shows an increase, and AmE a decrease, in frequency (see Tables 11.5 and 11.6). In BrE, both periphrastic and suffixed types show a numerical increase, although this is limited to the Learned General Prose and Fiction genres rather than across the board.

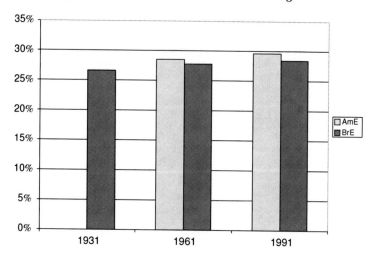

Figure 11.7 Periphrastic comparatives as a percentage of all comparative forms
(AmE: post-edited Frown, estimated Brown)

With respect to competition between the types of comparison, both regional varieties give modest, but not statistically significant, evidence of a shift towards periphrastic comparatives. In the case of BrE, data from the 1930s corpus Lanc-31 (B-LOB) suggest that this is part of a continuing trend through the twentieth century (see Figure 11.7).

One finding that is arguably more credible because it echoes previous findings, concerns patterns of selection among adjectives that, at one time or another, have allowed both modes of comparison. The adjective *worthy* provides an example of such vacillation. In LOB *worthy* occurs twice in comparative use, once in periphrastic and once in inflectional form:

(8)   He sowed passions, jealousies, loyalties, scandals, animosities and treacheries as effortlessly as some far *worthier* characters scatter boredom. [LOB C01]

(9)   How much greater the pity, then, that Charles II could not prove *more worthy* on taking up the Crown. [LOB D05]

Bauer (1994: 56–60) claims that across the twentieth century the degree of vacillation among such adjectives reduced as individual forms established a clearer preference for inflectional or periphrastic comparison. The Brown family corpora lend tentative support to this claim, with a reduction in the frequency of adjectives allowing at least one occurrence of each type within the same corpus (Table 11.7).

In general, adjectives that formerly allowed vacillation appear to be standardizing on the periphrastic alternant. The number of examples is

Table 11.7. *Number of adjectives exhibiting both inflectional and periphrastic comparison in the same corpus*

	1931	1961	1991/2
BrE	16	16	10
AmE	(no data)	12	9

admittedly small (on account of the size of the corpora), although there is some impressionistic support for the claim in the rather antiquated ring of some of the 1960s examples of inflectional comparison, such as *pleasanter*, *severer* and *slenderer*:

(10)   Across the bridge on the left I saw St. Sophia with its sturdy brown minarets and to the right of them the *slenderer* spires of the Blue Mosque. [Brown E13]

(11)   It would be *pleasanter* if such cruel and feudal performances as tiger and rhino hunts were dropped from future Royal programmes. [LOB B01]

The 1930s corpus furnishes other examples, such as *bitterer*, that sound dated:

(12)   ... and *bitterer* than all the physical torment would be the thought that they were separated from God for ever and ever ... [B-LOB G11]

To sum up what we have observed in the use of comparative forms: alongside the marginal shift in favour of analyticity, there is, as Bauer (1994: 56–60) suggests, a slight shift towards regularization (i.e. reduction in variation).

11.7   Conclusion

At the end of this book, we have to admit to a sense of incompletion. Like the changing language itself, the investigation of linguistic change is a trail that seems to have no end. We have made use of the resources that are available at present, and the time that is available, to present a synthesis of what can be known about the evolution of English grammar in the very recent past. But that synthesis is incomplete: many topics that might legitimately have found a place in this volume have been omitted. As new resources become available in electronic form, many of the threads of investigation followed in the present book will be taken up again by others, in studies of greater depth, breadth and precision – something that we obviously encourage.

   Throughout these chapters we have grappled with two questions: *What* has recently been happening to English grammar, particularly in the written language, and (more speculatively) *why?* Are there reasonable explanations of what has been happening? Many frequency changes do seem to be susceptible to plausible explanation, as we have tried to show in this chapter. But there still remain changes, and differences between the changes in AmE and BrE, which are puzzling and which would benefit from more thorough analysis of the corpora.

In another respect, however, we feel entitled to sound a more positive note. Corpora have changed our way of looking at the diachronic development of a language. Twenty years ago the major changes in Old and Middle English grammar were well documented and well understood. Grammatical change going on in contemporary English, on the other hand, was described impressionistically and unsystematically at best. In particular, hardly any reliable information was available on changing frequencies of use, and outside phonetics, where sociolinguistic studies of sound change in progress had shown the way, the development of utterance-based models of change was in its infancy.

As a result, only the major and dramatic stages in grammatical change came into focus, for example the extension of grammatical categories to new semantic classes of words or into new structural contexts (e.g. the progressive with *have to* or the copula *be*, or passive progressives involving three or more auxiliaries, such as the modal passive progressives or the present/past perfect passive progressive). Similarly, gradual developments, for example in grammaticalization, tended to become visible only as they were approaching completion and clear diagnostic examples became common. Thus, observers were understandably more sensitive to the new status of *gonna* and, to some extent, *wanna*, as here the auxiliarization process was reflected in phonetic contractions, than to the related process affecting *need to*, which had not advanced as far.

Arguably, a perspective focusing on the later stages of a grammatical change or even its endpoint is an unproductive one for the study of ongoing developments, where shifts in the usage frequency of competing variants, across varieties as well as across text types and genres, are the all-important factors which both reflect and shape the way in which a diachronic development is unfolding. Within such a statistically sensitive frame of reference, we have been able to show on numerous occasions that previous commentators were often correct about the fact that some grammatical category was undergoing change but frequently very wrong about the extent and causes of the development. For example, the use of the progressive with stative verbs, commonly cited as an innovation in present-day English (see section 6.5.2), turns out to be a relatively insignificant factor statistically. Other developments – passive progressives, the interpretive use, future progressives and, not least, the continuing entrenchment of the progressive in those environments in which it is already common – emerge as more important in the corpus analysis and have an important impact on the way we model grammatical change in theoretical terms. Similarly, as has been shown, much more is involved in the spread of *s*-genitives in Present-Day English than the commonly suspected tendency for this grammatical category to spread to inanimate nouns.

In fact, it seems that this insight can be generalized from these two individual instances. Wherever we have looked, the increases in frequency of forms observed in our corpora have been far in excess of new linguistic contexts of choice made available for their use. In other words, statistics does not seem to play a major role in the very early stages of grammatical innovation, but its role becomes paramount as the new forms are being integrated and spread through the system. In this way, it becomes understandable why the spread of *going to*, a form whose grammaticalization as a future marker was essentially complete by c. 1600, should still show up as a strong trend in our late-twentieth-century corpora.

Related issues arise with decline in frequency. The modal *must*, for example, has been declining to an extent that calls for an explanation in terms of grammatical change. However, as this modal has been losing frequency in both its deontic and its epistemic uses, there is as yet no categorical explanation for its decline – on the lines of functional specialization to one of its previously two uses, for example. Analysing the decline of *must* in its corpus context, however, has sharpened our understanding of what is most likely going on here – be it at the level of layering in overlapping processes of grammaticalization (*must – have (got) to – want to/need to*) or at the level of the discourse context (a reluctance to use openly 'authoritarian' exponents of obligation).

Where socio-cultural motivations are the dominant factors accounting for frequency changes – as in colloquialization, densification, 'Americanization' and democratization – corpora are absolutely indispensable tools for testing our explanatory hypotheses.

And yet, mysteries and challenges remain. One of the more challenging puzzles we have come across, for example, is the increase in frequency that seems to be a long-drawn-out aftermath of grammaticalization. Why is the *to*-infinitive still becoming more frequent today, more than a thousand years after grammaticalization took place (see section 9.1)? Why is the progressive, whose 'grammaticalization was in all essentials complete by the end of the seventeenth century' (Mair 2006b: 97), still increasing apace, including in those syntactic environments in which it has long been common? Is the progressive losing its purely aspectual character and taking on discoursal and attitudinal roles in the language (as might well be suggested by the 'interpretive' and other 'special' uses discussed in section 6.5.4)?

It is tempting to adopt the thesis that frequency changes take place under their own momentum: that increase begets increase, and decrease begets decrease, unless other factors interfere with the change. The argument, which sees interaction between use (communicative events) and user (cognitive resources) as a basis for language changes, runs roughly as follows. Increasing frequency feeds into the expansion of the language system through making peripheral combinations less peripheral, or central ones more central. As a result, users' resort to those usages is still more frequent.[36] A mirror-image process explains decrease and eventual atrophy: the language system has relatively central and relatively peripheral elements, and with evolving frequency of usage these can become more peripheral in the user's grammar – a process which in return feeds back into less frequent usage.

Sapir's claim (1921: 150) was: 'Language moves down time in a current of its own making. It has a drift.' We seem to have returned to this concept of drift, and given it a quantitative interpretation in trying to make sense of highly significant changes evident in the thirty-year period covered by the Brown family of corpora. For Sapir, linguistic drifts were primarily focused on decontextualized grammatical structure – for example the transition from the synthetic type to the analytical type that has characterized the history of English and – to a lesser extent – the history of most modern Indo-European languages. Using statistical techniques, other scholars (most prominently Biber and Finegan 1989) have investigated 'stylistic drifts' in the history of English writing. Perhaps it is time to give a more general application to this and investigate the role of 'frequency drifts' in processes of linguistic change at all levels.

The present study having focused mainly on change in the written language, the final challenge which arises is to determine the relationship between spoken and written English with regard to diachronic changes. Is writing ultimately dependent on speech, such that the grammar of written English will just lag behind spoken English to a greater or lesser extent but in the end succumb to the general trend? Or is the written language autonomous to some extent, with its history responding to factors which concern written communication only, such as the pressure to pack ever more information into the same number of words? The real-time study of spoken English, now at its beginning, will develop into a burgeoning subfield of corpus linguistics in the coming years and we are confident that in a few decades' time the answer to this question will involve far less speculation than it does at present.

---

[36] This hypothesis gains plausibility from work by Bybee and others since the 1970s (see Bybee 2007) reversing the former neglect of frequency in explanations of language change. The influence of frequency of use, in many studies discussed and illustrated in Bybee (2007), has varied effects on the language, one of the most important being the cognitive effect that 'repetition strengthens memory representations for linguistic forms and makes them more accessible' (p. 10). Addressing the issue of whether frequency is a cause or an effect, Bybee (pp. 17–18) comes to the conclusion that it is both. Frequency observed in texts 'is of course an effect'; but 'frequency or repetition of experiences has an impact on cognitive representations and in this way becomes a cause' [of language change] (p. 18). It seems a fairly natural assumption that one result of the strengthened cognitive representation of a linguistic form is that it gets used more often. This may explain why frequency change appears to take place 'under its own momentum'.

Table 11.8. *Summary table: postulated explanatory trends, together with the increases and decreases of frequency they help to explain*

Features increasing in frequency 1961–1991/2	Features decreasing in frequency 1961–1991/2
Grammaticalization	
'Semi-modals' in general; more particularly: *have to, be going to, want to, need to, supposed to*	(The declining frequency of modals, especially *must*, may be partly due to the grammaticalization of 'semi-modals')
Progressive, especially present progressive and modal progressive	
Get-passive (AmE)	
Help+ bare infinitive	*Help*+ to infinitive
Start/stop + gerund	
Let's	*Let us*
Colloquialization	
Contracted verbs (e.g. *it's*)	
Contracted negatives (e.g. *don't*)	
'Semi-modals' in general	
Progressive, especially present progressive and modal progressive	
Get-passive (AmE)	*Be*-passive
That relativization and zero relativization	*Wh*- relativization
Preposition stranding (in relative clauses)	Pied-piping (in relative clauses)
Not-negation (AmE)	*No*-negation
Questions	
1st and 2nd person pronouns (AmE)	
Let's	*Let us*
'Americanization'	
Have (main verb) with *do*-periphrasis	*Have* (main verb) constructed as auxiliary
Mandative subjunctive (BrE)	*Should* periphrasis for mandative subjunctive (BrE)
Contracted verbs and negatives	
Have to (epistemic) (BrE)	
Noun + common noun construction	
S- genitive	
Help + bare infinitive	*Help* + *to* infinitive
Want to, wanna	
[NOTE: The list might be extended to other features where AmE shows a more extreme or advanced change of frequency.]	*Be*-passive
Densification of content	
Nouns, especially plural nouns and proper nouns – in particular acronyms as proper nouns	Prepositions, especially *of*
	Pronouns (AmE)
Adjectives	
Adjective + noun, noun + common noun, adjective + adjective combinations	Determiners, especially definite articles
S-genitive	
Lexical density	
Abstract noun suffixes (nominalization)	

Table 11.8. *(cont.)*

Features increasing in frequency 1961–1991/2	Features decreasing in frequency 1961–1991/2
Other plausible trends	
Prescriptivism	
that relativization (especially AmE)	*which* relativization (especially AmE)
	be- passive
Democratization (including avoidance of gender discrimination)	
have to, *need to* (especially deontic)	*must* (especially deontic)
they as singular pronoun (= 'he or she')	*he* as generic singular pronoun
personal names (both given names and surnames)	titular nouns, including *Mr, Mrs* and *Miss*
Analyticization	
periphrastic comparison of adjectives (as a proportion of all adjective comparison)	inflectional comparison of adjectives (as a proportion of all adjective comparison)

[NOTE: The entry of the same feature under two headings of the table indicates that both trends may have contributed to the observed change of frequency. For example, the increase in 'semi-modals' can be attributed first to grammaticalization in the spoken language, and secondly to colloquialization causing their increased use to spread in the written language.]

Appendix I
The composition of the Brown Corpus

I Press: 88 samples (each of c. 2,000 words – see Note 1)

A. Press: Reportage	Daily	Weekly	Total
Political	10	4	14
Sports	5	2	7
Society	3	0	3
Spot News	7	2	9
Financial	3	1	4
Cultural	5	2	7
Total			**44**

B. Press: Editorial			
Institutional	7	3	10
Personal	7	3	10
Letters to the Editor	5	2	7
Total			**27**

C. Press: Reviews (theatre, books, music, dance)			
	14	3	17
Total			**17**

II General Prose: 206 samples

D. Religion			
Books			7
Periodicals			6
Tracts			4
Total			**17**

E. Skills and Hobbies			
Books			2
Periodicals			34
Total			**36**

F. Popular Lore			
Books			23
Periodicals			25
Total			**48**

G. Belles Lettres, Biography, Memoirs, etc.

Books	38
Periodicals	37
Total	75

H. Miscellaneous

Government Documents	24
Foundation Reports	2
Industry Reports	2
College Catalogue	1
Industry House organ	1
Total	30

III Learned: 80 samples
J. Learned

Natural Sciences	12
Medicine	5
Mathematics	4
Social and Behavioral Sciences	14
Political Science, Law, Education	15
Humanities	18
Technology and Engineering	12
Total	80

IV Fiction: 126 Samples
K. General Fiction

Novels	20
Short Stories	9
Total	29

L. Mystery and Detective Fiction

Novels	20
Short Stories	4
Total	24

M. Science Fiction

Novels	3
Short Stories	3
Total	6

N. Adventure and Western Fiction

Novels	15
Short Stories	14
Total	29

P. Romance and Love Story

Novels	14
Short Stories	15
Total	29

R. Humour

Novels	3
Essays, etc.	6
Total	**9**

GRAND TOTAL   **500**

NOTE 1: Each text sample consists of 2,000 words or just over 2,000 words. The rule followed by the compilers was that the sample ended at the first sentence break after the 2,000th word.

NOTE 2: The grouping of the 15 text categories into four subcorpora (I–IV) was not part of the original corpus design: instead, the corpus was simply divided into Informative (A–J) and Imaginative (K–R) super-genres.

NOTE 3: The other members of the Brown family of corpora – the LOB, F-LOB and Frown Corpora – follow the same design as the Brown Corpus, with one or two insignificant differences. Further details of all four corpora can be found in the four corpus manuals, online on the ICAME website at http://khnt.hit.uib.no/icame/manuals/.

Appendix II
The C8 tagset used for part-of-speech tagging of the four corpora

APPGE	possessive determiner, prenominal (e.g. *my, your, our*)
AT	article or determiner (e.g. *the, no*) [cannot function pronominally]
AT1	singular article or determiner (e.g. *a, an, every*) [cannot function pronominally]
BCL	before-clause marker (e.g. *in order [that], in order [to]*)
CC	coordinating conjunction (e.g. *and, or*)
CCB	adversative coordinating conjunction (*but*)
CS	subordinating conjunction (e.g. *if, because, unless, so, for*)
CSA	*as* (as conjunction)
CSN	*than* (as conjunction)
CST	*that* (as conjunction)
CSW	*whether* (as conjunction)
DA	after-determiner or post-determiner (e.g. *such, former, same*) [can function pronominally]
DA1	singular after-determiner (e.g. *little, much*) [can function pronominally]
DA2	plural after-determiner (e.g. *few, several, many*) [can function pronominally]
DAR	comparative after-determiner (e.g. *more, less, fewer*) [can function pronominally]
DAT	superlative after-determiner (e.g. *most, least, fewest*) [can function pronominally]
DB	before-determiner or pre-determiner (*all, half*) [can function pronominally]
DB2	plural before-determiner (*both*) [can function pronominally]
DD	determiner (e.g *any, some*) [can function pronominally]
DD1	singular determiner (e.g. *this, that, another*) [can function pronominally]
DD2	plural determiner (*these, those*) [can function pronominally]
DDL	*wh*-determiner, functioning as relative pronoun (*which*) [can function pronominally]
DDLGE	*wh*-determiner, functioning as relative pronoun, genitive (*whose*) [can function pronominally]
DDQ	*wh*-determiner, interrogative (*which, what*) [can function pronominally]
DDQGE	*wh*-determiner, interrogative, genitive (*whose*) [can function pronominally]

DDQV	*wh-ever* determiner, interrogative (*whichever, whatever*) [can function pronominally]
EX	existential *there*
FO	formula (e.g. O_2, $x = y^3$)
FU	unclassified word (e.g. TOOLONG, *ding-ding*)
FW	foreign word (e.g. *Lieder, amigo*)
GE	Germanic genitive marker – (*'s* or *'*)
IF	*for* (as a preposition)
II	preposition (general) (e.g. *on, from, at*)
IO	*of* (as a preposition)
IW	*with, without* (as prepositions)
JJ	general adjective (e.g. *old, good, unconscious*)
JJR	general comparative adjective (e.g. *older, better, stronger*)
JJT	general superlative adjective (e.g. *oldest, best, strongest*)
JK	catenative adjective (*able*, as part of *be able to*)
MC	cardinal number, neutral for number (e.g. *two, three, 271, . . .*)
MC1	singular cardinal number (*one, 1*)
MC2	plural cardinal number (e.g. *sixes, sevens, 50s, 1900's*)
MCGE	genitive cardinal number, neutral for number (*two's, 100's*)
MCMC	'hyphenated' number (*40–50, 1770–1827*)
MD	ordinal number (e.g. *first, second, next, last*)
MF	fraction, neutral for number (e.g. *quarters, two-thirds*)
ND1	singular noun of direction (e.g. *north, southeast*)
NN	common noun, neutral for number (e.g. *sheep, aircraft, headquarters*)
NN1	singular common noun (e.g. *book, child, time*)
NN2	plural common noun (e.g. *books, children, times*)
NNA	following noun of title/status (e.g. *M.A.*)
NNB	preceding noun of title/status (e.g. *Mrs., Prof.*)
NNL1	singular locative noun, as part of a name (e.g. *Island*, as part of *Coney Island, Street* as part of *Argyle Street*)
NNL2	plural locative noun, as part of a name (e.g. *Islands*, as part of *Virgin Islands*)
NNO	numeral noun, neutral for number (e.g. *dozen, hundred*)
NNO2	numeral noun, plural (e.g. *hundreds, thousands*)
NNT1	temporal noun, singular (e.g. *day, week, year*)
NNT2	temporal noun, plural (e.g. *days, weeks, years*)
NNU	unit of measurement noun, neutral for number (e.g. *in., cc, kg,* ° [degree(s)])
NNU1	singular unit of measurement noun (e.g. *inch, centimeter, hectare*)
NNU2	plural unit of measurement noun (e.g. *ins., feet, hectares*)
NP	proper noun, neutral for number (e.g. *IBM, Andes*)
NP1	singular proper noun (e.g. *London, Jane, Simpson*)
NP2	plural proper noun (e.g. *Browns, Reagans, Koreas*)
NPD1	singular weekday noun (e.g. *Sunday, Thursday*)
NPD2	plural weekday noun (e.g. *Sundays, Fridays*)
NPM1	singular month noun (e.g. *August, October*)
NPM2	plural month noun (e.g. *Augusts, Octobers*)

PN	indefinite pronoun, neutral for number (*none, neither*)
PN1	indefinite pronoun, singular (e.g. *anyone, everything, nobody, one*)
PNLO	objective [accusative, oblique] *wh*-pronoun, relative (*whom*)
PNLS	subjective [nominative] *wh*-pronoun, relative (*who*)
PNQO	objective [accusative, oblique] *wh*-pronoun, interrogative (*whom*)
PNQS	subjective [nominative] *wh*-pronoun, interrogative (*who*)
PNQV	*wh-ever* pronoun (*whoever, whomever*)
PNX1	reflexive indefinite pronoun (*oneself*)
PPGE	possessive personal pronoun (e.g. *mine, yours, ours*)
PPH1	3rd person singular neuter personal pronoun (*it*)
PPHO1	3rd person singular objective personal pronoun (*him, her*)
PPHO2	3rd person plural objective personal pronoun (*them*)
PPHS1	3rd person singular subjective personal pronoun (*he, she*)
PPHS2	3rd person plural subjective personal pronoun (*they*)
PPIO1	1st person singular objective personal pronoun (*me*)
PPIO2	1st person plural objective personal pronoun (*us*)
PPIS1	1st person singular subjective personal pronoun (*I*)
PPIS2	1st person plural subjective personal pronoun (*we*)
PPX1	singular reflexive personal pronoun (e.g. *yourself, itself, myself*)
PPX2	plural reflexive personal pronoun (e.g. *yourselves, themselves, ourselves*)
PPY	2nd person personal pronoun (*you, ye, youse*)
RA	adverb, after nominal head (e.g. *else, apiece, ago*)
REX	adverb introducing appositional constructions (e.g. *namely, e.g., i.e.*)
RG	premodifying degree adverb (e.g. *very, so, too*)
RGQ	*wh-* premodifying degree adverb (*how*)
RGQV	*wh-ever* premodifying degree adverb (*however*)
RGR	comparative premodifying degree adverb (*more, less* as in *more lonely, less grand*)
RGT	superlative premodifying degree adverb (*most, least* as in *most lonely, least grand*)
RL	locative adverb (e.g. *alongside, forward*)
RP	prepositional adverb, particle (e.g. *about, in, out*)
RPK	prepositional adverb, catenative (*about* in *be about to*)
RR	adverb (general) (e.g. *soon, quickly, far*)
RRQ	*wh-* adverb (general) (*where, when, why, how*)
RRQV	*wh-ever* adverb (general) (*wherever, whenever*)
RRR	comparative adverb (general) (e.g. *better, longer, sooner*)
RRT	superlative adverb (general) (e.g. *best, longest, soonest*)
RT	quasi-nominal adverb of time (e.g. *now, tomorrow*)
TO	infinitive marker (*to*)
UH	interjection or discourse particle (e.g. *oh, yes, um*)
VAB0	finite base form of verb *BE* (auxiliary): i.e. *be* as imperative or subjunctive
VABDR	*were* (auxiliary)
VABDZ	*was* (auxiliary)
VABG	*being* (auxiliary)
VABI	*be* as infinitive (auxiliary)
VABM	*am* (auxiliary)

VABN	*been* (auxiliary)
VABR	*are* (auxiliary)
VABZ	*is* (auxiliary)
VVBo	finite base form of *BE* (as lexical vb): i.e. *be* as imperative or subjunctive
VVBDR	*were* (lexical)
VVBDZ	*was* (lexical)
VVBG	*being* (lexical)
VVBI	*be* infinitive (lexical)
VVBM	*am* (lexical)
VVBN	*been* (lexical)
VVBR	*are* (lexical)
VVBZ	*is* (lexical)
VADo	finite base form of verb *DO* (auxiliary): indicative, imperative or subjunctive
VADD	*did* (auxiliary)
VADZ	*does* (auxiliary)
VVDo	finite base form of verb *DO* (lexical): indicative, imperative or subjunctive
VVDD	*did* (lexical)
VVDG	*doing*
VVDI	*do* infinitive (lexical)
VVDN	*done*
VVDZ	*does* (lexical)
VAHo	finite base form of *HAVE* (auxiliary): indicative, imperative or subjunctive
VAHD	*had* past tense (auxiliary)
VAHG	*having* (auxiliary)
VAHI	*have* infinitive (auxiliary)
VAHZ	*has* (auxiliary)
VVHo	finite base form of verb *HAVE* (lexical): indicative, imperative or subjunctive
VVHD	*had* past tense (lexical)
VVHG	*having* (lexical)
VVHI	*have* infinitive (lexical)
VVHN	*had* (past participle)
VVHZ	*has* (lexical)
VM	modal auxiliary (*can, will, would*, etc.)
VMK	modal catenative (*ought, used* [+ *to*])
VVo	finite base form of lexical verb (e.g. *give, work, go*)
VVD	past tense of lexical verb (e.g. *gave, worked, went*)
VVG	*-ing* participle of lexical verb (e.g. *giving, working, eating*)
VVGK	*-ing* participle catenative (*going* in *be going to*)
VVI	infinitive of lexical verb (e.g. [*to*] *give* . . . [*It will*] *work* . . .)
VVN	past participle of lexical verb (e.g. *given, worked, sung*)
VVNK	past participle catenative (e.g. *bound* in *be bound to*)
VVZ	*-s* form of lexical verb (e.g. *gives, works, defines*)
WPR	relativizer *that*
XX	negative particle *not, n't*

| ZZ1 | singular letter of the alphabet (e.g. *A*, *b*) |
| ZZ2 | plural letter of the alphabet (e.g. *A's*, *b's*) |

Punctuation tags

YBL	punctuation tag – left bracket	(, [
YBR	punctuation tag – right bracket	),]
YCOL	punctuation tag – colon	:
YCOM	punctuation tag – comma	,
YDSH	punctuation tag – dash	–
YEX	punctuation tag – exclamation mark	!
YLIP	punctuation tag – ellipsis	. . .
YQUE	punctuation tag – question mark	?
YQUO	punctuation tag – quotes	[", ', ", ']
YSCOL	punctuation tag – semicolon	;
YSTP	punctuation tag – full stop	.

Chapter 3

Table A3.1. *Subjunctive vs* should-*periphrasis in four parallel corpora (Figures for Brown and LOB are from Johansson and Norheim (1988: 29)*

	Brown	LOB	Frown	F-LOB
	subjunctive : *should*	subjunctive : *should*	subjunctive : *should*	subjunctive : *should*
ADVISE	2 : 1	0 : 3	0 : 0	0 : 3
ASK	5 : 0	1 : 2	5 : 0	1 : 3
BEG	1 : 0	0 : 0	1 : 0	0 : 0
DEMAND	19 : 0	2 : 3	14 : 0	8 : 6
DESIRE	1 : 1	0 : 1	1 : 0	0 : 0
DIRECT	2 : 0	0 : 1	0 : 0	0 : 1
INSIST	9 : 2	0 : 8	12 : 2	3 : 3
MOVE	1 : 0	1 : 0	0 : 0	0 : 0
ORDER	2 : 1	1 : 0	4 : 0	4 : 3
PROPOSE	9 : 1	0 : 5	4 : 1	1 : 7
RECOMMEND	10 : 1	1 : 13	8 : 1	8 : 22
REQUEST	6 : 0	2 : 0	7 : 0	6 : 2
REQUIRE	14 : 0	1 : 6	15 : 0	9 : 6
STIPULATE	2 : 0	0 : 1	1 : 0	1 : 1
SUGGEST	12 : 7	2 : 34	25 : 6	4 : 17
URGE	6 : 0	0 : 2	3 : 0	2 : 1
WISH	3 : 0	1 : 2	1 : 0	0 : 0
anxious	1 : 0	0 : 2	0 : 0	0 : 0
essential	2 : 1	1 : 7	0 : 0	0 : 1
important	4 : 3	0 : 0	4 : 0	1 : 3
necessary	5 : 1	0 : 5	0 : 0	1 : 0
sufficient	0 : 0	1 : 2	0 : 0	0 : 0
TOTAL	116 : 19	14 : 97	105 : 10	49 : 79
PERCENTAGES	85.9 : 14.1	12.6 : 87.4	91.3 : 8.7	38.3 : 61.7

Table A3.2. *Indicative*, should-*periphrasis and subjunctive after mandative expressions in ICE-GB*

	spoken part	written part
ADVISE	0 : 1 : 0	0 : 1 : 0
ASK	0 : 0 : 1	0 : 0 : 0
BEG	0 : 0 : 0	0 : 0 : 0
DEMAND	0 : 0 : 0	0 : 1 : 0
DESIRE	0 : 0 : 0	0 : 1 : 0
DIRECT	0 : 0 : 0	0 : 0 : 0
INSIST	2 : 0 : 1	4 : 0 : 3
MOVE	1 : 0 : 1	0 : 0 : 0
ORDER	0 : 0 : 0	0 : 0 : 0
PROPOSE	0 : 2 : 0	0 : 0 : 0
RECOMMEND	1 : 1 : 0	0 : 4 : 2
REQUEST	0 : 0 : 1	1 : 0 : 0
REQUIRE	0 : 2 : 0	1 : 0 : 2
STIPULATE	1 : 0 : 0	0 : 0 : 0
SUGGEST	2 : 6 : 0	2 : 1 : 3
URGE	0 : 1 : 1	0 : 0 : 0
WISH	0 : 0 : 0	0 : 0 : 0
anxious	0 : 1 : 0	0 : 0 : 0
essential	2 : 0 : 0	0 : 0 : 0
important	2 : 5 : 0	1 : 3 : 0
necessary	0 : 0 : 0	0 : 0 : 0
sufficient	1 : 0 : 0	0 : 0 : 0
TOTAL	12 : 19 : 5	9 : 11 : 10
PERCENTAGES	33.3 : 52.8 : 13.9	30 : 36.7 : 33.3

Chapter 4

Table A4.1. *Frequencies of modals in the four written corpora: comparing 1961 with 1991*[i]

	1961 frequency	1991/2 frequency	Change %[ii]
would	6,085	5,550	*** −8.3%
will	5,524	5,110	*** −7.0%
can	4,340	4,373	+1.3%
could	3,517	3,422	−2.2%
may	2,636	1,978	*** −24.6%
should	2,211	1,935	*** −12.1%
must	2,165	1,482	*** −31.2%
might	1,444	1,275	** −11.3%
shall	622	350	*** −43.5%
ought (to)	172	107	*** −37.5%
need(n't)	116	79	** −31.6%
TOTAL	28,832	25,661	*** −10.6%

[i]The figures in the columns headed by 1961 and 1991/2 are combined frequencies in each pair of million-word corpora; contracted forms, whether positive or negative, are included in the counts for individual modals. Thus the figures for *will* include the contracted forms *'ll* and *won't*.
[ii]*Change %* is based on normalized frequencies per million words, rather than raw frequencies.

Table A4.2. *Modal auxiliaries in AmE and BrE respectively*[i]

	American English			British English		
	Brown (1961)	Frown (1991)	Change %	LOB (1961)	F-LOB (1991)	Change %
would	3,053	2,868	* −5.2%	3,032	2,682	*** −11.4%
will	2,702	2,402	*** −10.3%	2,822	2,708	−3.9%
can	2,193	2,160	−0.7%	2,147	2,213	+3.2%
could	1,776	1,655	−6.0%	1,741	1,767	+1.6%
may	1,298	878	*** −31.8%	1,333	1,100	*** −17.4%
should	910	787	** −12.8%	1,301	1,148	** −11.7%
must	1,018	668	*** −33.8%	1,147	814	*** −29.0%
might	665	635	−3.7%	779	640	*** −17.7%
shall	267	150	*** −43.3%	355	200	*** −43.6%
ought (to)	69	49	−28.4%	103	58	*** −43.6%
need(n't)	40	35	−11.7%	76	44	** −42.0%
TOTAL	13,991	12,287	*** −11.4%	14,836	13,374	*** −9.8%

[i]*Change %* is here based on frequencies per million words.

Table A4.3. *Comparison of DSEU and DICE: modals in spoken BrE in the 1960s and the early 1990s*

	DSEU corpus (1960s)		DICE corpus (early 1990s)		Change (%age of DSEU)
	raw freq.	pmw	raw freq.	pmw	
will	541	3,981	483	3,741	−6.0%
would	550	4,047	577	4,469	+10.4%
can	526	3,871	497	3,850	−0.5%
could	237	1,744	195	1,510	−13.4%
should	186	1,369	147	1,139	−16.8%
may	162	1,192	58	449	*** −62.3%
must	156	1,148	63	488	*** −57.5%
might	113	832	94	728	−12.4%
shall	61	449	27	209	*** −53.4%
ought (to)	43	316	17	132	** −58.4%
need(n't)	3	22	1	8	−64.9%
TOTAL	2,578	18,971	2,159	16,723	−11.8%

Table A4.4. May – *change in frequency of senses (analysis of every third example)*

	Brown		Frown		LOB		F-LOB	
(a) Epistemic possibility	290	(67%)	221	(75%)	257	(58%)	267	(73%)
(b) Root possibility	63	(15%)	16	(5%)	84	(19%)	25	(7%)
(c) Permission	30	(7%)	26	(9%)	29	(7%)	28	(8%)
(d) Residual categories	13	(3%)	8	(3%)	36	(8%)	9	(2%)
(e) Unclear	36	(8%)	22	(8%)	38	(8%)	37	(10%)
TOTAL	432 (100%)		293 (100%)		444 (100%)		366 (100%)	
OVERALL CORPUS FREQUENCY	1,298		878		1,333		1,100	

Table A4.5. Should – *change in frequency of senses*

	Brown		Frown		LOB		F-LOB	
(a) Epistemic	89	(10%)	66	(8%)	147	(11%)	106	(9%)
(b) Root/Deontic	654	(72%)	622	(79%)	653	(50%)	749	(65%)
(c) Putative, quasi-subj.	88	(10%)	34	(4%)	263	(20%)	136	(12%)
(d) *should = would*	31	(3%)	13	(2%)	96	(7%)	34	(3%)
(e) Unclear	48	(5%)	52	(7%)	142	(11%)	122	(11%)
TOTAL	910 (100%)		787 (100%)		1,301 (100%)		1,147 (100%)	

Table A4.6. Must – *change in frequency of senses (analysis of every third example)*

	Brown	Frown	LOB	F-LOB
(a) Epistemic (necessity)	54 (16%)	33 (15%)	97 (25%)	91 (34%)
(b) Deontic (obligation/necessity)	245 (72%)	164 (73%)	264 (69%)	165 (61%)
(c) Unclear	40 (12%)	26 (12%)	21 (5%)	14 (5%)
TOTAL	339 (100%)	223 (100%)	382 (100%)	270 (100%)

Table A4.7. May, should *and* must – *changes in frequency of senses in spoken mini-corpora*

	may		should		must	
	DSEU	DICE	DSEU	DICE	DSEU	DICE
Epistemic	102	57	14	20	59	28
Deontic[i]	59	2	104	111	91	33
Other	7	0	62	14	–	–
Unclear	5	1	13	6	12	3
TOTAL	173	60	193	151	162	64

[i]The deontic category for *may* includes here both root/event possibility and permission. All examples are of 'permission' with the exception of four cases of root/event possibility in the DSEU column. The rather high frequency for *may* = 'permission' in DSEU is probably unrepresentative of spoken language in the 1960s generally. It is due in large measure to the use of 'polite' turn-taking formulae in adversarial broadcast discussion programmes: *May I ask . . . , May I finish please, if I may say so,* etc.

Chapter 5

Table A5.1. *Frequencies of semi-modals in the Brown family of corpora*

	American English			British English			Both		
	Brown (1961)	Frown (1991)	Change %[i]	LOB (1961)	F-LOB (1991)	Change %	1961 corpora	1991/2 corpora	Change %
BE able to[ii]	191	202	+6.7%	246	248	+0.9%	437	450	+3.0%
BE going to	216	332	*** +55.0%	248	245	−1.1%	464	577	** +24.3%
BE supposed to	48	55	+15.6%	22	47	** +113.9%	70	102	** +45.7%
BE to	344	217	*** −36.4%	451	376	** −16.5%	795	593	** −25.4%
(had) better	41	34	−16.4%	50	37	−25.9%	91	71	−22.0%
(HAVE) got to	45	52	+16.6%	41	27	−34.1%	86	79	−8.1%
HAVE to	627	639	+2.8%	757	825	+9.1%	1,384	1,464	* +5.8%
NEED to	69	154	*** +125.1%	53	194	*** +266.5%	122	348	** +185.2%
WANT to	323	552	*** +72.4%	357	423	* +18.6%	680	975	*** +43.4%
TOTAL	1,904	2,237	*** +18.5%	2,225	2,422	** +9.0%	4,129	4,659	** +12.3%

[i]Change % is based on normalized (not raw) frequencies.
[ii]The small italic capitals indicate the lemma rather than the base form *be*, *have*, etc. alone. Forms spelt *gonna*, *gotta* and *wanna* are counted with *BE going to*, *HAVE got to*, and *WANT to*, respectively.

Table A5.2. *Changing frequencies of semi-modals in the two British spoken mini-corpora: DSEU (1958–69) and DICE (1990–92)*

	DSEU (1958–69)		DICE (1990–92)		Change %
	raw freq.	pmw[i]	raw freq.	pmw	
BE able to	61	449	53	411	−8.5%
BE going to	197	1,450	305	2,363	*** +63.0%
BE to	13	96	12	93	−2.8%
(had) better	12	88	8	62	−29.8%
(HAVE) got to	72	530	67	519	−2.1%
HAVE to	148	1,089	185	1,433	* +31.6%
NEED to	7	52	33	256	*** +396.2%
WANT to	142	1,045	182	1,410	** +34.9%
BE supposed to	16	118	23	178	+50.8%
TOTAL	668	4,917	868	6,725	*** +36.8%

[i]The column marked pmw gives the normalized frequency of each semi-modal, scaled up to per million words, so as to be comparable with each of the corpora in the Brown family.

Table A5.3. *A study in apparent time: modals and semi-modals in the BNC demographic subcorpus*
Table corresponding to Figure 5.4. An 'apparent-time' study of age groups of speakers in the BNCdemog: distribution of modals and semi-modals according to age. (The sets of modals and semi-modals listed in Table 5.3 are aggregated here.)

Age of speakers	Total number of words	Modals		Semi-modals	
		raw freq.	pmw	raw freq.	pmw
0–14	353,843	7,057	19,944	3,195	9,029
15–24	497,234	10,276	20,666	4,147	8,340
25–34	686,035	15,246	22,223	5,543	8,080
35–44	701,033	15,866	22,632	5,300	7,560
45–59	728,450	15,729	21,592	5,216	7,160
60+	666,863	13,754	20,625	3,993	5,988
TOTAL	3,633,458[i]	77,928	21,447	27,394	7,539

[i]The total number of words in this table is smaller than that in BNCdemog as a whole (4.2 million words), because about 14% of the dialogue in this subcorpus is spoken by persons whose age is unknown, and is therefore excluded.

Chapter 6

Table A6.1. *Distribution of progressives across the paradigm in LOB, F-LOB, Brown and Frown (whole corpus frequencies)*

Active	Brown raw freq.	Frown raw freq.	AmE change %	LOB raw freq.	F-LOB raw freq.	BrE change %
Present	1,015	1,343	*** +33.5%	985	1,273	*** +29.4%
Past	1,241	1,228	−0.2%	1,299	1,182	* −8.8%
Present perfect	114	119	+5.3%	129	139	+8.0%
Past perfect	105	94	−9.7%	110	99	−9.8%
Modal	137	138	+1.6%	149	194	* +30.5%
Modal perfect	8	10	+26.1%	17	13	−23.3%
to-inf.[i]	51	52	+2.8%	59	70	+18.9%
Perfect *to*-inf.	0	1				
TOTAL	2,671	2,985	*** +12.7%	2,748	2,970	** +8.2%

Passive[ii]	Brown raw freq.	Frown raw freq.	AmE change %	LOB raw freq.	F-LOB raw freq.	BrE change %
Present	119	79	** −33.0%	123	179	** +45.9%
Past	61	51	−15.7%	73	80	+9.9%
Modal	0	0		2	1	−50.0%
TOTAL	180	130	** −27.2%	198	260	** +31.6%

Active + passive	Brown raw freq.	Frown raw freq.	AmE change %	LOB raw freq.	F-LOB raw freq.	BrE change %
Present	1,134	1,422	** +26.5%	1,108	1,452	** +31.4%
Past	1,302	1,279	−0.9%	1,372	1,262	* −7.8%
Present perfect	114	119	+5.3%	129	139	+8.0%
Past perfect	105	94	−9.7%	110	99	−9.8%
Modal	137	138	+1.6%	151	195	* +29.5%
Modal perfect	8	10	+26.1%	17	13	−23.3%
to-inf.	51	52	+2.8%	59	70	+18.9%
Perfect *to*-inf.	0	1				
TOTAL	2,851	3,115	*** +10.2%	2,946	3,230	** +9.9%

[i]This includes semi-modals, e.g. *I need to be going*, and catenatives, e.g. *It seems to be continuing*.
[ii]None of the corpora attested use of the progressive passive with modal perfect (e.g. *It will have been being used*), *to*-infinitives (e.g. *It needs/seems to be being used*) or perfect *to*-infinitives (e.g. *It needs/seems to have been being used*).

Table A6.2. *Frequencies of progressives relative to estimated count of non-progressives in LOB and F-LOB (For raw frequencies of the progressive, see Table A6.1)*[i]

	LOB raw freq. non-prog.	LOB % in prog.	F-LOB raw freq. non-prog.	F-LOB % in prog.	Change in proportion (%)
Active					
Present	29,255	3.4%	31,131	4.1%	** +21.5%
Past	34,809	3.7%	34,105	3.5%	** −7.1%
Present perfect	3,142	4.1%	3,166	4.4%	+6.9%
Past perfect	3,501	3.1%	3,386	2.9%	−6.9%
Modal	14,841	1.0%	13,374	1.5%	+44.5%
Passive					
Present	3,655	3.4%	2,970	6.0%	** +79.1%
Past	3,951	1.8%	3,694	2.2%	+17.2%

[i]The figures given in Table A6.2 for non-progressives are calculated on the basis of automatic retrieval algorithms applied to the POS-tagged (and post-edited) versions of the corpora. The simple past (active) and modal (active) were explicitly marked in the grammatically tagged versions of the corpora. Retrieval of perfect and passive forms of the non-progressive was achieved by specifying a tag for auxiliary (any form of BE or HAVE) and a following tag for past participle. However, since a whole variety of word sequences may intervene between the auxiliary and the participle (e.g. *he was, as far as I know, arrested on Monday evening; she has in all probability arrived home by now*), some cases will have been missed.

Table A6.3. *Distribution of all progressives in written AmE (1961–1991/92)*

	Brown (1961)		Frown (1991/92)		
Genre	raw freq.	pmw	raw freq.	pmw	Change %
Press	573	3,210	635	3,589	+11.8%
Gen. Prose	851	2,031	913	2,204	+8.5%
Learned	198	1,222	154	960	* −21.4%
Fiction	1,229	4,839	1,413	5,580	*** +15.3%
TOTAL	2,851	2,813	3,115	3,100	*** +10.2%

Table A6.4. *Genre distribution of progressives in spoken BrE: DSEU (1958–69) and DICE (1990–92)*

	DSEU		DICE		Change as %
Genre	raw freq.	pmw	raw freq.	pmw	of DSEU
Conversation (face-to-face)	437	6,293	576	8,906	*** +41.5%
Telephone conversation	68	6,890	123	12,935	*** +87.7%
Broadcast discussion	215	5,779	284	8,651	*** +49.7%
Broadcast interviews	37	6,917	35	5,892	−14.8%
Sport commentaries	67	4,623	123	7,619	*** +64.8%
OVERALL	824	6,043	1141	8,368	*** +38.5%

Table A6.5. *Distribution of present progressives (active) outside quotations, in LOB and F-LOB*[i]

Genre	LOB (1961)			F-LOB (1991)			Change as % of LOB (based on pmw)
	raw freq.	pmw	proportion of present prog.	raw freq.	pmw	proportion of present prog.	
Press	231	1,428	82.8%	258	1,629	76.1%	+14.0%
Gen. Prose	307	790	87.2%	421	1,103	85.7%	*** +39.6%
Learned	50	321	98.0%	71	458	92.2%	+42.7%
Fiction	35	186	11.6%	94	512	26.0%	*** +178.0%
TOTAL	623	697	63.2%	844	961	66.4%	*** +38.0%

[i]The frequency per million words, the proportion of present progressives and the significance of the change, are all measured against word counts that *exclude* quotations.

Table A6.6. *Contracted forms of present progressive (active) in LOB and F-LOB*[i]

Genre	LOB (1961)		F-LOB (1991)		Change	
	raw freq.	% of present prog.	raw freq.	% of present prog.	proportional	overall
Press	13	4.7%	37	10.9%	** +134.2%	*** +183.9%
Gen. Prose	17	4.8%	20	4.1%	−15.7%	+18.5%
Learned	0	0.0%	0	0.0%	0.0%	0.0%
Fiction	172	56.8%	217	59.3%	+4.4%	* +25.8%
TOTAL	202	20.5%	274	21.5%	+5.0%	*** +36.0%

[i]Note that 'proportion' and 'proportional change' in this and all subsequent tables refer to the frequency of the given feature in relation to the total number of present progressives (active) in each corpus.

Table A6.7. *Contracted forms of present progressive (active) outside quotations in LOB and F-LOB*

Genre	LOB (1961)		F-LOB (1991)		Change	
	raw freq.	% of present prog.	raw freq.	% of present prog.	proportional	overall
Press	6	2.6%	15	5.8%	+123.8%	* +155.3%
Gen. Prose	3	1.0%	10	2.4%	+143.1%	* +239.4%
Learned	0	0.0%	0	0.0%	0.0%	0.0%
Fiction	6	17.1%	35	36.8%	+117.2%	*** +497.5%
TOTAL	15	2.4%	60	7.1%	*** +195.3%	*** +307.1%

Table A6.8. *Contracted forms in all syntactic environments in LOB and F-LOB*

Genre	LOB (1961)		F-LOB (1991)		Change % of LOB
	raw freq.	pmw	raw freq.	pmw	
Press	325	1,833	752	4,222	*** +130.3%
Gen. Prose	609	1,474	711	1,721	** +16.8%
Learned	22	139	55	344	*** +148.6%
Fiction	4,186	16,351	4,978	19,362	*** +18.4%
TOTAL	5,142	5,115	6,496	6,444	*** +26.0%

Table A6.9. *Distribution of the present progressive (active) of verbs lending themselves to stative interpretation in LOB, F-LOB, Brown and Frown*

Verb class			LOB (1961) freq.	F-LOB (1991) freq.	Brown (1961) freq.	Frown (1991/2) freq.
perception/ sensation	(i) production	*look*	4	4	4	5
		sound	0	1	0	0
	(ii) experience	*see*	4	7	0	4
		imagine	0	1	0	1
		sub-total	8	13	4	10
Cognition/emotion/attitude		*feel*	2	1	0	6
		find	4	6	7	1
		forget	2	1	1	0
		hope	3	8	1	4
		intend	0	1	0	0
		long	2	1	2	1
		regret	1	0	0	0
		remember	0	0	0	1
		suppose	0	2	0	0
		think	15	9	9	19
		want	2	0	0	1
		wish	1	0	0	0
		witness	0	2	1	0
		sub-total	32	31	21	33
being/having		*average*	0	1	0	0
		be	7	10	2	14
		bore	0	1	0	2
		bug	0	1	0	0
		cost	2	1	1	1
		have	11	12	12	10
		have to	1	4	2	1
		rely	0	1	1	0
		require	0	1	0	0
		tend to	0	1	1	0
		sub-total	21	33	19	28
stance		*sit*	0	3	3	4
		stand	5	5	1	7
		lie	2	3	1	2
		live	10	10	7	4
		reside	0	1	1	0
		face	3	1	5	3
		hang	1	1	0	3
		loom	1	0	0	0
		verge on	0	1	0	0
		sub-total	22	25	18	23
TOTAL			83	102	62	94

Table A6.10. *Subject person and number of present progressives (active) in LOB and F-LOB*

	LOB		F-LOB		Change	
	raw freq.	% pres prog.	raw freq.	% pres prog.	proportional	overall
1sg. (*I*)						
Press	11	3.9%	18	5.3%	+34.7%	+63.2%
Gen. Prose	21	6.0%	14	2.9%	* −52.2%	−32.8%
Learned	3	5.9%	4	5.2%	−11.7%	+33.8%
Fiction	73	24.1%	77	21.0%	−12.7%	+5.2%
TOTAL	108	11.0%	113	8.9%	−19.0%	+4.9%
1pl. (*we*)						
Press	10	3.6%	26	7.7%	* +114.0%	** +159.3%
Gen. Prose	30	8.5%	49	10.0%	+17.1%	* +64.5%
Learned	5	9.8%	11	14.3%	+45.7%	+120.8%
Fiction	18	5.9%	32	8.7%	+47.2%	* +77.3%
TOTAL	63	6.4%	118	9.3%	* +44.9%	** +87.8%
2sg./pl. (*you*)						
Press	10	3.6%	6	1.8%	−50.6%	−40.2%
Gen. Prose	18	5.1%	28	5.7%	+11.5%	+56.7%
Learned	2	3.9%	1	1.3%	−66.9%	−49.8%
Fiction	81	26.7%	70	19.1%	* −28.5%	−13.8%
TOTAL	111	11.3%	105	8.2%	* −26.8%	−5.2%
3sg. (*he, she, it*, NPs)						
Press	158	56.6%	184	54.3%	−4.2%	+16.2%
Gen. Prose	159	45.2%	222	45.2%	+0.1%	** +40.6%
Learned	21	41.2%	39	50.6%	+23.0%	* +86.4%
Fiction	99	32.7%	146	39.9%	+22.1%	** +47.1%
TOTAL	437	44.4%	591	46.4%	+4.6%	** +35.6%
3pl. (*they*, NPs)						
Press	88	31.5%	103	30.4%	−3.7%	+16.7%
Gen. Prose	125	35.5%	178	36.3%	+2.1%	** +43.4%
Learned	20	39.2%	22	28.6%	−27.1%	+10.4%
Fiction	29	9.6%	40	10.9%	+14.2%	+37.6%
TOTAL	262	26.6%	343	26.9%	+1.3%	** +31.2%

Table A6.11. *Futurate use of present progressive (active) in LOB and F-LOB: clear cases only*

Genre	LOB (1961)		F-LOB (1991)	
	raw freq.	pmw	raw freq.	pmw
Press	11	62	10	56
Gen. Prose	2	5	7	17
Learned	0	0	1	6
Fiction	43	170	27	107
TOTAL	56	56	45	45

Table A6.12. *Futurate use of present progressive (active) in Brown and Frown: clear cases only (based on a 1 in 4 sample)*

Genre	Brown (1961)		Frown (1992)	
	raw freq.	pmw	raw freq.	pmw
Press	3	68	2	45
Gen. Prose	1	10	2	19
Learned	0	0	0	0
Fiction	3	47	14	218
TOTAL	7	28	18	71

Table A6.13. *Constructions referring to the future in corpora of recent British English (LOB and F-LOB): raw and proportional frequencies*

	LOB (1961)		F-LOB (1991)		
	raw freq.	% of future expressions surveyed	raw freq.	% of future expressions surveyed	change in proportion
will + *be* -*ing*	63	1.7%	89	2.6%	** +54.9%
will + inf.	2,756	76.6%	2,631	81.4%	+5.3%
shall + inf.	355	9.9%	200	6.2%	** −38.2%
BE going to (pres. tense)	174	4.8%	163	5.0%	+2.7%
BE TO (pres. tense)	252	7.0%	187	5.8%	* −18.6%
Futurate pres. prog. (estimated)	61	1.7%	52	1.6%	−6.5%
TOTAL	3,661	100.0%	3,332	100.0%	

Table A6.14. *Frequencies of modal +* be *-ing and modal +* infinitive *constructions in LOB and F-LOB: whole corpus frequencies*

	modal + *be -ing*			modal + infinitive		
	LOB (1961) raw freq.	F-LOB (1991) raw freq.	change %	LOB (1961) raw freq.	F-LOB (1991) raw freq.	change %
can	–	4		2,147	2,213	+3.2%
could	4	6	+49.6%	1,741	1,767	+1.6%
may	10	15	+49.6%	1,333	1,100	*** −17.4%
might	12	12	−0.3%	779	640	*** −17.7%
must	10	7	−29.9%	1,147	814	*** −29.0%
need	–	–		76	44	** −42.0%
ought (to)	–	–		103	58	*** −43.6%
shall	7	5	−28.8%	355	200	*** −43.6%
should	9	18	+99.5%	1,301	1,148	** −11.7%
will	66	89	* +35.0%	2,822	2,708	−3.9%
would	32	34	+6.0%	3,032	2,682	*** −11.4%
TOTAL	150	190	* +25.0%	14,836	13,374	*** −9.8%

Table A6.15. *Modal +* be *-ing and modal +* infinitive *in Brown/Frown: whole corpus frequencies*

	modal + *be -ing*			modal + infinitive		
	Brown (1961) raw freq.	Frown (1992) raw freq.	Change %	Brown (1961) raw freq.	Frown (1992) raw freq.	Change %
can	4	1	−74.8%	2,193	2,160	−0.7%
could	4	7	+76.5%	1,776	1,655	−6.0%
may	9	9	+0.9%	1,298	878	*** −31.8%
might	14	19	+36.9%	665	635	−3.7%
must	16	1	* −93.7%	1,018	668	*** −33.8%
need	–	–		40	35	−11.7%
ought (to)	–	–		69	49	−28.4%
shall	1	1	–	267	150	*** −43.3%
should	12	9	−24.4%	910	787	** −12.8%
will	41	48	+18.1%	2,702	2,402	*** −10.3%
would	36	43	+20.5%	3,053	2,868	* −5.2%
TOTAL	137	138	+1.6%	13,991	12,287	*** −11.4%

Table A6.16. *Distribution of interpretive use of the progressive (present tense), in LOB and F-LOB, based on clearest cases*

	LOB (1961) raw freq.	F-LOB (1991) raw freq.
Syntactic frame types	11	25
Other 'clearest cases'	41	72
TOTAL clearest cases	52	97

Table A6.17. *Functions of* will + be -ing*: estimated frequencies in LOB and F-LOB*

	LOB (1961) raw freq. (whole corpus)	F-LOB (1991) raw freq. (whole corpus)
Type 1: clear	7	4
Type 2: clear	26	45
Epistemic: clear	3	4
Unclear	28	36
TOTAL	64	89

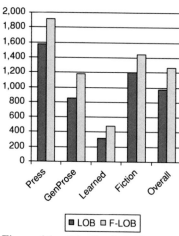

Figure A6.1 Distribution of present progressive (active) in LOB and F-LOB across subcorpora: frequencies pmw

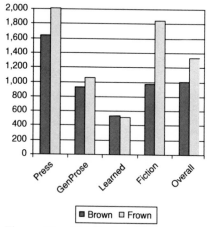

Figure A6.2 Distribution of present progressive (active) in Brown and Frown across subcorpora: frequencies pmw

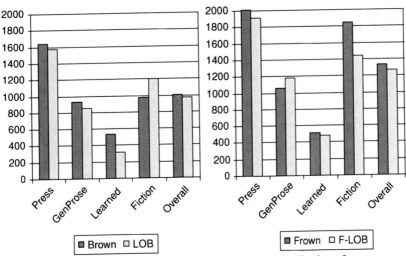

Figure A6.3 Distribution of present progressives (active) in 1961, Brown versus LOB: frequencies pmw

Figure A6.4 Distribution of present progressives (active) in 1991/2, Frown versus F-LOB: frequencies pmw

Chapter 7

Table A7.1. *Finite non-progressive be-passives in the Brown family of corpora*

Genre	LOB (1961)		F-LOB (1991)		Change %
	raw freq.	pmw	raw freq.	pmw	
Press	2,003	11,301	1,710	9,651	*** −14.6%
Gen. Prose	5,483	13,206	4,677	11,287	*** −14.5%
Learned	2,972	18,433	2,476	15,386	*** −16.5%
Fiction	1,312	5,182	1,243	4,909	−5.3%
TOTAL	11,770	11,690	10,106	10,058	*** −14.0%

Genre	Brown (1961)		Frown (1992)		Change %
	raw freq.	pmw	raw freq.	pmw	
Press	1,744	9,769	1,286	7,271	*** −25.6%
Gen. Prose	4,863	11,607	3,997	9,647	*** −16.9%
Learned	2,907	17,937	1,159	7,228	*** −59.7%
Fiction	1,264	4,975	1,227	4,847	−2.6%
TOTAL	10,778	10,634	7,669	7,633	*** −28.2%

(AmE automatic)

Table A7.2. *Composition of the DCPSE subcorpus*

Text category	1960/61/63		1990–92	
	no. of words[i]	%	no. of words	%
Broadcast discussions	16,009	27.8%	16,911	27.6%
Spontaneous commentary	13,879	24.1%	15,238	24.9%
Formal conversations	19,742	34.2%	20,759	33.9%
Informal conversations	3,977	6.9%	4,261	7.0%
Telephone conversations	4,070	7.1%	4,083	6.7%
TOTAL	57,677		61,252	

[i] Word counts here are those provided by the program ICECUP, the standard interface to the DCPSE.

Table A7.3. Get-*passives in the Brown family of corpora*

Genre	LOB (1961)		F-LOB (1991)	
	raw freq.	pmw	raw freq.	pmw
Press	5	28	11	62
Gen. Prose	10	24	18	43
Learned	2	12	4	25
Fiction	17	67	14	55
TOTAL	34	34	47	47

Genre	Brown (1961)		Frown (1992)	
	raw freq.	pmw	raw freq.	pmw
Press	6	34	14	79
Gen. Prose	4	10	16	39
Learned	0	0	3	19
Fiction	19	75	27	107
TOTAL	29	29	60	60

Chapter 8

Table A8.1. *Retrieved expanded predicates (types) in the Brown family of corpora*

light verb	deverbal nouns LOB	F-LOB	Brown	Frown
have	*bath, chat, drink, escape, feed, fight, glimpse, joke, look, quarrel, ride, row, shot, sleep, swear, swim, swing, talk, try, walk*	*care, chat, drag, drink, escape, fall, glance, glimpse, laugh, look, nap, puff, shower, stroll, talk, taste*	*bath, chat, drink, fear, fight, glimpse, joke, look, nap, row, talk*	*bath, drink, itch, look, nap, ride, talk, taste, walk*
take	*aim, glance, grip, look, nibble, risk, shower, sip, step, stroll, walk*	*bath, dive, drive, glance, gulp, leak, look, peek, risk, sip, step, stroll, swallow, swig, walk*	*bath, fall, glance, gulp, look, nap, ride, shower, sip, swallow, swig, swipe, walk*	*bath, drag, drive, fall, look, shower, sip, slap, stab, step, stroll, swallow, walk*
give	*bow, cackle, chuckle, cough, cry, glance, groan, hop, hug, jolt, kiss, laugh, leap, look, mumble, poke, rebuff, ring, roar, scratch, scream, screech, shake, shiver, shout, shrug, sigh, smack, smile, snort, sob, stare, twist, whistle, wink*	*bow, call, chuckle, cry, glance, grin, hug, jump, kiss, laugh, leap, look, nod, shake, shock, sigh, smile, snigger, stare, suck, tap, try, wave*	*glance, grin, gulp, hug, laugh, lift, lurch, nudge, pat, pout, pull, push, sigh, smile, thrust, wave, whack, wink, yell*	*grunt, hug, jerk, kick, laugh, look, nod, pat, plunge, shrug, try*

Table A8.2. *Expanded predicates across text types in the Brown family of corpora*

Genre	LOB (1961)		F-LOB (1991)	
	raw freq.	pmw	raw freq.	pmw
Press	16	90	10	56
Non-fiction	17	29	15	26
Fiction	100	395	84	332
TOTAL	133	132	109	108

Genre	Brown (1961)		Frown (1992)	
	raw freq.	pmw	raw freq.	pmw
Press	4	22	10	57
Non-fiction	23	40	15	26
Fiction	50	197	61	241
TOTAL	77	76	86	86

Genre	Total 1960s		Total 1990s	
	raw freq.	pmw	raw freq.	pmw
Press	20	56	20	56
Non-fiction	40	35	30	26
Fiction	150	296	145	286
TOTAL	210	104	195	97

Chapter 9

Table A9.1. To- *vs bare infinitives with* help *(all construction types) in five corpora*

	AmE	BrE
1930s	no data	72 : 12
1961	55 : 125	94 : 27
1991/92	44 : 203	77 : 122

(BrE vs AmE 1961 $p < 0.001$; BrE vs AmE 1991/92 $p < 0.05$; BrE diachr. $p < 0.001$; AmE diachr. $p < 0.001$)

Table A9.2. To-*inf. vs* V-*ing after* start

	AmE	BrE
1930s	no data	13 : 7
1961	47 : 49	36 : 52
1991/92	59 : 110	49 : 59

(AmE diachr. $p < 0.05$; all others not significant)

Table A9.3. Begin/start + *infinitive by speaker age in the spoken-demographic BNC*[i]

	begin		start	
Age	number of hits	pmw	number of hits	pmw
0–14	7	20	22	62
15–24	7	14	22	44
25–34	6	9	34	50
35–44	9	13	35	50
45–59	12	12	40	55
60+	22	22	32	48

[i] *Begin* + gerund was not included in the analysis because the spoken-demographic material contained only seven instances of the construction.

Table A9.4. Start/stop + *gerund in five corpora*

	Brown	Frown	B-LOB	LOB	F-LOB
start + -ing	49	110	7	52	59
stop + -ing	24	43	8	29	35

Table A9.5. To-*inf. vs* -ing *after* begin *and* start *in the spoken-demographic BNC and the spoken ANC*

	begin	start
ANC	153 : 17	432 : 1034
BNC	76 : 8	218 : 864

Chapter 10

Table A10.1a. *Comparison of tag frequencies in LOB and F-LOB: change in the frequency of parts of speech in BrE 1961–91*

Word class	LOB post-edited raw freq.	pmw	F-LOB post-edited raw freq.	pmw	Change %
Adjective	75,407	74,893	79,975	79,520	*** +6.2%
Adverb	62,707	62,280	59,166	58,830	*** −5.5%
Article	112,934	112,164	109,260	108,639	*** −3.1%
Conjunction	56,395	56,011	55,891	55,573	−0.8%
Determiner	31,878	31,661	29,438	29,271	*** −7.5%
Nouns	253,831	252,101	265,456	263,946	*** +4.7%
Numeral	15,514	15,408	15,483	15,395	−0.1%
Preposition	121,330	120,503	117,816	117,146	*** −2.8%
Pronoun	57,412	57,021	53,616	53,311	***−6.5%
Verb	179,900	178,674	177,980	176,968	** −1.0%
Misc.	42,295	42,007	43,016	42,771	** +1.8%
TOTAL	1,009,603		1,007,097		

Table A10.1b. *Comparison of tag frequencies in Brown and Frown: change in the frequency of parts of speech in AmE, 1961–92*

Word class	Brown estimated		Frown post-edited		Change %
	raw freq.	pmw	raw freq.	pmw	
Adjective	81,386	80,955	83,260	82,593	*** +2.0%
Adverb	56,369	56,071	54,895	54,455	** −2.9%
Article	115,504	114,893	107,395	106,534	*** −7.3%
Conjunction	57,328	57,025	55,429	54,985	*** −3.6%
Determiner	30,036	29,877	27,324	27,105	*** −9.3%
Nouns	268,727	265,136	279,147	277,794	*** +4.8%
Numeral	14,142	14,067	15,722	15,596	*** +10.9%
Preposition	121,850	121,205	115,842	114,914	* −5.2%
Pronoun	52,748	52,469	53,433	53,005	+1.0%
Verb	174,638	173,713	175,218	173,814	+0.1%
Misc.	39,709	39,499	43,715	43,365	*** +9.8%
TOTAL	1,012,437		1,011,380		

(automatic: adjusted using error coefficient – see explanation in Chapter 2, footnote 27)

Table A10.2. *Frequency of selected noun subcategories in the LOB and F-LOB Corpora*[i]

Singular common nouns

Subcorpus	LOB corpus		F-LOB corpus		
	raw freq.	pmw	raw freq.	pmw	Change %
Press	28,063	158,337	28,738	162,192	** +2.4%
Gen. Prose	65,678	158,189	67,486	162,861	*** +3.0%
Learned	27,254	169,033	27,572	171,332	+1.4%
Fiction	32,777	129,449	33,685	133,022	*** +2.8%
TOTAL	153,772	152,724	157,481	156,585	*** +2.5%

Plural common nouns

Subcorpus	LOB corpus		F-LOB corpus		
	raw freq.	pmw	raw freq.	pmw	Change %
Press	9,330	52,642	9,834	55,501	*** +5.4%
Gen. Prose	23,821	57,374	25,973	62,679	*** +9.2%
Learned	9,773	60,613	10,705	66,521	*** +9.7%
Fiction	8,037	31,741	9,183	36,264	*** +14.2%
TOTAL	50,961	50,614	55,695	55,378	*** +9.4%

Proper nouns

Subcorpus	LOB corpus		F-LOB corpus		
	raw freq.	pmw	raw freq.	pmw	Change %
Press	12,131	68,445	12,410	70,040	+2.3%
Gen. Prose	14,434	34,765	17,320	41,797	*** +20.2%
Learned	3,765	23,351	4,609	28,640	*** +22.7%
Fiction	9,229	36,449	9,667	38,175	** +4.7%
TOTAL	39,559	39,289	44,006	43,756	*** +11.4%

[i]This table was first published as Table 3 in Mair *et al.* (2002). It appears here with minor revisions.

Table A10.3a. *Noun combinations in the language of the Press (A–C)*[i]

sequence consisting of	BrE			AmE		
	LOB	F-LOB	Change %	Brown	Frown	Change %
N* NN*	5,769	6,172	** +7.0%	6,655	6,910	** +4.8%
N* N* NN*	860	1,016	*** +18.2%	1,295	1,053	*** −18.0%
N* N* N* NN*	142	167	*** +17.6%	248	170	*** −30.8%
N* N* N* N* NN*	19	27	+42.1%	40	24	* −39.5%
N* N* N* N* N* NN*	2	3	+50.0%	3	3	0.9%
N* N* N* N* N* N* NN*	–	1	–	–	1	–
TOTAL	6,792	7,386	*** +8.7%	8,241	8,161	−0.1%

[i]Tables A10.3a and A10.3b first appeared (in a slightly different form) in the handout for a paper delivered by Christian Mair at the AAACL/ICAME joint Conference at the University of Michigan, Ann Arbor, May 2005. The title of the paper was 'The corpus-based study of language change in progress: the extra value of part-of-speech tagged corpora'. The tables record frequencies of noun sequences in which the last noun (normally the head of the phrase) is a common noun, whereas the preceding nouns are unspecified nouns – both common and proper. The restriction of the head to common nouns excludes irrelevant proper noun sequences such as *George Bush, Mary Baker Eddy, Mrs Cummings, Mr Clinton.*

Table A10.3b. *Noun combinations in the language of Learned writing (J)*

sequence consisting of	BrE			AmE		
	LOB	F-LOB	Change %	Brown	Frown	Change %
N* NN*	4,638	5,046	*** + 9.0%	5,043	5,702	*** +14.3%
N* N* NN*	541	602	+11.5%	527	664	*** +27.3%
N* N* N* NN*	52	62	+19.5%	45	78	** +75.2%
N* N* N* N* NN*	8	8	0.2%	6	14	+35.8%
N* N* N* N* N* NN*	3	2	−33.2%	1	3	+203.2%
N* N* N* N* N* N* NN*	3[1]	–	–	–	1	–
TOTAL	5,245	5,720	*** +9.3%	5,622	6,462	*** +16.2%

[i]One of these three cases is an even longer sequence of eight nouns – a record for the four corpora.

Table A10.4a. *Increase of noun + common noun sequences between LOB and F-LOB*

Genre	LOB		F-LOB		
	raw freq.	pmw	raw freq.	pmw	Change %
Press	4,795	27,054	6,177	34,862	***+28.9%
Gen. Prose	8,202	19,755	11,362	27,419	***+38.8%
Learned	4,151	25,745	5,178	32,176	***+25.0%
Fiction	2,261	8,930	3,180	12,558	***+40.6%
TOTAL	19,409	19,277	25,897	25,750	***+33.6%

(NOTE: In this and the following table, the counts for common nouns exclude tags NNB, NNL, NNL1, NNL2 and NNA, which are invariably associated with naming expressions, and would be irrelevant here. In compound place-names such as *Appalachian Mountains*, the first word is counted as a proper noun, but the second is not.)

Table A10.4b. *Development of noun + common noun sequences between Brown and Frown*

Genre	Brown		Frown		
	raw freq.	pmw	raw freq.	pmw	Change %
Press	6,582	36,872	7,071	39,964	***+8.4%
Gen. Prose	10,391	24,802	12,988	31,347	***+26.4%
Learned	5,096	31,445	6,001	37,419	***+19.0%
Fiction	3,524	13,876	3,679	14,528	+4.7%
TOTAL	25,593	25,252	29,739	29,595	***+17.2%

(automatic)

Table A10.5. *Plural attributive nouns in AmE and BrE*

AmE			BrE		
Brown	Frown	Change %	LOB	F-LOB	Change %
794	1,003	***+27.4%	605	1,030	***+70.4%

(AmE automatic)

Table A10.6. *Frequency of proper noun + proper noun sequences*

AmE			BrE		
Brown	Frown	Change %	LOB	F-LOB	Change %
8,116	8,601	***+6.9%	5,976	7,178	***+20.3%

(AmE automatic)

Table A10.7a. *S-genitives in American English: Brown vs Frown*

Genre	Brown		Frown		Change %
	raw freq.	pmw	raw freq.	pmw	
Press	1,276	7,147	1,819	10,281	*** +43.9%
Gen. Prose	1,999	4,771	3,174	7,661	*** +60.6%
Learned	472	2,914	890	5,549	*** +90.5%
Fiction	1,358	5,348	1,357	5,359	+0.2%
TOTAL	5,105	5,037	7,240	7,205	*** +43.0%

(automatic)
NOTE: these figures include plural genitives (s') as well as singular ('s)

Table A10.7b. *S-genitives in British English: LOB vs F-LOB*

Genre	LOB		F-LOB		Change %
	raw freq.	pmw	raw freq.	pmw	
Press	1,290	7,278	1,751	9,882	*** +35.8%
Gen. Prose	1,929	4,646	2,448	5,908	*** +27.2%
Learned	497	3,082	669	4,157	*** +34.9%
Fiction	1,246	4,921	1,315	5,193	+5.5%
TOTAL	4,962	4,928	6,183	6,148	*** +24.7%

Table A10.8. Of-*genitive in AmE (Brown and Frown) and in BrE (LOB and F-LOB): a sample from 2% of all* of-phrases[i] *(approximate result only)*

variety	genitive type	1961 raw freq.	pmw	1991/92 raw freq.	pmw	Change %
AmE	of-genitive	153	7,542	116	5,723	* −23.6%
	s-genitive		5,002		7,155	*** +43.0%
BrE	of-genitive	124	6,158	95	4,723	* −23.3%
	s-genitive		4,928		6,148	*** +24.7%
AmE + BrE	s-genitive as %age of both s- and of-genitives		42.0%		56.0%	

(AmE automatic)
[i]For both AmE and BrE, a 2% sample of *of*-phrases was manually analysed, and those examples of *of*-phrases which were clearly paraphrasable by an *s*-genitive (allowing for some stylistic infelicity) were counted as *of*-genitives. For comparative purposes, ideally, a similar procedure should have been carried out on the *s*-genitives, but since a large majority of them are paraphrasable by *of*-phrases (80% is the figure arrived at by Hinrichs and Szmrecsanyi 2007) we deemed it unnecessary. The result is an approximation only, in view of the scaling-up of the count of *of*-genitives to pmw.

Table A10.9a. *Decreasing use of* wh- *relative pronouns* (who, whom, whose, which) *in AmE (Brown and Frown)*

Genre	Brown raw freq.	pmw	Frown raw freq.	pmw	Change %
Press	1,174	6,574	1,035	5,850	** −11.0%
Gen. Prose	2,823	6,738	2,278	5,498	*** −18.4%
Learned	1,079	6,658	785	4,895	*** −26.5%
Fiction	940	3,701	793	3,132	*** −15.4%
TOTAL	6,016	5,936	4,891	4,867	*** −18.0%

(automatic)

Table A10.9b. *Decreasing use of* wh- *relative pronouns* (who, whom, whose, which) *in BrE (LOB and F-LOB)*

	LOB		F-LOB		
Genre	raw freq.	pmw	raw freq.	pmw	Change %
Press	1,375	7,758	1,233	6,959	** −10.3%
Gen. Prose	3,369	8,114	3,039	7,334	*** −9.6%
Learned	1,217	7,548	1,225	7,612	+0.9%
Fiction	1,047	4,135	906	3,578	** −13.5%
TOTAL	7,008	6,960	6,403	6,367	*** −8.5%

Table A10.10. *The relative pronoun* which *in AmE (Brown and Frown) and in BrE (LOB and F-LOB)*

	1961		1991/2		
	raw freq.	pmw	raw freq.	pmw	Change %
AmE	3,496	3,449	2,273	2,262	*** −34.4%
BrE	4,406	4,376	3,987	3,964	*** −9.4%

(AmE automatic)

Table A10.11a. *Increasing use of* that-*relative clauses in AmE (Brown and Frown)*

	Brown		Frown		
Genre	raw freq.	pmw	raw freq.	pmw	Change %
Press	360	2,017	554	3,131	*** +55.3%
Gen. Prose	837	1,998	1,494	3,606	*** +80.5%
Learned	224	1,382	552	3,442	*** +149.0%
Fiction	429	1,689	575	2,271	*** +34.4%
TOTAL	1,850	1,825	3,175	3,160	*** +73.1%

Table A10.11b. *Increasing use of* that-*relative clauses in BrE (LOB and F-LOB)*

| Genre | LOB | | F-LOB | | |
	raw freq.	pmw	raw freq.	pmw	Change %
Press	199	1,123	223	1,259	+12.1%
Gen. Prose	558	1,344	649	1,566	** +16.5%
Learned	156	968	252	1,566	*** +61.8%
Fiction	440	1,738	434	1,714	−1.4%
TOTAL	1,353	1,344	1,558	1,549	*** +15.3%

Table A10.12a. *Zero relative clauses in AmE (Brown and Frown)*[i]

| Genre | Brown | | Frown | | |
	raw freq.	pmw	raw freq.	pmw	Change %
Press	164	919	194	1,096	+19.3%
Gen. Prose	407	971	414	999	+2.9%
Learned	64	395	65	405	+2.6%
Fiction	388	1,528	403	1,591	+4.2%
TOTAL	1,023	1,009	1,076	1,071	+6.1%

[i]Zero relatives with adverbial gaps are not included. The figures for zero relatives are a low approximation, as although the examples were individually post-edited to exclude mishits, the search template used in the CQP search failed to find certain less usual word sequences introducing zero relative clauses: e.g. Noun + generic *one*; Noun + Noun (as in *the picture Mary loved*). The template was as follows: [pos="NN.*"] [pos="A.*|D.*|PP.*S.*|PPY|PPH1" & word != "which|whom|whose"]. This formula does its best to capture a noun head followed by a number of word classes which can begin a zero relative clause. It can be glossed: 'a common noun followed by any of the following: article, subject pronoun, *you*, *it*, or a determiner-pronoun, but this last may not be *which*, *whom* or *whose*'.

Table A10.12b. *Zero relative clauses in BrE (LOB and F-LOB)*

| Genre | LOB | | F-LOB | | |
	raw freq.	pmw	raw freq.	pmw	Change %
Press	148	835	146	818	−2.0%
Gen. Prose	301	725	373	900	** +24.2%
Learned	61	378	63	391	+3.5%
Fiction	391	1,544	393	1,552	+0.5%
TOTAL	901	895	975	968	+8.2%

Table A10.13. *Pied-piping in* wh- *relative clauses (LOB and F-LOB)*

	LOB		F-LOB		
Genre	raw freq.	pmw	raw freq.	pmw	Change %
Press	221	1,247	150	847	***−32.3%
Gen. Prose	698	1,681	586	1,414	**−15.4%
Learned	305	1,892	300	1,864	−1.3%
Fiction	166	656	113	446	**−32.1%
TOTAL	1,390	1,381	1,149	1,142	***−17.1%

Chapter 11

Table A11.1. *Lexical density in AmE and BrE (1961–1991/2)*

	AmE			BrE		
	Brown: %age of all words	Frown: %age of all words	Change (as % of Brown)	LOB: %age of all words	F-LOB: %age of all words	Change (as % of LOB)
Press	58.0%	59.7%	***+2.9%	56.8%	57.8%	***+1.8%
Gen. Prose	54.6%	57.5%	***+5.3%	53.7%	55.4%	***+3.1%
Learned	56.0%	60.3%	***+7.7%	54.9%	57.6%	***+4.9%
Fiction	51.6%	52.5%	***+1.9%	51.2%	51.6%	+0.9%
TOTAL	54.7%	57.1%	***+4.4%	53.8%	55.2%	***+2.6%

(AmE: post-edited Frown, estimated Brown)

Table A11.2a. *Punctuation marks: a comparison of AmE and BrE changes 1961–91*

Punctuation mark	Brown (raw freq.)	Frown (raw freq.)	Change (as % of Brown)	LOB (raw freq.)	F-LOB (raw freq.)	Change (as % of) LOB
Full stop	49,180	51,330	***+4.9%	50,313	47,905	***−4.7%
Question mark	2,349	2,868	***+22.8%	2,584	2,827	***+9.5%
Exclam. mark	796	687	**−13.2%	1,030	823	***−20.0%
Colon	1,730	1,922	***+11.7%	1,937	2,433	***+25.7%
Semi-colon	2,838	2,183	***−22.7%	2,514	2,077	***−17.3%
Dash	3,436	3,403	−0.4%	3,942	3,454	***−12.3%
Hyphen	6,939	7,394	***+7.1%	7,540	7,222	*−4.1%
( ) brackets	2,348	4,036	***+72.9%	2,902	4,352	***+50.1%
[ ] brackets	109	317	***+192.4%	54	131	***+142.9%
Comma	58,328	60,989	***+5.1%	54,548	53,570	**−1.7%

(AmE: post-edited Frown, estimated Brown)

Table A11.2b. *Some punctuation marks: a comparison of B-LOB (BrE 1931) and F-LOB (BrE 1991)*

Punctuation mark	B-LOB (1931)	F-LOB (1991)	Change (as % of B-LOB)
Full stop	44,917	47,905	***+7.3%
Question mark	2,323	2,827	***+22.5%
Exclamation mark	1,410	823	***−41.3%
Colon	1,630	2,433	***+50.2%
Semi-colon	3,471	2,077	***−39.8%
Comma	62,191	53,570	***−13.3%

(B-LOB automatic)

Table A11.3. *Abstract nominalizations in AmE*

Genre	Brown (1961)		Frown (1991)		Change %
	raw freq.	pmw	raw freq.	pmw	
Press	5,482	30,708	5,139	29,045	**−5.4%
Gen. Prose	15,557	37,130	16,311	39,367	***+6.0%
Learned	7,665	47,297	8,712	54,323	***+14.9%
Fiction	3,113	12,255	2,808	11,089	***−9.5%
TOTAL	31,817	31,391	32,970	32,810	***+4.5%

(estimated)

Table A11.4. *Abstract nominalizations in BrE*

Genre	LOB (1961)		F-LOB (1991)		Change %
	raw freq.	pmw	raw freq.	pmw	
Press	4,962	27,997	4,996	28,197	+0.7%
Gen. Prose	12,782	30,786	15,006	36,213	***+17.6%
Learned	6,978	43,278	7,917	49,196	***+13.7%
Fiction	3,214	12,693	3,278	12,945	+2.0%
TOTAL	27,936	27,746	31,197	31,020	***+11.8%

Table A11.5. *Decline of titular nouns preceding personal names: raw frequencies*[i]

	AmE			BrE		
	Brown	Frown	Change %	LOB	F-LOB	Change %
Mr	841	543	***−34.8%	1,459	863	***−40.8%
Mrs	535	150	***−71.7%	288	240	*−16.7%
Miss	219	69	***−68.2%	310	79	***−74.5%
All titular nouns[ii]	2,652	1,686	***−35.9%	3,671	2,284	***−37.8%

[i]The new titular noun *Ms* occurs occasionally in the 1991/2 corpora: there are 44 occurrences in Frown, and 13 in F-LOB.
[ii]All titular nouns (both with and without the abbreviatory full stop) preceding personal names were counted.

References

NOTE: A superscript numeral before a date indicates the edition being referred to.

Aarts, Flor and Bas Aarts. 2002. 'Relative *whom*: "a mischief-maker".' In: Andreas Fischer, Gunnel Tottie and Hans-Martin Lehmann (eds.). *Text Types and Corpora*. Tübingen: Narr, pp. 123–130.

Aarts, Jan. 1991. 'Intuition-based and observation-based grammars.' In: Karin Aijmer and Bengt Altenberg (eds.). *English Corpus Linguistics: Studies in Honour of Jan Svartvik*. London and New York: Longman, pp. 44–62.

Aarts, Jan and Willem Meijs (eds.). 1984. *Corpus Linguistics. Recent Developments in the Use of Computer Corpora in English Language Research*. Amsterdam: Rodopi.

Adamczewski, Henri. 1982. *Grammaire linguistique de l'anglais*. Paris: Armand Colin.

Aitchison, Jean. 1991. *Language Change: Progress or Decay?* Cambridge: Cambridge University Press.

Akimoto, Minoji. 1989. *A Study of Verbo-nominal Structures in English*. Tokyo: Shinozaki Shorin.

Algeo, John. 1992. 'British and American mandative constructions.' In: Claudia Blank (ed.). *Language and Civilization: A Concerted Profusion of Essays and Studies in Honor of Otto Hietsch*. Vol. II. Frankfurt: Peter Lang, pp. 599–617.

1995. 'Having a look at the expanded predicate.' In: Bas Aarts and Charles F. Meyer (eds.). *The Verb in Contemporary English: Theory and Description*. Cambridge: Cambridge University Press, pp. 203–217.

Allerton, David J. 2002. *Stretched Verb Constructions in English* (Routledge Studies in Germanic Linguistics 7). London: Routledge.

Altenberg, Bengt. 1982. *The Genitive v. the of Construction: A Study of Syntactic Variation in 17th Century English* (Lund Studies in English 62). Lund: CWK Gleerup.

1991. 'A bibliography of publications relating to English computer corpora.' In: Johansson and Stenström, pp. 355–396.

Anderson, John M. 2001. 'Modals, subjunctives, and (non-)finiteness.' *English Language and Linguistics* 5(1), 159–166.

Arnaud, Réné. 2002. 'Letter writers of the Romantic Age and the modernization of English (A quantitative historical survey of the progressive).' http://web.univ-pau.fr/saes/pb/bibliographies/A/arnaud/romanticletterwriters.pdf [accessed 8 December 2007].

314

Ashley, Mike. 2000. *The Time Machines: The Story of the Science-Fiction Pulp Magazine from the Beginning to 1950. The History of the Science-Fiction Magazine*, Vol. 1. Liverpool: Liverpool University Press.

Auer, Anita. 2006. 'Precept and practice: The influence of prescriptivism on the English subjunctive.' In: Christiane Dalton-Puffer, Dieter Kastovsky, Nikolaus Ritt and Herbert Schendl (eds.). *Syntax, Style and Grammatical Norms. English from 1500–2000*. Bern: Peter Lang, pp. 33–53.

Axelsson, Margareta Westergren. 1998. *Contraction in British Newspapers in the Late 20th Century*. Uppsala: Acta Universitatis Upsaliensis.

Bailey, Richard W. 1996. *Nineteenth-Century English*. Ann Arbor: University of Michigan Press.

Barber, Charles. 1964. *Linguistic Change in Present-Day English*. Edinburgh and London: Oliver and Boyd.

Barbieri, Federica. 2005. 'Quotative use in American English.' *Journal of English Linguistics* 33(2), 222–256.

Barlow, Michael. 2003. *Concordancing and Corpus Analysis Using MP 2.2*. Houston, TX: Athelstan.

Bauer, Laurie. 1994. *Watching English Change: An Introduction to the Study of Linguistic Change in Standard Englishes in the Twentieth Century*. London: Longman.

Bell, Allan. 1984. 'Language style as audience design.' *Language in Society* 13(2), 145–204.

Bergenholtz, Henning and Burkhard Schaeder (eds.). 1979. *Empirische Textwissenschaft: Aufbau und Auswertung von Text-Corpora*. Königstein: Scriptor.

Berglund, Ylva. 1997. 'Future in Present-day English: Corpus-based evidence on the rivalry of expressions.' *ICAME Journal* 21, 7–20.

2000. '*Gonna* and *going to* in the spoken component of the *British National Corpus*.' In: Christian Mair and Marianne Hundt (eds.). *Corpus linguistics and linguistic theory*. Amsterdam: Rodopi, pp. 35–49.

Bertinetto, Pier Marco. 2000. 'The progressive in Romance, as compared with English.' In: Östen Dahl (ed.). *Tense and Aspect in the Language of Europe*. Berlin/New York: Mouton de Gruyter, pp. 559–604.

Bevier, Thyra Jane. 1931. 'American use of the subjunctive.' *American Speech* 6(3), 207–215.

Biber, Douglas 1987. 'A textual comparison of British and American writing.' *American Speech* 62(2), 99–119.

1988. *Variation across Speech and Writing*. Cambridge: Cambridge University Press.

1993. 'Representativeness in corpus design.' *Literary and Linguistic Computing* 8(4), 243–257.

2001. 'Dimensions of variation in 18th century registers.' In: Hans-Jürgen Diller and Manfred Görlach (eds.). *Towards a History of English as a History of Genres*. Heidelberg: C. Winter [reprinted in: Conrad and Biber (eds.), pp. 201–214].

2003a. 'Compressed noun-phrase structures in newspaper discourse: The competing demands of popularization vs. economy.' In: Jean Aitchison and Diana M. Lewis (eds.). *New Media Language*. London: Routledge, pp. 169–181.

2003b. 'Variation among university spoken and written registers: A new multi-dimensional analysis.' In: Pepi Leistyna and Charles F. Meyer (eds.).

Corpus Analysis. Language Structure and Language Use. Amsterdam: Rodopi, pp. 47–70.

2004. 'Modal use across registers and time.' In: Anne Curzan and Kimberly Emmons (eds.). *Studies in the History of the English Language II. Unfolding Conversations.* Berlin: Mouton de Gruyter, pp. 189–216.

Biber, Douglas and Victoria Clark. 2002. 'Historical shifts in modification patterns with complex noun phrase structures.' In: Teresa Fanego, María López-Couso and Javier Pérez-Guerra (eds.). *English Historical Morphology. Selected Papers from 11 ICEHL, Santiago de Compostela, 7–11 September, 2000.* Amsterdam: Benjamins, pp. 43–66.

Biber, Douglas, Susan Conrad and Randi Reppen. 1998. *Corpus Linguistics. Investigating Language Structure and Use.* Cambridge: Cambridge University Press.

Biber, Douglas and Edward Finegan. 1989. 'Drift and evolution of English style: A history of three genres.' *Language* 65(3), 487–517.

1997. 'Diachronic relations among speech-based and written registers in English.' In: Terttu Nevalainen and Lena Kahlas-Tarkka (eds.). *To Explain the Present. Studies in the Changing English Language in Honour of Matti Rissanen.* Helsinki: Mémoires de la Société Néophilologique de Helsinki, pp. 253–275.

Biber, Douglas, Stig Johansson, Geoffrey Leech, Susan Conrad and Edward Finegan. 1999. *The Longman Grammar of Spoken and Written English.* London: Longman.

Blake, Norman. 1996. *A History of the English Language.* Basingstoke: Macmillan.

Blyth, Carl, Sigrid Recktenwald and Jenny Wang. 1990. '"I'm like, 'Say what!'." A new quotative in American narrative discourse.' *American Speech* 65(3), 215–217.

Bodine, Anne. 1975. 'Androcentrism in prescriptive grammar: Singular "they," sex-indefinite "he," and "he or she".' *Language in Society* 4(2), 129–146.

Bolinger, Dwight. 1980. '*Wanna* and the gradience of auxiliaries.' In: Gunter Brettschneider and Christian Lehmann (eds.). *Wege zur Universalienforschung. Sprachwissenschaftliche Beiträge zum 60. Geburtstag von Hansjakob Seiler.* Tübingen: Narr, pp. 292–299.

Brinton, Laurel. 1996. 'Attitudes towards increasing segmentalization: Complex and phrasal verbs in English.' *Journal of English Linguistics* 24, 186–205.

Brinton, Laurel and Minoji Akimoto (eds.). 1999. *Collocational and Idiomatic Aspects of Composite Predicates in the History of English.* Amsterdam and Philadelphia: Benjamins.

Bruyndonx, Jim. 2001. *The Expanded Form in British English. Meanings and Constraints: A Corpus-illustrated Description.* Unpublished PhD thesis, Catholic University of Leuven.

Bryant Margaret M. (ed.). 1962. *Current American Usage.* New York: Funk & Wagnalls.

Buchstaller, Isabelle. 2006. 'Diagnostics of age-graded linguistic behaviour: The case of the quotative system.' *Journal of Sociolinguistics* 10(1), 3–30.

Bundt, Harry and William Black. 2000. *Abduction, Belief and Context in Dialogue: Studies in Computational Pragmatics.* Amsterdam: Benjamins.

Burchfield, Robert W. ³1996. *The New Fowler's Modern English Usage.* Oxford: Clarendon.

Butters, Ronald. 1980. 'Narrative *go* "say".' *American Speech* 55, 215–227.

1982. 'Editor's note [on *be like* "think"].' *American Speech* 57, 149.

Buyssens, Eric. 1968. *Les Deux Aspectifs de la Conjugaison Anglaise au XXe Siècle.* Brussels: Presses Universitaires de Bruxelles.

Bybee, Joan. 2007. *Frequency of Use and the Organization of Language.* New York: Oxford University Press.

Bybee, Joan and William Pagliuca. 1985. 'Cross-linguistic comparison and the development of grammatical meaning.' In: Jacek Fisiak (ed.). *Historical Semantics, Historical Word Formation.* The Hague: Mouton, pp. 59–83.

Bybee, Joan, Revere D. Perkins and William Pagliuca. 1994. *The Evolution of Grammar: Tense, Aspect and Modality in the Languages of the World.* Chicago: University of Chicago Press.

Carter, Ronald and Michael McCarthy. 1999. 'The English *get*-passive in spoken discourse.' *English Language and Linguistics* 3(1), 41–58.

Cattell, Norman Raymond. 1984. *Composite Predicates in English.* Sydney: Academic Press.

Chafe, Wallace. 1982. 'Integration and involvement in speaking, writing and oral literature.' In: Deborah Tannen (ed.). *Spoken and Written Language. Exploring Orality and Literacy.* Norwood, NJ: Ablex, pp. 35–53.

Chappell, Hilary.1980. 'Is the *get*-passive adversative?' *Papers in Linguistics: International Journal of Human Communication* 13(3), 411–452.

Charleston, Britta. 1960. *Studies on the Emotional and Affective Means of Expression in Modern English.* Bern: Francke.

Chomsky, Noam. 1965. *Aspects of the Theory of Syntax.* Cambridge, MA.: MIT Press.

Christ, Oliver. 1994. 'A modular and flexible architecture for an integrated corpus query system.' *Proceedings of* COMPLEX *'94: Third Conference on Computational Lexicography and Text Research (Budapest, July 7–10, 1994).* Budapest, pp. 23–32.

Claridge, Claudia. 2000. *Multi-word Verbs in Early Modern English. A Corpus-based Study.* Amsterdam: Rodopi.

2008. 'Historical corpora.' In: Lüdeling and Kytö (eds.), pp. 242–259.

Close, Reginald A. 1988. 'The future in English.' In: Wolf-Dietrich Bald (ed.). *Kernprobleme der Englischen Grammatik: Sprachliche Fakten und Ihre Vermittlung.* Munich: Langenscheidt-Longman, pp. 51–66.

Coates, Jennifer. 1983. *The Meanings of the Modal Auxiliaries.* London: Croom Helm.

Coates, Jennifer and Geoffrey Leech. 1980. 'The meanings of the modals in British and American English.' *York Papers in Linguistics* 8, 22–34.

Collins, Peter C. 1996. '*Get*-passives in English.' *English World-Wide* 15(1), 43–56.

Comrie, Bernard. 1976. *Aspect.* Cambridge: Cambridge University Press.

Conrad, Susan and Douglas Biber (eds.). 2001. *Variation in English. Multi-dimensional Studies.* Harlow: Longman.

Cort, Alison and David Denison. 2005. 'The category modal – a moving target?' Paper presented at the First International Conference on the Linguistics of Contemporary English, University of Edinburgh.

Crawford, William J. 2009. 'The mandative subjunctive.' In: Günter Rohdenburg and Julia Schlüter (eds.). *One Language, Two Grammars? Differences between*

British and American English. Cambridge: Cambridge University Press, pp. 257–276.

Croft, William. 2000. *Explaining Language Change. An Evolutionary Approach.* Harlow: Longman.

Crystal, David. 2004. *The Stories of English.* Woodstock and New York: Overlook Press.

Dahl, Östen. 1985. *Tense and Aspect Systems.* Oxford: Blackwell.

Danchev, Andrei and Merja Kytö. 2002. 'The go-futures in English and French as an areal feature.' *Nowele* 40, 9–60.

Davidse, Kristin and Liesbet Heyvaert. 2003. 'On the middle construction in English and Dutch.' In: Sylviane Granger, Jacques Lerot and Stephanie Petch-Tyson (eds.). *Corpus-Based Approaches to Contrastive Linguistics and Translation Studies.* Amsterdam: Rodopi, pp. 57–73.

de Haan, Pieter. 2002. '*Whom* is not dead?' In: Pam Peters, Peter Collins and Adam Smith (eds.). *New Frontiers of Corpus Research.* Amsterdam: Rodopi, pp. 215–228.

Declerck, Renaat. 1991a. *A Comprehensive Descriptive Grammar of English.* Tokyo: Kaitakusha.

   1991b. *Tense in English. Its Structure and Use in Discourse.* London and New York: Routledge.

Denison, David. 1993. *English Historical Syntax. Verbal Constructions.* London and New York: Longman.

   1998. 'Syntax.' In: Suzanne Romaine (ed), pp. 92–329.

   2001. 'Gradience and linguistic change.' In: Laurel Brinton (ed.). *Historical Linguistics. 1999.* Amsterdam/Philadelphia: Benjamins, pp. 119–144.

Dennis, Leah. 1940. 'The progressive tense: Frequency of its use in English.' *Publications of the Modern Language Association of America* 55, 855–865.

Depraetere, Ilse. 2003. 'On verbal concord with collective nouns in British English.' *English Language Linguistics*, 7(1), 85–127.

Ding, Daniel. 2002. 'The passive voice and social values in science.' *Journal of Technical Writing and Communication* 32(2), 137–154.

Dixon, Robert M. W. 1991. *A New Approach to English Grammar, on Semantic Principles.* Oxford: Clarendon.

   2005. *A Semantic Approach to English grammar.* Oxford: Oxford University Press.

Downing, Angela. 1996. 'The semantics of *get*-passives.' In: Ruqaiya Hasan, Carmel Cloran and David Butt (eds.). *Functional Descriptions. Theory in Practice.* Amsterdam and Philadelphia: Benjamins, pp. 179–205.

Elsness, Johan. 1994. 'On the progression of the progressive in early Modern English.' *ICAME Journal* 18, 5–25.

Elsom, John. 1984. 'The sad decline of the subjunctive.' *Contemporary Review* 245, 36–40.

Facchinetti, Roberta. 2002. '*Be able to* in Present-day British English.' In: Bernhard Kettemann and Georg Marko (eds.). *Teaching and Learning by Doing Corpus Analysis.* Amsterdam: Rodopi, pp. 117–130.

Facchinetti, Roberta, Manfred Krug and Frank Palmer (eds.). 2003. *Modality in Contemporary English.* Berlin: Mouton de Gruyter.

Fairclough, Norman. 1992. *Discourse and Social Change.* Cambridge: Polity.

Fanego, Teresa. 1996a. 'On the historical developments of English retrospective verbs.' *Neuphilologische Mitteilungen* 97, 71–79.

1996b. 'The development of gerunds as objects of subject-control verbs in English (1400–1760).' *Diachronica* 13, 29–62.

Fillmore, Charles. 1990. 'Epistemic stance and grammatical form in English conditional sentences.' *Papers from the 26th Regional Meeting of the Chicago Linguistic Society* 26, 137–162.

Filppula, Markku. 2002. The English progressive on the move. Paper presented at International Conference on English Historical Linguistics, Glasgow, August 2002.

Fischer, Olga. 1992. 'Syntax.' In: Norman Blake (ed.). *The Cambridge History of the English Language*. Vol. II: *1066–1476*. Cambridge: Cambridge University Press, pp. 207–408.

Fischer, Olga and Wim van der Wurff. 2006. 'Syntax.' In: Richard Hogg and David Denison (eds.). *A History of the English Language*. Cambridge: Cambridge University Press, pp. 109–198.

Fitzmaurice, Susan M. 2004. 'The meaning and uses of the progressive construction in an early eighteenth-century English Network.' In: Anne Curzan and Kimberly Emmons (eds.). *Studies in the History of the English Language II: Unfolding Conversations*. Berlin / New York: Mouton de Gruyter, pp. 131–174.

Fleisher, Nicolas. 2006. 'The origin of passive *get*.' *English Language and Linguistics* 10(2), 225–252.

Fligelstone, Steven, Mike Pacey and Paul Rayson. 1997. 'How to generalize the task of annotation.' In: Garside *et al.*, pp. 122–136.

Fong, Vivienne. 2004. 'The verbal cluster.' In: Lisa Lim and Joseph A. Foley (eds.). *Singapore English: A Grammatical Description*. Amsterdam and Philadelphia: Benjamins, pp. 75–104.

Foster, Brian. 1968. *The Changing English Language*. London: Macmillan.

Fowler, H. W. ^{2}1965 [1926]. *A Dictionary of Modern English Usage*. Oxford: Oxford University Press.

Francis, W. Nelson. 1979. 'Problems of assembling large computer corpora.' In: Bergenholtz and Schaeder, pp. 110–123.

1980. 'A tagged corpus – problems and prospects.' In: Greenbaum *et al.*, pp. 192–209.

Francis, W. Nelson and Henry Kučera. 1982. *Frequency Analysis of English Usage: Lexicon and Grammar*. Boston: Houghton Mifflin.

Fries, Charles Carpenter. 1940. *American English Grammar. The Grammatical Structure of Present-Day American English with Especial Reference to Social Differences or Class Dialects*. New York: Appleton-Century-Crofts.

Gachelin, Jean-Marc. 1997. 'The progressive and habitual aspects in Non-Standard Englishes.' In: Edgar Schneider (ed.). *Englishes around the World. General Studies, British Isles, North America. Studies in Honour of Manfred Görlach*. Amsterdam and Philadelphia: Benjamins, pp. 33–46.

Garretson, Gregory and Annelie Ädel. 2005. 'Who's speaking?: Evidentiality in US newspapers during the 2004 presidential campaign'. Paper presented at the ICAME 26 and AAACL6 conference, University of Michigan, Ann Arbor, 12–15 May 2005.

320 References

Garside, Roger, Geoffrey Leech and Anthony McEnery (eds.). 1997. *Corpus Annotation. Linguistic Information from Computer Text Corpora.* Harlow: Addison Wesley Longman.

Garside, Roger and Nicholas Smith. 1997. 'A hybrid grammatical tagger: CLAWS 4.' In: Garside *et al.*, pp. 102–121.

Geisler, Christer. 2007. 'A multivariate investigation of written British and American English.' Anonymous submission to Corpus Linguistics 2007, Birmingham, 27–30 July 2007.

Givón, Talmy. 1993. *English Grammar. A Function-Based Introduction.* Vol. II. Amsterdam and Philadelphia: Benjamins.

Gonzáles-Álvarez, Dolores. 2003. '*If he come* vs. *if he comes, if he shall come*: Some remarks on the subjunctive in conditional protases in Early Modern and Late Modern English.' *Neuphilologische Mitteilungen* 104, 303–313.

Granger, Sylviane. 1983. *The BE + Past Participle Construction in Spoken English.* Amsterdam: North Holland.

Green, Georgia. 1975. 'How to get people to do things with words: The whimperative question.' In: Peter Cole and Jerry L. Morgan (eds.). *Syntax and Semantics.* Vol. III: *Speech Acts.* New York: Academic Press, pp. 107–141.

Greenbaum, Sidney. 1986. 'The *Grammar of Contemporary English* and *A Comprehensive Grammar of the English Language*.' In: Gerhard Leitner (ed.). *The English Reference Grammar.* Tübingen: Niemeyer, pp. 6–14.

Greenbaum, Sidney, Geoffrey Leech and Jan Svartvik (eds.). 1980. *Studies in English Linguistics. For Randolph Quirk.* London: Longman.

Greenbaum, Sidney and Janet Whitcut. 1988. *Longman Guide to English Usage.* Harlow: Longman.

Gries, Stefan Thomas. 2002. *Multifactorial Analysis in Corpus Linguistics: A Study of Particle Placement.* New York and London: Continuum.

Grund, Peter and Terry Walker. 2006. 'The subjunctive in adverbial clauses in nineteenth-century English.' In: Merja Kytö, Mats Rydén and Erik Smitterberg (eds.). *Nineteenth-Century English. Stability and Change.* Cambridge: Cambridge University Press, pp. 89–109.

Haegeman, Liliane. 1985. 'The *get*-passive and Burzio's generalization.' *Lingua* 66, 53–77.

Halliday, M. A. K. and Christian Matthiessen. ³2004. *An Introduction to Functional Grammar.* London: Arnold [1st edn Halliday, M.A.K., 1985].

Hancil, Sylvie. 1996. 'Subjectivity, politeness and the progressive form.' *Proceedings of the Edinburgh Linguistics Department Conference 1996*, pp. 112–117.

Hardie, Andrew and Tony McEnery. 2004. 'The *were*-subjunctive in British rural dialects: Marrying corpus and questionnaire data.' *Computers and the Humanities* 37, 205–228.

Hardy, Donald E. 2004. 'The role of linguistics in interpretation: The case of grammatical voice.' *Belgian Journal of English Language and Literature* 2, 31–48.

Harsh, Wayne. 1968. *The Subjunctive in English.* Alabama: University of Alabama Press.

Heine, Bernd. 1993. *Auxiliaries: Cognitive Forces and Grammaticalization.* New York: Oxford University Press.

Heringer, Hans Jürgen. 1989. *Lesen, Lehren, Lernen: Eine Rezeptive Grammatik des Deutschen.* Tübingen: Niemeyer.

Heyvaert, Lisbet. 2003. *A Cognitive-Functional Approach to Nominalization in English.* Berlin: Mouton de Gruyter.

Hiltunen, Risto. 1999. 'Verbal phrases and phrasal verbs in Early Modern English.' In: Laurel Brinton and Minoji Akimoto (eds.), pp. 133–165.

Hinrichs, Lars, Nicholas Smith and Birgit Waibel. forthcoming. *The Part-of-speech-tagged 'Brown' Corpora: A Manual of Information, including Pointers to Successful Use.* https://webspace.utexas.edu/lh9896/public/hinrichs/Manual_final.pdf.

Hinrichs, Lars and Benedikt Szmrecsanyi. 2007. 'Recent changes in the function and frequency of Standard English genitive constructions: A multivariate analysis of tagged corpora.' *English Language and Linguistics* 11(3), 335–378.

Hirtle, Walter. 1967. *The Simple and Progressive Forms: An Analytical Approach.* Quebec: Presses de l'Université Laval.

Hoffmann, Achim. 1972. 'Die verbo-nominale Konstruktion: eine spezifische Form der nominalen Ausdrucksweise im modernen Englisch.' *Zeitschrift für Anglistik und Amerikanistik* 20, 158–183.

Hoffmann, Sebastian. 1997. *Mandative Sentences. A Study of Variation on the Basis of the British National Corpus.* Unpublished Lizentiats-Arbeit, Universität Zürich.

2005. *Grammaticalization and English Complex Prepositions: A Corpus-based Study.* London: Routledge.

Hofland, Knut and Stig Johansson. 1982. *Word Frequencies in British and American English.* Bergen: Norwegian Computer Centre for the Humanities.

Holmes, Janet. ²2001 [1992]. *An Introduction to Sociolinguistics.* London: Longman.

Hommerberg, Charlotte and Gunnel Tottie. 2007. '*Try to* or *try and*? Verb complementation in British and American English.' *ICAME Journal* 31, 45–64.

Hopper, Paul J. 1991. 'On some principles of grammaticalization.' In: Elizabeth Traugott and Bernd Heine (eds.). *Approaches to Grammaticalization.* Vol. I. Amsterdam: Benjamins, pp. 17–35.

Hopper, Paul J. and Elizabeth Closs Traugott. ²2003 [1993]. *Grammaticalization.* Cambridge: Cambridge University Press.

Hübler, Axel. 1992. 'On the *get*-passive.' In: Wilhelm G. Busse (ed.). *Anglistentag 1991. Proceedings.* Tübingen: Niemeyer, pp. 89–101.

1998. *The Expressivity of Grammar: Grammatical Devices Expressing Emotion across Time.* Berlin and New York: Mouton de Gruyter.

Huddleston, Rodney. 1980. 'Criteria for auxiliaries and modals.' In: Greenbaum *et al.*, pp. 65–78.

1984. *Introduction to the Grammar of English.* Cambridge: Cambridge University Press.

Huddleston, Rodney and Geoffrey K. Pullum. 2002. *The Cambridge Grammar of the English Language.* Cambridge: Cambridge University Press.

2005. *A Student's Introduction to English Grammar.* Cambridge: Cambridge University Press.

Hudson, Richard. 1994. 'About 37% of word-tokens are nouns.' *Language* 70, 331–339.

Hundt, Marianne. 1997. 'Has BrE been catching up with AmE over the past thirty years?' In: Magnus Ljung (ed.). *Corpus-based Studies in English. Papers from the 17th International Conference on English Language Research on Computerized Corpora (ICAME 17), Stockholm, May 15–19, 1996.* Amsterdam: Rodopi, pp. 135–151.

1998a. *New Zealand English Grammar. Fact or Fiction. A Corpus-Based Study of Morphosyntactic Variation.* Amsterdam: John Benjamins.

1998b. 'It is important that this study *(should) be* based on the analysis of parallel corpora: On the use of the mandative subjunctive in four major varieties of English.' In: Hans Lindquist, Staffan Klintborg, Magnus Levin and Maria Estling (eds.). *The Major Varieties of English* (Papers from MAVEN 97). Växjö: Acta Wexionensia, pp. 159–175.

2001. 'What corpora tell us about the grammaticalisation of voice in *get*-constructions.' *Studies in Language* 25(1), 49–88.

2004a. 'Animacy, agentivity, and the spread of the progressive in modern English.' *English Language and Linguistics* 8(1), 47–69.

2004b. 'The passival and the progressive passive: A case study of layering in the English aspect and voice systems.' In: Lindquist and Mair (eds.), pp. 79–120.

2006. '"Curtains like these are selling right in the City of Chicago for $1.50": The mediopassive in American 20th-century advertising language.' In: Antoinette Renouf and Andrew Kehoe (eds.). *The Changing Face of Corpus Linguistics.* Amsterdam: Rodopi, pp. 163–183.

2007. *English Mediopassive Constructions. A Cognitive, Corpus-Based Study of their Origin, Spread and Current Status.* Amsterdam: Rodopi.

2009a. 'Colonial lag, colonial innovation or simply language change?' In: Günter Rohdenburg and Julia Schlüter (eds.). *One Language, Two Grammars? Differences between British and American English.* Cambridge: Cambridge University Press, pp. 13–37.

2009b. 'Global feature – local norms? A case study on the progressive passive.' In: Lucia Siebers and Tobias Hoffmann (eds.). *World Englishes: Problems – Properties – Prospects.* Amsterdam and Philadelphia: Benjamins, pp. 287–308.

forthcoming a. '*These books (will) sell (well)* – the development of constraints on mediopassives formation in late Modern and Present Day English advertising copy.'

forthcoming b. 'How often do things *get V-ed* in Philippine and Singapore English? A case study on the *get*-passive in two outer-circle varieties of English.'

Hundt, Marianne and Christian Mair. 1999. '"Agile" and "uptight" genres: The corpus-based approach to language change in progress.' *International Journal of Corpus Linguistics* 4, 221–242.

Hundt, Marianne, Nadja Nesselhauf and Carolin Biewer (eds.). 2007. *Corpus Linguistics and the Web.* Amsterdam: Rodopi.

Jacobson, Sven. 1980. 'Issues in the study of syntactic variation.' In Jacobson, Sven, (ed.). *Papers from the Scandinavian Symposium on Syntactic Variation.* Stockholm: Almquist and Wiksell. pp. 23–36.

James, Francis. 1986. *Semantics of the English Subjunctive.* Vancouver: University of British Columbia Press.

Jespersen, Otto. 1909–49. *A Modern English Grammar on Historical Principles*, 7 vols. London: George Allen and Unwin/Copenhagen: Munksgaard.

1924. *The Philosophy of Grammar*. London: George Allen and Unwin.

1984. *Analytic Syntax*. Chicago, IL: University of Chicago Press [First published 1937].

Jin, Koichi. 2002. 'On the middle voice in present-day English.' In: Jacek Fisiak (ed.). *Studies in English Historical Linguistics and Philology. A Festschrift for Okio Oizumi*. Frankfurt: Peter Lang, pp. 139–155.

Johansson, Stig. 1980. *Plural Attributive Nouns in Present-Day English*. (Lund Studies in English 59). Lund: CWK Gleerup.

Johansson, Stig, Geoffrey Leech and Helen Goodluck. 1978. *Manual of Information for the Lancaster-Oslo/Bergen Corpus for Digital Computers*. Oslo: University of Oslo.

Johansson, Stig and Else Helene Norheim. 1988. 'The subjunctive in British and American English.' *ICAME Journal* 12, 27–36.

Johansson, Stig and Signe Oksefjell. 1996. 'Towards a unified account of the syntax and semantics of *get*.' In: Jenny Thomas and Michael Short (eds.). *Using Corpora for Language Research: Studies in Honour of Geoffrey Leech*. London: Longman, pp. 57–75.

Johansson, Stig and Anna-Brita Stenström (eds.). 1991. *English Computer Corpora: Selected Papers and Research Guide*. Berlin and New York: Mouton de Gruyter.

Johnson, Samuel. 1755. *A Dictionary of the English Language*. 2 vols. London.

Joseph, Brian D. 2004. 'The editor's department.' *Language* 80, 381–383.

Jucker, Andreas H. 1992. *Social Stylistics. Syntactic Variation in British Newspapers*. Berlin and New York: Mouton de Gruyter.

Kearns, Kate. 2003. 'Durative achievements and individual-level predicates on events.' *Linguistics and Philosophy* 26(5), 595–635.

Kennedy, Graeme. 1998. *An Introduction to Corpus Linguistics*. London: Longman.

2001. 'The distribution of agent marking and finiteness as possible contributors to the difficulty of passive voice structures.' In: Karin Aijmer (ed.). *A Wealth of English*. Göteborg: Acta Universitatis Gothoburgensis, pp. 39–46.

Killie, Kristin. 2004. 'Subjectivity and the English progressive.' *English Language and Linguistics* 8, 25–46.

Kohnen, Thomas. 2007. 'From Helsinki through the centuries: The design and development of English diachronic corpora.' In: Päivi Pahta, Irma Taavitsainen, Terttu Nevalainen and Jukka Tyrkkö (eds.). *Studies in Variation, Contacts and Change in English 2: Towards Multimedia in Corpus Studies*. http://www.helsinki.fi/varieng/journal/volumes/02/kohnen.

König, Ekkehard. 1980. 'On the context-dependence of the Progressive in English.' In: Christian Rohrer (ed.). *Time, Tense, and Quantifiers. Proceedings of the Stuttgart Conference on the Logic of Tense and Quantification*. Tübingen: Niemeyer, pp. 269–291.

1995. '*He is being obscure*: non-verbal predication and the progressive.' In: Pier Marco Bertinetto, Valentina Bianchi, Östen Dahl and Mario Squartini (eds.). *Temporal Reference, Aspect, and Actionality*. Vol. II: *Typological Approaches*. Turin: Rosenberg and Sellier, pp. 155–167.

König, Ekkehard and Peter Lutzeier. 1973. 'Bedeutung and Verwendung der Progressivform im heutigen Englisch.' *Lingua* 32, 277–308.

Kortmann, Bernd. 2006. 'Syntactic variation in English: A global perspective.' In: Bas Aarts and April MacMahon (eds.). *The Handbook of English Linguistics.* Oxford: Blackwell, pp. 603–624.

Kytö, Merja and Suzanne Romaine. 1997. 'Competing forms of adjective comparison in Modern English: What could be more quicker and easier and more effective?' In: Terttu Nevalainen and Leena Kahlas-Tarkka (eds.). *To Explain the Present: Studies in the Changing English Language in Honour of Matti Rissanen.* Helsinki: Société Néophilologique, pp. 329–352.

2000. 'Adjective comparison and standardization processes in American and British English from 1620 to the present.' In: Laura Wright (ed.). *The Development of Standard English 1300–1800: Theories, Descriptions, Conflicts.* Cambridge: Cambridge University Press, pp. 171–194.

Kytö, Merja, Juhani Rudanko and Erik Smitterberg. 2000. 'Building a bridge between the present and the past: A corpus of 19th century English.' *ICAME Journal* 24, 85–97.

Kranich, Svenja. 2007. 'Interpretative progressives in Late Modern English.' Paper presented at the 3rd Late Modern English Conference, Leiden, the Netherlands, 29 August–1 September 2007.

Krenn, Brigitte. 2000. *The Usual Suspects. Data-oriented Models for Identification and Representation of Lexical Collocations.* Saarbrücken: German Research Centre for Artificial Intelligence.

Krug, Manfred. 1996. 'Language change in progress: Contractions in journalese in 1961 and 1991/92.' In: Steven McGill (ed.). *Proceedings of the 1995 Graduate Research Conference on Language and Linguistics* (Exeter Working Papers in English Language Studies 1), pp. 17–28.

2000. *Emerging English Modals: A Corpus-based Study of Grammaticalization.* Berlin and New York: Mouton de Gruyter.

Labov, William. 1963. 'The social motivation of a sound change.' *Word* 19, 273–309.

1972. *Sociolinguistic Patterns.* Philadelphia PA: University of Pennsylvania Press.

1994. *Principles of Linguistic Change.* Vol. I: *Internal Factors.* Oxford: Blackwell.

2001. *Principles of Linguistic Change.* Vol. II: *Social Factors.* Oxford: Blackwell.

Labuhn, Ute. 2001. *Von Give a Laugh bis Have a Cry. Zu Aspektualität und Transitivität der V + N-Konstruktionen im Englischen.* Frankfurt/Main: Peter Lang.

Lakoff, Robin. 1971. 'Passive resistance.' *Papers from the Regional Meeting of the Chicago Linguistic Society* 8, 149–162.

1990. *Talking Power.* New York: Basic Books.

Lee, Yong Wey David. 2000. *Modelling Variation in Spoken and Written Language: the Multi-dimensional Approach Revisited.* Unpublished PhD thesis, Lancaster University.

Leech, Geoffrey. 1966. *English in Advertising. A Linguistic Study of Advertising in Great Britain.* London: Longman.

2003. 'Modality on the move: The English modal auxiliaries 1961–1992.' In: Facchinetti *et al.*, pp. 223–240.

³2004 [1971]. *Meaning and the English Verb.* London: Longman.

2004. 'Recent grammatical change in English: Data, description, theory.' In: Karin Aijmer and Bengt Altenberg (eds.). *Advances in Corpus Linguistics*. Amsterdam: Rodopi, pp. 61–81.

2007. 'New resources, or just better old ones? The Holy Grail of representativeness,' In: Hundt *et al.* 2007, pp. 133–149.

Leech, Geoffrey and Jennifer Coates. 1980. 'Semantic indeterminacy and the modals.' In: Greenbaum *et al.*, pp. 79–90.

Leech, Geoffrey and Jonathan Culpeper. 1997. 'The comparison of adjectives in recent British English.' In: Terttu Nevalainen and Leena Kahlas-Tarkka (eds.). *To Explain the Present. Studies in the Changing English Language in Honour of Matti Rissanen*. Helsinki: Societé Neophilologique, pp. 353–373.

Leech, Geoffrey and Roger Fallon. 1992. 'Computer corpora: What do they tell us about culture?' *ICAME Journal* 16, 1–22 [reprinted in: Geoffrey Sampson and Diana McCarthy (eds.). 2004. *Corpus Linguistics. Readings in a Widening Discipline*. London and New York: Continuum, pp. 160–173].

Leech, Geoffrey, Brian Francis and Xunfeng Xu. 1994. 'The use of computer corpora in the textual demonstrability of gradience in linguistic categories.' In: Catherine Fuchs and Bernard Victorri (eds.). *Continuity in Linguistic Semantics*. Amsterdam: Benjamins, pp. 57–76.

Leech, Geoffrey, Paul Rayson and Andrew Wilson. 2001. *Word Frequencies in Written and Spoken English*. Harlow: Longman.

Leech, Geoffrey and Nicholas Smith. 2005. 'Extending the possibilities of corpus-based research on English in the twentieth century: A prequel for LOB and F-LOB.' *ICAME Journal* 29, 83–98.

2006. 'Recent grammatical change in written English 1961–1992.' In: Antoinette Renouf and Andrew Kehoe (eds.). *The Changing Face of Corpus Linguistics*. Amsterdam: Rodopi., pp. 185–204.

Leonard, Rosemary. 1968. *The Types and Currency of Noun + Noun Sequences in Prose Usage 1750–1950*. Unpublished MPhil thesis, University of London.

1984. *The Interpretation of English Noun Sequences on the Computer*. Amsterdam: North-Holland.

Levin, Magnus. 2001. *Agreement with Collective Nouns in English*. Lund: Lund Studies in English.

2006. 'Collective nouns and language change.' *English Language and Linguistics* 10, 321–343.

Lindquist, Hans. 2000. 'Livelier or more lively? Syntactic and contextual factors influencing the comparison of disyllabic adjectives.' In: John M. Kirk (ed.). *Corpora Galore: Analyses and Techniques in Describing English*. Papers from the Nineteenth International Conference on English Language Research on Computerised Corpora (ICAME 1998). Amsterdam: Rodopi, pp. 125–132.

Lindquist, Hans and Christian Mair. 2004a. 'Introduction.' In: Lindquist and Mair (eds.), pp. ix–xiv.

(eds.). 2004b. *Corpus Approaches to Grammaticalization in English*. Amsterdam: Benjamins.

Live, Anna H. 1973. 'The take-have phrasal in English.' *Linguistics* 95, 31–50.

Ljung, Magnus. 1980. *Reflections on the English Progressive* (Gothenburg Studies in English 46). Gothenburg: Acta Universitatis Gothoburgensis.

Los, Bettelou. 2005. *The Rise of the to Infinitive*. Oxford: Oxford University Press.

Lüdeling, Anke and Merja Kytö. 2008. *Corpus Linguistics: An International Handbook*. Berlin: Mouton de Gruyter.

Lyons, John. 1982. 'Deixis and subjectivity: *Loquor, ergo sum?*' In: Robert J. Jarvella and Wolfgang Klein (eds.). *Speech, Place and Action*. New York: Wiley, pp. 101–124.

Mair, Christian. 1997. 'The spread of the *going-to*-future in written English: A corpus-based investigation into language change in progress.' In: Raymond Hickey and Stanislaw Puppel (eds.). *Language History and Linguistic Modelling. A Festschrift for Jacek Fisiak*. Berlin: Mouton de Gruyter, pp. 1537–1543.

2002. 'Three changing patterns of verb complementation in Late Modern English: A real-time study based on matching text corpora.' *English Language and Linguistics* 6, 105–131.

2004. 'Corpus linguistics and grammaticalization theory: Statistics, frequencies and beyond.' In: Christian Mair and Hans Lindquist (eds.). *Corpus Approaches to Grammaticalization in English*. Amsterdam: Benjamins, pp. 121–150.

2006a. 'Tracking ongoing grammatical change and recent diversification in Present-Day Standard English: The complementary role of small and large corpora.' In: Antoinette Renouf and Andrew Kehoe (eds.). *The Changing Face of Corpus Linguistics*. Amsterdam: Rodopi, pp. 355–375.

2006b. *Twentieth-Century English. History, Variation and Standardization*. Cambridge: Cambridge University Press.

Mair, Christian and Marianne Hundt. 1995. 'Why is the progressive becoming more frequent in English? A corpus-based investigation of language change in progress.' *Zeitschrift für Anglistik und Amerikanistik* 43(2), 111–122.

Mair, Christian, Marianne Hundt, Geoffrey Leech and Nicholas Smith. 2002. 'Short-term diachronic shifts in part-of-speech frequencies: A comparison of the tagged LOB and F-LOB corpora.' *International Journal of Corpus Linguistics* 7(2), 245–264.

Mair, Christian and Geoffrey Leech. 2006. 'Current change in English syntax.' In: Bas Aarts and April MacMahon (eds.). *The Handbook of English Linguistics*. Oxford: Blackwell, pp. 318–342.

Makkai, Adam. 1977. 'The passing of the syntactic age: A first look at the ecology of the English verb *take*.' In: Adam Makkai (ed.). *Linguistics at the Crossroads*. Padua: Liviana, pp. 79–104.

Marmaridou, Sophia A. S. 1991. *What's so Proper about Names?* Athens: Parousia.

Mazaud, Carolin. 2004. *Complex Premodifiers in Present-Day English. A Corpus-based Study*. Unpublished PhD thesis, Heidelberg University.

McArthur, Tom (ed.). 1992. *The Oxford Companion to the English Language*. Oxford and New York: Oxford University Press.

McCarthy, Michael. 1998. *Spoken Language and Applied Linguistics*. Cambridge: Cambridge University Press.

McEnery, Anthony and Zhonghua Xiao. 2005. 'Help or help to: What do corpora have to say?' *English Studies* 86(2), 161–187.

Meints, Kerstin. 2003. 'To get or to be? Use and acquisition of *get* versus *be* passives: Evidence from children and adults.' In: Hubert Cuyckens, Thomas Berg, René

Dirven and Klaus-Uwe Panther (eds.). *Motivation in Language*. Amsterdam and Philadelphia: Benjamins, pp. 123–150.

Meyerhoff, Myriam and Nancy Niedzielski. 2003. 'The globalization of vernacular variation.' *Journal of Sociolinguistics* 7, 534–555.

Mindt, Dieter. 2000. *An Empirical Grammar of the English Verb System*. Berlin: Cornelsen.

Misztal, Barbara. 2000. *Informality. Social Theory and Contemporary Practice*. London: Routledge.

Mitchell, Bruce. 1985. *Old English Syntax*. 2 vols. Oxford: Oxford University Press.

Mitchell, Bruce and Fred C. Robinson. ⁵1992. *A Guide to Old English*. Oxford: Blackwell.

Moens, Marc and Mark Steedman. 1988. 'Temporal ontology and temporal reference.' *Computational Linguistics* 14(2), 15–28.

Möhlig, Ruth and Monika Klages. 2002. 'Detransitivization in the history of English from a semantic perspective.' In: Javier Pérez-Guerra, Teresa Fanego and María José Lopez Couso (eds.). *English Historical Syntax and Morphology*. Amsterdam and Philadelphia: Benjamins, pp. 231–254.

Mondorf, Britta. 2007. 'Recalcitrant problems of comparative alternation and new insights emerging from Internet data.' In: Hundt *et al.* 2007, pp. 211–232.

Mossé, Fernand. 1938. *Histoire de la forme périphrastique être + participe présent en germanique*. 2 vols. Paris: Klincksieck.

Mukherjee, Joybrato. 2004. 'Corpus data in a usage-based cognitive grammar.' In: Karin Aijmer and Bengt Altenberg (eds.). *Advances in Corpus Linguistics. Papers from the 23rd International Conference on English Language Research on Computerized Corpora*. Amsterdam: Rodopi, pp. 85–100.

2005. *English Ditransitive Verbs*. Amsterdam: Rodopi.

Müller, Ernst-August. 1978. *Funktionsverbgefüge vom Typ 'give a smile' und ähnliche Konstruktionen. Eine Textorientierte Untersuchung im Rahmen eines doppelschichtigen Semantikmodells*. Frankfurt/Main: Peter Lang.

Mustanoja, Tauno F. 1960. *A Middle English Syntax. Part I: Parts of Speech*. Helsinki: Société Néophilologique.

Myhill, John. 1995. 'Change and continuity in the functions of the American English modals.' *Linguistics. An Interdisciplinary Journal of the Language Sciences* 33, 157–211.

1996. 'The development of the strong obligation system in American English.' *American Speech* 71(4), 339–388.

Nakamura, Junsaku. 1991. 'The relationship among genres in the LOB corpus based upon the distribution of grammatical tags.' *JACET Bulletin* 22, 44–74.

Nehls, Dietrich. 1988. 'On the development of the grammatical category of verbal aspect in English.' In: Josef Klegraf and Dietrich Nehls (eds.). *Essays on the English Language and Applied Linguistics on the Occasion of Gerhard Nickel's 60th Birthday*. Heidelberg: Groos, pp. 173–198.

Nesselhauf, Nadja. 2007. 'The spread of the progressive and its "future" use.' *English Language and Linguistics* 11(1), 191–207.

Nevalainen, Terttu and Helena Raumolin-Brunberg. 2002. 'The rise of *who* in Early Modern English.' In: Patricia Poussa (ed.). *Relativization on the North Sea Littoral*. Munich: Lincom Europa, pp. 109–121.

Nickel, Gerhard. 1968. 'Complex verbal structures in English.' *International Review of Applied Linguistics* 6, 1–21 [reprinted in Dietrich Nehls (ed.). *Studies in Descriptive English Grammar*. Heidelberg: Julius Groos, 1978, pp. 63–83].

Nokkonen, Soili. 2006. 'The semantic variation of NEED TO in four recent British corpora.' *International Journal of Corpus Linguistics* 11, 29–71.

Nuñez Pertejo, Paloma. 2004. *The Progressive in the History of English: with Special Reference to the Early Modern English Period. A Corpus Based Study*. München: Lincom Europa.

Oldireva Gustafsson, Larisa. 2006. 'The passive in nineteenth-century scientific writing.' In: Merja Kytö, Mats Rydén and Eric Smitterberg (eds.). *Nineteenth-Century English. Stability and Change*. Cambridge: Cambridge University Press, pp. 110–135.

Olofsson, Arne. 1990. 'A participle caught in the act: On the prepositional use of *following*.' *Studia Neophilologica* 62, 23–35.

Olsson, Yngve. 1961. *On the Syntax of the English Verb with Special Reference to "have a look" and Similar Complex Structures* (Gothenburg Studies in English 12). Stockholm: Almquist and Wiksell.

Övergaard, Gerd. 1995. *The Mandative Subjunctive in American and British English in the 20th Century* (Studia Anglistica Upsaliensia 94). Uppsala: Acta Universitatis Upsaliensis.

Palmer, Frank R. ²1990 [1979]. *Modality and the English Modals*. London and New York: Longman.

   1999. 'Mood and modality: Basic principles.' In: Keith Brown and Jim Miller (eds.). *Concise Encyclopedia of Grammatical Categories*. Amsterdam: Elsevier, pp. 229–235.

   ²2001 [1986]. *Mood and Modality*. Cambridge: Cambridge University Press.

   2003. 'Modality in English: Theoretical, descriptive and typological issues.' In: Facchinetti *et al.*, pp. 1–17.

Pauwels, Anne. 1998. 'Feminist language planning: Has it been worthwhile?' at http://www.linguistik-online.de/heft1_99/pauwels.htm. Linguistik online1, 1/98. Viewed 1 April 2009.

Peters, Pam. 1998. 'The survival of the subjunctive: Evidence of its use in Australia and elsewhere.' *English World-Wide* 19(1), 87–103.

   2000. 'Paradigm split.' In: Christian Mair and Marianne Hundt (eds.). *Corpus Linguistics and Linguistic Theory*. Papers from the Twentieth International Conference on English Language Research on Computerized Corpora (ICAME 1999). Amsterdam: Rodopi, pp. 301–312.

   2004. *The Cambridge Guide to English Usage*. Cambridge: Cambridge University Press.

Popper, Karl R. ²1979 [1972]. *Objective Knowledge: An Evolutionary Approach*. Oxford: Clarendon Press.

Potter, Simeon. ²1975 [1969]. *Changing English*. London: Deutsch.

Poutsma, Hendrik. 1926. *A Grammar of Late Modern English. For the Use of Continental, Especially Dutch, Students. Pt. 2, The Parts of Speech, Section 2, The Verb and the Particles*. Groningen: Noordhoff.

Pratt, Lynda and David Denison. 2000. 'The language of the Southey-Coleridge circle.' *Language Sciences* 22, 401–422.

Prince, Ellen F. 1972. 'A note on aspect in English: The take-a-walk construction.' In: Senta Plötz (ed.). *Transformationelle Analyse*. Frankfurt/Main: Athenäum, pp. 409–420.

Quirk, Randolph. 1995. *Grammatical and Lexical Variance in English*. London: Longman.

Quirk, Randolph, Sidney Greenbaum, Geoffrey Leech and Jan Svartvik. 1985. *A Comprehensive Grammar of the English Language*. London and New York: Longman.

Quirk, Randolph and Jan Rusiecki. 1982. 'Grammatical data by elicitation.' In: John Anderson (ed.). *Language Form and Linguistic Variation. Papers Dedicated to Angus McIntosh*. Amsterdam: Benjamins, pp. 379–394.

Raab-Fischer, Roswitha. 1995. 'Löst der Genitiv die *of*-Phrase ab? Eine korpusgestützte Studie zum Sprachwandel im heutigen Englisch.' *Zeitschrift für Anglistik und Amerikanistik* 43, 123–132.

Radford, Andrew. 1988. *Transformational Grammar. A First Course*. Cambridge: Cambridge University Press.

Rayson, Paul, Dawn Archer, Scott Piao and Tony McEnery. 2004. 'The UCREL semantic analysis system.' In: *Proceedings of the Workshop on Beyond Named Entity Recognition Semantic Labelling for NLP Tasks, in association with the Fourth International Conference on Language Resources and Evaluation. (LREC2004), 25 May, 2004*. Lisbon, pp. 7–12.

Rayson, Paul, Andrew Wilson and Geoffrey Leech. 2002. 'Grammatical word class variation within the British National Corpus Sampler.' In: Pam Peters, Peter Collins and Adam Smith (eds.). *New Frontiers of Corpus Research. Papers from the Twenty First International Conference on English Language Research on Computerized Corpora – Sydney 2000*. Amsterdam: Rodopi, pp. 295–306.

Renský, Miroslav. 1966. 'English verbo-nominal phrases: Some structural and stylistic aspects.' *Travaux Linguistiques de Prague* 1, 289–299.

Rickford, John R., Norma Mendoza-Denton, Thomas A. Wasow and Juli Espinoza. 1995. 'Syntactic variation and change in progress: Loss of the verbal coda in topic restricting *as far as* constructions.' *Language* 71, 102–131.

Rinzler, Simone. 2004. 'Pragmatique d'un genre: Communication institutionelle, monologisme et aspect passif.' *Anglophonia* 16, 207–225.

Rissanen, Matti. 1986. 'The choice of relative pronouns in seventeenth century American English.' In: Jacek Fisiak (ed.). *Historical Syntax*. Berlin: Mouton de Gruyter, pp. 417–435.

1999. 'Syntax.' In: Roger Lass (ed.). *The Cambridge History of the English Language*. Vol. 3: *1476–1776*. Cambridge: Cambridge University Press, pp. 187–331.

Rohdenburg, Günter. 1990. 'Aspekte einer vergleichenden Typologie des Englischen und Deutschen: Kritische Anmerkungen zu einem Buch von John A. Hawkins.' In: Claus Gnutzmann (ed.). *Kontrastive Linguistik*. Frankfurt, Bern, New York and Paris: Peter Lang, pp. 133–152.

1995. 'On the replacement of finite complement clauses by infinitives in English.' *English Studies* 16, 367–388.

1996. 'Cognitive complexity and increased grammatical explicitness in English.' *Cognitive Linguistics* 7, 149–182.

2006. 'The role of functional constraints in the evolution of the English complementation system.' In: Christiane Dalton-Puffer, Dieter Kastovsky, Nikolaus Rittand and Herbert Schendl (eds.). *Syntax, Style and Grammatical Norms.* Bern, Berlin, Frankfurt/Main and Wien: Peter Lang, pp. 143–166.

Romaine, Suzanne (ed.). 1998. *The Cambridge History of the English Language.* Vol. IV: 1776–1997. Cambridge: Cambridge University Press.

Romaine, Suzanne and Deborah Lange. 1991. 'The use of *like* as a marker of reported speech and thought: A case of grammaticalization in progress.' *American Speech* 66, 227–279.

Römer, Ute. 2005. *Progressives, Patterns, Pedagogy: A Corpus-Driven Approach to English Progressive Forms, Functions, Contexts and Didactics.* Amsterdam and Philadelphia: Benjamins.

Rosenbach, Anette. 2002. *Genitive Variation in English: Conceptual Factors in Synchronic and Diachronic Studies.* Berlin: Mouton de Gruyter.

2003. 'Aspects of iconicity and economy in the choice between the *s*-genitive and the *of*-genitive in English.' In: Günter Rohdenburg and Britta Mondorf (eds.). *Determinants of Grammatical Variation in English.* Berlin: Mouton de Gruyter, pp. 379–412.

2006. 'On the track of noun+noun constructions in Modern English.' In: Christoph Houswitschka, Gabriele Knappe and Anja Müller (eds.). *Anglistentag 2005 Bamberg. Proceedings.* Trier: Wissenschaftlicher Verlag, pp. 543–557.

Rudanko, Juhani. 1999. *Diachronic Studies of English Complementation Patterns.* Lanham, MD: University Press of America.

2000. *Corpora and Complementation.* Lanham, MD: University Press of America.

2006. 'Watching English grammar change: A case study on complement selection in British and American English.' *English Language and Linguistics* 10, 31–48.

Ryan, William M. 1961. 'Pseudo-subjunctive *were*.' *American Speech* 36, 48–53.

Rydén, Mats. 1975. 'Noun-name collocations in British English newspaper language.' *Studia Neophilologica* 47, 14–39.

1997. 'On the panchronic core meaning of the English progressive.' In: Terttu Nevalainen and Leena Kahlas-Tarkka (eds.). *To Explain the Present: Studies in the Changing English Language in Honour of Matti Rissanen.* Helsinki: Société Néophilologique, pp. 419–429.

Sadock, Jerrold M. 1974. *Towards a Linguistic Theory of Speech Acts.* New York: Academic Press.

Sag, Ivan. 1973. 'On the state of progress on progressives and statives.' In: Charles-James Bailey and Roger Shuy (eds.). *New Ways of Analyzing Variation in English.* Washington: Georgetown University Press, pp. 83–95.

Salton, Gerard. 1989. *Automatic Text Processing.* Reading, MA: Addison-Wesley.

Samuels, Michael. 1972. *Linguistic Evolution. With Special Reference to English.* Cambridge: Cambridge University Press.

Sankoff, David. 1988. 'Sociolinguistics and syntactic variation.' In Newmeyer, Frederick J. (ed.). *Linguistics. The Cambridge Survey.* Vol. 4: *Language. the Socio-Cultural Context.* Cambridge: Cambridge University Press, pp. 140–161.

Sapir, Edward. 1921. *Language. An Introduction to the Study of Speech.* London: Harvest Books [original publisher Harcourt, Brace and World Inc.].

Scheffer, Johannes. 1975. *The Progressive in English.* Amsterdam: North-Holland.

Schlüter, Julia. 2009. 'The conditional subjunctive.' In: Günter Rohdenburg and Julia Schlüter (eds.). *One Language, Two Grammars? Differences between British and American English*. Cambridge: Cambridge University Press, pp. 277–305.

Schneider, Edgar W. 2005. 'The subjunctive in Philippine English.' In: Danilo T. Dayag and J. Stephen Quakenbusch (eds.). *Linguistics and Language Education in the Philippines and Beyond. A Festschrift in Honor of Ma. Lourdes S. Bautista*. Manila: Linguistic Society of the Philippines, pp. 27–40.

Scott, Mike. 1999. *WordSmith Tools*. Oxford: Oxford University Press.

Seoane, Elena. 2006a. 'Changing styles: On the recent evolution of scientific British and American English.' In: Christiane Dalton-Puffer, Dieter Kastovsky, Nikolaus Ritt and Herbert Schendl (eds.). *Syntax, Style and Grammatical Norms. English from 1500–2000*. Bern: Peter Lang, pp. 191–211.

2006b. 'Information structure and word order change: The passive as an information-rearranging strategy in the history of English.' In: Ans van Kemenade and Bettelou Los (eds.). *The Handbook of the History of English*. Oxford: Blackwell, pp. 360–391.

Seoane, Elena and Lucia Loureiro-Porto. 2005. 'On the colloquialization of scientific British and American English.' *ESP Across Cultures* 2, 106–118.

Seoane, Elena and Christopher Williams. 2006. 'Changing the rules: A comparison of recent trends in English in academic scientific discourse and prescriptive legal discourse.' In: Marina Dossena and Irma Taavitsainen (eds.). *Diachronic Perspectives on Domain-Specific English*. Bern: Peter Lang, pp. 255–276.

Seoane-Posse, Elena. 2002. 'On the evolution of scientific American and British English, with special reference to recent and ongoing changes in the use of the passive voice.' Paper presented at the 12th International Conference on English Historical Linguistics, University of Glasgow, 21–26 August, 2002.

Serpollet, Noëlle. 2001. 'The mandative subjunctive in British English seems to be alive and kicking... Is it due to American influence?' In: Paul Rayson, Andrew Wilson, Tony McEnery, Andrew Hardie and Shereen Khoja (eds.). *Proceedings of the Corpus Linguistics 2001 Conference*. Lancaster University: UCREL Technical Papers 13, 531–542.

2003. Should *and the Subjunctive: A Corpus-Based Approach to Mandative Constructions in English*. Unpublished PhD thesis, Lancaster University.

Shibatani, Masayoshi. 1985. 'Passives and related constructions: A prototype analysis.' *Language* 61(4), 821–848.

Sigley, Robert. 1997. 'Text categories and where you can stick them: A crude formality index.' *International Journal of Corpus Linguistics* 2(2), 199–237.

Smith, Nicholas. 2002. 'Ever moving on. Changes in the progressive in recent British English.' In: Pam Peters, Peter Collins and Adam Smith (eds.). *New Frontiers of Corpus Research*. Amsterdam: Rodopi, pp. 317–330.

2003a. 'Changes in the modals and semi-modals of strong obligation and epistemic necessity in recent British English.' In: Facchinetti *et al.*, pp. 241–266.

2003b. 'A quirky progressive? A corpus-based exploration of the *will* + *be* + -*ing* construction in recent and present-day English.' In: Dawn Archer,

Paul Rayson and Andrew Wilson (eds.). *Proceedings of the Corpus Linguistics 2003 conference*. Lancaster University: UCREL Technical Papers 16, pp. 714–723.

2005. *A Corpus-Based Investigation of Recent Change in the Use of the Progressive in British English*. Unpublished PhD thesis, Lancaster University.

Smith, Nicholas and Paul Rayson. 2007. 'Recent change and variation in the British English use of the progressive passive.' *ICAME Journal* 31, 129–159.

Smitterberg, Erik. 2005. *The Progressive in 19th-Century English: A Process of Integration*. Amsterdam and New York: Rodopi.

Stein, Gabriele. 1991. 'The phrasal verb type "to have a look" in Modern English.' *International Review of Applied Linguistics* 29, 1–29.

Stein, Gabriele and Randolph Quirk. 1991. 'On having a look in a corpus.' In: Karin Aijmer and Bengt Altenberg (eds.). *English Corpus Linguistics. Studies in Honour of Jan Svartvik*, London: Longman, pp. 197–203.

Strang, Barbara M. H. 1970. *A History of English*. London: Routledge.

1982. 'Some aspects of the history of the be+ing construction.' In: John Anderson (ed.). *Language Form and Linguistic Variation. Papers Dedicated to Angus McIntosh*. Amsterdam and Philadelphia: Benjamins, pp. 427–474.

Strunk, William, Jr and E. B. White. ³1979 [1959]. *The Elements of Style*. New York: Longman.

Stubbs, Michael. 1996. *Text and Corpus Analysis: Computer-assisted Studies of Language and Culture*. Oxford: Blackwell.

2001. 'Texts, corpora and problems of interpretation: A response to Widdowson.' *Applied Linguistics* 22(2), 149–172.

Sussex, Roland. 1982. 'A note on the get-passive construction.' *Australian Journal of Linguistics* 2, 83–92.

Svartvik, Jan. 1966. *On Voice in the English Verb*. The Hague and Paris: Mouton.

Svartvik, Jan and Randolph Quirk (eds.). 1980. *A Corpus of English Conversation*. (Lund Studies in English, Volume 56). Lund: C. W. K. Gleerup.

Sweetser, Eve. 1990. *From Etymology to Pragmatics. Metaphorical and Cultural Aspects of Semantic Structure*. Cambridge: Cambridge University Press.

Szmrecsanyi, Benedikt. 2003. '*Be going to* vs. *will/ shall*: Does syntax matter?' *Journal of English Linguistics* 31, 295–323.

Taavitsainen, Irma and Päivi Pahta. 2000. 'Conventions of professional writing: The medical case report in a historical perspective.' *Journal of English Linguistics* 28, 60–76.

Taeymans, Martine. 2004. 'An investigation into the marginal modals *dare* and *need* in British present-day English.' In: Olga Fischer, Muriel Norde and Harry Perridon (eds.). *Up and Down the Cline. The Nature of Grammaticalization*. Amsterdam: Benjamins, pp. 97–114.

Tagliamonte, Sali. 2004. 'Have to, gotta, must? Grammaticalisation, variation and specialization in English deontic modality.' In: Hans Lindquist and Christian Mair (eds.), pp. 33–55.

Tognini-Bonelli, Elena. 2001. *Corpus Linguistics at Work*. Amsterdam: Benjamins.

Tottie, Gunnel. 1991. *Negation in Speech and Writing. A Study in Variation*. San Diego: Academic Press.

2002. *An Introduction to American English*. Oxford: Blackwell.

2009. 'How different are American and British English grammar? And how are they different?' In: Günter Rohdenburg and Julia Schlüter (eds.). *One Language, Two Grammars? Differences between British and American English.* Cambridge: Cambridge University Press, pp. 341–363.

Tottie, Gunnel and Sebastian Hoffmann. 2006. 'Tag Questions in British and American English.' *Journal of English Linguistics* 34(4), 283–311.

Traugott, Elizabeth Closs. 1972. *A History of English Syntax.* New York: Holt, Rinehart and Winston.

1989. 'On the rise of epistemic meanings in English: An example of subjectification in semantic changes.' *Language* 65(1), 31–55.

1995. 'Subjectification in grammaticalisation.' In: Dieter Stein and Susan Wright (eds.). *Subjectivity and Subjectivisation. Linguistic Perspectives.* Cambridge: Cambridge University Press, pp. 31–54.

Trudgill, Peter and Jean Hannah. ⁴2002 [1982]. *International English. A Guide to Varieties of Standard English.* London: Arnold.

Trudgill, Peter, Terttu Nevalainen and Ilse Wischer. 2002. 'Dynamic *have* in North American and British Isles English.' *English Language and Linguistics* 6(1), 1–15.

Turner, John F. 1980. 'The marked subjunctive in contemporary English.' *Studia Neophilologica* 52, 271–277.

Urdang, Laurence. 1991. '"If I were a king ..." I'd be in a subjunctive mood.' *Verbatim* 17, 12–14.

Ure, J. M. 1971. 'Lexical density and register differentiation.' In: G. E. Perren and J. L. M. Trim (eds.). *Applications of Linguistics.* Cambridge: Cambridge University Press, pp. 443–452.

Váradi, Tamás. 2001. 'The linguistic relevance of corpus linguistics.' In: Paul Rayson, Andrew Wilson, Tony McEnery, Andrew Hardie and Shereen Khoja (eds.). *Proceedings of the Corpus Linguistics 2001 Conference.* Lancaster University: UCREL Technical Papers 13, pp. 587–593.

Varela Pérez, José Ramón. 2007. 'Negation of main verb *have*: Evidence of a change in progress in spoken and written British English.' *Neuphilologische Mitteilungen* 108, 223–246.

Visser, Fredericus Th. 1963–1973. *An Historical Syntax of the English Language.* 3 vols. Leiden: E. J. Brill.

Vosberg, Uwe. 2003a. 'Cognitive complexity and the establishment of -ing constructions with retrospective verbs in Modern English.' In: Marina Dossena and Charles Jones (eds.). *Insights into Late Modern English.* Bern: Peter Lang, pp. 197–220.

2003b. 'The role of extractions and horror aequi in the evolution of -ing complements in Modern English.' In: Günter Rohdenburg and Britta Mondorf (eds.). *Determinants of Grammatical Variation in English.* (Topics in English Linguistics 43.) Berlin: Mouton de Gruyter, pp. 305–327.

2006a. *Die Große Komplementverschiebung. Außersemantische Einflüsse auf die Entwicklung satzwertiger Ergänzungen im Neuenglischen.* Tübingen: Narr.

2006b. 'The Great Complement Shift. Extra-semantic factors determining the evolution of sentential complement variants in Modern English.' In: *English and American Studies in German 2005.* (Summaries of Theses and Monographs. A Supplement to Anglia.) Tübingen: Niemeyer, pp. 19–22.

Warner, Anthony. 1995. 'Predicting the progressive passive: Parametric change within a lexicalist framework.' *Language* 71, 533–557.

Weiner, E. Judith and William Labov. 1983. 'Constraints on the agentless passive.' *Journal of Linguistics* 19(1), 29–58.

Wekker, Herman C. 1976. *The Expression of Future Time in Contemporary British English*. Amsterdam: North-Holland.

Westin, Ingrid. 2002. *Language Change in English Newspaper Editorials*. Amsterdam and New York: Rodopi.

Westin, Ingrid and Christer Geisler. 2002. 'A multi-dimensional study of diachronic variation in British newspaper editorials.' *ICAME Journal* 26, 115–134.

Wierzbicka, Anna. 1982. 'Why can you have a drink when you can't *have an eat?' *Language* 58, 753–799.

Williams, Christopher. 2002. *Non-progressive and Progressive Aspect in English*. Fasano di Puglia: Schena Editore.

Wright, Susan. 1994. 'The mystery of the modal progressive.' In: Dieter Kastovsky (ed.). *Studies in Early Modern English*. Berlin and New York: Mouton de Gruyter, pp. 467–485.

1995. 'Subjectivity and experiential syntax.' In: Dieter Stein and Susan Wright (eds.). *Subjectivity and Subjectivisation. Linguistic Perspectives*, Cambridge: Cambridge University Press, pp. 467–485.

Yoshimura, Kimihiro and John R. Taylor. 2004. 'What makes a good middle? The role of qualia in the interpretation and acceptability of middle expressions in English.' *English Language and Linguistics* 8(2), 293–321.

Ziegeler, Deborah. 1999. 'Agentivity and the history of the English progressive.' *Transactions of the Philological Society* 97, 51–101.

Index

A Representative Corpus of Historical
  English Registers xxi, 29, 45, 71, 78,
  121, 132, 154
ability 112, 113
abstract nouns 250–2
abstraction 107
academic writing 42, 164 *see also* Learned
  subcorpus
accelerating change 43
acronyms 206, 212, 213
adjectives 208–9
adversative 147, 156
advertising language 161
Aktionsart *see* aspect, progressive (aspect)
American English xxiii, 5, 9, 11, 22, 25, 28,
  44, 71, 73, 121, 122, 136, 141, 142, 189,
  229–30, 244, 252, 289, 294, 295, 303
  and passim
  see also spoken English, American; written
  English, American
American mass print media 257
American National Corpus 190, 197, 302
Americanism 20, 205
Americanization 11, 22, 43, 237, 252–9
analytical grammar 7
analyticization 263, 264–7
ANC – *see* American National Corpus
annotation of corpora 9, 33, 37 *see also*
  tags
anti-colloquialization 245–6
apparent time 12, 103, 198, 287
apposition 216, 257
archaism 80
ARCHER *see* A Representative Corpus of
  Historical English Registers
articles 208
aspect 118, 119, 120, 127 *see also* progressive
  (aspect)
attributive adjectives 216, 254
attributive nouns 215
  plural 219–21
audience design 252
Australian English 28, 258

automatic processing, automatic tagging 33,
  38, 207–8, 276–80
auxiliarization 268
auxiliary verbs 92–8, 129

Baker, Paul xxii
bar charts 35
Barber, Charles 16
bare infinitive 238 *see also* infinitive;
  to-infinitive
Bauer, Laurie 17, 266–7
be able to 96, 98, 111–13, 286, 287
(be) going to 78, 91, 101, 102, 107–8, 140,
  141, 256, 269, 286, 287, 294
be-passive 47, 48, 49, 141, 145, 148–54, 164,
  244, 297 *see also* passive
be supposed to 96, 105, 286, 287
be to (semi-modal) 95, 98, 102, 108, 140, 286,
  287, 294
begin 195, 301, 302
Biber, Douglas 27, 61, 84, 101, 172, 210,
  239–40, 247 *see also* Biber *et al.*
Biber *et al.* (1999) 123, 125, 127, 142, 211,
  218, 226, 241, 247
B-LOB Corpus xxi, 10, 108, 188, 201, 255
BNC *see* British National Corpus
BNCdemog 45, 101, 103, 106
BNC Sampler Corpus 33, 37
brackets 246
Briticism 56, 57, 70, 193
British English xxiii, 5, 9, 10, 11, 28, 30, 44,
  71, 73, 76, 121, 122, 141, 142, 189, 205,
  252–9, 303 *and passim*
British National Corpus (BNC) xxi, 12, 14,
  45, 71, 137, 164, 173, 174, 176, 178,
  190, 197, 287, 302
broadcast discussion 125, 126
broadcast interviews 126
Brown Corpus xix, 9, 24, 25, 26, 28, 29, 34,
  50 *and passim*
Brown family of corpora, the xix–xxii, 9, 10,
  12, 24–31, 43, 48, 98, 116, 204 *and*
  passim

335

Lightning Source UK Ltd.
Milton Keynes UK
UKOW050331300113

205579UK00001B/40/P